Tamed Frontiers

Tamed Frontiers

Economy, Society, and Civil Rights in Upper Amazonia

Fernando Santos-Granero
Frederica Barclay

Westview
PRESS
A Member of the Perseus Books Group

Copyright © 2000 by Westview Press, A Member of the Perseus Books Group

Published in 2000 in the United States of America by Westview Press, 5500 Central Avenue, Boulder, Colorado 80301-2877, and in the United Kingdom by Westview Press, 12 Hid's Copse Road, Cumnor Hill, Oxford OX2 9JJ

Library of Congress Cataloging-in-Publication Data
Santos-Granero, Fernando, 1955–
    Tamed frontiers : economy, society, and civil rights in upper
Amazonia / Fernando Santos-Granero, Frederica Barclay.
        p.   cm.
    Includes bibliographical references (349–369) and index.
    ISBN 0-8133-3717-8
    1. Loreto (Peru : Dept.)—Economic conditions.   2. Loreto (Peru :
Dept.)—Social conditions.   3. Civil society—Peru—Loreto (Dept.)
4. Civil rights—Peru—Loreto (Dept.)   I. Barclay, Frederica.
II. Title.
HC228.L6S26   1999
330.985'440633—dc21   99-16846
                                                                          CIP

10   9   8   7   6   5   4   3   2   1

Contents

Tables and Illustrations

Figures

Photos

Women packing barbasco roots for export in the baling yard of Israel and
  Company, circa 1947 118

Maps

Boxes

Acknowledgments

Many institutions and individuals have made this book possible. We are much indebted to The Ford Foundation, which financed the first phase of this research. The Smithsonian Tropical Research Institute (STRI) generously supported additional research and the writing of this book. Without the unfailing backing of Ira Rubinoff and Anthony Coates, STRI's director and deputy director, respectively, the writing of this book would have not been possible. For that we are extremely grateful.

Many friends and colleagues assisted us in the process of gathering information for this volume. Alberto Chirif, Martha Rodríguez Achung, Joaquín García, Alejandra Schindler, Humberto Morey, Michelle McKinley, Camilo Domínguez, Verónica Barclay, and David Barclay helped us to obtain indispensable bibliographic references or information not accessible from Panama, or called our attention to sources relevant to different aspects of our research. Javier Dávila, poet, journalist, and editor of *Proceso*, placed at our disposal his copies of that news magazine, which began publication in Loreto in 1966 and is not available in public libraries. Aeltsje Kuipers was kind enough to present us with valuable documentation on Loreto's economy gathered by her late husband, Jan Vogelzang, who had been a close adviser to the region's peasant organizations as part of the Dutch technical cooperation service.

Germán Lequerica, a distinguished Loretan poet, shared his knowledge on the functioning of the large merchant houses of Iquitos, for one of which he worked during his youth. He also put at our disposal his personal contacts, which made it possible to interview former *fundo* owners and employees. The information they provided us on the workings of the region's agroextractive export economy proved to be invaluable for our research. In turn, María Elena Dávila provided us with priceless, firsthand recollections about the daily life in Loreto's *fundos* during the late 1930s and 1940s. Finally, combining ingeniousness, patience, and a large dose of charm, Santiago (Shanti) Arévalo, our research assistant while in Iquitos, was able to gather restricted statistical data from public and private institutions that would have otherwise remained beyond our reach. To all of these friends our warmest thanks.

This book was written in English. Anthony Coates generously volunteered to check our grammar and edit our style. A geologist with a broad range of intellectual interests and with a love for fine language and conciseness, Tony not only helped us to better the text but made very useful suggestions as to how to improve the presentation of the information. In addition, his positive commentaries after reading each of the chapters that we handed him, and the way in which he was increasingly drawn by the book's subject, constituted for us a secret source of encouragement. For all this we are particularly thankful.

Finally, we are greatly indebted to Amparo Menéndez-Carrión, Heraclio Bonilla, Olga Linares, and Marianne Schmink, who read the first draft of this book. Their insightful comments allowed us to clarify obscure points, trim the text, and sharpen our arguments. However, we assume full responsibility for any errors or shortcomings.

This book is dedicated to the people of Loreto, whose many voices we hope to have captured.

—*FS-G and FB*
Panama, 1999

Glossary of Spanish Terms

Andullo   rectangular skein made of strips of naturally coagulated hevea latex.

Arroba   measure of weight equivalent to 15 kilograms

Arrojo   primitive tapping technique consisting of pounding the trunk of the rubber tree, making irregular cuts on it, and tightly wrapping it with vines in order to force the latex to flow into containers placed on the ground; in Brazil, *arrocho.*

Barbasco   also *cube*; generic term for a wide variety of plants used traditionally as fish poison; more specifically, *Lonchocarpus nicou.*

Caboclo (pl. *caboclos*)   in Brazil, derogatory term designating Amazonian peasants of mixed ethnic descent.

Canon   canon, or quit-rent, paid by a miner to the owner of the land in exchange for rights of exploitation.

Casa aviadora   in Brazil, commercial firm devoted to supplying goods on credit in exchange for forest products.

Casa fuerte   powerful merchant house devoted to the import-export trade.

Caserío (pl. *caseríos*)   riverine villages or hamlets.

Cauchero (pl. *caucheros*)   extractors of castilloa rubber.

Caucho   rubber from *Castilloa elastica* or *Castilloa ulei*; known in the international market as black rubber; *caucho en planchas* means slabs of artificially coagulated castilloa latex; *sernambí de caucho* means balls made of strips of artificially coagulated castilloa latex.

Comadre (pl. *comadres*)   female coparent; see *compadrazgo.*

Compadrazgo   spiritual bond established between the parents of a child and the man and woman who are chosen to become the child's godparents in the ceremony of baptism under the Catholic ritual.

Compadre (pl. *compadres*)   male coparent; see *compadrazgo.*

Comunidad nativa (pl. *comunidades nativas*)   official term used to designate Amazonian indigenous settlements beginning in 1974.

Conquistar   recruitment of tribal Indians as workers through a combination of force and persuasion.

Correría (pl. *correrías*)   punitive raid or slave-raid carried out against tribal peoples.

Estrada   trail in the form of a loop 8–10 kilometers long that starts and ends in a tapper's hut and comprises up to 200 hevea rubber trees.

Fundo (pl. *fundos*)   in Loreto, agroextractive riverine landholdings.

Habilitación   supply and credit system by which individuals are engaged to perform a certain service in exchange for advances in goods or cash and that leads to relationships of debt-peonage or debt-merchandise; in Brazil, *aviamento.*

Habilitado   outfitted; person who is engaged to perform a certain service in exchange for advances in goods or cash; in Brazil, *aviado.*

Habilitador outfitter; person who supplies credit in goods or cash in exchange for a certain service; in Brazil, *aviador*.

Hacienda (pl. *haciendas*) large landholding.

Jebe débil rubber from *Hevea guayanensis* and *Hevea benthamiana*; known in the international market as weak Pará; *jebe débil fino* means balls of smoked weak hevea latex; *sernambí de jebe débil* means skeins made of strips of naturally coagulated weak hevea latex.

Jebe rubber from *Hevea brasiliensis*; known in the international market as Pará rubber; *jebe fino* means balls of smoked hevea latex; *jebe entrefino* means balls of smoked hevea latex of inferior quality; *sernambí de jebe* means rectangular skeins made of bits and strips of naturally coagulated hevea latex (see *andullos*)

Padrinazgo spiritual bond established between a baptized child and his or her godparents under the Catholic ritual.

Patrón (pl. *patrones*) patron, master, or boss; also *patrón de caserío, gran patrón*.

Pueblo joven (pl. *pueblos jóvenes*) young town; euphemism for shantytown.

Quintal measure of weight equivalent to 46 kilograms.

Regatón (pl. *regatones*) small fluvial trader.

Ribereño (pl. *ribereños*) in Loreto, riverine Amazonian peasants of mixed ethnic descent.

Selva alta literally, "high jungle"; area east of the Andes between 400 and 2,500 meters above sea level.

Selva baja literally, "low jungle"; floodplain area east of the Andes less than 400 meters above sea level.

Seringueiro in Brazil, hevea rubber tapper.

Úmisha in Loreto, ritual felling of a decorated palm tree trunk as part of the celebration of Carnival and Saint John's Day.

Introduction

The incorporation of Amazonian territories into national economies as a result of the expansion of market forces has not been a homogeneous process. Rather, it has been an uneven development producing a variety of socioeconomic arrangements. Behind these variations are differences in temporal scales, economic agents involved, types of productive activities carried out, linkages with the national and international markets, and the strategic importance attributed by the state to the integration of various areas. The combination of these factors has induced different degrees of economic, social, and political integration. This heterogeneity is seldom acknowledged, however, and all Amazonian regional economies tend to be portrayed as "frontier" economies.

In this book we analyze the evolution of the political economy and civil society of Loreto to see whether it fits the frontier model. Originally composed of the present-day departments of Loreto, Ucayali, and San Martín, Loreto today occupies the northeastern portion of the original department (see Map 1). For the purpose of this study we consider Loreto and Ucayali to be a single region. Although Ucayali separated from Loreto in 1980, both departments are located in the *selva baja*—the tropical forest area east of the Andes below 400 meters above sea level—and share a common history. We exclude San Martín, which separated from Loreto in 1904, for it is located in the selva alta region—the area east of the Andes between 2,500 meters and 400 meters above sea level—and has a very different economic and social profile.

The radical transformations experienced by Loreto since its opening as a new colonization frontier in 1851 has, we contend, led to the "taming" of its frontier traits. Because Loreto is not the only "tamed frontier" within the Amazon Basin, we insist upon the need to study these economies so as to devise better strategies with which to offset the negative traits displayed by present-day tropical forest frontier economies.

Violent and Tamed Frontiers

The notion of the "frontier" evokes two sets of related but not always consistent ideas. The first set derives from the Latin root of the word *frons*, meaning forehead or front. Thus, the term came to signify that part of the country that fronts, faces,

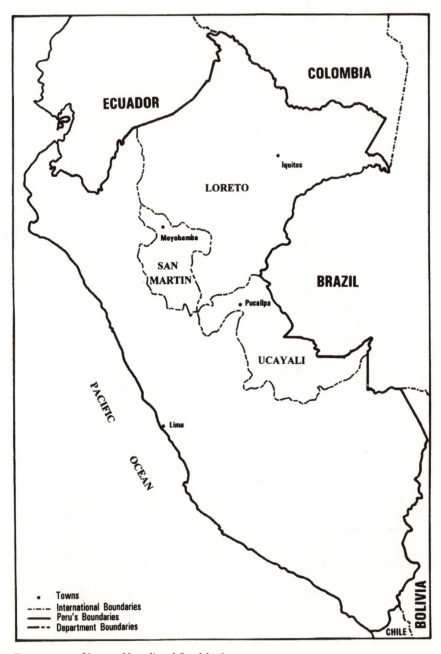

Departments of Loreto, Ucayali and San Martin

or borders on another country (*Oxford Universal Dictionary Illustrated*). The same root is present in the term "front," which in its military connotation denotes "the foremost part of the ground occupied, or of the field of operations; the part next to the enemy" (ibidem). Briefly, based on the notion of "facing someone or something," these two terms underscore a contrast between us and others, either under the guise of an opposition between fellows and aliens, or between friends and foes. In addition, *frons* is associated with the Latin *limes*, which in Roman times referred to the boundaries separating the dominion of the empire, where civilization reigned, from the still unconquered lands, where barbarism prevailed. Hence, the terms "frontier" and "front" further qualifies the us-them opposition as one between "civilized" and "savage."

The second set of ideas conjures up the image of an uninhabited area with plenty of resources waiting for someone to grab them; an area where enterprising pioneers and shrewd adventurers can find countless opportunities for fast enrichment. In a more romantic vein, it also evokes the image of a land where total freedom prevails; an area not constrained by traditional social structures and mores, where one is what one does. Frederick J. Turner (1920) praised many of these elements in his classic work on the American frontier. Within this same set of ideas, but somewhat in opposition with the romantic view, the term "frontier" also summons the notion of a lawless land where the strong impose their will over the weak—in short, an area characterized by disorder, violence, and instability.

The above clusters of associations surrounding the notion of "frontier" are present in various forms in studies of the process of frontier expansion in the Amazon Basin, particularly in Brazilian Amazonia. In his influential work, *Os Indios e a Civilização,* Darcy Ribeiro (1970) analyzed the impact that the advancing "frontiers of civilization" had over the indigenous peoples of Brazilian Amazonia. He characterized the process as a violent expansion of a market economy, leading to the extermination or disappearance of numerous tribal peoples; or to the "ethnic transfiguration" of surviving groups. Ribeiro contended that the specific outcome of the confrontation between tribal peoples and the national society depended as much on the "cultural predisposition" of the former as on the type of economic front (extractive, pastoral, agricultural) through which the latter becomes manifest in the region (1971: 12–3). The analysis of these different pioneer fronts, and of Amazonian frontier economies, has been the subject of numerous studies.

In *The Struggle for Land*, Joe Foweraker (1981: ix) presented a general panorama of the advance of pioneer frontiers into Brazilian Amazonia, regarded by him as the world's "last great frontier." He argued that the process of integration of these frontiers into the national economy involves a transition from precapitalist to capitalist forms of production. This transition, however, does not go uncontested (1981: 171). The struggle for land and control of labor, confronting local populations to peasant immigrants and large entrepreneurs, is an intrinsically violent process. According to Foweraker, violence results from "a ruthless search for gain by evil and unprincipled entrepreneurs and politicians, who do not include the costs of violence in their calculations" (1981: 169). In turn, the constant expropriation of local and immigrant peasants by powerful entrepreneurs and companies fuels the process of frontier expansion in a cycle that according to the author is self-perpetuating. This is what he defines as the "drama of the frontier."

More recently, Marianne Schmink and Charles Wood (1992) have offered a more complex and subtle picture of the process of frontier expansion in their book *Contested Frontiers in Amazonia*, based on a comprehensive and detailed study of the southern portion of the Brazilian state of Pará. They define the dynamics of this process as a "contest for resources among social groups capable of mobilizing varying degrees of power" (1992: xxvi). The authors argue that the confrontation between a diversity of social actors—Indians, peasants, miners, ranchers, and entrepreneurs—competing for a variety of resources has resulted not in "a single process of linear change but instead [in] a diversity of contested frontiers with highly varied outcomes" (1992: 13). By considering the diverse sources of power mobilized by these different actors at the regional, national, and international levels, and by examining concrete examples of conflicting interests, Schmink and Wood present a rich and evocative portrayal of the frequently violent confrontations that characterize frontier economies in Brazilian Amazonia.

The ideas developed by Stephen Bunker (1984) on the extractive character of these economies have further contributed to the notion of frontier violence and confrontation. In *Underdeveloping the Amazon*, Bunker (1985) argues that extractive economies not only do not foster stable communities, local accumulation, and economic agglomeration but also increasingly impoverish the environmental and social basis of the frontier with each subsequent extractive cycle. Incapable of generating "self-sustaining autonomous development," extractive frontier economies, according to Bunker, are doomed to repeat themselves.

The aforementioned authors, plus other scholars, have thus emphasized the frontier and extractive character of regional economies in Brazilian Amazonia, resulting in a set of features that conspire against development. First, these economies are highly dependent for their functioning and reproduction on external demand and capital, whether national or international. Second, because of the dependent and cyclical nature of extractive booms, they do not permit local capital accumulation and the emergence of a bourgeoisie with deep-rooted interests in the region. Third, they are based on precapitalist social relations of production and exchange. These stifle the emergence of a domestic market that could foster economic diversification and industrialization. Fourth, frontier economies do not generate permanent demographic fronts or promote internal articulation because of the itinerant character of extractive activities. Lastly, the presence of the state in frontier areas is either weak or subservient to the interests of the economically powerful. Lawlessness, characterized by the disenfranchisement of a large portion of the local population and by recurrent and violent confrontation over valuable resources, is the inevitable result.

As we hope to demonstrate, none of the above traits are present in the contemporary economy of Loreto. Although the initial stages of the evolution of Loreto's economy followed the pattern of frontier expansion common in Amazonia, its subsequent development took a very different track, one that could no longer be characterized as a frontier economy. One of the principal objectives of this book is thus to uncover the factors that have induced the transformation of Loreto's frontier economy into a more integrated, diversified, stable, capitalist, and civil regional economy.

The process we are calling the "taming of the frontier" does not involve conquering a given space and subjugating its people to alien economic dynamics, as occurs during the opening of frontiers in Amazonia. It does not involve violent acts such as the expropriation of local populations, the imposition of imported values, the rapacious depletion of the environment, and the transformation of the landscape to conform to outlandish models. In short, it is not based on the kind of confrontation between fellows and foreigners, friends and enemies, civilized and savage. On the contrary, the taming of the frontier implies the suppression or containment of the worse traits identified with frontier economies. Above all, it involves the extension of civil rights and the empowerment of previously disenfranchised and oppressed sectors of the population, such as took place in Loreto beginning in the 1960s.

If the "violent frontier" approach has become hegemonic in Amazonian studies, it is because scholars have favored the analysis of areas recently opened to colonization or of old colonization areas that have been reopened as a result of new road construction. This focus has reinforced the belief that the process of occupation and integration of the Amazon Basin can only create unstable, underdeveloped, and confrontational frontier economies that are self-perpetuating. The history of Loreto's economy demonstrates that this need not be the case; that Amazonian regional economies are not doomed to continuously reproduce their violent and transient "frontier" character.

This volume is divided into three parts, each devoted to the study of one of the stages in the development of Loreto's political economy. Part 1, corresponding to the 1851–1914 period, examines the events that led to the opening of the region to international navigation and trade. We define this period as that of the coming-of-age of Peru's most important frontier economy and place special emphasis on the features of the rubber extractive economy that emerged after 1870. Part 2 analyzes the agroextractive export economy that originated around 1915, after the rubber bust, and disintegrated in the early 1960s. In this transition period Loreto's economy was still very much a frontier economy, although some of its more violent traits had disappeared or were attenuated. Part 3 is devoted to the study of the factors that led to the formation of Loreto's agroextractive industrial economy beginning in 1963 and to the taming of the frontier. We have chosen to end our study in 1990, with the accession of Pres. Alberto Fujimori and the triumph of a neoliberal political paradigm. The ensuing economic and political changes mark the beginning of a new stage, the characteristics of which, although still too early to be properly assessed, are examined in the Epilogue.

PART ONE

Coming of Age, 1851–1914

Part 1 analyzes the events that led to the opening up of Loreto and to the subsequent development of a frontier economy based mainly on the extraction and export of rubber. The analysis of the coming-of-age of Peru's most important Amazonian economy begins with an examination of the reasons that led Peru to sign a treaty with Brazil in 1851, opening the Amazon River to ships from both countries. It ends with the collapse of the rubber economy in 1914 as a result of the flooding of the market with cultivated rubber from the British colonies of Southeast Asia. The state played a crucial role in connecting Loreto, until then a marginal and extremely isolated region, with the international market. It also established the conditions that allowed the region to rapidly increase its exports of rubber when the international demand soared in the 1870s. Thus, much of Part 1 revolves around the political economy of rubber extraction and trade, with special emphasis on state action, the resource base, the labor force, and the trading elite. Comparison with the better-known Brazilian case reveals the distinctive features of Loreto's economy, placing them in a broader perspective.

In Chapter 1 we examine the role played by the state in transforming Loreto into Peru's most dynamic nineteenth-century frontier economy. Contrary to the prevailing view that the state had little interest in its Amazon territories and did nothing to integrate them until well into the twentieth century, we maintain that it started taking measures to assert its influence in the region not long after Peru's independence from Spain in 1821. Through laws promoting colonization, agriculture, and commerce and by improving transportation and other services, the government was responding to two geopolitical imperatives: (1) to stop Brazil's expansion toward the west, and (2) to neutralize Ecuadorian and Colombian diplomatic claims over the upper Amazon region.

In Chapter 2 we explore the ecological basis of the rubber economy in general and that of Loreto in particular. We question two widely held perceptions. First, that Loreto's rubber economy was based on the exploitation of only two latex-producing species: *Castilloa sp.* and *Hevea brasiliensis*. Second, that most of Loreto's rubber exports consisted of latex obtained from *Castilloa sp*. We argue instead that

Loreto's economic boom was based on the tapping of several species and that the region's rubber economy experienced a process of "heveaization."

In Chapter 3 we address the issues of labor recruitment, retention, and organization in a frontier region not fully incorporated into the capitalist sphere, where no free labor market existed, and where there was a recurrent shortage of disciplined workers. We question the widespread notion that *habilitación* (debt-peonage) and *correrías* (slave-raids) were the only means of recruiting laborers for rubber extraction. We also question the view—derived from the labor situation in the estates of the infamous rubber baron, Julio César Arana—that Loreto's rubber economy was an "economy of terror" based on the indiscriminate use of physical violence. We instead argue that all modes of recruitment and retention of laborers combined in different proportions persuasion and violence and that control over laborers rather than natural resources, given the relative abundance of rubber and the shortage of disciplined labor, became the crux of the rubber economy. In such a context *habilitado* peons became simultaneously the rubber extractors' only capital and asset and the traders' only security.

In Chapter 4 we examine Loreto's trade, placing emphasis on the so-called grand commerce and on the pivotal role played by the import-export merchant houses of Iquitos, whose owners composed the region's trading elite. Two commonly accepted views about Loreto's commerce are brought into question here: first, that in the absence of local capital accumulation the region's trade was monopolized by foreign, particularly British, capital, which controlled credit, fluvial-maritime navigation, imports and exports; and second, that the structure of Loreto's commerce was identical to that of Brazilian commerce.

In Chapter 5 we question the general view that throughout the rubber boom the state had little presence in the region, weak control over its economy, and a precarious political hold. Instead, despite the 1879 war with Chile, a large external debt, and a stagnated economy, the Civilist governments of the time managed to extend their control in the Amazon, preserving the region's territorial integrity, regulating its economy, and crushing all armed attempts to overthrow its authority. The state's economic policies pitted the government against the region's economic elite, namely on the issues of taxes and tariffs, access to land and resources, and labor relations. We conclude that Civilist governments, despite their failure to carry out their economic program, had a powerful influence over the region and were quite successful in regulating those aspects of the rubber economy that they deemed necessary for the country's welfare.

In summary, Part 1 analyzes the formative stage of Loreto's economy from 1851 until the collapse of the rubber economy in 1914, during which the economy bore many of the traits generally attributed to frontier economies. These include the prevalence of extractive over productive activities; dependence on external demand and capital; persistence of precapitalist, coercive forms of production and exchange; lack of a domestic market; low levels of internal articulation and of articulation to the rest of the country; mostly unstable demographic fronts; self-serving and transient elites; and a state of lawlessness characterized by the existence of large disenfranchised social sectors and the settlement of conflicts through violence.

However, we also maintain that despite its shortcomings the rubber boom contributed to the integration of the region. This was achieved through the foundation and consolidation of important urban centers, the creation of extensive trading fluvial networks, the establishment of quite stable demographic and economic fronts along the navigable rivers, the incorporation into the marketplace of large numbers of previously isolated tribal Indians, and the expansion of state presence in the region. Our findings, based on an analysis of empirical data, also confirm some of the extremely insightful conclusions to which Barham and Coomes (1994b, 1996) and Coomes and Barham (1994) have arrived in their recent works on the Amazonian rubber economy through "deductive reasoning and conceptual argumentation," namely, that the rubber economy allowed for local capital accumulation and that the debt-peonage or debt-merchandise relationship was a relatively efficient labor arrangement "in the high risk, high transaction cost environment of the Amazon" (Barham and Coomes 1994b: 71). Some of the traits that characterized Loreto's frontier economy during the rubber era were to survive in the following stage (1915–1962). Others persisted in more subdued ways or began to disappear as a result of the important transformations experienced by Loreto after the rubber bust.

1

"Paying Preferential Attention": The State and the Rearing of Loreto

In 1767, after the Jesuits were expelled from the province of Maynas (the name given to Loreto in colonial times), the region fell into chaos. Most of the missions the Jesuits had founded were abandoned; a large portion of the catechized Indian population reverted to a "tribal" lifestyle; and the economic and political links with the colonial administrative centers of Quito and Lima were weakened significantly. The Franciscans, who succeeded the Jesuits, lacked the human, logistical, and economic resources to exert control upon a region that included the present-day departments of Loreto, Ucayali, and San Martín. Francisco de Requena, the province's governor since 1791, tried to reorganize the region and infuse it with new life, but his efforts met with failure. In 1802 he recommended to the Spanish Crown that it transfer jurisdiction over Maynas, from the Audiencia of Quito to the Viceroyalty of Peru, in order to tighten its control of the region. Although the Crown heeded Requena's recommendation, Maynas continued to remain largely outside the sphere of influence of the colonial administration. The upheavals caused by the wars of independence, the desertion of the Spanish authorities, and the expulsion, by the new national government, of the few foreign Franciscan missionaries that had been working in the region deepened Maynas's isolation. During the first decades of republican governance, the situation in the province did not improve; it continued to be an isolated, poorly colonized area.

Contrary to the prevailing view, however, the government was not disinterested in the region. As a result of Brazil's uninterrupted expansion toward the west, and of Ecuador's and Colombia's claims over the area north of the upper Amazon River, Peru took some important measures to guarantee its sovereignty over Loreto. Foremost among these was the signing of a treaty with Brazil in 1851 that settled most of the frontier disputes between them and opened the Amazon River to navigation by ships from both countries. This had the effect of neutralizing Ecuador's and Colombia's territorial claims. But the government went further in its efforts to assert a presence in the region. During the following decades, it founded a navy station in the hamlet of Iquitos, purchased steamships from Great Britain and the United States, explored the Amazon and its tributaries, and stimulated European colonization. Some of these measures, such as the colonization policies, failed to achieve their objectives. Others, such as the foundation of the navy station at Iquitos, were extremely successful; in due time Iquitos became the capital of Loreto and one of Peru's largest cities (see Map 1.1).

Because of a deepening fiscal crisis, by the early 1870s the government was unable to continue subsidizing all these activities. By then, however, it had already created the conditions for the effective articulation of the region with the marketplace. We argue that this proved to be a momentous achievement, for it facilitated Loreto's rapid involvement in rubber extraction and export once the international demand for that product soared during the 1870s. This heavy-handed government intervention should lead us to revise the accepted view that during the nineteenth century Peru showed little interest in integrating its Amazon territories; the idea that it had no clear geopolitical agenda, and that it had little or no presence in peripheral regions, is clearly mistaken.

Geopolitics and Early Governmental Actions

In 1853 Pres. Rufino Echenique asserted that the Amazon River valley required "preferential attention" and that the state should "endeavor to exploit and populate its fertile plains" (Larrabure i Correa: II, 46–52). In order to achieve this goal, Echenique passed an important piece of legislation dealing with colonization, land concessions, fluvial exploration and navigation, and geographic and political administration. This law regulated matters that had been the object of previously fragmentary and ineffective legislation. By addressing them in an integral fashion, the 15 April 1853 law became the first systematic policy for the control and occupation of the Amazon region, particularly of Loreto.

One of the antecedents of this law was the treaty signed in 1851 by Peru and the Empire of Brazil (Larrabure i Correa: II, 18–23). Though formally the treaty's focus was on fluvial navigation and commerce, its most important clause was that in which both states agreed to respect the principle of *uti possidetis* (actual possession) as the basis for the future demarcation of their common Amazonian frontiers. This agreement, which allowed Brazil to take possession of territories previously disputed by Peru, was, however, an important move in the geopolitical chess game that Peru was playing with Ecuador, Colombia, and Brazil for the control of the upper tract of the Amazon River. By signing a treaty with the most powerful of these countries, and in return for the territories it ceded, Peru was able to enlist Brazil's nonwritten support for its territorial claims vis-à-vis Ecuador and Colombia. Thus, when the Ecuadorian government presented a diplomatic complaint to the Brazilian Foreign Office, its laconic answer was that "the Government of Brazil has dealt with the one who was in possession of those territories." (Larrabure i Correa: I, 83).

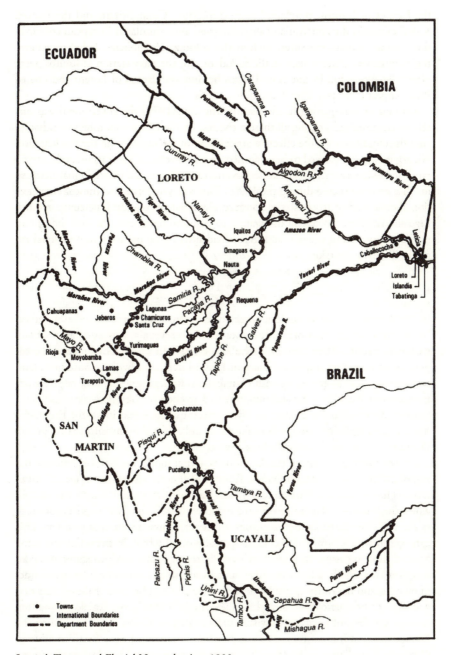

Loreto's Towns and Fluvial Network, circa 1900

Apart from this boundary agreement, the 1851 international treaty between Peru and Brazil dealt with navigation rights along the Amazon. In previous years the U.S. government had supported an initiative by a group of American entrepreneurs interested in having access to Brazil's rubber production to establish a steamship line along the Amazon River (Santos 1980: 54). Fearful of the effects that this would have on its sovereignty over the Amazon region and its resources, Brazil thought it wise to enlist the support of Peru in order to strengthen both countries' rights over the Amazon Basin. The treaty opened the Amazon and its tributaries to navigation by steamboats of both states, exonerated from import duties their respective merchandise, and committed both countries to contract jointly the services of a steamship line. The latter would have to make regular trips from the city of Belém, at the mouth of the Amazon, up to the Peruvian port of Nauta, at the confluence of the Marañon and Ucayali Rivers. Both states agreed to subsidize the company during the first five years of its existence.

Echenique's 1853 law ratified the 1851 treaty and effectively ordered the opening of the Peruvian portion of the Amazon to Brazilian steamboats. It appointed the small towns of Loreto, on the border with Brazil, and Nauta as the only Peruvian ports authorized to engage in international trade. It also reserved the right of exploration of the Amazon's tributaries to Peruvian vessels. In order to undertake this exploration and to serve the smaller ports on the Ucayali and Huallaga Rivers, the Peruvian government had ordered, earlier that same year, the construction of two steamboats in the United States (Larrabure i Correa: II, 41). This marked the beginning of a strategy to develop a national fluvial fleet, which was to have important consequences in the following years. Finally, this law also hastened the negotiations to contract the services of a shipping line that would serve the Amazon.

One month before the 1853 law was passed by Congress, President Echenique had approved the creation of the Political and Military Government of Loreto (Larrabure i Correa: I, 19–20). This new jurisdiction was detached from the vast, postindependence department of Amazonas and comprised all of the territory traversed by the Amazon and Marañon Rivers and their northern and southern tributaries. The 1853 law divided Loreto into ten districts: four along the Huallaga, four along the Amazon-Marañon axis, and two along the Ucayali. The governor's residence was established in the small port of Loreto, which also harbored a forty-man garrison. By then, however, the largest population, the bulk of the economic activity, and the most important towns within the region, such as Moyobamba, were located in the Huallaga districts—the area along the eastern slopes of the Andes known in colonial times as the Upper Mission. The rest of the territory of the new government of Loreto, previously known as the Lower Mission, was scarcely populated, with the only existing towns being the remnants of a few Jesuit missions. These were a string of scattered riverine hamlets inhabited by a small number of "catechized" Indian families (descendants of the mission Indians of colonial times) and a few mestizo and white settlers. Nauta, founded in 1830, was the only port town created in postindependence times. Though the external and internal boundaries of Loreto were changed several times in subsequent years, the spirit that fostered the law remained alive, and the region of Loreto maintained a distinct identity.

In order to increase the population, Echenique's 1853 law, taking a cue from an earlier 1832 law (Larrabure i Correa: I, 17), contemplated stimulating colonization of the region through national and foreign, preferably European, immigration. The law enabled the state to sign contracts with private entrepreneurs for the recruitment and settlement of colonists in the Amazon Basin. For each settler introduced, the contractor was to receive a premium. In addition, the state committed to cover the costs of travel and installation of the immigrants, grant them lands, provide them tools, and exempt them from property and other taxes. Though the government signed a few of these contracts (Registro 1902: 111–4) and issued new immigration and colonization laws in ensuing years, none of them were effective in attracting European colonists, mainly because the region was considered to be too isolated from the market and from "civilized" life. In contrast, the 1853 navigation treaty with Brazil, and the direct intervention of the state in the creation of a fluvial fleet, had an almost immediate effect on the commercial development of the region, insofar as it provided the local white-mestizo population with an outlet for its produce.

On the basis of the 1851 treaty, Brazil contracted in 1852 the services of the Amazon Navigation Company, which was incorporated with a capital of 1,200 *contos*, or approximately £80,000 (Larrabure i Correa: II, 26–29). Peru protested the fact that Brazil had acted unilaterally but ratified the contract with some modifications in 1853 (Larrabure i Correa: II, 24–5, 29–40). In Brazil the company was known as the Amazon Navigation and Trade Company. According to Santos (1980: 55–6), it had been organized in Belém on an ad hoc basis by a well-known Brazilian banker, the Barão de Mauá. During the following five years, the company served both countries along two navigation lines: Belém-Manaus and Manaus-Nauta. Along the latter, the company was obliged by contract to make up to six trips per year. The Peruvian and Brazilian states subsidized the company on an equal-share basis, Peru's contribution being 20,000 pesos per year (Larrabure i Correa: II, 24–41). At the time, silver pesos were equivalent to U.S. silver dollars and were exchanged at a rate of $5 per sterling pound (Bonilla 1976: IV, 107).

This subsidy was meant to compensate the company for the presumed insufficiency of cargo and passengers during the first years of operation. However, despite the fact that some contemporary observers (Raimondi 1862: 197) considered this to be an unfair and costly deal, Peru regarded it as an indispensable first step toward attaining geopolitical goals in the region. Among them was the development of its own national fluvial fleet, for which the Brazilian contract was good experience. This explains why Peru requested the introduction of a clause into the contract that denied the company exclusive rights of navigation along the Amazon (Larrabure i Correa II, 40). The steamships ordered in the United States by the Peruvian government early in 1853 arrived in 1854. Though they proved to be badly designed for use in the region—they sunk in 1857 (Romero 1983: 15)—they helped, together with those of the Brazilian company, to stimulate internal and external trade.

Before 1853 the export commerce in the region had been almost negligible due to the lack both of roads, through which to transport the local production to the Pacific Coast, as well as adequate boats to transport it in large volumes to Brazil or to the Atlantic markets. Fluvial trade was mainly internal, based on large wooden canoes driven by indigenous rowers and controlled by local retail merchants, the *regatones*. The advent of steam navigation brought forth an astonishing increase in internal and external trade and provided a market for the region's exportable goods. These included Panama hats, sarsaparilla (*Smilax sp.*), as well as salted fish, tobacco, cotton, hammocks, turtle egg oil, quinine, vanilla, wax, and small quantities of rubber (Herrera 1905: 120–34). As we see in Table 1.1, the increase in exports went hand in hand with a considerable growth in imports. Among them were tools, cotton textiles, clothing, footwear, foodstuffs, and liquors (Herrera 1905: 133). Steam navigation also generated new economic opportunities for the riverine population, mainly the production of firewood, coal, and local foodstuffs to supply passing vessels.

As a result of the new commercial dynamism, the small ports of Loreto and Nauta became, together with the city of Moyobamba, the most active trading cen-

Table 1.1   Loreto's Import and Export Trade, 1853–1870

Year	Imports	Exports	Total (pesos)[a]
1853	150	1,280	1,430
1854	350	74,907	75,257
1855	8,500	64,522	73,022
1856	21,000	180,848	201,848
1857	25,000	245,586	270,586
1858	49,350	246,775	296,125
1859	89,500	237,055	326,555
1860	150,000	159,889	309,889
1861	142,500	156,260	298,760
1862	100,000	120,388	220,388
1863	82,787	242,893	325,680
1864	126,922	274,754	401,676
1865	308,518	245,431	553,949
1866	303,292	238,394	541,686
1867	324,533	207,535	532,068
1868	190,726	276,747	467,473
1869	293,730	312,154	605,885
1870	616,065	508,106	1,120,171

SOURCE: Herrera 1905: 137-8

NOTES: [a] In the 1850s silver pesos were equivalent to U.S. silver dollars. The latter were exchanged at a rate of $5 per pound sterling (Bonilla 1976: IV, 107).

[b] In 1863 the Peruvian currency changed from "pesos" to "soles" (Romero 1983: 20).

[c] Throughout the 1870s the exchange rate was approximately 5 soles per pound sterling (Bonilla 1976: IV, 200; Romero 1983: 68; Bardella 1989: 77).

ters of the region. Loreto attracted a significant number of Portuguese and Brazilian merchants, and Nauta became the headquarters of at least two merchant houses (Raimondi 1862: 346, 319). Some intermediate outposts also experienced a certain economic prosperity, expressed in the initiation of cattle-raising and the production of *aguardiente*, an unrefined liquor distilled from sugarcane (Raimondi 1869: 318–9). Due to the fact that "third-country" vessels were not allowed to travel along the Amazon, the whole of the region's exports was sold to Brazil, from where some of them were reexported. Contemporary travelers reported that this situation allowed Brazilian merchants to pay low prices for Peruvian exports (Raimondi 1869: 261).

In 1858 Peru and Brazil signed a new treaty that seemed to maintain the status quo (Larrabure i Correa: II, 57–63). However, in contrast to the 1853 treaty, the new agreement did not commit both countries to contract and subsidize jointly a navigation company. Thus, when the contract with Amazon Navigation and Trade expired, Peru renewed it in 1859 for only two years. The new contract established that the company was to make twelve trips a year to Yurimaguas, a port on the Huallaga River close to its confluence with the Amazon. Peru was to pay the company 10,000 pesos per trip, that is, around £1,300 (Larrabure i Correa: II, 63–6; Bonilla 1976: IV, 110). Though this arrangement was considered outrageously onerous by contemporary observers (Raimondi 1862: 271), it seems clear in retrospect that Peru was trying to buy time in order to develop its own fleet.

State Investment and the Founding of Iquitos

The plans for a fluvial fleet were accelerated by the outbreak, in 1859, of war with Ecuador. Two years earlier, Ecuador had ceded lands west of the Bobonaza and Pastaza Rivers to British creditors as partial payment of its external debt. As these lands were considered by Peru to be within its boundaries, it broke diplomatic relations with Ecuador and prepared for war. In 1860 Peru besieged and invaded the Ecuadorian port of Guayaquil, thus putting an abrupt end to the war. In the ensuing political chaos, the two states signed the Treaty of Mapasingue, whereby Ecuador recognized Peruvian sovereignty over the territories traversed by the northern tributaries of the Marañon and Amazon Rivers up to the point at which they were navigable. However, the Ecuadorian postwar Congress did not ratify the treaty. It was not until 1887 that both countries agreed to submit their differences to the king of Spain (Martínez Riaza, 1998a).

In the aftermath of the confrontation, Peru was determined to augment its presence in Loreto. This was achieved through four measures: (1) the militarization of the region; (2) the formation of an embryonic national fluvial fleet; (3) the foundation of a naval captainship and workshop in the hamlet of Iquitos; and (4) the creation of the Amazon Hydrographic Commission. By means of the first measure, issued in 1861, the former political-military government of Loreto was turned into the Military Maritime Department under a navy officer with the rank of colonel

(Larrabure i Correa: II, 23–4). The second goal was partially achieved when in 1861 Peru ordered the construction of four new boats in England, which arrived in Iquitos in 1863 and 1864. The boats' names (*Morona, Pastaza, Napo,* and *Putumayo*) represented a symbolic claim of sovereignty over the major northern tributaries of the Marañon and Amazon that were disputed by Ecuador.

Napo and *Putumayo* were dedicated to the exploration and charting of the Amazon and its tributaries; *Morona* and *Pastaza*, with a larger carrying capacity, were designed for internal fluvial trade, though they could also double as gunboats (Romero 1983: 23–4). From 1863 onward the latter pair made regular trips between Yurimaguas and the Brazilian frontier town of Tabatinga. Conceived of as "messengers of civilization and progress" but also meant as a deterrent against invasions by its neighbors, these vessels enabled Peru to renew the region's fluvial trade. This had been disrupted since 1860, when the contract with the Brazilian navigation line was canceled (Larrabure i Correa: II, 70–2). As can be deduced from Table 1.1 above, the arrival of *Morona* and *Pastaza* reversed this trend by stimulating a dramatic increase in the region's import-export trade.

In 1832 the Peruvian Congress had approved the construction of a shipyard in a site close to the confluence of the Ucayali and Marañon Rivers (Larrabure i Correa: I, 17–18). This objective was retained in the 1861 law that transformed Loreto into a Military Maritime Department. In addition, the 1861 law approved the construction of a navy station, a naval workshop, and a nautical school. Although the law stated that all of these facilities should be erected on the site established by the 1832 law, a commission of navy officers and engineers was appointed to determine the best place to found the new naval complex. On the basis of Iquitos's topographic characteristics and the availability of resources, the commission recommended that the facilities be located in that small hamlet along the Amazon farther downriver.

The building of the complex began in 1862. When the four steamboats ordered by the Peruvian state finally gathered in Iquitos in 1864, the navy station was officially inaugurated (Larrabure i Correa: II, 70). By 1869 the naval workshop included a steam-powered sawmill, a carpenter's shop, a foundry and forge, a brick furnace, and a floating dock. In 1862, when construction started, Iquitos had a population of 862, of which 25 percent where foreigners, mainly British sailors, mechanics, and engineers (Rodríguez Achung 1986: 23). However, shortly thereafter the local population and economy experienced spectacular growth, and the new city displaced Nauta as Peru's most important Amazon port, then Moyobamba as capital of the department. This would have been impossible without the heavy investment that the state made in the region, largely based on revenues from guano exports (Bonilla 1994). This subsidy amounted to 300,000 pesos or approximately £50,000 per year (Raimondi 1869: 322; Bonilla 1976: IV, 122), an impressive sum if we consider that in 1862 the annual budget of the municipality of Callao, Peru's main port, totaled 77,620 pesos (Memoria 1862: Doc. 11). An additional investment of 300,000 *soles*—the new name of the Peruvian currency after 1863—was made in 1868 for the construction of a fort in the town of Leticia, close to the border with Brazil (García Rosell 1905: 622).

Thus three events—the purchase of steamboats, the foundation of the navy station at Iquitos, and the building of the fort at Leticia—enabled Peru to launch a program of exploration of the region's rivers and resources. In 1867 it created the Amazon Hydrographic Commission, appointing John Tucker as president. Tucker had been rear admiral of the Confederate Navy during the U.S. Civil War and was in the service of the Peru Navy since the 1866 war between Spain and Peru (Raimondi 1879: III, 380). The Commission was administered under the Ministry of War and Navy; its members, together with naval officers stationed in Iquitos, explored all of the major northern and southern tributaries of the Marañon and Amazon Rivers. They charted the region's rivers and determined their navigability, the availability of resources, the extent of the indigenous population, and the location of *varaderos*—portages or short land trails linking the headwaters of neighboring rivers.

The investment made by the state in this exploration program bore fruits far beyond their expectations. In the following seven years (until 1873, when it carried out its two last expeditions), Peru managed to reconnoiter, describe, and map most of the upper Amazon's fluvial network (Tizón i Bueno 1905: 547). In later years, rubber extractors and merchants were to profit from the knowledge acquired along this pioneering period. Thus, unintentionally, the state established the conditions for the development of rubber extraction activities in the remotest corners of Loreto.

In 1868 Peru, following a similar measure taken by the Brazilian state two years earlier, opened its portion of the Amazon River to international navigation (Larrabure i Correa: II, 5). The fact that the Amazon had been closed to foreign vessels up till then had impaired Loreto's export trade, as it was captive to Brazilian navigation companies. The Peruvian boats had replaced those belonging to Amazon Navigation and Trade, making regular trips to the Brazilian border town of Tabatinga and, occasionally, to Manaus and Belém. However, the Brazilian markets were still the only ones in which Loreto's production could be placed. By then, three Brazilian companies were operating along the Brazilian section of the Amazon (Santos 1980: 55). Two other British companies, the Red Cross Line and the Booth Line, made regular trips between Liverpool and Belém (Santos 1980: 58). The opening of Amazon waters to international navigation did not immediately attract foreign navigation companies. By 1872, however, the British-owned Amazon Steam Navigation Company started operating in the area. With newer and faster ships, that company defeated its Brazilian competitors in only two years (Weinstein 1983: 62). In 1874 it bought out its three Brazilian rivals, for a time enjoying a virtual monopoly over the regular fluvial navigation of the Brazilian Amazon.

The End of Government Support

In the early 1870s Peru entered a period of financial crisis. Excessive public expenditures, fiscal deficits, and the undertaking of substantial foreign loans led the country into almost complete bankruptcy (Bonilla 1994: 320). By 1872 the government could no longer afford to remit the monthly subsidy to the navy station at Iquitos (Romero 1983: 62). The facts that the inhabitants of Loreto were exempted from paying property and other taxes (Larrabure i Correa: I, 229–31), and that the import-export trade was also exonerated from tariffs, made matters even worse. By 1876, in little more than a decade, the population of Iquitos had more than trebled, reaching 2,950 (Rodríguez Achung 1986: 23). Most of the population depended in some way on the state, either as employees, suppliers, or providers of services.

From 1872 on the general commander of Loreto had to resort to expensive private credit from the merchant houses of Iquitos and Yurimaguas to pay salaries and keep the naval workshop running (Romero 1983: 57, 60, 64). With the increase in commerce, some of these merchant houses had seen their capitals go up to 100,000 soles (approximately £20,000), and they were becoming the most important economic agents within the region (Raimondi 1869: 322). But in 1877 that source of credit also closed, as the state bonds, which backed the loans, had lost all value. The government therefore decided to sell its boats and lease the Iquitos naval workshop to a group of local merchants who, by contract, committed to create a steamship line as the Peruvian Navigation Company (Larrabure i Correa: II, 92–8).

In consideration for this detrimental contract, the government committed to support the company with an annual subsidy of £24,000 for a period of fifteen years. In turn the company's boats had to make regular trips along three routes: Iquitos-Yurimaguas (on the Huallaga River), Iquitos-Sarayacu (on the Ucayali River), and Iquitos-Belém. It also committed to increase its fleet by ordering the construction of new vessels. Although the general commander of Loreto objected that the contract meant, in essence, the virtual dismantling of the navy station, it was subscribed to in 1877. The contractual terms were very onerous for the government, and the payment it received for its four-boat fleet (£7,600) was equivalent to only 2.1 percent of the annual subsidies the state had committed to pay (Romero 1983: 69). It is, therefore, not surprising that the contract was widely criticized and that in 1880 the fiscal superintendent annulled it (Bedoya 1905, in Larrabure i Correa: III, 6).

Peru's financial crisis and, as a consequence, Loreto's, deepened as a result of the war with Chile (1879–1882). Not until after the war did Loreto's administration start obtaining enough revenue to operate regularly and make new investments in the region. This was largely due to the increase in rubber prices and exports, as well as to the establishment of a customhouse in Iquitos.

Between 1853, when the first shipments of rubber were made, and 1868, when the Amazon was opened to international traffic, rubber exports had remained minimal, with an average of less than 5 metric tons per year (Pennano 1988: 178–9). But the opening of the Amazon boosted rubber exports. By 1884, two years after the establishment of the Iquitos customhouse, volume rose to 540 metric tons. Compared to the 10,643 metric tons exported from Brazilian Amazonia that same year (Weinstein 1983: 197), that might seem insignificant. However, the impact of rubber extraction on the Loreto economy was as massive and pervasive as that experienced by the economies of the Brazilian states of Pará and Amazonas.

The government's vision of Loreto as a prosperous agrarian economy in the hands of enterprising and industrious European immigrants never materialized. However, its policies had two important effects. First, it forestalled Ecuador and Colombia from having an effective presence in the region. Second, it made the region accessible and, thus, available for exploitation. Without its favored status and the state intervening to establish certain basic conditions and infrastructure, Loreto would have continued to be an economic hinterland, subordinated to extraregional urban centers such as Moyobamba, Manaus, or Belém. But for the state's investments in the creation and rearing of the region, Loreto would have remained peripheral to the rubber economy, and once the latter came to an end it would have reverted to its original remote, isolated condition. Instead, during the rubber boom Iquitos became a leading trade center, handling not only most of the rubber produced in Peruvian Amazonia but also that extracted from the Amazon lowlands of Ecuador and Colombia.

In brief, thanks to government intervention Loreto was transformed from a backwater into a new, promising frontier economy. As we shall see, however, the rubber economy that flourished from 1870 to 1914 had mixed results. On the one hand it stimulated colonization, commerce, and urban growth; on the other it promoted coercive forms of labor and the exploitation of the region's indigenous population.

2

"A Magical Product":
The Ecological Basis of the
Rubber Economy

Rubber extraction and exportation in Loreto grew steadily from 1870 on thanks to increasing demand in the United States and the industrialized countries of Europe. At the beginning of the nineteenth century, rubber began to be used for insulation of underwater telegraph cables and for the crafting of some specialized products (Pennano 1988: 65). Later on it was employed in the manufacture of waterproof garments and footwear. However, not till 1844, when Charles Goodyear patented the process of vulcanization that stabilized rubber chemically, making it less vulnerable to temperature changes, did the range of rubber's industrial applications increase exponentially (Pennano 1988: 74). It was soon used in roofing, paving, cabling, and the manufacture of surgical instruments and steam machine parts (Dean 1987: 9). In 1884 Charles Macintosh introduced the first bicycle tires, and the bicycle craze swept Europe and the United States. The demand for rubber increased even more after 1895, when cars began to be furnished with rubber tires (Pennano 1988: 76).

As a consequence of increasing demand, rubber prices rose steadily between 1877 and 1888. In 1885 Loreto's rubber exports exceeded 1,000 metric tons (Pennano 1988: 178–9). In previous years rubber had been slowly displacing the region's other export products, and by 1886 it represented 88.5 percent of the total value of Loreto's exports (Palacios 1890b: 493). Shortly after that rubber became Loreto's only export. The private income and public revenue generated by the rubber trade brought a welcome relief to cash-strapped Loreto, which since 1872 had not received state funds. It also attracted many laborers from small towns located on the eastern slopes of the Andes along the Huallaga Basin, as well as from the Andean highlands and the Pacific Coast. By the turn of the century rubber was referred to by contemporary observers as "a magical product" that had saved Loreto's economy from an early death; it was also hailed as the "golden key to national happiness" (Pesce 1904: 46). But what was the exact nature of this "magical product," known in the market by the generic, and frequently confusing, label of "rubber"?

In the second half of the eighteenth century French naturalist Charles La Condamine had drawn attention to the properties of rubber and its usage by Amerindians. La Condamine was unaware that the rubber objects he had seen on the Pacific Coast of Ecuador and along the Amazon River were made from the latex of trees belonging to two different genera, later classified as *Castilloa* and *Hevea*. From then on French, German, and English explorers and naturalists started collecting, describing, and classifying these and other latex-producing Amazonian trees and plants, disagreeing strongly among themselves over questions of classifications and species names.

The taxonomic confusion persisted well into the second half of the nineteenth century, when several species were being tapped simultaneously and tappers knew little about their different botanical characteristics. By the beginning of the twentieth century, however, the existence of five main genera was finally agreed upon: *Hevea, Castilloa, Sapium, Ficus,* and *Manihot* (Domínguez and Gómez 1990: 82). Intensive experimentation by tappers, scientists, and manufacturers alike led to the selection of five species belonging to *Hevea* and *Castilloa*. These became the most sought-after species, accounting for the bulk of rubber production in the Amazon Basin: *Hevea brasiliensis*, known as "Pará rubber" in the international market, *seringa* in Brazil, and *jebe* in the upper Amazon countries; *Hevea benthamiana* and *Hevea guyanensis*, known as "weak Pará," *seringa fraca*, or *jebe débil*; and *Castilloa elastica* and *Castilloa ulei*, known as "black rubber" in the international market and as *caucho* throughout Amazonia. Species of *Sapium* and *Ficus*, producers of white, pink, and gray rubbers, were also exploited but to a much lesser extent (Domínguez and Gómez 1990: 82–4).

While acknowledging the existence of various latex-producing species, students of the rubber economy have often tended to play down this diversity, collapsing all species under the generic term "rubber" or highlighting one species as emblematic of a given region's economy. Thus, for instance, Weinstein (1983: 185), in her otherwise rich and insightful study, assumes that the Brazilian rubber economy was almost entirely based on the exploitation of hevea; she makes only one reference to the gathering of castilloa in the area of the Tocantins River in eastern Brazil. We know, however, that from the 1890s onward the gathering of castilloa increased at a faster rate than that of hevea; by 1906, in fact, *caucho* accounted for 16 percent of Brazilian rubber exports (Dean 1987: 38). Similarly, Weinstein (1983: 26) characterizes the Peruvian rubber economy as being totally based on the collection of castilloa, implicitly presenting it as the antithesis of the hevea-producing Brazilian economy.

This dichotomization is not new. In the early twentieth century observers stressed the contrast between the "riskier and more nomadic" activities of the Peruvian *caucheros*, who fell and drained castilloa trees, and the "more sedentary and beneficent" operations of the Brazilian *seringueiros*, who opened up rubber trails and periodically tapped hevea trees (Pesce 1903: 93). A Peruvian government official asserted that "*seringa*-producing Brazil has become wealthy and mighty [while] *caucho*-producing Peru still does not collect its copious riches" (Quiroz, in Fuentes 1906: 426). Modern authors have presented a less monolithic view of the Peruvian rubber economy, arguing that the exploitation of *caucho* and *jebe* coexisted, resulting in different tapping techniques, settlement patterns, and working ethoses (San Román 1975: 141; Pennano 1988: 53). In our opinion, this is still too narrow a view. For one, it does not acknowledge the importance that the exploitation of other rubber species, such as weak heveas, had for the region's economy. For another, it ignores the dramatic fluctuations in species tapped and areas exploited in Loreto's rubber production.

To understand the complexities of rubber production in upper Amazonia it is important to examine the geographic distribution of the different rubber-producing species, focusing on their botanical potential and constraints. As we shall see, their diverse natural properties encouraged the development of different techniques for the tapping and processing of latex. These techniques, in turn, resulted in various qualities of rubber, differentially priced on the international market. The geographic distribution and natural potential of these species, combined with other economic considerations, gave rise to a series of rubber extractive fronts, which differed in settlement patterns, labor arrangements, and profitability.

They also differed in sustainability of economic activities and resulting stability. Although some rubber fronts persisted over time, others appeared and disappeared as resources became progressively depleted, new areas were incorporated into production, and market demands changed. In brief, rather than talking about *the* rubber boom, which suggests a monoproducing and homogeneous economy, it is more appropriate to talk about diversity in modes of producing rubber. Their different combinations not only account for the significant variations that exist among rubber regions within the Amazon Basin but also explain changes within a particular region over time.

Botanical Properties of Latex-Producing Trees

It is said that the main latex-producing species of the Amazon Basin are distributed in three distinct areas (see Wolf and Wolf 1936; San Román 1975; Dean 1987; Domínguez and Gómez 1990). *Castilloa elastica* and *ulei* occurs along the slopes and plains east of the Andes in a north-south arch stretching from eastern Colombia to eastern Bolivia. *Hevea brasiliensis* is found south of the Amazon River in an area extending from the Ucayali River in the west to Matto Grosso in the east and down to the Mamoré River. In turn, *Hevea guyanensis* and *benthamiana* occur north of the Amazon, from the Napo River in the west to the Guyanas in the east and as far as the Orinoco River.

This, however, is a very broad generalization. A closer inspection of particular areas shows a much greater complexity. Thus, in Loreto castilloa extraction was reported as far east as the lower tracts of the Putumayo and Caqueta Rivers (Domínguez and Gómez 1990: 85), the right bank of the Yavari (Memorial 1904:

500) and the upper tracts of the Yurua and Purus Rivers (Mavila 1902: 549). It was even reported in Brazil along the upper Madeira and as far east as the Tocantins, close to the mouth of the Amazon (Domínguez and Gómez 1990: 82). In turn, tapping of hevea was reported as far west as the right bank of the Marañon River, the inner lands between the Ucayali and the Huallaga, and even on the left bank of the latter river, in the environs of the town of Yurimaguas (Collier 1981: 48). Finally, exploitation of weak heveas was reported in the middle Caqueta and Putumayo Rivers. But it was also reported as far south as the Huallaga and Yavari Rivers (Fuentes 1905a: 62) and as close to the Andean foothills as the Pachitea and Pichis Rivers, located beyond the boundaries of the department of Loreto (San Román 1975: 125).

These different species have also been associated with particular habitats. *Castilloa* is supposed to thrive in well-drained soils of the terra firme, the interfluvial and headwater areas from 1,000 to 300–500 meters above sea level (Domínguez and Gómez 1990: 84). Although generally dispersed, castilloa is also found in more or less homogeneous stands, particularly in the lower lands (ibidem). In contrast, hevea is associated with the low riparian or interfluvial plains that are seasonally flooded, where it grows in low-density stands. However, it is well known that a variety of this species was exploited in the terra firme areas of the Acre region, where it produced a highly appreciated quality of rubber (ibidem: 93). The habitats of weak heveas are more variable, but in general terms they grow in well-drained soils of the terra firme or on riverbanks that experience only short periods of flooding (ibidem: 96).

In brief, although in theory different latex-producing species tend to occur in different areas and habitats, on the ground it is possible to find individuals of all four rubber-yielding species in a relatively small area. However, proximity does not imply that these species are similar in terms of the quality of their latex, their productivity, or the techniques through which they were exploited.

In hevea the latex corpuscles that contain rubber hydrocarbons are located in the bark, forming long, intercommunicated conduits (Domínguez and Gómez 1990: 90). This allows latex to flow freely when the trunk is incised. At the onset of the rubber boom hevea was tapped with a primitive method known as *arrocho* in Brazil and *arrojo* in Peru and Colombia. This consisted of pounding the trunk, making irregular cuts on it, and tightly wrapping it with vines in order to force the latex to flow into containers placed on the ground. There it coagulated naturally in contact with air (Domínguez and Gómez 1990: 97). This technique damaged the trees and led to their eventual deaths. In Brazil, the increase of rubber prices that took place in the 1850s and 1860s stimulated private appropriation of natural hevea-rich forests and the abandonment of the *arrocho* technique in favor of a more sustainable extractive system (Santos 1980: 80).

The new system of extracting and processing the latex of hevea was made possible by its botanical properties. It entailed the identification and marking of individual trees and the opening of *estradas*, or rubber trails. In Brazil these trails consisted of 100–200 trees; in Loreto they comprised 60–150 trees (Weinstein 1983: 16;

Fuentes 1906: 415). *Estradas* were loops 8–10 kilometers long starting and ending in the tapper's hut. Each tapper was in charge of two or three trails. The tapping and processing of the latex under the new system—for which more detailed accounts are presented by Pennano (1988: 55–6) and Domínguez and Gómez (1990: 100)—consisted of the following operations. Early every morning the tapper walked along one of his trails, making several oblique incisions in the trees with a special knife. Then the tapper attached a small tin cup at the base of the cuts in order to collect the flowing latex. Once back at his hut the tapper started a second round to collect the latex accumulated in the cups, which could amount to a gallon. In the afternoon the tapper started the process of smoking the latex collected earlier. This was achieved by fabricating a rounded clay mold along the midlength of a pole and slowly pouring upon it layer after layer of liquid latex while rotating the pole over a tin chimney that channeled the heavy smoke produced by the burning of different oily nuts and woods. Through this process the latex slowly coagulated. After several days a large rubber ball of 50–60 kilograms was detached from the pole by breaking the inner clay mold. This smoked latex was known as "fine Pará," or *jebe fino* quality. In order to allow the hevea trees to recover, tappers alternated their daily rounds among their various trails.

Although smoked balls constituted the most appreciated and highly priced form of hevea rubber, this was not the only quality obtained from this species. Less well processed or impure rubber balls were classified as "entrefine" (*entrefino*) and brought a lower price at market. A third quality of hevea rubber, classified as "scrappy," "coarse," or "negroheads" (*sernambí de jebe*) flowed from badly made incisions or injuries resulting from disease or remained attached to the collecting cups. It thus naturally coagulated in contact with air. The bits and strips of rubber so coagulated were wrapped into skeins weighing an average of 15 kilograms. These were known locally as *andullos*.

Hevea tappers worked eleven hours a day, six days a week (except for rainy days), during the whole of the dry season, which in different parts of Loreto could last between four and eight months. The rest of the year was devoted to other productive activities, mainly horticultural farming, hunting, and fishing. In some isolated fronts, such as the Yavari or the Pacaya-Samiria, many tappers preferred to abandon their working post during the rains and settle temporarily in towns along the larger rivers (Fuentes 1908: 57). Even though the productivity of hevea decreased with time, trees could be periodically tapped for several decades. The tolerance of hevea to prolonged periodic tapping gave rise to the tapping-trail technique. In turn, this encouraged sedentary settlement patterns, as well as a reasonably sustainable economy that combined extraction of latex with the small production of agricultural foodstuffs.

As for *Hevea brasiliensis*, the trees of weak hevea species could be regularly tapped. However, weak hevea species are more difficult to tap because their latex does not flow as easily. Not only are weak heveas less productive, but they cannot stand long periods of tapping. In addition, rubber processed from the latex of weak heveas is less elastic and tends to lose more weight than that of hevea. In Loreto, weak heveas were reported to be particularly abundant in the Putumayo Basin (von Hassel 1902a: 106). As they were not systematically exploited until the beginning of the twentieth century, weak heveas provided an alternative source of rubber in those areas in which castilloa stands had been depleted.

In Loreto, collection of weak hevea latex was carried out through two different techniques. The first was similar to that for hevea. During the early years of the twentieth century, Colombian extractors working in the middle Putumayo opened trails, incised the trees regularly, and smoked the latex in a fashion similar to that used to obtain fine Pará rubber balls (Domínguez and Gómez 1990: 97). Rubber thus processed was known in the international market as "weak fine," or *jebe débil fino*. However, the smoking of weak hevea latex proved not to be sufficiently profitable, because its processing required the same amount of work as fine Pará, but the final product brought a much lower price. For this reason, the smoking of weak heveas was abandoned quite early.

The second technique, applied along both the Putumayo and Napo Rivers, was also based on the opening of tapping trails (von Hassel 1903: 233; Domínguez and Gómez 1990: 98). Tappers marked a number of weak hevea trees, making numerous and deep incisions on them. Several days later they collected the latex that had flowed to the ground and coagulated naturally. The strips of rubber thus collected were pounded in a stream to free them of impurities. They were then wrapped in skeins and exposed to the effects of sun and air. The dark, elongated skeins obtained were locally known as "Putumayo tails" (*rabos del Putumayo*) and classified in the market as *sernambí de jebe débil*, or "weak scrappy." Although weak hevea trees could be tapped in this way with some frequency, they died in a much shorter time than did hevea. Thus, even though weak hevea was exploited using more or less well-established tapping trails, it did not induce the formation of stable economic fronts like those associated with hevea and characteristic of the Brazilian Amazon and the lower tracts of its southern tributaries.

Castilloa differs from the heveas in several respects. Firstly, in castilloa latex corpuscles containing rubber hydrocarbons form isolated, unconnected cells (Domínguez and Gómez 1990: 90). For this reason, when incised, their latex does not flow easily and in large volumes. In order to collect a significant amount of raw rubber, castilloa trees must be profusely and profoundly cut. Second, whereas heveas can be incised more or less regularly for a period of several months per year, castilloa can be tapped only twice per year if the tree is to survive. Finally, incised castilloa trees are prone to attack from a variety of pests, a fact that rapidly leads to their deaths. These botanical characteristics severely limited the sustainable exploitation of castilloa and resulted in what many authors considered a "barbarous" method of exploitation, that is, the felling and total draining of the trees.

There were two standard methods for extracting and processing the latex of castilloas. The first consisted of making a clearing around the tree, then felling two or three smaller neighboring trees over which the target castilloa would fall after being cut close to its roots (Lamb 1974: 100–2; Domínguez and Gómez 1990: 88). This facilitated the thorough tapping of its trunk. Several trees could be felled thus in a single day. Next day, the trunk and the larger branches were incised profusely in a transversal manner so as to extract all of the latex. This was collected in buckets and taken to the tappers' encampment, where it was deposited in carefully excavated quadrangular holes 30–40 centimeters deep. In the holes the latex was mixed with an infusion of a wild vine (*sacha-camote*), which acted as a natural coagulant. Some tappers added common soap to the mix to accelerate the coagulation process, but this was considered to be a noxious practice, for it diminished the elasticity of the final product. The rubber produced in this way was known as "Peruvian slabs," or *caucho en planchas*, and generally weighed 60 kilograms. Slabs could be further processed by pressing them for four to six days in order to squeeze out all of the water and serum they contained. Later they were cut into strips that were allowed to dry in the sun and were finally wrapped into "Peruvian balls," or *sernambí de caucho*. Though Peruvian slabs and balls fetched lower prices at market than did hevea rubber, the fact that castilloa trees produced up to 250 kilograms in one blow—in contrast to the 5 kilograms produced by a hevea tree per tapping season—compensated for the loss of the tree.

Castilloa trees could also be tapped without being cut down (Fuentes 1906: 414–5). In such cases, the ground surrounding them was cleared and incisions were made in both their superficial roots and trunks, thereby allowing the latex to flow downward into narrow canals previously dug into the ground. This latex was allowed to coagulate upon contact with the air. The strips thus formed were later collected and wrapped in skeins. These were also known as Peruvian balls and carried a higher price than rubber slabs. Both methods caused great damage to the trees; however, whereas the felling of the trees allowed for their eventual regrowth, incising them led to their definitive deaths.

Neither modes of castilloa exploitation promoted permanent settlement of the land. Castilloa collectors were organized in small teams of up to three men. Because *caucho* could be gathered all year long, extracting teams were in constant movement along any given area, exploring the inner lands in search of castilloa stands, which comprised from five to forty trees. Once a stand was identified, its trees were marked as a sign of property and a camp was established. Other wandering teams generally respected marked trees. Having depleted the available castilloa trees, rubber-collecting teams moved to another area. Thus, nomadic castilloa collectors presented a sharp contrast with sedentary hevea tappers. This contrast provided the grounds for the portraying of these two types of rubber extractors as almost different human "species," around whom developed two radically distinct rubber "cultures."

The natural properties of the different rubber-producing species combined with different gathering techniques resulted in the production of seven different qualities of rubber, each with different prices at market. The number of rubber qualities quoted in the market changed through time, as demonstrated by the fact that weak hevea rubbers began to be accepted only after 1900. As shown in Table 2.1, the

Table 2.1 Prices of Rubber According to Quality in Iquitos, 1904–1910

*Value in soles per arroba**

Rubber quality	1904	1905	1910
Hevea			
Fine Pará	55.0	55.0	75.5
Entrefine	52.0	nd	nd
Fine scrappy	43.0	42.5	45.5
Weak heveas			
Weak fine	nd	37.5	47.0
Weak scrappy	nd	nd	33.0
Castilloa			
Peruvian balls	40.0	45.0	55.0
Peruvian slabs	8.3	7.5	nd

SOURCES: Flores Marín 1987: 85–6; Fuentes 1906: 414–5; Bonilla 1974: 74.
NOTES: * 1 *arroba* = 15 kilograms
** In 1897 the silver standard was replaced by the gold standard and the exchange rate was set at one Peruvian pound (equivalent to 10 soles) per pound sterling. This rate was maintained until at least 1914 (see Bonilla 1976: I, 319; III, 285).

structure of prices of rubber qualities was also labile. Thus, though it can be asserted that fine Pará and Peruvian slabs occupied the extreme positions within the price hierarchy, the relative position of the other rubber qualities varied through time.

The Heveaization of Rubber Production and Trade

Loreto's rubber economy experienced important changes in the species exploited and exported during the long period between 1870 and 1914. It also experienced changes in the areas under exploitation. At the onset of the rubber boom, the region's economy was mainly based on the extraction of castilloa, which in the 1880s and 1890s represented, on average, 75 percent of the region's total rubber exports (see Table 2.2). In the 1860s and 1870s, when rubber was still not Loreto's main export, the first castilloa forests exploited were those located along the shores of the northern tributaries of the Marañon and Amazon Rivers (especially the Pastaza, Tigre, Itaya, Nanay, and Napo Rivers) and of one of its southern tributaries, the Ucayali River (Butt 1873: 103–9; Memorial 1904: 496; Stiglich 1904a: 301–2). In some of these rivers, such as the Napo and the Nanay, hevea was also exploited on a small scale (Raigada 1875: 171).

By the 1880s castilloa trees became scarce in these areas. As a result, rubber tappers from the north started moving downriver toward the Amazon and into the Yavari in an eastward direction in search for new castilloa stands (Memorial 1904: 496). In turn, *caucheros* operating along the Ucayali started moving to its tributaries. Thus, by 1884 as many as 1,500 *caucheros* were reported to have entered the

Table 2.2 Rubber Exports of the Three Main Species Expressed as Percentage of Total Exported Rubber, 1886–1913

Species	1886	1889	1892	1895	1898	1900	1901	1903	1904	1908	1909	1910	1911	1912	1913
Hevea	12.5	31.9	12.3	17.0	48.9	53.7	57.6	48.4	49.4	40.0	44.4	44.6	49.7	46.3	37.3
Weak hevea	—	—	—	—	—	—	0.3	0.9	—	23.0	20.6	19.3	16.3	23.0	26.1
Castilloa	87.5	68.1	87.7	83.0	51.1	46.3	42.1	50.7	50.6	37.0	35.0	36.1	34.0	30.7	36.6

SOURCES: Mavila 1902: 548; Maurtua 1911: 147; Bonilla 1974: 78; Pennano 1988: 183–4; Appendix 1.

Pachitea River, an affluent of the middle Ucayali (Samanez y Ocampo 1980: 75). In the following decade, the Ucayali rubber tappers also moved eastward. The discovery of a portage between the headwaters of the right-bank tributaries of the Ucayali and those of the Yavari, Yurua, and Purus made this eastward move easier. Many entered into the area of the Tapiche, an affluent of the lower Ucayali River. By 1904 this river, which in 1894 was only inhabited by indigenous peoples, had a population of more than 5,000 collectors (Memorial 1904: 497). Others went to the Yaquerana, a tributary of the upper Yavari, where in 1893 as many as 2,000 *caucheros* were reported to have established themselves (García Rossell 1905: 631).

The *caucheros'* move toward the southeast did not mean that the areas north of the Amazon were totally abandoned. We know that by 1898 Loreto exported castilloa rubber from both the old rubber areas of the Tigre, Itaya, Nanay, Napo, and Putumayo Rivers, as well as from the more recently opened areas of the Yavari, Yurua, and Purus Rivers (Pesce 1904: 29). Furthermore, some of the old castilloa areas began to be resettled at this time. The Pastaza River region, which had been abandoned during the 1870s due to the depletion of castilloa, started to be reexploited by 1890 thanks to the regeneration of its stands (Palacios 1890b: 526). This was also the case of the Utiquenea River, an affluent of the middle Ucayali, depleted of *caucho* trees in the 1870s and exploited once more thirty years later (Stiglich 1904a: 301–2).

Even more important, at the turn of the century many areas formerly exploited by castilloa collectors began to be gradually occupied by hevea tappers. There was an opportunistic relationship between these two kinds of extractors, by which the exploration and exploitation of an area by castilloa collectors created the conditions for the establishment of hevea tappers (Fuentes 1906: 423). In effect, *caucheros* subjugated or eliminated hostile indigenous peoples, explored the land, established trading posts, and promoted the extension of fluvial traffic as well as the arrival of a host of small and large traders, thereby facilitating the subsequent settlement of hevea tappers. The case of the Tigre River, an old castilloa-collecting area that by 1905 had become a hevea-producing zone, constitutes but one example of this widespread process (Mavila 1904: 250).

For most of the 1880s and 1890s, hevea exports represented in average around 24 percent of total rubber exports. The turn of the century, however, brought forth a first important transformation of the structure of Loreto's rubber exports. By 1900 the weight of castilloa diminished both in absolute and proportional terms. In contrast, the production of hevea increased spectacularly, accounting for 54 percent of the rubber trade (see Table 2.2; Appendix 1). The stereotypical image of Loreto's rubber economy as based on *caucho* extraction is valid only until this date. In the following years hevea and weak hevea rubber came to dominate Loreto's exports.

There are three reasons that explain the decline of *caucho* exports. First, in the last decades of the nineteenth century castilloa trees disappeared in many of the older areas, and in some of them hevea collectors replaced castilloa extractors. Second, due to the growing scarcity of castilloa, many *caucheros* started adulterating the product, either by adding large quantities of soap when processing the latex or by including stones, gravel, and *fariña* (coarse flour made from bitter or sweet manioc) in order to increase the weight of rubber slabs. As a result of these practices, by 1888 European and United States rubber importers stopped buying *caucho* almost completely (Palacios 1890b: 488–9). Although the crisis was overcome through a stricter control of rubber quality, the market remained reluctant to accept *caucho*. These factors led castilloa rubber exports to fall by 1900 to less than half that of 1886.

Finally, the move toward the floodplains of eastern Loreto, particularly those of the Yavari River, also contributed to the decline of *caucho* exports. These areas, rich in hevea but relatively poor in castilloa stands, were rapidly swept and depleted by the *caucheros*, who by the turn of the century began moving southward into the upper Yurua region. They were replaced in the Yavari area by small and large hevea tappers. By 1898–1899 many of the castilloa extractors of the Yavari were granted credit by the merchant houses of Iquitos in order to work the newly opened Yurua area (Memorial 1904: 498). In the Yurua, castilloa was also scarce. The 1901 crisis in rubber prices made it impossible for many of the tappers in this area to pay their Iquitos creditors. They were thus forced to move even farther south toward the upper Purus region, and from there into the Madre de Dios River basin, beyond the limits of the department of Loreto.

All the factors mentioned above account for the increase, both in absolute and relative terms, of the production and export of hevea rubber vis-à-vis castilloa. This does not mean that *caucho* stopped being extracted in Loreto. On their southward move to the Madre de Dios region, caucheros entered into previously unexplored areas and discovered new stands of castilloa. They found a new connection between Loreto and the Madre de Dios Basin through the Chandless River—the previous one being the Mishagua portage connecting the Urubamba and Manu Rivers. They also opened numerous trails between the upper tracts of the Yurua and Purus Rivers and the lower Urubamba–upper Ucayali area (Memorial 1904: 498). This discovery allowed the development of new castilloa rubber fronts along the Mishagua, Sepahua, and Tamaya Rivers.

A second important transformation furthering the process of heveaization took place in the early 1900s. During this period the exportation of weak hevea increased from a mere 0.3 percent of the total rubber exports of the region in 1901 to an impressive 23 percent in 1908 (see Table 2.2). Weak hevea was exploited in several areas within Loreto, but its irruption into the market was the result of the maneuvers of an ambitious Peruvian merchant, Julio C. Arana, who incorporated the rubber production of the middle Putumayo River into the region's economy. As indicated in Chapter 3, Arana had by 1905 forced most prominent Colombian *caucheros* from the middle Putumayo—those who had previously been his clients or partners—to sell their rubber estates. He thus became the virtual owner of the entire area traversed by the Caraparana and Igaraparana Rivers. Since castilloa stands in this vast region had by then been depleted, Arana shifted to the large-scale exploitation of weak heveas, accounting for the impressive increase of these species in Loreto's rubber exports.

The increase of weak hevea production, together with the existing production of fine hevea, replaced castilloa as Loreto's main rubber export. From 1900 onward the exportation of hevea qualities represented about 65 percent of the region's total rubber exports. In 1911, a year after the first crash in the price of rubber, the composition of Loreto's rubber exports was as follows: Almost 50 percent was hevea rubber produced within numerous small outposts, large estates, and a few vast concessions organized on stable tapping trails. Outposts and estates were mainly located in the older rubber fronts of the Marañon, Amazon, and lower Ucayali Rivers, whereas many concessions were granted in newer fronts, such as the Yavari River. A further 16 percent of rubber exports was weak hevea rubber, produced either in small *fundos*, or landholdings, located in the older rubber fronts, such as the lower Napo, or in large rubber outposts located in newer peripheral fronts, such as the middle Putumayo. Finally, castilloa rubber accounted for 34 percent of total production, generated by a variety of small to large tappers constantly on the move, either in the older rubber fronts, where castilloa trees had regenerated, or in the new fronts opened on the southeastern fringes of the region.

The increased exploitation of hevea constituted a major change in Loreto's rubber economy. Although this fact is ignored by many present-day authors, contemporary observers were conscious of this important phenomenon. In 1903 Luis Pesce noted "the large decrease in the exportation of *caucho* that has been noted in these past years with respect to the increasing exportation of *jebe*, especially in the upper regions of the Amazon, Marañon, Ucayali, Yavari, Yurua, Tarahuaca, Purus, etc." (1904: 34). In 1906 Emilio Castre asserted that "the export of *jebe* surpasses that of *caucho*. *Jebe* is nowadays the commercial life of Loreto" (1906: 165).

In summary, Loreto's rubber economy was not homogeneous either in terms of the species tapped or the areas exploited. In addition, it experienced dramatic transformations through time. From being based primarily on the production of castilloa, it developed into a mainly hevea-producing economy. This gave rise to the emergence and consolidation of permanent economic fronts along the region's larger rivers. Furthermore, having developed in the west along the Marañon and its northern and southern tributaries, including the Ucayali, the rubber trade expanded toward the Amazon in both a northeastern (Putumayo) and southeastern (Yavari) direction. This contributed to the colonization of the region's most remote areas and thus to the preservation of the region's territorial integrity. Finally, the exploitation of different species in different areas at different times gave rise to a variety of rubber fronts having diverse labor arrangements; the nature and implications of these shall be examined in Chapter 3.

3

"Having No Other Capital Than Our Personnel": Labor Recruitment and Control

The most important problem of Loreto's turn-of-the-century economy was the lack of a free labor market and the recurrent shortage of disciplined workers. This was a general problem of Latin American economies of the time except in some large cities and in a few rural areas well articulated to the marketplace through modern mining or export agriculture. In economies that lacked a mass of disciplined laborers dispossessed of means of production, all forms of recruitment, retention, and organization of laborers entailed a dose of coercion. This was certainly true of Loreto. However, we question the widespread notion—derived from the cruel treatment of indigenous laborers in the estates of the ill-reputed rubber extractor Julio C. Arana—that Loreto's was an "economy of terror." We argue instead that all forms of labor recruitment, retention, and control combined persuasion and coercion.

Previous studies on the Peruvian rubber economy, based on general accounts provided by nineteenth-century observers, have contrasted two basic forms of labor recruitment: *habilitación* (debt-peonage), and *correrías* (slave-raids). In the highly schematic descriptions of these systems, debt-peonage and enslavement are presented as well-defined and exclusive situations. Thus, some authors have asserted that *habilitación* was the system used to engage mestizo workers, whereas *correrías* constituted the standard practice to enroll the indigenous population (Varese 1973: 245–6). Such generalizations have had the effect of presenting an extremely abstract image of the labor situation prevalent in Loreto during the rubber era, which does not account for spatial and temporal differences.

We contend that the advance of merchandise with the resulting creation of a debt, which characterizes the *habilitación* system, was a crucial component of all labor arrangements, not only in the engagement of mestizo laborers. We further argue that slave-raids against tribal Indians were not meant to capture men to serve as rubber tappers, as has been stated, but of women and children who were first transformed into sexual and/or domestic servants and only later into *habilitado* peons. Finally, we suggest that there were other forms of labor recruitment and labor arrangements, like the engagement of indigenous groups through the mediation of their headmen under the fiction of reciprocal exchange.

Although debt-peonage and enslavement differed in important ways as mechanisms of labor recruitment, they blended and supported one another as a means of controlling labor. In this sense, debt-peonage and enslavement, persuasion and violence constituted two faces of the same coin. Because of the publicity that the cruel treatment of Arana's indigenous laborers received at the time, and because the Putumayo case has been taken as representative of the labor situation in Loreto as a whole, we will also analyze the factors that led to this extreme exploitation. We question Michael Taussig's (1987) widely accepted view that this "economy of terror" was typical of a situation of colonial frontier encounter in which white dominators and Indian subordinates, interlocked in exploitative relationships, simultaneously despised and feared one another. We argue that if this were so, first, the Colombian extractors that preceded Arana in the area would have resorted to the same methods, and, second, the same kind of situation would have sprung up wherever rubber extractors attempted to engage tribal Indians—which was certainly not the case.

We conclude this chapter with a discussion of the crucial role played by labor in the functioning of Loreto's rubber economy. Because rubber was relatively abundant, yet disciplined laborers were scarce, control over labor rather than over rubber trees became the crux of the rubber economy. Under these circumstances laborers became the rubber extractors' main capital and asset. By the same token, they became the rubber traders' only security. Through the "transfer of debts"—a legal formula that allowed the debt of a peon to be sold and bought by a third party—peons could be forfeited by bankrupt rubber extractors and quickly converted into cash. It was through these precapitalist labor arrangements, characteristic of labor-intensive rather than capital-intensive economies, that almost the entire indigenous population of Loreto was persuaded or forced to enter into market relations.

Available Labor and the Debt-Peonage System

In order to better understand the variety of labor arrangements that arose during the rubber boom, it is necessary to present an overall view of the complex ethnic and social panorama of the region. In 1859, when Antonio Raimondi (1859, 1862), an Italian naturalist commissioned by the government to draw a detailed map of the country, visited Loreto for the first time, the region had a population of 49,963, distributed in twelve districts and sixty-one villages, towns, and cities. In addition, Raimondi estimated that there were a maximum of 40,000 tribal Indians scattered in the region's forests (Mattos 1874: 63). The bulk of the population living in towns and villages (85 percent) was located in the Huallaga Basin, along the western fringe of Loreto, in the present-day department of San Martín; the rest was dispersed along the region's vast eastern section comprising the Marañon, Amazon, Ucayali, and Napo Rivers.

By then, Loreto's population was divided into four social groups that had strong ethnic overtones: whites, mestizos, catechized Indians, and tribal Indians. Whites constituted a powerful, mainly urban minority composed of landowners and merchants who controlled the region's economic and political life. Mestizos were a larger group descended from Spaniards, Andean, and Amazonian Indians whose origins go back to the foundation of the city of Moyobamba in 1540. They were not a uniform group. Most were small farmers living in the region's towns and cities, but some were larger landowners and traders who shared power with the dominant white group. Catechized Indians consisted of various groups of acculturated indigenous peoples who had been reduced in mission posts during colonial times and shared the fact of being Christian, speaking Quechua, and maintaining some old mission mores and traditions. They mostly lived in former mission posts and represented around 42 percent of the population living in towns (Raimondi 1859,1862). Although they had lost part of their cultural heritage, catechized Indians still preserved an indigenous identity and were classified as "Indians" by their white and mestizo neighbors.

Finally, tribal Indians were indigenous groups who had avoided European domination or who, after experiencing it, had managed to escape it. They lived in small settlements scattered in the forest, avoiding contact with white-mestizos; and represented around 45 percent of Loreto's total population. Together, catechized and tribal Indians represented 67 percent of the region's population. In the regional ethnic classification system, these four groups were conceived of as forming part of a continuum according to their degree of "civilization," with whites and mestizos grouped together as "civilized," catechized Indians occupying an intermediate, "semicivilized" position, and tribal Indians classed as "savages" (Stiglich 1904b: 428).

At the onset of the rubber boom, poor mestizos and catechized Indians constituted the most important source of labor. However, their insertion into the rubber economy differed markedly. Whites and mestizos migrated to the newly opened rubber-producing areas, mostly as a result of the decline of export agriculture (mainly tobacco and cotton) and the Panama hat industry, but they were also attracted by the bright prospects of rubber extraction. Many Moyobambinos, as the mestizos of the Huallaga were known, became peons for large rubber extractors under the *habilitación* system. But despite their hardworking habits, Moyobambinos were not considered as the most desirable workers. As an observer put it, whereas "Indians are loyal, reliable and stay with the *caucheros* for a long time, mestizos are intelligent and bright, but do not support their *patrones* for more than the time necessary to obtain some cash, which they then use to have a good time or to become independent" (Fuentes 1906: 437). In effect, most Moyobambinos aimed at accumulating some capital and becoming independent extractors. In such cases, they worked in small teams composed of family members and/or partners, which sometimes included a few *habilitado* laborers.

Given that mestizos were not considered to be reliable peons, the burden of rubber extraction fell on the backs of catechized Indians. The most important ethnic groups within this category were the Hibitos, Cholones, Lamista, Tabaloso, Jebero, Chayahuita, Chamicuro, Aguano, Shipibo, Setebo, Conibo, Cocama, Cocamilla, Urarina, Omagua, Iquitos, and Yumbos. Catechized Indians provided the bulk of the region's labor force long before the outset of the rubber boom. In colonial times catechized Indians were forced by law to provide their services to third parties. In 1825, four years after the independence of Peru from Spain, the new republican government issued a decree forbidding all forms of personal servitude or coercive labor that in the past had been imposed upon indigenous peoples (Mattos 1874: 68). The decree specifically forbade local authorities to force Indians to work for third parties. However, although they were nominally free and generally demanded to be paid in-kind in advance, catechized Indians continued to provide the bulk of the region's labor force. Thus, at the onset of the rubber boom they were the first to be recruited by rubber extractors and traders.

With the increase of rubber exports in the 1880s, the recruitment of mestizos and catechized Indian peons accelerated. The town of Moyobamba, by then the capital of Loreto, experienced an acute population decline, from 15,000 inhabitants in 1859 to 7,000 in 1904 (Fuentes 1906: 216). In turn, the indigenous villages from the Huallaga Basin became deserted. Jeberos, which had a population of 3,000 in 1859, shrank to 300 in 1903, and Lagunas decreased from 1,000 to 130 (Derteano 1903: 604–5). Emigration was mainly male, a phenomenon that generated a scarcity of men in the Huallaga Basin.

A local authority reported that most of these men were "snatched from their homes . . . in order to engage them in rubber extraction" (Derteano 1903: 607). In effect, though most mestizos who migrated downriver did so by their own means, most catechized Indians were recruited through the *habilitación* system. Recruitment, known as *enganche* (hooking), consisted of persuading people to accept manufactured merchandise as an advance for a given service, including the extraction of castilloa and the tapping of hevea. These could be mestizos or catechized Indians. However, the latter were more prone to enter into this kind of labor arrangement. Catechized Indians—neither isolated self-subsistence tribal Indians scarcely involved in the region's mercantile activities nor mestizo peasants who regularly sold their surplus agricultural production in the local market—had become dependent on manufactured goods for their livelihood but lacked the means to obtain them. Working for local *patrones* and traders was one of the few means to obtain these goods. Thus, offers of merchandise generally proved to be irresistible.

Would-be *patrones* who lacked capital or did not control indigenous laborers resorted to local traders or commercial firms to procure credit in merchandise that would allow them to engage indigenous peons through the *habilitación* system. Such credit also took the form of *habilitación*. *Patrones* thus outfitted committed themselves to pay their debts with rubber. According to Hildebrando Fuentes

(1906: 422), at the onset of the rubber boom it was quite easy to obtain credit from such sources. It sufficed to have a "good reputation" in order to secure credit in merchandise and/or money from 20,000 soles up to 50,000 soles. Since during the 1870s the exchange rate was around 5 soles per sterling pound, this meant the respectable sum of £4,000–10,000. Having secured credit, the newly outfitted *patrón* would "go to one of the region's towns, such as Iquitos itself, Moyobamba, Lamas, Tarapoto, Jeberos, etc. and begin to conquer and engage laborers, a task that might take six months and sometimes even a whole year" (ibidem). The use of the term "conquer" (*conquistar*) in this context plays with the two meanings that this word has in Spanish (to conquer a people or to seduce a woman) and attests to the ambivalent nature of labor recruitment, which combined persuasion and force (see Taussig 1987: 28–29).

Whether the recruited laborers were mestizos or catechized Indians, the advances furnished not only served the purpose of outfitting or enabling them to carry out the required task but also created a debt that provided *patrones* with a legal instrument to oblige them to perform. Once the *habilitado* peon delivered the promised products, the value of these was discounted from his original debt. If the peon had a positive balance, his *patrón* settled his account and attempted to persuade him to accept new merchandise in order to continue working for him. More frequently, peons had negative balances and were forced to accept new merchandise and continue working. As the goods furnished by the *patrones* were always overvalued, whereas the rubber obtained from their peons was constantly undervalued, it was almost impossible for the *habilitado* peons to settle their debts. Furthermore, as the goods provided included the foodstuffs peons needed to subsist while working, there was little chance for them to escape this vicious circle. Thus, debt-peonage tended to become a permanent condition, and the hold that *patrones* had over their peons became tighter and tighter.

Mestizos, who were better acquainted with the legal system and who were attributed a higher status than Indians, were spared the more exploitative aspects of *enganche* and *habilitación*. In contrast, the engagement and retention of catechized Indians, who were less knowledgeable of their legal rights, often included a certain dose of coercion. This was the case with catechized Indians who were reluctant to work for *patrones*, fearing the implications of the *habilitación* system. In such cases, rubber *patrones* resorted to other recruitment strategies. This could include securing the support of local authorities to force potential catechized Indian peons to accept advances in merchandise against their will. It also included providing much-appreciated alcohol during indigenous religious festivities, then persuading the drunken participants to accept merchandise in advance (Stocks 1981: 92–3).

Considered the most fit working force for rubber extraction, the catechized Huallaga Indians were engaged en masse in this activity and removed farther and farther east to work in the newly opened rubber fronts. The more indebted they became, the greater the hold their *patrones* had over them, and the harder it was for them to regain their independence. Under such circumstances, many catechized Indians attempted to flee; if they were caught, then physical punishments were added to the legal hold of indebtedness as an element to retain them. Thus, Joseph Woodroffe notes that the flogging of peons with whips made out of tapir hide was "a practice common in the country" (1914: 73).

So in demand were catechized Indians that from the very onset of the rubber boom it was usual for a bankrupt extractor to pass his indigenous peons to other *patrones* through the "transfer of debts." Through this mechanism would-be *patrones* or *patronas* in need of additional laborers "bought" from the former employer his peons' debts. In order for this transfer to be legal, the parties involved had to sign a contract in the presence of a local authority (Woodroffe 1914: 90). Such transfers could take place several times in the life of an indebted peon. Moreover, quite often sons of indebted peons were forced to assume their fathers' debts upon death. This system, which led to a veiled form of slavery, was denounced by some of the higher regional authorities, as well as by missionaries and other contemporary observers.

Because of the accelerated increase in the international demand for rubber, very soon the available mestizo and catechized Indian labor force became insufficient. The opening of new fronts in the eastern areas of Loreto at the turn of the century provided what seemed to be an almost inexhaustible source of rubber; given the increasing demand, a greater amount of capital was pumped into the economy and made readily available to local entrepreneurs. Natural resources and capital were abundant, but labor was scarce. This scarcity, however, was not the result, as many have assumed, of a lack of population in the region. It instead derived from the inexistence of a labor market based on free laborers not only detached from their means of production but also accustomed to carrying out disciplined, routine work for a third party.

Most of the available disciplined labor force, the mestizo and catechized Indian population of the Huallaga Basin, was already engaged in rubber extraction. Moreover, in the new rubber fronts opened in the Napo, Putumayo, Yavari, Yurua, Purus, upper Ucayali, and Urubamba Rivers there was no significant population of this kind. These areas had been either out of reach of the colonial administration or controlled only sporadically by Jesuit and Franciscan missionaries. As a result, there were few ancient mission posts and, accordingly, a very reduced rural population that could be depended upon as an immediate source of labor. Although many upriver "civilized" Indians were driven to the new fronts, there was still a serious shortage of workers. It was then that *patrones* attempted to recruit "savage," or tribal, Indians.

Modes of Recruitment of Tribal Indians

The relationship between rubber extractors and tribal Indians was not easy. Most natives had experienced, albeit indirectly, the effects of colonial rule—epidemics, raids, displacement—and feared and distrusted foreigners. In addition, they rejected the ideas of working permanently on a single task and of receiving orders. In brief, they lacked the labor discipline characteristic of class societies. In some cases, tribal Indians raided the rubber extractors' temporary camps in order to steal manufactured goods, particularly iron tools that were much more efficient than traditional stone, wood, and bone instruments (Fuentes 1906: 305). In other cases, they engaged in *habilitado* relationships only to obtain certain goods considered indispensable, such as steel utensils, cloth, and shotguns. Once they obtained these goods, they shunned further contact with foreigners (Stiglich 1904b: 399). For this reason, rubber extractors and traders started introducing poor-quality merchandise that required rapid replacement. The epitome of such goods was the so-called trade-gun, a muzzle-loader with wound-wire barrels, which was made in Europe especially for the Amazonian rubber trade and fell apart after fifty shots (Wolf and Wolf 1936: 45; Casement 1985: 52).

The reluctance of tribal Indians to enter into permanent relations with foreigners is at the core of what became a regional institution: *correrías*, or slave-raids. This has led scholars studying the rubber boom to assume that *correrías* constituted the main mechanism of labor recruitment in remote areas (Varese 1973: 245–6; San Román 1975: 142; Flores Marín 1987: 63; Pennano 1988: 193–4; Chibnik 1994: 40). As we shall see, this was not quite so.

Far from being an invention of the rubber era, *correrías* had a long tradition in Loreto. They were modeled upon the raids that the powerful riverine indigenous societies, such as the Piro, Conibo, and Omagua, used to carry out against the smaller groups of the terra firme during pre-Hispanic times (Santos-Granero 1992: 11–2). In these raids adult men were killed, and women and children were captured to work as "servants" for their captors' families. However, these servants were eventually incorporated into their captors' society through marriage. Early in colonial times the Jesuit missionaries organized similar raiding groups composed of catechized Indians in order to retrieve what were known as "apostates," or converted indigenous people who rejected their newly acquired faith and escaped mission subjection (ibidem: 155–76). In later times, when the population of the riverine missions declined due to recurring epidemics, Jesuits also resorted to this method to capture uncontacted indigenous peoples and replenish mission populations. Raids were also conducted as punishment against hostile indigenous groups that rejected the missionaries' presence and against already reduced groups that defied missionary rule.

In early republican times, long before the rubber boom, *correrías* were once again carried out to capture indigenous children who were then raised as domestic servants (see Larrabure I Correa: I, 249). This and the exchange of indigenous children for iron tools gave place to somewhat intense trafficking. With the beginning of the rubber boom, raids against uncontacted indigenous peoples acquired the same multipurpose characteristics as the old mission *correrías*. In this new context, raids were conducted in territories where indigenous peoples had resisted invasion and permanent labor relations; they were also conducted against indigenous groups that had robbed rubber encampments or killed solitary rubber extractors (León 1905: 355;

Fuentes 1906: 305). Raiding groups were mainly composed of mestizos and cate-chized Indians under the command of a *patrón* or one of his foremen.

Although initially *correrías* had a punitive and clearing-out purpose, early on raid-ing rubber *patrones* began taking captives among the survivors, causing some au-thors to assume that the main objective of these raids was to obtain laborers for the rubber-tapping industry. This was not so. Turn-of-the-century sources are consistent as to the objectives of *correrías*. Germán Stiglich reports, "Those who conduct these *correrías* approach [the indigenous settlements] during the day to raid them at night and capture boys and girls in order to sell them." (1904b: 396). Jorge von Hassel presents a more detailed description of the slave traffic that resulted from *correrías*: "Rubber extractors call '*correrías*' the raids they perform against Indian hamlets, raids in which they kill men and take with them women and children, and that at present constitute a splendid business in the Amazonian region, for young savages aged 8 to 14 fetch a price that fluctuates between 200 and 400 silver soles [£20–40]" (1902b: 399). Fuentes adds that "only children and young women are spared from the massacre, and [are] taken to the city or to the rubber post where they are civilized" (1906: 305). This was so because, as Fuentes (1908: 141) and other observers noted, captured adult men and women did not get used to their "new lives" in the rubber camps and constantly attempted to flee.

Most of the women captured in *correrías* became concubines, servants, or camp sex slaves for the rubber *patrones*, their foremen, and their most loyal peons. Most male migrants arriving in the area were single or had left their wives behind. Con-temporary sources report a permanent scarcity of women in the peripheral rubber fronts (Pesce 1904: 232). Captured indigenous women filled this void. Though some tribal Indian women became virtual spouses for their masters and were pub-licly acknowledged as such, most of them were treated as slaves, being transferred from one man to another as payment for game debts, retribution for services ren-dered, and even through public raffles (Sala 1897: 56, 81).

Other women, as well as boys, were sold as domestic servants to town-dwellers. Fuentes informs that "most of the servants of Iquitos are Indians caught in the fa-mous *correrías*" (1906: 305). Another source states that "growing up in a more civ-ilized environment, as that of the white peoples, the Indian boys get so used to their demands that it is only then that they become useful" (Stiglich 1904b: 396). In ef-fect, it was only after being "civilized" that these captured boys were engaged by their *patrones* into an *habilitado* relationship and became as effective and valuable rubber workers as catechized Indians. Thus, rather than providing *patrones* with readily available laborers, *correrías* constituted a long-term investment aimed at "producing" a trained and loyal labor force that could be put to work in a variety of activities.

Peter Gow was the first to point out, in reference to labor shortage in the lower Urubamba and upper Ucayali Rivers, that "slave raiding did not provide such labor force, for the only slaves taken in these raids were women and children, and they did not collect much rubber" (1991: 41). He argues instead that in this area the most important mechanism of recruitment of tribal Indian laborers was through the establishment of alliances and *habilitado* relationships with prominent indigenous headmen. As we shall see, this kind of arrangement was not exceptional and also developed in other areas inhabited by tribal Indians. The case of Venancio Amaringo Campa, an Ashaninka leader from the upper Ucayali River, constitutes one of the most outstanding examples of an indigenous headman acting as broker between the rubber *patrones* and his followers (see Box 3.1).

Box 3.1   The Ashaninka Headman Venancio Amaringo Campa

Venancio Amaringo Campa was an Ashaninka chieftain who at the turn of century ruled over a large indigenous settlement known as Washington and located at the mouth of the Unini River, an affluent of the upper Ucayali. In 1897 Father Sala reported that Venancio was working for Carlos Fermín Fitzcarrald, the Peruvian rubber baron who controlled rubber extraction in the Manu River. Sala narrates how this chief, heading an expedition of four large canoes and twenty-five followers armed with rifles, intercepted his party in order to capture a minor Chinese trader who was traveling with him and who was indebted to Fitzcarrald (1897: 79). He further notes that Venancio spoke Ashaninka, Quechua, and Spanish and that he wore a hat, a neckerchief, and a black parasol, signs of his privileged position vis-à-vis the white world.

In 1900 Pedro Portillo, prefect of Ayacucho, met Venancio in the upper Ucayali River (1900: 497–500). He reports that by then the indigenous leader was taking his people to the Cujar River, a tributary of the Purus, to collect rubber for Delfín Fitzcarrald, brother of the late rubber baron. Venancio's four wives, his children, one of his brothers and forty "savage laborers" composed the expedition. Portillo managed to convince Venancio to accompany him to Washington. He describes this settlement as located at a strategic site that could be made into an impregnable fortress. He notes that it normally had a population of 500 but that between June and November, the dry season, most of it was taken by Venancio to the Sepahua, Cujar or Purus Rivers in order to collect rubber for different local *patrones*. During those months only fifty to sixty men remained to guard the settlement, presumably from attacks by other indigenous headmen from his own and other ethnic groups. When Portillo asked Venancio for fifty of his "subjects" to accompany him downriver, he replied that due to his commitment to gather rubber for Fitzcarrald's brother he could not part with the required men.

In 1901, while visiting a small tributary of the Purus River, Almirón reported that he had encountered "Venancio Amaringo Campa, chief of the Unini River, together with one hundred families of this tribe, who were engaged in the extraction of caucho" (1905: 376). By then Venancio was working for Carlos Scharff, Fitzcarrald's former henchman (Gow 1991: 41). Scharff had become an important rubber extractor and trader, who controlled twelve outposts in the Purus River and a total of 2,000 "civilized" and indigenous laborers (Flores Marín 1987: 158).

(continues)

Box 3.1   *(continued)*

A year later La Combe (1902: 233), commissioned by the government to explore the Ucayali River, reported having stopped briefly in Washington on his way upriver. Venancio was considered to be such an important contact in the area that La Combe was bringing with him a letter of introduction written by Portillo, who had been appointed prefect of Loreto. By then Venancio Amaringo Campa began to call himself Venancio Atahualpa, perhaps in reference to Juan Santos Atahualpa, the famous Andean messianic leader who in the mid-eighteenth century had expelled the Spaniards from the region with the support of the Ashaninka and other local indigenous peoples.

In Washington La Combe was told that Venancio had gone to the Sepahua River. A week later the explorer met Venancio leading a convoy of canoes downriver. They were loaded with indigenous boys and women, whom La Combe suspected had been captured by the headman in the Sepahua area (ibidem: 235). Some time afterward he found out through two of Venancio's "slaves" that together with other rubber extractors the chief had spread the news among local indigenous peoples that Peruvian authorities were coming in a war steamship in order to steal their women (ibidem: 246). La Combe suggests that Venancio's aim was to frighten enslaved indigenous people so that they would not resort to the authorities to obtain their freedom.

In 1904 Father Alemani (1904: 261) reported that Venancio's settlement had been abandoned. After inquiring about the headman's whereabouts, he was told that the latter had gone together with more than one hundred of his men to extract rubber in the Manu or Madre de Dios Rivers. This suggests that by then Venancio had become an independent extractor. In fact, Gow (1991: 41) claims that Venancio constituted one of those exceptional cases in which an indigenous headman turned into a rubber *patrón*. In any case, it seems that Venancio was not independent for a long time. In 1910 Maúrtua reported that the workforce engaged by the rubber *patrones* of the Purus River consisted of local indigenous peoples, and "the tribes that at present obey old Venancio, chief of the Campa of the Shepahua and Mishahua rivers" (1911: 171). This was the last information on the whereabouts of this indigenous leader, who was so influential at the time that even the highest regional authorities sought his support.

In order to persuade indigenous headmen to work for them, rubber *patrones* took advantage of the tribal Indians' desire for Western manufactured goods, as well as of the traditional mediating role of native Amazonian leaders. A local *patrón* would outfit an important headman, providing him with goods in exchange for a certain amount of rubber. The chief distributed part of these goods among his followers, retaining the rest as a sort of commission. He then led his men in a rubber-gathering expedition that could last up to six months (Sala 1897: 70; Portillo 1900: 498). Once the stated amount of rubber was collected, the headman transported it to the *patrón's* rubber post. When his account was settled, he profited a second time by retaining part of the goods received, handing out the rest among his followers. An indigenous headman could expand his business and power by persuading other minor headmen to get involved in rubber extraction, acting as a broker between them and the *patrón* or *patrones* for whom he worked. This was achieved thanks to the generalized desire for manufactured goods, as well as through the use of a certain dose of implied or actual violence based on their recent acquisition of firearms from the *patrones*.

In effect, powerful chiefs who engaged in mercantile relations with white or mestizo *patrones* became a real threat to neighboring headmen and their people, whether of the same or other ethnic groups. On their own initiative or at the request of *patrones*, such headmen often engaged in *correrías* against neighbors in order to obtain women and children. Father Sala (1897: 91) reports, for instance, that the Asheninka inhabitants of the Gran Pajonal were very fearful of the slave-raids carried out by chief Venancio Amaringo. Contemporary sources are full of accounts of Ashaninka leaders from the Ucayali River raiding the interior Ashaninka and Asheninka (Samanez y Ocampo 1980: 83); of Conibo headmen enslaving the Amahuaca and Ashaninka (ibidem: 82); and of Piro chiefs raiding the Ashaninka, Conibo, and Machiguenga (ibidem: 66; Gow 1991: 38).

Correrías conducted during the rubber boom era were based on the traditional indigenous mechanism of acquiring "servants" ("slaves" being a rendering of native terms that does not appropriately describe the social standing of these captives). However, whether led by indigenous leaders or white-mestizo *patrones*, these *correrías* distorted the pre-Hispanic model, insofar as under the new circumstances most captives became, at least before being "civilized," actual "slaves" who could be sold and bought at pleasure, rather than family "servants" and potential spouses.

To avoid being subjected to *correrías* carried out by enterprising indigenous leaders, some headmen opted to establish similar exchange relations with other local rubber *patrones*, so as to be able to acquire firearms and confront their rivals on equal terms. This increased inter- and intratribal violence to previously unknown levels. In summary, either through the imposition of powerful headmen or through imitation of their strategies, many indigenous leaders and their followers became involved in the rubber economy. This undoubtedly benefited the *patrones*, who were thus able to obtain laborers for the extraction of rubber. As Father Sala remarked: "A trader who knows how to handle his *curaca* [chief], rises as foam in a whirlpool of dirty water" (1897: 81). It also benefited some indigenous leaders who, because of their charisma or by implied threats, were able to mobilize followers to work for the rubber *patrones* while maintaining their own autonomy. As we shall see, however, not every indigenous leader was able to maintain such a large degree of independence. Many were totally subordinated through violence, becoming virtual slaves of their former outfitters. This was clearly the case in Arana's Putumayo estates (see Taussig 1987; García Jordán 1993, 1994).

Coercion and Terror in the Putumayo Basin

The story of how the Huitoto of the Putumayo area were engaged in rubber extraction in the early 1880s is told in an extremely rich oral account published by Camilo Domínguez and Augusto Gómez (1990: 202–26). The narrator, Aquileo

Tovar, was a mestizo of Huitoto descent who grew up in a rubber post in the Putu-mayo area. According to his account, the Huitoto were persuaded to tap castilloa rubber by Crisóstomo Hernández and Benjamín Larrañaga, two pioneering Colom-bian *patrones* who offered permanent access to manufactured goods, especially iron tools and firearms. Hernández was a black man who had worked as a tapper for a rubber *patrón* in the Caqueta River. Fleeing from justice and accompanied by his Carijona concubine, he moved to the headwaters of the Caraparana River, a left-hand tributary of the Putumayo. There he established relations with Iferenanvique, a Huitoto-Murui headman. Hernández settled in the area and learned the Huitoto language. Eventually, the indigenous leader manifested his interest in acquiring "the things the whites fabricate." Hernández replied that if he and his people collected rubber for him, he could get them the goods they wanted.

After selling in the Caqueta River the first load of rubber collected by Iferenan-vique's people, Hernández came back with a large cargo of manufactured goods. He told the headman to distribute these among his people as compensation for the rubber they had collected. Iferenanvique refused and replied: "In this case you are our chief. Please be kind and open the bundles so that we can see their content, and you will be the one who issues the orders and I shall command my people to do whatever you command" (1990: 214). Next day, amid a large celebration, Hernán-dez opened the bundles. From each he took an item and presented it to the chief, asking him to distribute the rest among his followers. According to this story, when members of other neighboring Huitoto longhouse groups heard about how Ifere-nanvique's people had acquired foreign goods, they came to visit Hernández en masse, anxious to collect rubber for him under the *habilitación* system.

Later on, Hernández founded a rubber post named El Encanto, which became the center of his operations. He also contracted ten white overseers to keep the ac-counts of the tappers that belonged to the different Huitoto groups working for him. Tovar asserts that in this way most of the Huitoto of the Caraparana River were "conquered," meaning "seduced" by the allurement of foreign goods into partici-pating in the rubber economy. He further underscores the fact that Hernández did not use force to persuade the Huitoto to work for him; his only request to the headmen was that they provide his overseers with women. The fact that the Huitoto leaders agreed to do so constitutes a sign that from their point of view they were es-tablishing an alliance with the foreign traders that transcended mere economic dimensions.

Tovar's account of how Benjamín Larrañaga persuaded the Huitoto of the Igara-parana River, another left-hand tributary of the Putumayo, to gather rubber for him and of how he founded the post of La Chorrera is very similar. There is good evi-dence that violence was not completely absent in the establishment and administra-tion of Hernández's and Larrañaga's rubber operations (Casement 1988: 19; Taussig 1987: 27). Thus, it is reported that in the early 1902 Larrañaga, before becoming as-sociated with Arana, had to confront a partial, though unsuccessful, uprising of his *habilitado* indigenous peons, who complained about exacting working conditions

(Portillo 1909: 26–7). Shortly thereafter, and in revenge for the killing of two of his foremen, Larrañaga managed to persuade twenty-five rebel Huitoto headmen to come talk with him in La Chorrera, where he ordered their executions.

In spite of these violent acts, what Tovar's story indicates is that the Huitoto headmen, as in the case of the indigenous leaders of the lower Urubamba and upper Ucayali Rivers, entered voluntarily into *habilitado* relationships with the Colombian rubber *patrones*. Acting as middlemen between the *patrones* and their respective peoples, these headmen managed to persuade their followers to get involved in the region's mercantile economy while protecting them from the more negative aspects of such a link. Benefiting both economically (more goods) and politically (greater influence) from their role as brokers between *patrones* and their followers, indigenous headmen seemed to have conceived of their relationship with rubber extractors as one of advantageous reciprocal exchange. This situation changed when Julio C. Arana, the Peruvian rubber trader, took control of the area.

The Arana case constitutes one of the best-known success stories of Panama hat trader–turned–rubber merchant and, later, rubber extractor (Collier 1981: 40–7). In 1878, at the age of fourteen, Arana started working with his father in the business of manufacturing and trading Panama hats. Three years later he moved to Yurimaguas, where he became "general trader and exporter in the upper portion of the Amazon River, both in inland Peru and Brazil" (Arana 1913: 7). As such, he was one of the first traders to outfit rubber extractors in the recently opened Yavari River (Collier 1981: 47). By the time he was twenty, Arana had already made several trips to Brazil, where he made his first connections with the mercantile community of Manaus. In later years he expanded his business by obtaining credit from the trading firms of that city. In 1889 he moved his business to Iquitos, and in 1890 he associated with the Colombian trader Juan B. Vega (ibidem: 8).

Arana's firm made its first purchases of Putumayo rubber in 1899 (Arana 1913: 8). The outbreak of the Colombian civil war (1899–1902, the so-called war of the one thousand days), which cut off the Putumayo area from the Colombian highland towns it had depended upon, favored Peruvian interests in general and Arana's commercial interests in particular. In 1899 as many as 300 Peruvian *caucheros*, taking advantage of the situation, entered the area between the Putumayo and Caqueta Rivers. In order to enhance its influence in this area, the Peruvian government appointed a local governor, who doubled as customs officer (Domínguez and Gómez 1990: 176). As a result of being cut off from traditional suppliers, the Colombian *patrones* of the Putumayo River became more and more dependent on Arana. At first, he bought their rubber in Iquitos, but he soon mounted regular trips to the Putumayo with his firm's steamboats to buy it in situ (Wolf and Wolf 1936: 87; Arana 1913: 13).

Arana thus became the *habilitador*, or outfitter, of most of the Colombian *patrones* who had been working the Putumayo area since the early 1880s. From 1901 onward Arana changed strategy, taking advantage of his clients' indebtedness and forcing Larrañaga and other Colombian *patrones* to partner with him for the extraction of rubber (Pennano 1988: 163). Starting in 1903, however, Arana, through forfeit or buyout at very low prices, acquired the rubber estates of many of his Colombian partners, including those belonging to Larrañaga, which he acquired in 1905 (Arana 1913: 14).

There is general agreement that after Arana's takeover of the Putumayo there was a radical change in the treatment of the extant indigenous labor force. However, there has been little analysis of the factors that led to the transformation. Some authors have attributed the change to the "iniquity" of the Peruvian extractors (Domínguez and Gómez 1990: 174). According to this view, "In a few years [during the 1890s] Peruvians had annihilated Loreto's indigenous population and razed all of the region's latex-producing trees. This situation led Iquitos-based rubber firms to make increasingly frequent forays into Colombian, Ecuadorian and Brazilian territories" (ibidem). The change is also attributed to the greediness of Arana and his Colombian partners, Vega and Larrañaga (ibidem: 183). Although Arana's greed is not in question, these authors, by attributing such an important transformation to the character of Peruvian *caucheros*, overlook other, more important ecological and economic factors. Furthermore, as we have seen, it is clearly not accurate to state that by the turn of the century the indigenous population and the castilloa stands of Loreto had been annihilated.

Other scholars have suggested that the violence inflicted upon the indigenous population by Peruvian *caucheros*, particularly by Arana, was associated with the fact that they mainly exploited castilloa rubber. Barbara Weinstein argues that as castilloa is "a type of tree destroyed by the tapping process," *caucheros* "had no incentive to create long-term commercial ties with indigenous inhabitants" (1983: 26). In a more recent work, Bradford Barham and Oliver Coomes retake this argument, asserting that "the greater potential for coercive relations of labor in caucho than hevea was the product of distinct property relations and the labor incorporated into extraction" (1994b: 58). As an extreme example they mention Julio C. Arana and his Peruvian Amazon Rubber Company. As we shall see, this case proves exactly the contrary. Although it was not difficult to engage tribal Indians in the gathering of castilloa rubber, it was much more difficult to persuade them to carry out the routine and monotonous activities demanded by the tapping of heveas.

Before Arana's takeover of the Putumayo, Colombian *patrones* were mainly dedicated to the exploitation of castilloa and the production of rubber slabs (Domínguez and Gómez 1990: 221–2). By the end of the nineteenth century the region's casti-lloa stands had been depleted. For that reason some Colombian extractors, when the international market began to accept rubber obtained from weak heveas in 1900, started exploiting the new resource. By 1903 some Colombian *patrones* had opened weak hevea rubber trails and were producing smoked rubber balls "exactly the same in appearance as those produced in the [fine hevea] trails on the Amazon" (ibidem: 97). Since 1902 Arana and his new partner, Larrañaga, had also been opening trails and tapping weak hevea latex, "using for its processing the system put into practice throughout the Amazon" (Espinar 1902:

221). Later on, the process of smoking latex to form rubber balls was abandoned in favor of natural coagulation and the preparation of rubber skeins known as *rabos* (tails) or *chorizos* (sausages) (Domínguez and Gómez 1994: 188–90). The reason for this change was that smoked weak hevea rubber balls demanded the same investment of labor as fine Pará rubber balls but achieved a much lower price due to its inferior quality. In both cases, however, weak hevea trees were organized in trails and were tapped routinely.

This shift from the nomadic collection of castilloa to the sedentary and regular tapping of weak heveas demanded a radical change in the organization and regimentation of the existing indigenous labor. In the past, rubber *patrones* could do with a temporary, loosely disciplined labor force, but they now needed a permanent work force that could tap trees daily. The new organization of labor imposed by Arana was based, in a perverted way, on the model developed by the preceding Colombian *patrones*: the engagement of indigenous peons through the *habilitación* of their headmen.

Enrique Espinar, a Peruvian naval officer, offers an early description of how labor was organized in Arana and Larrañaga's posts. According to his account (1902: 221), in 1902 the firm controlled eighteen indigenous "groupings" belonging to five indigenous "nations": Huitoto, Bora, Andoque, Momanos (Muinane?), and Nevaje (Mai huna?). Each grouping was headed by an indigenous leader, referred to as *capitán*, and comprised more than 300 laborers. In turn, groupings were divided into two to four sections, each section in the charge of a chief, always an armed "civilized young man." They supervised the headman of the grouping and made sure that the indigenous laborers worked regularly.

The shift toward the exploitation of weak heveas, together with the tightening of the previous mechanisms of control, involved a drastic modification in the indigenous laborers' way of life. Whereas formerly they had maintained their freedom of movement, combining castilloa gathering with other traditional subsistence activities, under the new conditions indigenous peons were required to work exclusively in the tapping of weak heveas and were thus confined to the environs of the rubber sections. In addition, whereas previously they were asked to hand in a set amount of castilloa rubber slabs every three or four months, they were now requested to deliver a fixed quota every two to four weeks (Pineda Camacho 1993: 58).

The ideas of working permanently in a single activity, of not being able to produce their own foodstuffs, and of being restricted in freedom of movement and control of their time were alien and repugnant to Amerindians. In time, the loss of personal autonomy and extreme dependence on foreigners generated overt resistance. Fuentes reported that "Huitoto men are not well-disposed to the extraction of *jebe* in rubber trails by means of tin cups as is customary among *shiringueros*" (1908: 118). He added that in order to recover their freedom, and knowing that the whites' only interest in their territories was the collection of latex, the Huitoto tended to destroy the trees to force them to leave.

Resistance to the extraction of weak heveas explains why Arana and his partners had difficulties retaining Indian laborers (Casement, in Taussig 1987: 31). At the beginning, Indian escapees sought refuge among other Colombian *patrones*, who were still mostly devoted to the collection of castilloa, or fled toward the Caqueta River (Domínguez and Gómez 1990: 194). But when Arana bought out the operations of almost all the Colombian extractors living in the area, there were few places an escapee could hide. Moreover, as there were no official authorities, Colombian or Peruvian, who had the power or will to inspect and regulate the working conditions of the indigenous laborers, Arana was free to impose stricter measures of recruitment, control, and regimentation of his workforce.

Although the requirements of weak hevea collection resulted in the imposition of new labor arrangements, it was nevertheless Arana's plan to register his firm as a British company, which called for a complete reorganization of the means of labor control. After attaining total control of the Putumayo in 1905, Arana traveled to London to persuade British investors to participate in his venture. To achieve this, he had to show that his was a sound and extremely profitable business. Thus, he had to augment rubber production. With this in mind, Arana had introduced three modifications to the previous model of labor administration. First, he hired new white section chiefs who were not paid a salary but rather earned commissions on the basis of the volume of rubber they managed to obtain from indigenous laborers during each *fábrico*, or three-month collecting season (Casement 1988: 38; Woodroffe 1914: 160). Second, in 1904 Arana hired thirty-six Barbadians who, provided with arms and under the orders of the section chiefs, acted as overseers (Casement 1988: 4). Last, beginning in 1904 Arana's men trained 400 young indigenous men to police and punish unproductive or rebellious Indian tappers (Collier 1981: 62). In order to ensure that they would carry out work without hesitation, the henchmen, known as *muchachos* (boys), were assigned to control tappers who belonged either to a different clan or to a different ethnic group from their own.

The results of these organizational changes were impressive. In 1903 Arana's Putumayo estates produced 201 metric tons of rubber; in only two years the production more than doubled to 470 metric tons (House Documents 1913: 19). Rubber production continued to increase, and by 1906 it peaked at 645 metric tons (ibidem). This output was maintained in 1907 (627 metric tons), the year in which Arana's firm was incorporated in Great Britain as the Peruvian Amazon Rubber Company—later renamed the Peruvian Amazon Company (Collier 1981: 120–121). However, as soon as Arana attained his objective, rubber production plummeted and continued to decrease steadily. From 627 metric tons in 1907, rubber production dropped to 489 in 1908, 399 in 1909, and 380 in 1910 (ibidem), the year in which Roger Casement was commissioned by the British government to investigate the labor situation in the Putumayo Basin.

This would explain why after 1907 the treatment of the indigenous labor force in Arana's estates became less harsh. In effect, Rómulo Paredes, the lawyer-journalist who was among the first to denounce the Putumayo scandals and who in 1911 presided over the government commission that investigated the labor situations on Arana's estates, asserted that the first atrocities date from the time Arana partnered with the Colombian Larrañaga (1901). He added that the killings and cruel punishments continued till 1906, "the time in which they assumed a most horrifying extent"; although they were not eradicated, they gradually diminished after 1907 (House Documents 1913: 189).

During that period the relationship with *habilitado* indigenous headmen experienced a dramatic change. When the Barbadian overseers arrived in 1905, they found many leaders and elder men and women were still highly respected due to their experience and wisdom, as well as to their ability to counsel followers (Casement 1988: 52). However, as pressures upon the indigenous laborers mounted, elders and headmen began to exhort them to flee or resist. As a result, these leaders were classified as "dangerous," and many were killed. Those who escaped execution lost their previous autonomy and were forced to hand in larger volumes of rubber. When they or their people failed to meet assigned quotas, they were flogged, put into stocks, hanged, or even burned alive. These atrocities became standard practice throughout Arana's estates and were thought to be an indispensable element in the process of subduing recalcitrant or openly rebellious indigenous groups. It was the shift from castilloa to weak hevea tapping, Arana's need to attract British investors, and Huitoto resistance to conform to the new labor regimentation—rather than the colonial encounter between people who feared and distrusted one another (Taussig 1987)—that turned the economy of the Putumayo basin into an "economy of terror."

Whether through the direct outfitting of peons by means of the *habilitación* system, the long-term "production" of peons by means of slave-raids, or the engagement of whole indigenous groups through the brokerage of indigenous headmen, it was critical for rubber *patrones* to ensure the recruitment and retention of much-needed labor. This was so not only because of the obvious reason that someone had to collect the rubber but also because the control of laborers became the *patrón's* only possibility for obtaining credit. In other words, laborers became simultaneously a *patrón's* capital, asset, and security.

Peons as Capital, Asset, and Security

At the onset of the rubber boom it was not difficult to obtain credit from the large merchant houses of Manaus or Iquitos in order to undertake rubber extraction (Fuentes 1906: 422). Credit enabled *patrones* to engage mestizos and catechized Indians as rubber tappers through the *habilitación* system. In ensuing years, an increase in the frequency of credit default led merchant houses to be more reluctant to grant credits without some kind of collateral. Land could not be used as collateral because, until the Ley de Terrenos de Montaña was passed in 1898, the government had not permitted the acquisition of land in the Amazon area, and very few people possessed legal title to the lands they occupied and exploited.

Even after this and other land laws were passed (1900), land was still not used as collateral, because castilloa extractors were forced to move constantly in search of new stands. Thus, they had no incentive to seek legal rights over the lands they were currently exploiting. As to the more sedentary hevea tappers, the 1900 land law specifically established that hevea-rich rubber lands or already opened hevea trails could in no case be granted as property and could only be leased from the state (Laos 1902: 183–5). Therefore, although hevea estates offered certain assurances to creditors, they had little value as security. This was an important difference, for in Brazil it was possible to acquire property title to hevea rubber estates (Woodroffe 1914: 229; Fuentes 1906: 435–6).

In this context, then, control over laborers became a precondition for obtaining credit. In a 1904 petition to the prefect of Loreto, the region's most important rubber *patrones* and traders claimed that "no merchant house outfits someone who lacks peons" (1904: 500), indicating that laborers had come to be considered as collateral. This transformation was possible due to the institution of transfer of debts, where the debt of a peon could be legally transferred to a third party so as to obtain ready cash or discount a debt. As with uncollectable debts, *patrones* "sold" the debts of their peons at a loss of around 20 percent (Woodroffe 1914: 111). Insofar as peons' debts could be sold and bought for ready cash, they could also be offered as security against a loan (ibidem: 229). In the first case, what was being negotiated was the future labor of the transferred peons; in the second, it was the possibility of forfeiting the peons' debts in order to recover a loan. Only in very rare cases did trader-creditors retain forfeited laborers, their actual value residing in the fact that they could be readily converted into cash (Castre 1906: 157)

If laborers were the trader's only security, they were also the rubber *patrón's* only "capital," allowing him to obtain the necessary credit in money or merchandise, either to outfit his peons and keep his operation functioning or to expand his operation by engaging new workers. Joseph Woodroffe (1914: 233) notes that during the first decade of the twentieth century the commercial houses of Manaus granted credit of up to one *conto* (approximately £66) per laborer and up to two *contos* for the rubber *patrón*. Around the same time, it was reported that in Loreto "the wealth of a rubber *patrón* . . . is valued according to the number of peons he owns at the rate of 1,000 soles [£100] each" (Robledo 1903: 64).

The facts that rubber extractors claimed they had "no other capital than their personnel" (Memorial 1904: 500) and that laborers were scarce has prompted many to point out the apparent irrationality of *patrones* such as Arana, in whose estates the maiming and killing of indigenous laborers constituted standard practice. Thus, for instance, Casement suggested that the violence inflicted upon laborers in Arana's rubber estates was like "killing the goose that lays the golden eggs" (1985: 50).

In order to understand this apparent paradox it is necessary to reexamine the composition of the region's labor force. Loreto's potential workforce could be divided into two main categories: civilized and savage. The former comprised mestizos and catechized Indians; the latter, isolated tribal Indians. Catechized Indians were the most valued laborers, not only for their knowledge of the forest but also because they were familiar with mercantile activities and relations.

From the *patrones'* perspective, this had two advantages. First, catechized Indians depended on industrial goods to satisfy many of their basic needs (tools, utensils, clothes, firearms, etc.). Insofar as the *patrones* were the only source of such goods, catechized Indians were forced to work for them on a regular basis. Second, they were disciplined laborers, with a long tradition of working for whites and mestizos; hence, they had become inculcated with the physical habits characteristic of hired labor: performance of a single task, long workdays, routine actions, and fixed schedules. Moreover, most catechized Indians had come to accept domination and had adjusted to the subordinate role of peons. This does not mean that they always accepted their role unquestioningly or without resistance. And it does not mean they were never punished for attempting to flee or for failing to meet their quotas. However, there is no evidence that catechized Indians were routinely subjected to the types of physical violence employed against tribal Indian laborers.

Due to constant expansion in the rubber economy, the incorporation of new and remote rubber fronts, as well as the high mortality rates prevalent among rubber collectors, the civilized labor force became increasingly scarce and, as a result, even more valuable. It was under those circumstances that rubber *patrones* attempted to engage tribal Indians in the task of rubber extraction. Although *correrías* were effective in obtaining children and young women, they clearly did not provide the kind of ready laborers needed by rubber *patrones*. The establishment of relationships with influential indigenous headmen proved to be a more effective means for recruiting tribal Indians. However, this kind of laborer had the important disadvantage of not being used to the performance of the steady and repetitive tasks required by the rubber economy, particularly the tapping of heveas. They also had the disadvantage of not being strongly dependent on manufactured goods. These factors made "savage" Indians less valuable a workforce than "civilized" Indians.

When the desire for manufactured goods proved not compelling enough to retain tribal Indian laborers, rubber *patrones* resorted to other (mostly violent) means. The use of violence and terror against tribal Indian peons had a double purpose: to force them to work on a permanent basis and, more importantly, to instill a new labor discipline. The use of quotas, ritualistic weighing of the rubber collected, public floggings, stocks, and other punishments in the Putumayo area were meant to underscore the tenets of that new work ethic. However, the continued resistance of tribal Indians proved that it was not an easy task to convert them into "civilized" and, thus, more "useful" laborers.

The notion that tribal Indians were less valuable than catechized Indians was enhanced by the fact that the cost of engaging tribal Indians, known as *gastos de conquista*, or "conquering expenses," in Arana's account books, was considerably less than that entailed in the engagement of civilized Indians. By the same token, the profit obtained from tribal Indians was considerably higher, thereby allowing for a rapid recovery of expenses incurred during recruitment. Given that tribal Indians were far more numerous than catechized Indians, and given that their cost of replacement was relatively low, they came to be considered as expendable. In the case of the Putumayo Basin, the notion that indigenous laborers were expendable became widespread after 1905, when Arana was pressed to show his British partners that his operation was highly profitable.

Nonetheless, although the relationship between *patrones* and tribal Indian peons entailed at least the threat of physical violence, even in areas like the Putumayo it continued to be framed within the *habilitación* system. In other words, even in cases where tribal Indian peons were subjected and treated as slaves, their relationship with *patrones* was presented as one of exchange within the framework of *habilitación*. We contend this was so because it was through the idiom of *habilitación* that the highly unequal and exploitative relationship between *patrones* and peons was legitimized in the eyes of the latter.

The relationship with savage Indians was based on the fiction that *patrones* were traders who exchanged manufactured goods for rubber provided by their Indian partners within the framework of indigenous symmetrical reciprocity. This form of trade, which was widespread in Peruvian Amazonia both at the intra- and intertribal levels, was based on deferred exchange between established trading partners (Harner 1973: 125–32; Bodley 1973; Zarzar and Román 1983; Santos-Granero 1992). Because the notions of trading partners and deferred exchange were not alien to Amerindians, during the initial phases of contact rubber *patrones* could advance the *habilitación* system as if it were a traditional form of trade, thereby disguising its exploitative component.

The near impossibility of redeeming debts has led some authors to claim that debt-peonage constituted a sort of quasislavery (San Román 1975: 148; Pennano 1988: 60). This, however, is only partly true. To start with, *patrones* did not "possess" their peons; they could sell only their debts, not their bodies. Moreover, indebted peons who wanted to end their relationship with a given *patrón* could seek out another *patrón* willing to redeem or buy their debts. There is plenty of evidence that this was not uncommon, particularly among catechized Indian peons (Woodroffe 1914: 233).

If debt-peonage led in fact to a state of quasislavery, why did rubber *patrones* such as Arana, who could have enslaved his peons through sheer force, not do so?

Since Arana subjected the indigenous population of the area by force and terror, converting local Indians into virtual slaves, one would have expected Arana to dispense with the Huitoto headmen as brokers and with *habilitación* as a system of recruitment and retention of laborers. But Huitoto headmen, although subjugated and without power of negotiation, were still held in high respect by followers. Arana's section chiefs took advantage of this and kept headmen as hostages or threatened to flog them in order to ensure that their people would not flee and would continue to work. Moreover, even at the height of the violence inflicted upon the Huitoto the relationship between the company and the indigenous tappers was not only expressed—it was also realized—as one of exchange of rubber for manufactured goods. Although the terms of this exchange were totally arbitrary, and even though the rubber brought in by a given individual frequently was not discounted from his debt in the company's accounts (Woodroffe 1914: 159), the company continued to supply goods to its laborers. Even as late as 1912 the distribution of goods at the end of each collecting season was occasion for great celebrations that lasted several days (Taussig 1987: 71–2).

The fact that the *habilitación* system was maintained amid extreme violence and cruelty against the Indian workforce has prompted Taussig to ponder: "Why this fiction of trade should exercise so much power is one of the great oddities of political economy and to this day there has been no way of disentangling the paradox that the rubber traders, although they strove tirelessly to create and maintain this fictional reality, were just as ready to claim the flesh of a debtor's body" (1987: 65). The answer to this seeming contradiction is that *habilitación* and terror were not antithetical mechanisms; both were necessary to ensure that the tribal Indian population continued to collect weak hevea rubber. If Arana maintained the fiction of *habilitación* and exchange, it was because he had realized that even on a large scale terror alone not only was too costly (the maintenance of a large body of guardians, overseers, and section chiefs) but also would not keep the system working.

Arana was also aware of the fascination that foreign goods exerted upon his Huitoto laborers, who needed to think that they were receiving something in exchange for the rubber they collected—something highly valued that could be obtained only by working for his company. Although most contemporary observers were appalled at the cheapness of the goods provided to tribal Indians in exchange for their rubber, from an indigenous perspective the timesaving utensils and firearms obtained were invaluable. The realization that slavery was a very costly system in a context where it was not legal and could not be enforced by law also explains why indigenous children captured in *correrías* were later incorporated into the *habilitación* system and treated as *habilitado* peons, rather than as the actual slaves they were immediately after being captured. In effect, though there are numerous reports of children and young women being sold or transferred as payment of a debt or a service, there are none that refer to the sale of adult indigenous workers originally captured in *correrías*.

Correrías were not meant to procure slaves but to produce peons. Although captured children were instilled with an ideology of subordination and brought up to become domestic servants or rural peons, they were still considered part of their masters' household. Since their rearing required an "investment" before they became useful laborers, *patrones* conceived of them as being more valuable than enslaved tribal Indians and, therefore, treated them less harshly. When they grew up they were assigned a variety of tasks. Those who became domestic servants were compensated for their services with a few goods. Those who became peons were integrated into the *habilitación* system, receiving goods in advance for their work. These servants and peons were attached to their masters by a combination of paternalistic and economic bonds, and neither they nor their offspring could be bought or sold.

However, whether slaves turned into *habilitado* peons or *habilitado* peons turned into quasislaves, the result was the same: the subjection of tribal Indians, their engagement in mercantile activities, and their transformation into disciplined, docile laborers. This is what contemporary commentators referred to as the "civilizing" effect of the rubber economy (Pesce 1903: 92–3; Stiglich 1904b: 436). According to these authors, to civilize "savage" Indians is to "conquer" or "seduce" them into entering into contact with the marketplace, to make them indebted by creating in them new material needs, and to persuade them to drop their arms and participate in the regional economy. In other words, from this point of view, to "civilize" was to transform hostile, unproductive, autonomous, and free Indians into pacific, productive, indebted, and subservient peons.

In a recent work on the Amazonian rubber economy Coomes and Barham (1994: 241) have put forward the provocative argument that "the much-criticized debt-merchandise contract provided the basis for a stable and relatively efficient relationship among the trader, the patron and the tapper." In their view, the debt-merchandise or debt-peonage contract became the most widespread labor arrangement for rubber extraction "because no other alternative contract could meet the needs of creditors and borrowers at lower cost in this high risk, high transaction cost environment where both labor and capital were scarce" (Barham and Coomes 1994b: 63). The analysis of the case of Loreto confirms this view.

Whereas the means of labor recruitment varied widely depending on the type of population being considered, the relationship between *patrones* and their peons was always based upon the *habilitación* system. Although the terms of exchange involved in the *habilitado* relationship also changed according to the type of population involved, even in the most coercive situations—such as that in Arana's Putumayo estates—labor relationships continued to be embedded in the *habilitación* system. As we shall see, *habilitación* continued to be the dominant type of labor arrangement throughout most of the post–rubber bust era, because the shortage of labor that sustained it persisted until the 1940s, when it gradually began to change.

4

"Commerce Is the Most Powerful Agent": The Hegemonic Role of Merchant Houses

Most students of the Peruvian rubber boom agree with the statement that commerce was "the most powerful agent" of Loreto's turn-of-the-century economy (Palacios 1890b: 471). They also agree that Loreto's trade was monopolized by the merchant houses of Iquitos, that is, by firms engaged in international trade either as importers or exporters, often combining both. Owners of merchant houses made up the upper layer of the region's commercial elite; together with the military and higher government officials, they dominated the region's political and economic life. Unfortunately, most studies of the rubber boom provide little concrete information about how these firms worked; instead they give only a general, decontextualized, frequently atemporal picture of their structure and functions.

Among the unsubstantiated generalizations about the Peruvian rubber trade and the large merchant houses of Iquitos, two stand out because they have taken deep root among nonspecialists. First is the assertion that the region's merchant houses were mere "agencies" of larger European and North American trading firms; in this formulation, Loreto's rubber economy was controlled by foreign capital, particularly British (Bonilla 1974: 75; San Román 1975: 161; Pennano 1988: 78). Second is the notion that the structure of production, trade, and credit in Peruvian Amazonia was not essentially different from that prevalent in Brazil (Haring 1986a: 127).

These take their cue from generalizations, frequently phrased as denunciations, put forward by contemporary observers, be they local authorities, travelers, or merchants. Valid only for particular moments in the evolution of Loreto's rubber economy, they have been taken as characteristic of the entire period. In other cases, views are informed by the theoretical and ideological approaches of those studying Loreto's rubber economy, mostly "dependency" or "enclave" theories (see also Barham and Coomes 1994a: 76). Although the aforementioned assertions might not be totally inexact, we shall argue that they cannot be taken at face value; they are not substantiated by solid information on the functioning of specific merchant houses, and they fail to incorporate the temporal dimension.

In this chapter, we attempt to fill this void by analyzing the internal differences characterizing Loreto's so-called grand commerce. Constituted by the major import-export merchant houses, this commerce varied markedly in terms of the traders' national origin, their relationship with foreign capital, and the scale of their operations. The histories of the commercial trajectories of some of these firms (see Boxes 4.1–4.9) reveal divergent ways in which they began doing business in the region, invested their capital, and adapted their strategies according to economic and political changes at the regional, national, and international levels.

Our analysis thus casts doubt on previous generalizations, questioning the received wisdom about Loreto's rubber economy. Despite the important role that Great Britain played in the rubber economy, not one of the large merchant houses of Iquitos was British. Great Britain monopolized maritime navigation between the Brazilian port of Belém and the ports of Europe and the United States; although it controlled navigation along the Amazon, British companies navigating along this route did not operate as a trust. Furthermore, although Great Britain was an important supplier of credit it never absorbed more than 50 percent of Loreto's rubber exports or provided more than 50 percent of its imports. Our analysis demonstrates that the most important foreign-owned merchant houses in Loreto, in fact, were French and German. More importantly, it shows that some of the largest rubber-trading firms were owned by Peruvians; together, the largest Peruvian firms controlled around a third of the region's rubber exports.

Our analysis of how the largest merchant houses of Iquitos were organized and how they functioned demonstrates that Loreto's grand commerce differed substantially from that of Brazil. Whereas in Brazil imports, exports, and outfitting of rubber extractors rested in the hands of three different types of agents, in Loreto all functions were carried out simultaneously by the largest firms. Moreover, whereas in Brazil 50 percent of the rubber export trade was directly controlled by European and United States rubber-importing companies through their agents, in Loreto overseas rubber importers had no direct control over rubber exports. This concentration of multiple functions, as well as the greater autonomy with respect to overseas rubber importers, were possible, in our opinion, because Peru was a relatively small rubber producer. This fact had important consequences for the survival and performance of Loreto's grand commerce after the collapse of the rubber economy.

Composition of the Region's Grand Commerce

There is little information on Loreto's commercial firms after the 1851 treaty with Brazil on fluvial navigation until the turn of the century. In a report on his 1859 trip to Loreto, Italian naturalist Antonio Raimondi noted the positive effects the treaty had for the region's commerce. He mentions the existence in Moyobamba of several merchants who exported Panama hats directly to Brazil or sold them to foreign merchant houses, mainly Portuguese-Brazilian, established in Nauta (Raimondi 1862:

171; 1859: 98). Almost ten years later, during his 1868 trip, Raimondi (1869: 315) reported that thanks to the inauguration of a regular steamship line between Iquitos and Yurimaguas several merchant houses had been established in the latter. In Nauta, which had prospered with the opening of the Peruvian Amazon to international navigation, he reported the existence of two important merchant houses. In Iquitos—still little more than a village—he reported the existence of a large number of well-stocked wholesale commercial firms, some of which had a capital of some 50,000–100,000 pesos, or £8,000–16,000 (ibidem: 319, 322). Most of the commercial activity revolved around the exportation of Panama hats, tobacco, cotton, and salted fish to Brazil and Europe. As a result of the sustained increase in international trade, Brazil, France, and Germany appointed consular representatives in the city of Moyobamba.

Raimondi (1862: 172) pointed out that the Panama hat commerce enriched some of Moyobamba's merchants. It also constituted a means of capital accumulation for some of the merchants established in other towns within the Huallaga Basin, such as Tarapoto and Yurimaguas. This contradicts those who assert that before the rubber boom proper (i.e., 1890) commerce in the region was "vegetative, without funds of its own, linked to the houses of Manaus and Belém, and dependent on their good will, their credit, but also on their exorbitant profit margins" (Roux 1994: 240). It also contradicts the claim, "When commercial traffic became more substantial and rewarding thanks to the rubber boom, it was the middlemen or representatives of European firms who took in their expert hands these affairs, confining local commerce to accessory roles such as that of deceiving the customs for small profits" (ibidem).

As is apparent from the commercial biographies of the Huallaga-area traders who became heads of some of the most outstanding and long-lived merchant houses of Iquitos (see Boxes 4.1, 4.2, and 4.3), this is not an adequate representation of Loreto's commerce before the rubber boom. It provides a monolithic portrayal of Loreto's rubber traders, concealing the great diversity found among the Iquitos merchant houses in terms of national and ethnic backgrounds, time in which they started doing business in the region, origin of their capital, connections with the international market for capital and goods, and scale of their operations.

Based on these criteria, we identify four distinct groups of traders who established merchant houses in Iquitos. Peruvian merchants of Spanish stock constituted the first group. They were mainly native to the Huallaga area and were able to accumulate capital in the 1870s and early 1880s through the Panama hat trade and the export of such agricultural and forest products as tobacco, cotton, and sarsaparilla. These merchants were among the first to become involved in the rubber trade. They were independent importers, exporters, and shippers who started doing business with their own capital and expanded their activities with credit from Brazilian and European firms. Presently, they would incorporate and operate some of the most powerful merchant houses of Iquitos, both in terms of amount of capital managed and proportion of import-export trade controlled.

Box 4.1 The Rubber Merchant Luis Felipe Morey Arias

Luis Felipe Morey Arias was born in Tarapoto in 1854, of a Spanish father, who was a navy officer, and an Ecuadorian mother. His family belonged to the upper echelons of regional society. At age ten he was sent to Pará, Brazil, to attend school. This connection proved to be very helpful in L. F. Morey's later commercial career. In 1868 he returned to Loreto, where he was employed at the naval workshop of Iquitos (Anonymous 1938: 39). After a short time there, he went back to Tarapoto, where he became actively engaged in the commerce of tobacco and Panama hats, for which he made regular trips to Pará. By 1877, at twenty-three, he was already an important member of Loreto's mercantile community. That year the local government was experiencing the effects of an acute fiscal crisis that had begun in 1871. Loreto's commander had to turn to the trading community to obtain credit to cover the expenses of the administration. L. F. Morey was one of the three traders to answer his pleas, providing him with the largest credit, £520, which by then represented a respectable 22 percent of Loreto's monthly budget (Romero 1983: 64, 61).

In 1885 L. F. Morey associated with his brothers, Adolfo and Juan Abelardo, to incorporate in the town of Yurimaguas the rubber-trading firm Morey Brothers. Three years later this company was dissolved (Anonymous 1938: 39). In the following decades and until his death in 1936, L. F. Morey founded or invested in eleven commercial firms in Peru, Brazil, and the United States. Some were small merchant houses dedicated to the rubber trade in particular river basins. Their main assets were a trading post, one or two steamlaunches, and in some cases a rubber estate. Such were the cases of Morey and Dávila, which was founded in 1888 in Yurimaguas and operated in the lower Huallaga River; and of Morey, Dublé and Company, founded in 1889 in Masisea and which operated in the upper Ucayali River (Anonymous 1938: 39).

Other firms were based in Iquitos or Manaus and had branches in particular river basins. This was the case of Vega, Morey, and Company, formed in Iquitos in 1890 in association with his brother-in-law, Juan C. del Aguila, and the Colombian rubber extractor and trader Juan B. Vega. The incorporation of this firm was considered to be one of the most important commercial fusions of its time, and it is said that "because of the volume of its trade [this firm] led the commercial life of Iquitos for a long period" (Anonymous 1938: 40). There were also the cases of Morey and del Aguila, founded in 1892 in Iquitos and with a branch in Perseverancia in the Yavari River, and of Morey and Aguila, founded in Manaus in 1899 and which had a branch in Nuevo Iquitos in the Yurua River (Anonymous 1938: 40).

L. F. Morey also ventured into shipping. About 1892 he purchased the firm Marcial A. Pinón and Company, whose owner was one of the traders who in 1877 bought the state fluvial fleet. Among the assets of this firm were several steamboats. This takeover was considered one of the largest commercial transactions of its time (Anonymous 1938: 40). In 1896 L. F. Morey associated with Frenchman Charles Mourraille and Peruvian Cecilio Hernández to purchase the steamboat *Huáscar* and establish a direct navigation line between Iquitos and Liverpool (ibidem). This partnership, however, seems to have had only a brief existence. In the late 1890s he associated with Enrique

(continues)

Box 4.1 *(continued)*

S. Llosa to form E. S. Llosa and Company, a firm that owned the rubber estate Irene and a steamship by the name of *Veloz* (Anonymous 1938: 40). With a carrying capacity of 128 tons, that boat was considered to be "one of the fastest commercial vessels of Iquitos" (La Combe 1902: 343, 225–6). It traveled regularly along the Amazon and Ucayali Rivers, both between Iquitos and the frontier with Brazil and between Iquitos and the confluence of the Tambo with the Ucayali River.

In 1899 L. F. Morey moved with his family to Iquitos, which three years earlier had become the capital of Loreto. There he founded Luis Felipe Morey and Sons. This firm became one of the *casas fuertes,* or "powerful merchant houses," of Iquitos. His daughter Irene managed the firm very successfully, and son Manuel was in charge of supervising the firm's fluvial commercial network (Morey Menacho n.d.: 7). In 1900 the company became Loreto's fourth largest rubber exporter, controlling 13 percent of its rubber exports (see Table 4.3). It operated both in Peru and Brazil, and one of its two large steamboats navigated under the Brazilian flag (Capelo 1900: 35). In 1901 it was among the first to outfit castilloa extractors entering the Madre de Dios region, reorganizing for that purpose its trading posts of Mishagua and Unión Loretana, which were located along the tributaries of the lower Urubamba River (Robledo 1903: 61).

By then L. F. Morey had amassed a fortune and was able to extend his investments beyond the country's frontiers. In 1901, on his way to Lima after being elected senator for Loreto, he became a silent partner of the Manaus import-export firm of Ernest Kingdom and Company, together with Edmund Reeks and Harris A. Astlet (Anonymous 1938: 40). Five years later he bought E. Kingdom's share of the New York–based rubber import firm H. A. Astlet and Company, which had agents in Manaus and later became Sidney Fall and Company (ibidem).

In 1903 Stiglich (1907: 197) referred to the premises of L. F. Morey and Sons as the "best building" in Iquitos. One year later this firm was listed as importer-exporter, shipper, wholesale-retail trader, and customs broker and appeared as the region's third largest payer of *patente industrial,* a tax of 5 percent over the annual profits made by merchants, manufacturers, and professionals (Matrícula 1910: 58). In the following two years the company reported no profits in Iquitos, but its Yavari and Apayacu branches fared well enough as to pay taxes (Matrícula 1910: 59, 71–2). By 1907 the firm's share of the region's rubber export trade had decreased to 4 percent (Table 4.4). However, in the following years it recovered financially.

L. F. Morey was one of the few large rubber traders who ventured into rubber extraction. He owned several rubber estates, mostly along the Marañon and Ucayali rivers, which he registered after the rubber bust (Padrón 1939). By 1928 he owned fourteen large landholdings totaling 167,225 hectares.

L. F. Morey continued to be an eminent member of Iquitos's trading community well after the 1914 rubber bust. He was not only an extremely successful merchant but also a very active public man. He was appointed president of Loreto's Departmental Board (Junta Departamental) and elected president of the chamber of commerce of Iquitos, house representative for the province of San Martín, and senator for the department of Loreto. He and his wife had more than 300 godchildren, for whom they opened the doors of their home once a week. He died in 1936, but his firm continued to be one of the region's leading merchant houses until at least 1940 (Guía 1940).

Box 4.2   The Rubber Merchant Adolfo Morey Arias

Adolfo Morey Arias, brother of Luis Felipe Morey, was another local merchant who accumulated wealth on the basis of the Panama hat commerce, later investing it in the rubber trade. Born in Tarapoto in 1862, in the early 1880s he moved to Yurimaguas, where together with sister Manuela he founded a small commercial firm engaged in the export of hats and tobacco to Brazil (Anonymous 1992: 6). In 1885, together with his brothers Luis Felipe and Juan Abelardo, he founded a rubber-trading firm in Yurimaguas (Anonymous 1938: 40). During his stay in Yurimaguas, A. Morey participated actively in the city's commercial and political life, becoming subprefect of the province of Alto Amazonas in 1887 (Rumrrill et al. 1986: 275).

In 1888 he moved to Iquitos, where he founded A. Morey and Company with a branch office in Yurimaguas (Anonymous 1938: 207). Two years later his firm was listed among the twenty-five largest merchant houses of Iquitos (Capelo 1900). By then it controlled 6 percent of Loreto's rubber exports (see Table 4.3). Since the incorporation of his firm, A. Morey showed an inclination to invest in the shipping sector; he owned two small steamlaunches, and together with Anselmo del Aguila, also a Huallaga-born trader, he owned a third launch, which navigated under the Brazilian flag (Capelo 1900; Palacios Rodríguez 1991: 528). By 1904 A. Morey had augmented the firm's merchant fleet to four steamships valued at the quite impressive amount of £20,100 (Larrabure i Correa: II, 7). These boats were built to order for him during 1900–1903 in British, French, and German shipyards. With a carrying capacity of 211 tons, which represented 22 percent of the total tonnage of Loreto's merchant fleet, A. Morey became by far the largest private shipowner of the region, surpassing such important foreign-owned merchant houses as Wesche and Company and Marius, Lévy and Company (Larrabure i Correa: II, 7). In 1905 his company was described as "the oldest and most prestigious" of the two shipping firms that navigated regularly between Yurimaguas and Iquitos (Fuentes 1906: 302). In 1906 he further increased the tonnage of his fleet (Fuentes 1908: 10).

In 1904 A. Morey and Company occupied the sixth position as contributor of taxes in Iquitos, and a year later its Yurimaguas branch was mentioned as the third largest contributor of taxes in that city (García Córdova 1905: 40). In 1908 the company was still among the largest contributors of taxes of Iquitos (Matrícula 1910). Although by then Morey's firm was still involved in a vast range of commercial activities, fluvial navigation had become the hub of its business. In effect, by 1907 his share of the region's rubber trade had dropped to 3 percent (Larrabure i Correa: XIV, 244). After the 1914 rubber bust A. Morey expanded his shipping business, venturing into oceanic navigation and establishing lines between Iquitos, Europe, the United States, and the Peruvian Pacific Coast.

A. Morey also participated in regional politics, being elected as alternate congressman for Loreto during three consecutive periods between 1901 and 1918 (Tuesta 1994). His firm also managed to survive the rubber crisis, and he continued to be active in regional commerce and shipping until his death in 1943.

Box 4.3   The Rubber Merchant Cecilio Hernández Isla

The commercial trajectory of Cecilio Hernández is similar to those of the Morey brothers, Luis Felipe and Adolfo. Born in Chachapoyas but linked to important families residing in the Huallaga Basin, in the early 1880s he moved to Iquitos, where he established an important merchant house. In the late 1880s he associated with French merchants Charles Mourraille and Paul Magne, with whom he incorporated an import-export firm. By 1894 the company was among the most important in the region, having chartered the sole transatlantic steamship that had arrived in Iquitos directly from Europe (Palacios Rodríguez 1990: 513, 609). The firm already owned a large, eighty-six-ton steamship, a forty-nine-ton vessel, and a small, six-ton boat, which originally navigated under the Brazilian flag (ibidem: 528). Two years later, Mourraille, Hernández, Magne, and Company added to its fleet a smaller steamlaunch (Ibarra 1897: 516). These boats collected rubber extracted along the Napo, Tigre, and Putumayo Rivers and outfitted local rubber *patrones* with imported merchandise.

Sometime in the 1890s Mourraille, Hernández, Magne, and Company associated with Julio C. Arana, though each of the partner firms retained its separate commercial identity. The connection with Arana was established through Hernández, who was the uncle of Arana's wife (Collier 1981: 41). This new importing and merchant banking enterprise became one of the most powerful in the region (ibidem: 51). In 1896, however, Arana broke this partnership. That year Hernández associated briefly with Luis Felipe Morey to establish a navigation line between Iquitos and Liverpool (Anonymous 1938: 40). Again, this partnership seems to have been based on family ties, since two of Hernández's sons married two of L. F. Morey's daughters (Morey Meñacho n.d.: 14).

In 1897 Hernández, Mourraille, and Magne, who had maintained their original partnership, sold their largest steamship to Fermín Fitzcarrald and his partner, Bolivian rubber baron Nicolás Suárez (La Combe 1902: 355–6). Apparently, that marked the end of Mourraille's participation in this commercial society, for in 1899 only Hernández and Magne remained associated (Capelo 1900). By then they owned a medium-sized steamboat, a large scow or open barge used to transport additional freight, and an ice-making factory, located in Iquitos and valued at £2,300 (Capelo 1900: 31). By 1900 Hernández, Magne, and Company handled 9 percent of Loreto's rubber exports (see Table 4.3).

In the early 1900s Hernández broke his partnership with Magne and founded a new firm, Cecilio Hernández and Son (Anonymous 1938: 44). The new company was involved in import-export trade, fluvial navigation, wholesale-retail commerce, and customs brokerage. By 1904 it was the sixth largest taxpayer in the city of Iquitos (Fuentes 1908: 29–30). However, Hernández was not as powerful as in the past, and in 1907 his share of the region's rubber trade dropped to 3 percent (Larrabure i Correa XIV, 244). Nevertheless, by 1908 it was still listed among the ten largest taxpayers of Iquitos (Matrícula 1910).

Early on, Hernández was part of the small group of powerful merchants that controlled the region's rubber trade. By 1890 he had achieved such prominence within the trading community of Iquitos that he was invited by Prefect Samuel Palacios

(continues)

Box 4.3   *(continued)*

Mendiburu, together with eighteen other national and foreign local merchants, to constitute the chamber of commerce of Iquitos (Proceso 1968, No. 8). As with the Morey brothers, Hernández also became involved in regional politics. In 1896 he was appointed secretary of government for the administration of the insurgent Col. Ricardo Seminario and, in 1906, mayor of Iquitos. Hernández and Son survived the rubber bust, becoming in subsequent years a pioneer in the development of new export lines (Anonymous 1938: 44). The company continued doing business in the region until at least the early 1930s.

The second group was formed by merchants of Portuguese-Brazilian origin, some of whom established themselves in Loreto before the rubber boom to profit from the Panama hat trade. The most important members of this group were not agents of Brazilian firms, although they often operated on the basis of credit obtained from merchant houses in Belém and Manaus. In most cases, members of this group remained as owners of small to medium-sized merchant houses.

The third group was European merchants who, with a few exceptions, arrived in the area from the mid–1880s onward, mostly with their own capital. In most cases, they were associated with important European establishments; in a few instances they acted as agents of European-based firms. The most important merchants within this group were Ashkenazi Jews, mainly from France. Together with the Peruvian traders, they owned the largest merchant houses of Iquitos.

Sephardic Jewish traders from the Mediterranean composed the fourth group. Most arrived in Loreto during the 1890s, often after a more or less prolonged stay in Brazil. They were originally engaged in minor river trade and depended on credit provided by the larger commercial firms in Iquitos and Manaus. In some cases, however, they were able to accumulate capital through the rubber trade and established their own firms. Though many owned small merchant houses and remained in the lower echelons of the mercantile community of Iquitos, a few traders were extremely successful. Presently, some of them would be counted among Iquitos's most prominent members, being elected to important positions within the chamber of commerce and holding key public offices.

Among the Peruvian group, the most outstanding merchants were Luis Felipe Morey, Adolfo Morey, Cecilio Hernández, and Julio C. Arana. In reconstructing the commercial careers of the first three, we see that these native traders, far from being relegated to a minor function as a result of the arrival of European merchants, retained leading roles in the region's mercantile life.

The Portuguese-Brazilian merchants were among the first foreigners to settle in the region. As with the Peruvians, they initially were involved with Panama hats and later with the rubber economy, both as traders and as extractors. On the whole, however, there is little information about the activities of these merchants, which suggests they were not very important within Loreto's mercantile community. In effect, the little evidence we have depicts them as small to medium-sized importer-exporters, often engaged only in the import trade and minor fluvial commerce (see Boxes 4.4 and 4.5).

None of the Portuguese-Brazilian merchant houses of Iquitos, such as those belonging to Venancio F. Pereira, Antonio R. da Cunha, J. Mendes de Almeida, and Teixeira y Soares can be found among those cited by Roberto Santos (1980) and Barbara Weinstein (1983) as based in Belém or Manaus. And there is no evidence that the Portuguese-Brazilians who settled in Loreto acted as agents or associates of Brazilian commercial firms. This does not preclude the possibility that they had links and obtained credit with such firms, but it suggests that merchant houses in Belém and Manaus had no direct presence in Iquitos in the form of commercial branches or agencies, as has been argued (Roux 1994: 167).

In contrast, the European merchants quickly positioned themselves at the top of the regional mercantile community. However, they were not a homogeneous group:

Box 4.4   The Rubber Merchant Joaquín Antúnez de Brito

Joaquín Antúnez de Brito was a medium-sized Portuguese-Brazilian merchant who began operating in Loreto at the outset of the rubber boom. Of Portuguese origin, he associated with Frenchman Charles Mourraille in 1884. Their Iquitos-based firm, Mourraille, Brito, and Company, owned *Mayo*, a steamlaunch that traded along the Amazon and Ucayali Rivers (Samanez y Ocampo 1980: 75). It carried imported merchandise upriver to supply minor traders and extractors who were outfitted by the company. On its way downriver it came loaded with the rubber gathered by *habilitado* extractors. *Mayo* was one of the first boats to make regular trips to the mouth of the Pachitea River, an area that had been opened to rubber extraction around 1882 and where several smaller commercial firms had recently been established (ibidem). In the 1890s Brito and Mourraille split. By 1894 Brito owned a small, thirteen-ton steamlaunch (Palacios Rodríguez 1990: 528). Two years later he was reported as owning *Putumayo,* a steamship that traded along the Napo River route and was later sold to Arana, Larrañaga, and Company (Ibarra 1897: 516; Larrabure i Correa: II, 7).

It seems that Brito did not do well in the trading business after that, for in 1900 he was not listed among those owning merchant houses in Iquitos. However, as with other Portuguese-Brazilians, he seems to have done better in the business of hevea extraction. By 1902, under land legislation promulgated in 1899, Brito obtained three estates, Santa Clara, Palmella, and Bogotá along the Peruvian side of the Yavari River. These properties, which covered 1,578 hectares and contained forty producing rubber trails, were dedicated to the exploitation of fine pará rubber (Registro 1902: 29–30, 34–5; Fuentes 1908: 147–8). By 1908 Brito was listed as a minor contributor of taxes among the rubber extractors and traders of the Yavari River and as a small industrialist in the city of Iquitos, though no information is provided as to the nature of his industry (Matrícula 1910). After this date we have been unable to find references to Brito's commercial activities, suggesting that he left the region after the rubber bust.

Box 4.5   The Rubber Merchant Manuel Rocha

Manuel Rocha and his sons, of Portuguese origin, were among the most successful Portuguese-Brazilian merchants operating in Loreto. Sometime before 1890 Rocha established an important trading post and factory at the mouth of the Yavari River (Ydiáquez 1890: 100). By 1900 his firm, M. Rocha and Sons, was listed as one of the twenty-five merchants houses extant in Iquitos (Capelo 1900). At that time this company owned the *Portugal,* which, with a carrying capacity of 134 tons, was the largest private steamship of the time to navigate under the Peruvian flag (Capelo 1900). It also owned a smaller steamlaunch. By 1904 the company had bought a new, smaller steamlaunch. Although the total carrying capacity of the firm's vessels was reduced to twenty-three tons, they were valued at the still respectable sum of £5,000 (Larrabure i Correa: II, 7). After the death of Manuel Rocha around 1904, the firm changed its name to Rocha and Brothers. That year it was still listed among the exclusive group of merchant houses that combined import-export activities with fluvial transportation, and it occupied the seventh place among Iquitos's taxpayers (Fuentes 1908: 29–30). In 1906 Arturo, one of the Rocha brothers, figured as vice consul of the Kingdom of Portugal (Fuentes 1908: 221). Although the company was able to retain a small merchant fleet (Fuentes 1908: 10), by 1908 its profits had decreased so much that its fiscal contribution became almost insignificant (Matrícula 1910). The 1910 rubber crisis must have eliminated the company as a large trader in Iquitos, for it is not registered in any of the later lists of local merchants. Nonetheless, unlike the Brito brothers, the Rochas settled permanently in Loreto and remained there even after the rubber bust.

They differed in the times that they settled in the region, the type of economic activities they engaged in, and, more notoriously, the capital they controlled. Although national origin seems not to have determined the success of individual merchants, there was a certain connection between the different national groupings and their respective weights in the region's commerce. Thus, it is possible to identify three distinct European merchant subgroups: Spanish-Italian, British, and German-French.

The first was the least important among the Europeans devoted to the rubber trade. Although some Spaniards, such as the Barcia brothers, became important rubber traders, most of them confined themselves to small import and retail commerce. This is also true of most of the Italians with some notable exceptions, such as Luis Pinasco, who as an importer and retail trader in 1908 was listed as the tenth largest contributor of taxes in Iquitos (Matrícula 1910). Joseph Woodroffe confirms this general picture, asserting that owners of "eating houses, taverns and vendors of canned goods [were] mostly Italians and Spaniards" (1914: 33). All in all, Spaniards and Italians occupied the lower rung among European traders.

Contrary to the prevailing view, British merchants in Loreto never achieved a leading position, having a very minor presence in the lists of Iquitos's trading firms from 1900, 1904, and 1908. Although during the late 1860s Raimondi underscored the importance of the British community in the nascent port city of Iquitos, by 1903 the urban census reported the existence of only fourteen British subjects (Fuentes 1906: 462). In the 1904 register of Iquitos's fiscal contributors, only three British merchant houses were listed: Albert Banister, Abraham Dan, and David Cazes (Fuentes 1908: 29–30; Maúrtua 1911: 156). Of these, only Cazes, a Sephardim from Gibraltar who acted as British consul in Iquitos, was a merchant of some weight (Collier 1981: 152). His merchant house, the Iquitos Trading Company, is first mentioned in 1900 as owning a twenty-ton steamlaunch (Capelo 1900). In 1904 his house occupied the fifth position in terms of fiscal contribution, and in 1906 it was reported as owning two vessels with a total carrying capacity of 100 tons (Fuentes 1908: 10). By 1907 the Iquitos Trading Company had become the fifth-largest rubber-export firm, controlling almost 10 percent of Loreto's rubber exports (see Table 4.4). However, Cazes must have died or left the region shortly thereafter, for his firm was not listed among those extant in Iquitos in 1908. The two other British merchants were confined to the import business and appear as very minor contributors of taxes.

German and French traders (mostly Ashkenazi Jews) were the most prominent among the European traders and owned the most versatile and powerful merchant houses in Iquitos. Frenchman Charles Mourraille stands out as being one of the first to arrive in the region (see Box 4.6). Despite Mourraille's foreign origins, his commercial enterprises were incorporated in Peru and were not ancillary to larger European trading firms. Furthermore, during his active life in Loreto he was frequently associated with Peruvian merchants. In contrast, Wesche and Company, Kahn and Polack, Kahn and Company, and Marius and Lévy, the most important foreign-owned merchant houses in Iquitos, had a strong foothold in Europe (see Boxes 4.7, 4.8, and 4.9). Some were incorporated in Europe and maintained a branch office in Iquitos, others were incorporated in Peru but had agents in Europe, whereas some were in partnership with European firms. However, none were associated with British firms.

Sephardic Jews from the Mediterranean formed the fourth group of trading firms. In the 1820s many Sephardim migrated to Brazil, where they became engaged in commerce (Kelly and London 1983: 314). Most of them came from Morocco (Rabat and Fez), Spanish Morocco (Tetuan and Ceuta), French Morocco (Casablanca), Tangier, Malta, and Turkey (Rosenzweig 1967: 23–5; Trahtemberg n.d.: 184; Segal 1997: 90). According to Weinstein (1983: 50–1), by the second half of the nineteenth century most minor fluvial traders of Pará were Sephardim. They were frequently employed by Portuguese commercial firms, known as *casas aviadoras*, which were specialized in outfitting rubber extractors through the *aviamento* or *habilitación* system and as middlemen between the latter and the import and export houses. These firms supplied Jewish merchants "with the goods they peddled, and sold the rubber they received in return to foreign exporters" (ibidem).

By the mid-1890s most of the small-scale Brazilian fluvial rubber trade was controlled by Jewish traders (Pennano 1988: 58). In the face of local prejudice and

---

Box 4.6   The Rubber Merchant Charles Mourraille

It is not clear when French trader Charles Mourraille arrived in Loreto, but as early as 1862 he was reported as owning a house in Iquitos (Sotomayor et al. 1949: 21). Although ten years later he still had a house there, it is probable that by then he lived in Moyobamba, which was still Loreto's capital, where he was appointed consul of France (LC: IX, 411; Izquierdo Ríos 1976: 69).

Little is known about the commercial activities of Mourraille during the early years. We know, however, that in 1877 he associated with the Peruvians Marcial Pinón del Aguila, Antonio Nájar, and Manuel del Aguila to incorporate the Peruvian Navigation Company. That firm bought the state's regional fluvial fleet for £7,600 and leased the state's naval workshop and warehouses at £1,200 per year for a fifteen-year period (Romero 1983: 63, 69). In addition, the company agreed to deposit £10,000 as security. All in all, the partners had to disburse a total of £18,800, which was a substantial sum at the time. However, as many contemporary observers pointed out, this was a very low price for what they obtained, and according to Fuentes (1906: 456) it was this deal that allowed Mourraille to amass his fortune.

Because of the decline of the Panama hat trade and the increasing importance of Iquitos as a rubber-trading center, in the 1880s most consular representatives moved from Moyobamba to Iquitos. Among them was Mourraille (Izquierdo Ríos 1976: 69). By 1884 he had entered into a partnership with Joaquín Antúnez de Brito, a Portuguese rubber merchant and extractor. In 1885–1886 he became briefly associated with Colombian Enrique Reyes, a former quinine extractor and rubber trader. By then Mourraille's firm was considered by the Colombians as "an important and rich merchant house of Iquitos" (Reyes 1985: 166). Olivier Ordinaire, a French diplomat who visited Iquitos in 1885, was more emphatic, stating that he "had the satisfaction of verifying that the most prosperous merchant house in Iquitos … was a French firm, that of Mr. Charles Mourraille" (1988: 154). At that time Mourraille owned several steamboats devoted to trading rubber along the Amazon and its tributaries.

In the late 1880s Mourraille established a commercial partnership with Peruvian Cecilio Hernández and Frenchman Paul Magne. In the 1890s the company entered into brief partnerships, first with Julio C. Arana and later with Luis Felipe Morey, the most important Peruvian rubber traders of Loreto. Like other prominent merchants, Mourraille was involved in local politics. In 1882 he was invited by Prefect Tadeo Terry to organize an ad hoc commission to determine the value of duties and tariffs to be charged in the region. And in 1896, in the context of the federalist revolution of Col. Ricardo Seminario, he was appointed president of the chamber of commerce of Iquitos (Barletti 1993: 20). In 1897 his company sold one of its large steamboats to rubber barons Fermín Fitzcarrald and Nicolás Suárez. After that, Mourraille, Hernández, Magne, and Company dissolved, and Mourraille is no longer mentioned in the documentation of the time, a fact that suggests that he either left the region or died.

---

protests against what was perceived as a near-monopoly, Brazil imposed a flat tax of US$500 on each of these merchants. As a result, they were all but eliminated from the fluvial rubber trade. Some became town-based *aviadores*, or outfitters, but most engaged in urban retail commerce. It was in the 1890s that some of these Sephardic

Box 4.7   The Merchant House Wesche and Company

The German trader Herman Wesche founded Wesche and Company in 1882 (Guzmán Rivera 1929). There is very little information on its origins or the activities it carried out during the early years of its existence. Fuentes (1908: 26) asserts that Wesche and Company was associated to a European establishment owned by Charles Ahrenfeldt "forming one and the same society." Unfortunately, he does not inform us where the latter firm was located. What we know is that Herman Wesche resided in Iquitos and eventually married into a local family.

By 1894 it was reported that whereas each of the six most important merchant houses of Iquitos had a capital of no less than 100,000 soles, Wesche and Company stood out by having in circulation close to ten times this amount (Palacios Rodríguez 1990: 519). Given the exchange rate at the time, this represented close to £100,000 invested in the *habilitación* network either in cash or merchandise (Bardella 1989: 119). Not only did the firm have large working capital, but in 1897 it owned at least three large steamships. The *Laura*, with a carrying capacity of forty tons, navigated along the Napo River route (Ibarra 1897: 516). The *Carlos*, at eighty tons, could transport up to 200 passengers and was assigned to the Ucayali trade (Sala 1897: 43). Lastly, the *Herman*, at 120 tons, was one of the largest privately owned steamships of the time; it not only served the company but was leased to such large rubber extractor-traders as Fermín Fitzcarrald (ibidem: 185). This latter vessel belonged to Wesche and Company since at least 1894 (Palacios Rodríguez 1990: 528).

In 1900 Wesche and Company still owned the two larger steamships as well as four large scows (Capelo 1900). While the *Carlos* navigated under the Peruvian flag, the *Herman* was registered in Brazil. This suggests that Wesche and Company outfitted rubber extractors and traded along some of the Brazilian tributaries of the Amazon, which by then could only be navigated by Brazilian-registered vessels. In 1900 the company was the region's second largest exporter, handling 15 percent of its rubber exports (Table 4.3). In 1901 Wesche and Company also owned a sawmill, a workshop, and shipyard that rivaled with those belonging to the state (La Combe 1902: 224; Plane 1903: 329). In 1904 the company was listed as importer-exporter, wholesale-retail trader, shipper, and customs broker and appeared as Iquitos's largest contributor of taxes (Fuentes 1908: 29–30). Wesche and Company also provided other services; it acted as a discount broker and a shipping company, dispatching cargo for third parties (La Combe 1902: 218, 248).

By 1904 the company's fluvial fleet had been greatly diminished, and its total carrying capacity placed it in the fourth position beneath such Peruvian shippers as A. Morey, L. F. Morey and J. C. Arana (Larrabure i Correa: II, 7). However, the company still had Loreto's largest naval workshop. A year later, it was reported that Wesche and Company had plans to build a new and more modern shipyard that would provide the region's shippers with services that up until then could only be obtained in Brazil (Fuentes 1905a: 57). By 1907 the company's share of Loreto's rubber trade had diminished, though it still controlled 10 percent of its exports. Moreover, in 1908 it continued to be listed among the most powerful merchant houses of Iquitos, second only to Julio C. Arana's firm (see Table 4.4; Matrícula 1910).

(continues)

Box 4.7   *(continued)*

Between 1905 and 1913 Wesche and Company acquired or registered a number of small and large rubber estates, particularly along the Marañon River (Padrón 1939). Of these, the two largest were Samiria with an extension of 144,800 hectares and Parinari with 20,880 hectares; in 1912 the government ratified its property titles (Ballón 1991: I, 280–1). The fact that these two estates were dedicated to the tapping of hevea rubber since at least 1905 makes Wesche and Company a pioneer among merchant houses that became directly involved in the collection and processing of rubber (Matrícula 1910: 43). In effect, Wesche and Company, J. C. Arana, L. F. Morey, and Marius and Lévy were the first companies to start rubber-collecting operations in the early 1900s; most others did so only after the 1910 rubber price crisis. In addition, Flores Marín (1987: 56) reports that Wesche and Company was one of the few merchant houses operating in the Peruvian Amazon that attempted to establish rubber plantations, mainly in the area of the Samiria River.

Herman Wesche returned to Germany in 1914. It is not known whether he left Iquitos because of the rubber crisis or because Germany entered into war. Herman Wesche never returned to Peru. In the early 1920s Emilio Strassberger, the company's former manager, acquired the assets of the firm, founding E. Strassberger and Company, which continued to be a leading merchant house.

Box 4.8   The Merchant Houses Kahn and Company and Kahn and Polack

Kahn and Company was a first-rank merchant house owned by three Ashkenazi Jewish brothers, Edmond, Joseph, and Ferdinand Kahn. Born in the French region of Alsace-Lorraine, the three brothers must have settled in Loreto in the early 1880s, for in 1890 they were mentioned among the nineteen important merchants who founded the chamber of commerce of Iquitos (Proceso 1968, No. 8). Until at least 1894, they owned a joint company under the name Kahn Brothers, which was mentioned as one of the most important merchant houses of Iquitos (Palacios Rodríguez 1990: 519). In the early stages of their commercial operations in the region, the three brothers resided in Iquitos and handled their business directly. Ferdinand, at least, continued to do so for a long time, for during the federalist revolution of 1896 he is mentioned as a member of the new board of directors of the chamber of commerce (Navarro Cáuper 1988a: 4). By 1899 he had become head of the company (Anonymous 1938: 213). However, around 1906 it was reported that a French representative, Marcel Oury, managed the company (Fuentes 1908: 211).

Kahn and Company controlled a large share of the region's rubber exports, 13 percent in 1900 and 11 percent in 1907 (see Tables 4.3, 4.4), and as such was among the five top commercial houses of Iquitos. In 1904 it became the region's fourth largest contributor of taxes (Fuentes 1908: 29–30). Four years later it was the third (Matrícula 1910). However, unlike other first-rank firms, Kahn and Company did not diversify, concentrating mainly on the import-export trade. This in no way affected its prospects. In fact, unlike other European firms, Kahn and Company managed to survive the rubber bust. Under the management of Gerome Cahen (or Kahen), cousin of the owner, who became the firm's administrator around 1913, Kahn and Company

(continues)

Box 4.8 *(continued)*

---

continued to be active in the region until at least 1949 (Anonymous 1938: 213; Sotomayor et al. 1949). It is not clear whether the Kahn brothers left the region before or after the rubber bust. What is certain, however, is that at some point they did return to France (Rosenzweig, in Segal 1997: Appendix 2).

Kahn and Polack was owned by Samuel Kahn and Michel Polack, also French Ashkenazi Jews (Segal 1997: 114). It is probable that Samuel Kahn was related to the Kahn brothers, for Gerome Cahen, who was related to the three Kahn brothers, worked for Kahn and Polack before working for Kahn and Co. As with this latter firm, it is not known when Kahn and Polack started operating in the region. According to Fuentes (1908: 26), that company was partnered to a homonymous firm based in Paris, suggesting that the Iquitos company acted only as an agent for a more powerful French house. This was probably the case. Neither Samuel Kahn nor Michel Polack are listed among the Jewish traders who settled in Iquitos during the rubber boom (Rosenzweig, in Segal 1997: Appendix 2). Moreover, it is reported that since at least 1896 the French company had also a branch office in Manaus (Anonymous 1938: 213). In 1903 two French representatives, Marcel Cohen and Alberto Weill, managed the Iquitos office (Segal 1997: 114). Three years later Lucien Bernard replaced them (Fuentes 1908: 211).

In contrast to Kahn and Company, Kahn and Polack diversified early on, carrying out all the activities characteristic of the most powerful merchant houses of Iquitos, including shipping and wholesale-retail trade (Fuentes 1908: 29–30; Matrícula 1910). The process of diversification was gradual. In 1900 the firm was not listed among Loreto's shippers. By 1904, however, it had acquired two vessels, and by 1906 it possessed a steamship and two large scows, increasing the carrying capacity of its fleet to 174 tons (Larrabure i Correa: II, 7; Fuentes 1908: 10). Although the tonnage of the fleet of this foreign company was not negligible, it still was well behind those of such Peruvian shippers as J. C. Arana and A. F. Morey.

In 1904 Kahn and Polack became the region's second largest contributor of taxes, after Wesche and Company (Fuentes 1908: 29–30). In 1908 it continued to be among the largest foreign taxpayers (Matrícula 1910). Like other merchant houses, Kahn and Polack also acquired rubber estates, particularly on the Marañon and Ucayali Rivers. However, most of them were obtained after the rubber bust and in some cases even as late as 1926 (Padrón 1910). Kahn and Polack must have ceased operating in Loreto shortly thereafter, for it is not listed in the 1928 *Guía de Iquitos Comercial* (Rodríguez 1928).

Box 4.9   The Merchant House Marius, Lévy, and Schuler

The firm Marius and Lévy was owned by two French merchants of Ashkenazi Jewish origin. Its headquarters was located in Paris (Fuentes 1908: 26). Little is known as to when and under what conditions they established themselves in Loreto. We know, however, that since at least 1892 it owned a rubber trading post in the confluence of the Itecuahi and Yavari Rivers (Plane 1903: 332). However, by then the company

(continues)

Box 4.9   *(continued)*

---

must have been operating in Loreto for many years, for in 1894 it was listed among the six most powerful merchant houses of Iquitos (Palacios Rodríguez 1990: 519).

The company's trading activities must have been substantial, for although it only owned a small steamlaunch, it leased two other steamboats from Peruvian commercial firms and a 164-ton steamship from a Brazilian company (Ibarra 1897: 516). In 1900 the company enlarged its fleet by acquiring two medium-sized steamboats with a total carrying capacity of 97 tons (Capelo 1900). That year it became the region's largest rubber exporter, controlling 16 percent of the region's exports (Table 4.3). This is not surprising, as by 1902 Marius and Lévy had granted credit to a diversity of rubber *patrones* and minor traders for a total of £500,000 (Plane 1903: 326).

By 1903 Marius and Lévy was the most powerful merchant house operating in the Yavari River basin, above other Brazilian-based firms such as Salomon Braun, established in 1897, or the successors of Henri Lajeneusse. In this frontier area it owned two small rubber estates, Palmera and Alianza, with a total of forty-eight trails (Fuentes 1908: 148). By then the company also had a rubber trading post in the confluence of the Aguarico and Napo Rivers (von Hassel 1903: 237). It is probable, however, that this post was established much earlier, for Marius and Lévy had been active in this trading route since 1896. Through it, the company outfitted rubber *patrones* working along the upper Napo River and its tributaries, mostly Ecuadorian but also Peruvian and Colombian (Barclay 1995b: 20).

Until 1903 the Frenchman Isidore Lévy, probably a kinsman of one of the main partners, represented the company in Iquitos (Segal 1997: 115). A year later a third partner, Pierre Schuler, also a French Ashkenazi, was incorporated into the firm, which changed its name to Marius, Lévy, and Schuler. Fuentes (1908: 26) asserts that the firm's Iquitos office constituted a branch of Marius, Lévy, and Schuler of Paris. However, unlike the founding partners, Schuler resided in Iquitos. Under its new name the company was listed in 1904 as the third largest taxpayer of Iquitos, together with L. F. Morey, J. C. Arana, and Pinto Brothers (Fuentes 1908: 29–30; Maúrtua 1911: 156). It then carried out all the commercial activities characteristic of the top merchant houses of Iquitos. However, four years later, Marius, Lévy, and Schuler had dropped its activities as shippers and wholesale-retail traders, focusing on the import-export trade and customs brokerage.

This in no way can be interpreted as the result of decreasing profits, since in 1907 the firm was still a leading rubber exporter, controlling 14 percent of the region's exports; a year later it was listed as the region's third largest taxpayer. By then the company seems to have sold its Yavari rubber estates, though it retained a rubber trading post called Soledad, which was still one of the most profitable of the area (see Table 4.4; Matrícula 1910: 72). This is the last reference we have on this firm.

It is not clear whether Marius, Lévy, and Schuler closed shop shortly after the 1914 rubber price drop or continued doing business for some time after the rubber bust. We know that Pierre Schuler stayed in Iquitos after the rubber bust; in 1921 he acted as consul for France and Belgium (Torres Videla 1923: 174). In 1929 he was mentioned as a prominent member of the Masonic Lodge of Iquitos (Guzmán Rivera 1929). According to one source, the assets of Marius, Lévy, and Schuler were "conceded" to Kahn and Company in 1935 (Segal 1997: 115). However, the company must have closed much earlier, for in 1928 it was no longer listed among Iquitos's merchant houses (Rodríguez 1928).

merchants, as well as new Sephardic immigrants, settled in Loreto, where there was no legislation limiting their mercantile activities. Alfredo Rosenzweig (1967: 24) estimates in 150 the number of Jewish immigrants (both Sephardic and Ashkenazi) in Loreto; others estimate their number in more than 300 (Trahtemberg n.d.: 184).

Jewish merchants who owned commercial houses in Belém and Manaus sent many of the Sephardim immigrants to Iquitos (Segal 1997: 92). Most became small river traders, known in Loreto as *regatones*. Woodroffe reported that around 1905 "the trade in articles for the rivers [was] almost wholly in the hands of Moroccan Jews" (1914: 33). Others settled as minor traders in the small towns scattered along the region's larger rivers. By 1895 most lived in Yurimaguas, a strategically located town linking Iquitos with Moyobamba (Segal 1997: 92). Others lived in Contamana, on the Ucayali River, where, according to Germán Stiglich (1904a: 311), commerce "is very limited and is in the hands of Jews." These town merchants granted credit in goods to local rubber extractors during the rainy, nonworking season and were paid with rubber by the end of the collecting season (ibidem). Finally, a few were able to capitalize themselves and establish merchant houses in Iquitos. Such was the case for many of the Sephardim merchants that settled in Yurimaguas (Segal 1997: 93).

In 1900 there were four important Iquitos trading firms belonging to Sephardims of Moroccan origin: Pinto Brothers, Farache Brothers, Toledano Brothers, and Benasayag, Toledano and Company. Of these, the first three were listed by Plane (1903: 325) as Brazilian-Moroccans, which suggests they had operated in Brazil. There is little information on the dates these companies were founded. The only firm mentioned prior to the 1900s is that of the Pinto brothers—Moisés, Abraham, Jaime, and Samuel, who had migrated from Tangiers—which in 1894 was among the top-ranking houses in Iquitos (Palacios Rodríguez 1990: 519). With the exception of Toledano Brothers, all were import-export companies; none owned ships. By 1904 Pinto Brothers and Benasayag, Toledano had each managed to acquire a medium vessel, and the former had come to be the third-highest contributor of taxes in Iquitos, alongside three other large Peruvian and foreign firms (Larrabure i Correa: II, 7; Maúrtua 1911:156). Farache Brothers and Toledano Brothers continued doing small-scale business as before.

In addition, several other firms, owned by Mediterranean Sephardim and mainly dedicated to the import trade, were established at this time: Toledano and Delmar, Nahon and Gabay, Abensur and Company, and Israel and Company. Of these, the one belonging to Víctor Israel, an English-speaking Sephardim born in Malta but listed as Turkish, was the most successful (Rosenzweig 1967: 25; Maúrtua 1911: 156). Together with two brothers, Rafael and Isaac, Víctor Israel founded a small import trading firm in Iquitos at the turn of the century. By 1904 the company was not even making enough profits to pay income taxes. However, in the following years its profits increased spectacularly, so that by 1908 Israel and Company was the eighth-highest fiscal contributor in Iquitos, slightly above more traditional and powerful commercial houses such as that belonging to Adolfo Morey (Matrícula

1910). Later on, Víctor Israel acquired a small fluvial fleet and established himself as one of the most important rubber traders on the Napo River, outfitting both Peruvian and Ecuadorian extractors (Muratorio 1987: 136). Israel and Company survived the rubber crisis; after the rubber bust Víctor Israel became one of the region's most prominent traders and an important public figure (Trahtemberg n.d.: 190).

In contrast with Brazilian Amazonia, where prejudice and anti-Semitism seem to have played an important role in excluding Jewish merchants from the small fluvial trade and larger urban-based commerce, in Peruvian Amazonia they flourished and attained high standing. By the end of the rubber boom merchants of Jewish descent, either European Ashkenazi or Mediterranean Sephardim, owned most of the top merchant houses in Iquitos. There is no evidence that this was held against them or that there was any attempt to curtail their economic power. In fact, they occupied important positions in the city's mercantile community and were well represented in the chamber of commerce. Most lived with or married native women and left a prolific progeny in the region.

Changing Fortunes of Traders and Trading Houses

From the commercial biographies of the largest merchants of Iquitos, it is clear that what was known as Loreto's grand commerce was neither homogenous nor static. Data on the origin of the owners of Iquitos' top-ten trading firms (in terms of percentage of rubber trade controlled) for the period 1900–1908 show how the four groups of merchant houses fared differently through time and thus carried different weight within the regional economy (see Table 4.1).

In general terms, by 1900 the Peruvian merchant houses—which during the 1880s pioneered the regional rubber trade—had been equaled by European-based or European-owned firms that settled in Loreto the following decade. The early Portuguese-Brazilian merchant houses had diminished in importance, a trend that was to continue in subsequent years, whereas the Mediterranean firms, formerly confined to minor commerce, had made their way into the exclusive group of the *casas fuertes*, or "strong houses." This situation remained largely unchanged until 1908, when traditional Peruvian merchant houses were displaced as major importer-ex-

Table 4.1   Top-Ten Merchant Houses of Iquitos by Origin of Owners, 1900–1908

Origin	1900	1904	1908
Peruvian	4*	4	1
European	4	5	6
Mediterranean	1	1	3
Portuguese-Brazilian	1	—	—

SOURCES: Capelo 1900; Fuentes 1908: 29–30; Matrícula 1910.
NOTES: * Includes Juan B. Vega, a Colombian extractor and trader, who had been associated to Luis F. Morey and later partnered with Julio C. Arana.

porters by European firms. However, Arana's company, reinforced since 1907 with British capital, was able not only to keep its place in this exclusive group but also to surpass by far the most powerful of the European firms. In 1908 Arana's company was expected to pay almost five times more in taxes than the next largest, a European merchant house.

The formerly top-ranking Peruvian firms, though retaining their import-export activities, instead specialized in regional shipping. Thus, in 1904 the Morey brothers—Adolfo and Luis Felipe—controlled 44 percent of the tonnage of the region's private merchant fleet (Larrabure i Correa: II, 7). And in 1906, when total tonnage increased by 66 percent, these two firms still controlled 27 percent (Fuentes 1908: 10). On the whole, by 1906 Peruvian firms owned 57 percent of total tonnage (see Table 4.2). European companies followed (35 percent), whereas Mediterranean and Portuguese-Brazilian firms had an almost insignificant share of the business. Despite Peruvian supremacy in merchant fluvial transport, by the end of the rubber boom European companies had managed to gain control of a large portion of Loreto's internal and international trade. They were followed only by Sephardim-owned firms, which had experienced a spectacular growth during a very short period.

This point becomes clear if we consider the rubber export trade alone. Export data for the first decade of the twentieth century show that a few merchant houses controlled most of the rubber trade. Thus, in 1900 and in 1907 Iquitos's eight top export houses controlled some 85 percent of the region's total rubber exports (see Tables 4.3 and 4.4). However, the composition of the houses belonging to this exclusive group varied throughout the 1900s. During this period, the number of European houses within the group increased from four to six. Likewise, their share of the group's exports increased from 60 percent to 67 percent. In contrast, the number of Peruvian houses decreased from three to two (those of Arana and L. F. Morey), although the share of rubber handled by Peruvian firms remained almost the same, around 28 percent. This was largely due to the dramatic expansion of Arana's company, which that same year had been registered in London as the Peruvian Amazon Rubber Company.

Table 4.2   Tonnage of Steamboats Belonging to Iquitos's Merchant Houses by Origin of Owners, 1900–1906

Origin	1900	1904	1906
Peruvian	370.0	488.8	696.6
European	308.5	150.2	429.7
Mediterranean	—	77.8	60.8
Portuguese-Brazilian	198.0	23.2	41.6
Total tonnage	876.5	740.0	1,228.7

SOURCES: Capelo 1900: 35; Larrabure i Correa: II, 7; Fuentes 1908: 10.

Table 4.3   Major Rubber-Export Merchant Houses, 1900

Merchant houses	Rubber exports (tons)	Rubber exports (%)
Marius & Lévy	142.9	16.1
Wesche & Co	132.9	15.0
Kahn & Co.	118.9	13.4
L.F. Morey & Sons	114.5	12.9
Hernández, Magne & Co.	82.7	9.3
Pinto Brothers	54.6	6.1
Adolfo Morey & Co.	52.2	5.9
Kahn & Polack	51.9	5.8
Others (17 houses)	137.4	15.5
Total (25 houses)	888.0	100.0

SOURCE: Plane 1903: 324.

Tables 4.3 and 4.4 also demonstrate that Portuguese-Brazilian and Sephardim merchant houses, with the notable exception of Pinto Brothers, had little weight in the rubber export trade and that their relative importance in the region's commerce derived mainly from their activities as importers and wholesalers. In summary, during almost 50 years of the rubber boom, Loreto's grand commerce experienced important changes, both in composition and in the respective weights of its components. These transformations have seldom been acknowledged, leading different authors to render biased portrayals of the region's commerce according to the period being analyzed.

Table 4.4   Major Rubber-Export Merchant Houses, 1907

Merchant houses	Rubber exports (tons)	Rubber exports (%)
Arana & Brothers	540.9	23.2
Marius, Lévy & Schuler	323.4	13.9
Kahn & Co.	247.5	10.6
Wesche & Co.	228.1	9.8
Iquitos Trading Co.	225.4	9.7
Kahn & Polack	174.7	7.5
Barcia & Brothers	120.9	5.2
Luis F. Morey	98.8	4.2
Others (19 houses)	371.0	15.9
Total (27 houses)	2,330.7	100.0

SOURCE: Larrabure i Correa: XIV, 244–5.

NOTE: It must be noted that the rubber exports of Arana & Brothers were probably larger, since part of the production of the company's Putumayo estates was exported directly to Manaus and thus was not registered in the custom house of Iquitos.

The Issue of Foreign Control

Conventional wisdom holds that foreign, especially British, firms controlled sources of credit, fluvial-maritime navigation, import-export trade, and rubber extraction, thus monopolizing Loreto's rubber trade. This erroneous view derives from (1) the overgeneralized depiction of Loreto's commerce offered by observers of the time; and (2) an uncritical extrapolation to Loreto of the characteristics of the better-known Brazilian case. We contend that the simple pictures presented by such observers as Prefect Hildebrando Fuentes (1908) were meant to illustrate two extreme forms through which Loreto's trading firms had access to credit; they do not account for the situation of the large, Iquitos-based Peruvian merchant houses. We further argue, in contrast to the Brazil case, that even though Great Britain had a strong hold over the rubber economy and directly controlled a large portion of the international rubber trade, in Loreto its influence was indirect. Finally, we contend that the structure and functioning of Loreto's rubber trade, as a result of its peripheral position as a rubber-producing region, differed substantially from that of Brazilian Amazonia.

Sources of Credit

According to Fuentes (1908: 25–6), Loreto's grand commerce involved two types of rubber-trading firms. The first type was composed of large, first-rank firms that acted as agents or associates of overseas, mostly European, companies. In general, the Iquitos partners were in charge of outfitting rubber *patrones* and traders, collecting their production, and shipping it to the Atlantic Coast; parent firms handled transatlantic shipping and the sales of rubber to manufacturers. Branch offices enjoyed unlimited credit from parent firms, which provided agents and associates credit to operate at 5–6 percent annual interest.

By year's end the houses, after selling the rubber and deducting operation costs, which included repayment of any loans, then divided the profits. A certain percentage was assigned as a bonus to the Iquitos partners and to some of the higher-ranking employees of the branch office; another portion was allocated to the branch's reserve fund; the rest was divided among the partners of the European parent firm. As in Brazil (Weinstein 1983: 281, 292, 308), companies acting as agents could be, but not always were, one and the same with the firm they represented and thus did not always bear the same name as the parent firm. Additionally, branch offices might change names over time, as a result of the death or withdrawal of one of its partners. Finally, overseas companies could choose to change agents for a variety of reasons.

Among this type of firms, Fuentes (1908: 26) mentions Wesche and Company, Marius, Lévy, and Schuler, Kahn and Polack, and Pinto Brothers. The relationship of these branch offices to overseas parent firms attests to the existence of various arrangements. According to Fuentes, the German firm Wesche and Company was associated to the European firm of Charles Ahrenfeldt. In contrast, the others were associated with homonymous parent firms. In addition, while Wesche and Company, Marius, Lévy, and Schuler, and Kahn and Polack seemed to have been headed by hired administrators, Pinto Bothers, at least during the initial stages of operations in Iquitos, was run directly by the owners. It is worthwhile noting that despite the much-proclaimed British control of Loreto's rubber trade there were no British firms acting as agents for overseas companies.

The second type, independent merchant houses, did not act as agents but were related to foreign firms that furnished them credit (Fuentes 1908: 26). In contrast to the first type, these firms were provided only limited credit, either in money or merchandise. If the credit was cash, the firm was charged 5–6 percent annual interest plus 2 percent commission; if merchandise, they were charged 5 percent annual interest plus 5 percent commission. Additionally, as most of Loreto's merchant houses paid their credits in rubber, foreign creditors charged a 2 percent commission for selling it.

Fuentes (1908: 26) implies that smaller, second-rank merchant houses constituted this type of rubber-trading company and that all Peruvian firms fell within the same category. In effect, the only example he mentions is that of Ponciano Sánchez, a minor Peruvian trader who operated in the lower Amazon and Yavari Rivers. However, after reconstructing the commercial trajectory of this trader, it becomes apparent that he can hardly be taken to represent the situation of the large, Iquitos-based Peruvian merchant houses.

The earliest information on Ponciano Sánchez dates to 1895, when it appears he had a government contract to deliver mail by boat in the area of Caballococha, a small town on the Amazon close to the border with Brazil (Memoria 1899: Anexo 24). Four years later, he was listed as owning *Eloisa*, a 13-ton steamlaunch (Capelo 1900: 35). Enrique Espinar (1901: 55) describes *Eloisa* as a merchant boat trading along the Yavari River. This suggests that by then Sánchez had become a *regatón*, or minor fluvial trader. In the early 1900s Peruvian fluvial trading boats, such as *Eloisa*, were successfully competing with Brazilian peers in the recently opened Yavari River basin (Stiglich 1904a: 337). By 1906 Sánchez appears as owner and captain of a 49-ton steamship, suggesting his business had prospered (Fuentes 1908: 10). However, he was still a minor merchant, as becomes apparent from the fact that he personally commanded his boat and that he dealt directly with his riverine clients.

By 1906 Sánchez had probably established a wholesale-retail firm in Caballococha; two years later he was listed as the largest trader and number-one contributor of taxes in that town (Matrícula 1910: 75). It must also have been around 1906 that he established a commercial relationship with the British firms John Lilly and Company and Fernando Hesser, which furnished him credit to expand his business (Fuentes 1908: 26). As a result, sometime between 1906 and 1908 Sánchez established a merchant house in Iquitos, which was registered as dedicated to import, export, and shipping (Matrícula 1910: 44). Nevertheless, his new Iquitos firm was smaller than its Caballococha branch; whereas he contributed £50 for the former, he was taxed £100 for the latter. By expanding his original wholesale-retail business to venture into the import-export trade and shipping, Sánchez was becoming a first-rank merchant. However, he was a latecomer, and at the time of the rubber bust his was still a second-rank firm.

Fuentes's description of Loreto's rubber-trading firms has contributed to the widely accepted notion that foreign firms and capital dominated the region's commerce. This, however, seems to be a hasty conclusion. We contend that the two categories of rubber-trading firms depicted by Fuentes do not account for the large, Iquitos-based Peruvian merchant houses, which controlled a large share of the region's rubber export trade. As becomes apparent from the commercial trajectories of L. F. Morey, A. Morey, C. Hernández, and Julio C. Arana, their firms were neither agents of foreign houses nor small companies operating at a local level (see Boxes 4.1, 4.2, and 4.3).

The owners of these firms had capitalized before the onset of the rubber boom through the export of tobacco, Panama hats, and other local products. When in the 1870s the international demand for rubber soared, these merchants were able to take advantage of their knowledge of the region's trading system, their contacts with overseas commercial firms, and their capital and infrastructure to rapidly achieve a high position within the rubber trade. In fact, during the first decades of the rubber boom and until the 1890s, these merchants controlled much of the region's rubber trade and shipping business. Even later, when overseas companies came to hold a larger share of the region's rubber trade, Peruvian firms continued to control 27 percent of it (see Tables 4.3 and 4.4).

Large Peruvian merchants operated by themselves or in association with other Peruvian or foreign traders. Often they were simultaneously associated with several merchants. Through these joint ventures they were able to access more capital, enhance their fluvial fleets, outfit a larger number of rubber extractors, extend their influence to a variety of rubber fronts, and spread the many risks involved in rubber trading. It is worth noting that these partnerships never involved first-rank, European-based companies; when foreign traders were involved, they were immigrants who had settled and incorporated their firms in Loreto. This in no way means that Peruvian merchant houses did not resort to foreign credit. Many of the small and medium-sized merchant houses, whether Peruvian- or foreign-owned, worked mostly with credit provided by Brazilian, European, and, to a much lesser extent, North American firms. Even the largest Peruvian firms operated on the basis of credit. This, however, does not mean that they were controlled by overseas enterprises. As Joseph Wechsberg has pointed out, "Late nineteenth century commerce in general was based on credit" (1966: 58). This also included British commerce, as noted by Walter Bagehot, an outstanding English political economist who, in 1873, asserted that "English trade is essentially a trade in borrowed capital" (in Wechsberg 1966: 58).

A key component of the international commercial credit network was the merchant bank. According to Wechsberg (1966: 7–8), merchant banks guaranteed certain transactions by accepting bills of exchange. For this reason, they were also known as "accepting houses." In exchange for their services, they charged a 1–2 percent commission. Merchant bankers only dealt with large-scale firms dedicated to the trading of strategic goods such as rubber. In this case, a merchant bank would purchase and ship manufactured goods for its client, who would issue a bill of exchange to back the operation. The rubber-trading merchant house would then send a shipment of rubber to the bank, which was commissioned to place it on the market. From the profits made on this operation the bank paid the suppliers of manufactured goods, deducted any commissions owed for the transactions, and credited the rest to the client's account.

An alternative to the merchant bank was the overseas rubber-buying firm, for example, import companies that advanced credit in cash against future deliveries of rubber. In these cases, the company extended a letter of credit, which the Peruvian firm could use to purchase merchandise from an export company. Alternatively, overseas rubber-buying firms could be import-export houses, whereby credit was provided directly in merchandise. Having capital of their own, first-rank Peruvian merchant houses generally relied on overseas credit to acquire expensive infrastructure and equipment, such as steamships, or to expand the scale of their operations. By working on credit, these merchant houses were following standard economic practices; thus, it would be inexact to represent them as subordinated to foreign capital.

Fluvial-Maritime Navigation

It has been asserted that foreign control was not only exerted in the field of credit but also in fluvial-maritime transportation. There are, however, two contradictory views about this topic. Some authors (San Román 1975: 161–2; Pennano 1988: 78) have stressed that British companies dominated fluvial-maritime transport and that this monopoly allowed them to control the import-export trade and eventually the entire rubber industry. In contrast, others (Roux 1994: 162) assert that Loreto's rubber economy was wholly dependent on Manaus and Belém thanks to Brazil's monopoly of fluvial transport. This seeming contradiction derives from Jean-Claude Roux's reading of the reports of Col. Samuel Palacios (1890a; 1890b), who was commissioned by the government to analyze the situation in Loreto and issue recommendations to reorganize its administration. In his second report, Palacios criticized Loreto's mercantile community for failing to establish its own navigation company. This would have allowed them to avoid "the exclusive tutelage of Brazil's commerce" and spared them from "suffering patiently the whims of the *single* company that operates in the Amazon" (1890b: 494; emphasis in original).

The "single" company quoted by Palacios (1890b: 507) was the Compañía de Navegación del Amazonas Ltda. Taking a cue from Palacios, Roux assumed the company was Brazilian, yet it was one and the same with the Amazon Steam Navigation Company, a British company incorporated in 1872, the board of directors residing in London (Mavila 1902: 540). The company had acquired the monopoly of navigation along the Amazon in 1874 (Weinstein 1983: 62) and received subsidies from the Brazilian state (Mavila 1902: 540). To conform to Brazilian legislation, the company was registered in Brazil, and its vessels navigated under the Brazilian flag (Capelo 1900: 29; Mavila 1902: 543). This led not only Palacios (1890b: 507) but also Larrabure i Correa (Larrabure i Correa: II, 6), to assert that the company was Brazilian and incorporated with Brazilian capital, leading Roux to depict Loreto's rubber trade as Brazilian-dominated.

In fact, the problems mentioned by Palacios as arising from the lack of a national fluvial fleet—and assumed by Roux as problems that besieged Loreto's economy during all of the rubber boom—derived from a series of Brazilian regulations that directly affected Loreto's merchants and commerce. Three were considered the most noxious: (1) restrictions on foreign navigation along the Brazilian tributaries of the Amazon; (2) taxation of foreign vessels navigating along their section of the Amazon; and (3) taxation and inspection of merchandise being transshipped in Brazilian ports (Palacios 1890b: 506; Barandiarán 1890: 434). In his first report, Palacios (1890a: 410–11) made several recommendations to overcome these problems. As a result, a new Navigation and Commerce Treaty was signed in 1891 between Peru and Brazil, eliminating Brazilian regulations that affected Peruvian commerce. The treaty, ratified in 1896, remained in force until 1905 (Larrabure i Correa: II, 115).

One of the treaty's most important consequences was to encourage Loreto's merchant houses to acquire larger steamboats. As a result, by 1900 Loreto's private merchant fleet increased its carrying capacity to 877 tons and, by 1906, to 1,229 tons (see Table 4.2). Peruvian vessels still faced some restrictions on navigation along some of the Brazilian tributaries (Mavila 1902: 543). However, the merchant houses of Iquitos circumvented these limitations by registering some of their steamships in Brazil (ibidem: 544; Capelo 1900). Thus, contrary to Roux's contention, Peru was not dependent on Brazil's presumed monopoly of fluvial navigation; moreover, from 1900 onward it developed its own merchant fluvial fleet.

Likewise, the issue of British control of fluvial-maritime navigation in the Amazon Basin should also be placed in perspective. From 1874 until the 1890s the British-owned Amazon Steam Navigation Company was the only company to navigate along the Belém-Iquitos route. Two other British companies, the Booth Steamship Company and the Red Cross Line, connected Liverpool and other European ports with Belém. However, by the early 1890s Booth had extended its operations to include fluvial navigation, establishing a direct line between Liverpool and Manaus and, from there, to Iquitos by means of lighter vessels (Collier 1981: 60). Later on, the Red Cross Line did the same. From 1898 onward these two companies made direct trips between Iquitos and Liverpool, thus sparing Loreto's merchants from the burdensome transshipping of rubber in Manaus and Belém (Pennano 1988: 182).

In 1900 the Amazon Steam Navigation Company employed eight of its vessels in the Iquitos route; the Booth and Red Cross lines employed three and two boats, respectively (Capelo 1900: 29). By 1902 the Booth and Red Cross firms merged, forming the Iquitos Booth Steam Ship Navigation Company, which operated along the Manaus-Iquitos route with the same five boats (Mavila 1902: 540). The company made three monthly trips from Liverpool to Manaus, following alternatively the Le Havre–Oporto–Lisbon–Madeira and the Hamburg-Lisbon-Madeira routes. It also connected New York with Manaus every twenty days (Monnier 1994: 182). The fact that the British company called on Portuguese, French, German, and North American ports illustrates that monopoly of navigation was not synonymous with monopoly of the import-export trade. This is confirmed by the evidence on the origin of Loreto's imports and the destination of its exports.

Guido Pennano (1988: 77) asserts (with no source quoted) that the Amazon Steam and the Iquitos Booth companies eventually merged, suggesting that they formed a trustlike monopoly. This is a dubious conclusion, derived, perhaps, from the fact that in 1905 Iquitos Booth was reported as acting as agent for Amazon Steam Navigation Company in Iquitos (Larrabure i Correa: VII, 693–4). However, from 1905 to 1908 these two companies were registered separately by local authorities and tax collectors (Matrícula 1910: 62–3). Moreover, Roberto Santos (1980: 58) asserts that Amazon Steam Navigation Company continued operating as an independent company until 1911, when it closed down and was replaced by the Amazon River Company. Thus, although international fluvial navigation was in British hands, a single company did not monopolize it; moreover, the several companies navigating along the Belém-Manaus-Iquitos route did not operate as a trust.

The situation was different in the maritime sections of the Iquitos-Europe and Iquitos–United States routes, which from 1902 were definitely monopolized by the Iquitos Booth Steam Ship Navigation Company. This led Fuentes (1908: 17–8), among other contemporary observers, to denounce the company's high freight fares, arguing that only because of the high price of rubber could these be afforded and that, as a result, commerce in the rest of Loreto's products, such as tobacco and cotton, was suppressed. He also blamed this monopoly for the high prices of imported merchandise and, accordingly, for the high cost of living in the region.

Import-Export Trade

Taking their cue from Fuentes and other contemporary sources, some authors (San Román 1975: 161; Pennano 1988: 78) have suggested that domination in the fluvial-maritime transportation led to British control of the import-export sector, which they present as irrefutable proof of hegemony over Loreto's economy. This viewpoint should also be qualified. First, as we have seen, none of Loreto's major merchant houses were British or acted as agents for British companies. In 1900, for instance, 35 percent of Loreto's exports was controlled by French merchant houses, 28 percent by Peruvian firms, 15 percent by German companies, and the remaining 22 percent by an assortment of smaller Peruvian and foreign-owned firms (see Table 4.3). Six years later, the share of Loreto's rubber exports by national groups remained much the same (see Table 4.4).

Second, export figures according to country of destination show that between 1904 and 1914 Great Britain absorbed on average 48 percent of Loreto's rubber exports. Although we have no similar information prior to 1904, there is no indication that Britain had a more hegemonic role in earlier times. Based on figures mostly provided by British consuls, on average about half of Loreto's rubber production was sold to countries other than Great Britain (see Table 4.5). Moreover, beginning in 1907 there was a gradual decline in the share of Loreto's rubber exports absorbed by Great Britain, in favor first of France and later of the United States. Throughout this same period, France absorbed on average 39 percent of Loreto's rubber exports and, in some years (1908–1911), even surpassed Great Britain as the largest buyer.

In short, at least in the case of Loreto, British monopoly over maritime navigation did not lead to monopoly over the rubber trade. Neither did it lead to the monopoly over the import trade. According to Aníbal Maúrtua (1911: 149), in 1905 imports from Great Britain represented 39 percent of the value of Loreto's total imports, followed by Germany (23 percent), France (16 percent), the United States (11 percent), Brazil (5 percent), and others (5 percent).

Rubber Extraction

It has been argued (Pennano 1988: 78) that control of navigation allowed British capital to achieve "an absolute control of the trading system" and that it was "a fundamental and key step to achieve subsequent control of the rubber industry." According to this view, "control of the [rubber] sector and industry was virtually in foreign hands . . . and not under control of the region's large number of small hevea and castilloa producers and extractors" (1988: 114). In support of this argument, Pennano provides a list of foreign-owned, vertically integrated enterprises dedicated simultaneously to rubber extraction and trade in the different Amazon countries. However, of the five companies operating in Brazil, Bolivia, and Peru that he discusses in more detail, not one is reported as having prospered. This confirms what Weinstein (1983: 171–80) had already argued for the Brazilian case, namely, that foreign attempts at vertical integration of the rubber economy were seldom successful.

The assumption—that vertical integration was the basic form of organization of the Peruvian rubber economy—is mainly derived from data on the area of Madre de Dios, where a few British, French, and North American enterprises obtained land concessions from Peru during the late 1900s. These, however, operated for a brief period and were not very successful. The only example of a successful operation of this kind in Loreto was not a foreign company but that of J.C. Arana, who through his Putumayo estates and his commercial firm managed to simultaneously control rubber production, transport, and trade. Although he later registered his company in Great Britain, obtaining fresh capital to expand his operations, Arana's firm can hardly be described as British-controlled. Arana did not transfer his property rights over the Putumayo estates to the newly formed British company (Wolf and Wolf

Table 4.5 Destination of Loreto's Rubber Exports, 1904–1914

						Percentage distribution				
Destination	*1904*	*1905*	*1906*	*1907*	*1908*	*1910*	*1911*	*1912*	*1913*	*1914*
Great Britain	53.6	57.2	59.6	54.0	44.7	46.4	42.3	46.6	44.9	26.1
France	30.4	33.3	37.1	40.7	46.4	48.4	48.3	36.8	36.7	26.5
Germany	5.9	—	—	4.5	8.9	1.3	6.1	11.7	9.8	7.1
United States	2.4	2.9	3.3	0.8	—	3.9	3.3	4.9	8.6	40.3
Brazil	7.7	6.6	—	—	—	—	—	—	—	—
Total %	100.0	100.0	100.0	100.0	100.0	100.0	100.0	100.0	100.0	100.0
Total volume (metric tons)	2,161	2,187	2,348	2,896	2,263	2,294	2,082	2,814	2,349	1,570

SOURCES: Maúrtua 1911: 148–9; Bonilla 1974: 77; Pennano 1988: 188.

1936: 90); and as one of the British directors remarked peevishly, he "had absolute control of the company" (Collier 1981: 218).

There are a few other examples of enterprises that attempted to control both ends of the rubber industry—such as the Comptoir Colonial Français, which was incorporated in 1899 and exploited rubber properties on both sides of the Yavari River (Weinstein 1983: 172)—but none was a success. As to the foreign-owned merchant houses of Iquitos, it was reported during the early twentieth century that "in general . . . they do not own rubber estates and are not engaged directly in the collection of rubber" (Plane 1903: 326). However, a few of the first-rank merchant houses did engage in the tapping of hevea in a timid attempt at vertical integration. This was the case of Marius and Lévy and Wesche and Company, which acquired several rubber estates along the Yavari and Marañon Rivers, respectively.

However, these experiments at vertical integration were a failure. In short, rubber production in Loreto was never controlled directly by foreign enterprises and remained largely in the hands of a variety of independent rubber extractors outfitted by the merchant houses of Iquitos.

Foreign Control in Peru and Brazil

If some authors overemphasize British control over Loreto's rubber economy, this is largely due to the fact that they have in mind the Brazilian case. That, however, cannot present a starker contrast to Loreto. Both Santos (1980) and Weinstein (1983) have argued that one of the main characteristics of the Brazilian rubber trade was that the import, export, and outfitting activities were divided among three distinct types of commercial firms: importers, exporters, and *aviadores*. Importers, mostly Portuguese, worked with their own capital or on the basis of credit obtained from European and North American firms (Santos 1980: 130). They were essentially wholesalers of foreign wet and dry goods and supplied merchandise on credit to the *aviador* houses (Weinstein 1983: 19).

Aviadores were mostly Portuguese-Brazilians with a long trading experience in the region. They outfitted rubber extractors and minor traders with goods supplied by importers, channeling the rubber they obtained in exchange to the export houses (Weinstein 1983: 18). In addition, they controlled most of the region's fluvial merchant fleet. Export houses were in the hands of British and, to a lesser extent, North American traders, who acted as agents "for rubber-buying firms in New York or Liverpool, although a few functioned independently" (ibidem: 19). Some of these establishments also provided informal banking services or ventured into the import trade. However, according to Weinstein, "both these functions were secondary to the firm's central concern: the purchase of rubber and its transfer . . . overseas" (ibidem: 19).

The separation of the import, export, and outfitting functions in Pará started at the onset of the rubber boom, which in Brazil dates to the mid-nineteenth century. Foreign intervention in the export sector dates to the 1850s (Weinstein 1983: 62), whereas the first *aviador* houses exclusively dedicated to the outfitting of rubber extractors and traders appeared during the 1860s (ibidem: 58). By the 1870s the process of specialization of Belém's mercantile community deepened with the appearance of new and well-funded export houses and an increase in the number of *aviador* houses (ibidem: 67). According to Weinstein (1983: 145), the process of takeover of Pará's export sector by foreign firms was completed the following decade. Although the division of functions allowed for some exceptions, both Santos and Weinstein are emphatic in asserting that there were no merchant houses in Brazil that performed the wide range of activities associated with rubber trade: import, export, and outfitting, as well as wholesale-retail commerce, shipping, and banking.

Santos (1980: 123–6) has suggested that the division of functions resulted from the need to spread and reduce financial risks. This hypothesis is challenged by the evidence in Loreto, where the tendency was to concentrate and combine functions rather than to separate them. Of the fifty-one merchant houses existing in Iquitos in 1904, slightly more than half of them were devoted exclusively to the import trade (Maúrtua 1911: 156; see Table 7.4). However, all of the fifteen top merchant houses were multifunctional. Of these, 53 percent performed five of the functions associated with rubber trade: import, export, shipping, wholesale-retail trade, and outfitting. An additional 33 percent combined four of the functions. None of these top-ranking firms specialized in any single activity. Hence, it can be asserted that in Loreto the means of increasing gains while reducing financial risks came not through specialization but through diversification. This allowed profits to be made from a range of activities and compensated for losses incurred in one activity through gains in another.

This strategy proved highly successful, since the most powerful and stable merchant houses of Iquitos were those that opted for a multifunctional organization. This is not to say, however, that these firms were invulnerable to risks. Whether due to internal managerial miscalculations or to external factors associated with changes in the international market, even the most powerful merchant houses could incur losses. When losses were high, some merchant houses were forced to sell part of their assets, such as steamboats or rubber estates. Sometimes losses were substantial and affected a large number of firms. This was the case when the price of rubber experienced a sharp decrease, as in 1878, 1885, 1893, 1901–1902, and 1907–1908. However, even though such crises forced out many of the smaller, more specialized firms, they did not impair the functioning of the larger, diversified establishments.

Weinstein (1983: 138, 145) provides an alternative and more plausible explanation to the division of functions that took place in Brazil's rubber economy, suggesting it resulted from the attempts of European and North American rubber importers to monopolize the export sector. As noted, this process started in the 1850s and peaked in the 1880s. By then, the three largest foreign export houses of Belém "handled approximately half of Pará's annual rubber exports," whereas the remaining 50 percent "was usually divided among the four or five smaller foreign houses and the handful of *aviadores* . . . who dabbled in exports" (ibidem: 145). Insofar as Brazil was the world's largest supplier of rubber, direct control over its exports was crucial to ensuring a steady supply and keeping rubber prices low. This explains why rubber importers and manufacturers from industrialized countries established agents in Brazil's most important rubber-trading centers.

In contrast, Loreto's rubber exports between 1902 and 1914 never amounted to more than 8 percent of Brazil's exports, on average representing only 6 percent (see Table 4.7). As Loreto's exports during that period accounted for 90 percent of Peru's total rubber sales on average (see Table 4.6), it can be asserted that Peru as a whole was a secondary rubber supplier. Thus, monopoly over its rubber exports would have added little to the already strong hold over Brazilian production held by Great Britain and the United States.

*   *   *

Iquitos's trading firms not only linked the region with the international market but also played a positive role in articulating internally the region's economy. As outfitters and wholesalers, the merchant houses of Iquitos financed the operations of most rubber *patrones* in Loreto. This was achieved directly, as with the largest extractors, or indirectly, through the outfitting of intermediary fluvial traders and small local merchants. As shippers, merchant houses connected Iquitos with the larger rivers of the region and the remotest tributaries. At the beginning of the rubber boom, boats belonging to the merchant houses of Iquitos were dedicated mainly to collecting the rubber of their *habilitado* extractors. As the rubber economy expanded farther and farther away from Iquitos with the opening of new rubber fronts, however, the largest merchant houses found it useful to establish trading posts in strategic sites.

Table 4.6   Loreto's Share of Peru's Rubber Exports, 1902–1914 (in metric tons)

Year	Loreto's rubber exports	Peru's rubber exports	Loreto's % of Peru's exports
1902	1,684	1,782	94.5
1903	1,990	2,108	94.4
1904	2,161	2,221	97.3
1905	2,349	2,540	92.5
1906	1,930	2,576	75.0
1907	2,896	3,029	95.6
1908	2,385	2,516	94.8
1909	2,522	2,802	90.0
1910	2,294	2,651	86.5
1911	2,019	2,161	93.4
1912	2,814	3,194	88.1
1913	2,349	2,781	84.5
1914	1,570	2,272	69.1

SOURCE: Pennano 1988: 178–9, 182–3; elaborated by the authors.

Table 4.7   Loreto's and Brazil's Rubber Exports, 1902–1914 (in metric tons)

Year	Loreto's rubber exports	Brazil's rubber exports	Loreto's % of Brazil's exports
1902	1,684	28,700	5.9
1903	1,990	31,095	6.4
1904	2,161	30,650	7.1
1905	2,349	35,000	6.7
1906	1,930	36,000	5.4
1907	2,896	38,000	7.6
1908	2,385	38,860	6.1
1909	2,522	42,000	6.0
1910	2,294	40,800	5.6
1911	2,019	37,730	5.4
1912	2,814	43,370	6.5
1913	2,349	39,560	5.9
1914	1,570	36,700	4.3

SOURCES: Pennano 1988: 182–3; Santos: 1980: 236.

Thus, large merchant houses and their agents formed a trading network with sedentary local traders and itinerant fluvial peddlers, linking the various rubber fronts dispersed throughout the region. At the center of this vast commercial web was the town of Iquitos, seat of the region's economic and political elite.

Owners of large merchant houses in Iquitos thus became the privileged interlocutors of local military and civil authorities by virtue of the crucial role they played in linking Iquitos externally with the international market and internally with a series of more or less integrated extractive fronts. Their interests may not always have coincided, as we shall see in Chapter 5, but together large merchants and local authorities constituted the dominant group that ran the region's economic and political affairs. Connections between them were articulated through the chamber of commerce of Iquitos, founded in 1890 by Prefect Samuel Palacios (1890b: 471) only two years after the chamber of commerce of Lima was created (Basadre 1964: VI, 2805).

These two groups—merchants and local functionaries—also constituted the core of Iquitos's social life. They gathered in exclusive locales such as the Shooting Club and the Iquitos Social Club, which were "composed of most of the privileged children of the region, merchants being the foremost among them, and in general of the most select of this port's male society" (Capelo 1900: 27). Members of the Iquitos mercantile community expressed increasing economic power by building large premises for their firms and relatively sumptuous private residences. Thus, Ernesto La Combe (1902: 221) noted that whereas before 1900 most of them lived precariously and possessed modest stores, by 1901 they had started to construct fine, expensive houses, competing among themselves in size, materials, and design. La Combe saw this tendency as positive, in that it anchored foreigners, stimulating them to marry local women and settle permanently in the region.

Despite efforts at beautification, Iquitos was reported to be an ugly, dirty, and chaotic city as late as 1905 (Woodroffe 1914: 29). Only in subsequent years, thanks to increasing customs revenue, did the local government start investing in basic infrastructures, including running water, sewage, electricity, and paving. By 1913 Woodroffe (ibidem: 34–5) reported that Iquitos had undergone a radical change; it had acquired all the comforts of any modern city. Merchants played an important role in the process of modernization, both as contributors of taxes and as advisers to local government. La Combe may have been correct in that many of the foreigners arriving in the region during the rubber boom stayed on. However, most small, foreign-owned merchant houses closed shop once it became apparent that the rubber crisis, which culminated in 1920, was irreversible.

To summarize, Loreto's rubber economy was not monopolized by British capital. Credit, import-export trade, and production of rubber was not in the hands of British firms. In fact, Great Britain absorbed on average only half the region's rubber exports and provided half its imports. Although British companies monopolized maritime navigation and for a long period controlled most of the fluvial traffic, those cruising the Amazon did not operate as a trust. Foreign capital, which played an important role in the region's import-export trade and in the outfitting of rubber extractors, was mainly French and German. Even those foreign firms, however, did not monopolize the rubber trade; they had to share the market with important Peruvian trading houses. Having accumulated capital during the early stages of the opening of the region to international trade, the larger Peruvian firms controlled around a third of the region's rubber exports during the 1900s.

The Peruvian rubber economy was far more independent from foreign control than was the Brazilian rubber economy. Because Loreto was a relatively small producer, rubber import firms from industrialized countries were not keen on establishing direct control over the region's rubber trade. This explains, in turn, why the large merchant houses of Iquitos were able to integrate a diversity of commercial functions; and also why several Peruvian merchant houses were able to thrive as part of this powerful group. The facts that none of these trading firms was involved in large-scale extraction of rubber (with the exception of a few rubber barons) and that this activity remained in the hands of a myriad of small and medium-sized independent extractors, also contributed to the openness of Loreto's economy. We argue that this and the existence of a process of accumulation of capital made it possible for Loreto to survive the collapse of the rubber economy.

In effect, as Bradford Barham and Oliver Coomes (1994b, 1996) have convincingly argued, not all rubber traders and extractors were mindless profligates; contrary to widespread opinion, many were able to capitalize. Traders and extractors made important investments in infrastructure (ships, workshops, ports, warehouses, commercial premises, trading posts) during this period. Many lost value after the 1914 rubber crisis, but they still constituted a powerful incentive for many large and medium-sized merchant houses to stay in the region after 1920, when Loreto ceased exporting rubber altogether. Their greater independence with respect to European and U.S. rubber importers also made it possible for these companies to take root in the region. Together with a new wave of traders, and in association with the landed elite that sprang up after the rubber crisis, these merchant houses were to dominate Loreto's economy for the next half-century (1914–1962).

5

"Extending Its Control":
State Regulation and Local Resistance

Between 1851 and 1872 the Peruvian state devised and enacted a series of interrelated laws stating the conditions under which the colonization of Loreto, and the exploitation of its resources, were to take place. Implementation of these policies was financed through the export of guano, the country's most important source of revenues since the 1840s. The state followed a geopolitical strategy aimed at forestalling Ecuadorian and Colombian claims over the upper Amazon. By 1872, however, Peru had become heavily indebted. The international market was overstocked with guano; the price of this resource had dropped, and the country was unable to raise more international loans by issuing new bonds against future guano exports (Bonilla 1994: 169–190). War with Chile (1879–1881) aggravated the crisis.

After the war, which devastated the national economy and resulted in important human and territorial losses, the government ceased having a comprehensive, long-term plan for the region. This has led some authors to assert that the state had only "precarious political control" of the region (Bonilla 1974: 71), that it "played a minor role in the rubber trade" (Walker 1987: 77), and even that the region "was left in a state of vacancy by public authorities" (Roux 1994: 225). These assertions are rarely substantiated by a credible analysis of specific instances of state failure or impotence in carrying out its functions; even when they are backed by evidence, the temporal dimension is overlooked. Thus, specific situations are presented as representative of an entire period.

During the 1870–1914 period the state devoted itself to "extending its control" (Palacios 1890b: 521) over the region: primarily, to defend its sovereignty, to repress regional political movements that questioned its authority, and to regulate the rubber economy. In the geopolitical domain the state did seem to have an overall strategy. It was also extremely effective in putting down revolts and revolutions calling for larger political and economic autonomy for the region. In contrast, efforts to regulate the rubber economy, the topic of this chapter, were more reactive than proactive. Yet in our opinion this was less the result of an inherent weakness than it was an adherence to a liberal political paradigm by successive Civilist governments ruling Peru from the early 1870s until the 1914 rubber bust.

Even though they subscribed to a laissez-faire ideology with respect to the economy, the ruling Civilist governments deliberately set out to integrate the country's Amazon territories to the national patrimony by building railroads, promoting European immigration, and advancing export agriculture. These policies, however, failed, in part due to lack of funds, in part to adverse ecological and social conditions. Indeed, Civilist governments saw the flourishing rubber economy as the antithesis of its integration program. This, as well as the state's liberal stance, influenced heavily the way in which the state intervened. Thus, it made a point to control aspects of the rubber economy considered crucial for the preservation of the country's interests, namely, the collection of taxes and the regulation of access to land and natural resources.

In contrast, the state was much less assertive in regulating labor relationships and in protecting the indigenous labor force. This ambivalent position is reflected in the conflicts between the state and the region's economic elite, that is, the large rubber extractors and traders associated with the chamber of commerce in Iquitos. The government, we conclude, was quite effective in collecting taxes and tariffs and in preserving the land as public property, which was destined for agricultural use. By refusing to confront the elite on the issue of labor, however, it not only sanctioned the harsh exploitation of the indigenous population under the *habilitación* system but also contributed to the reproduction of precapitalist relations of production well into the twentieth century.

The Battle Over Taxes and Tariffs

During the rubber boom Peruvian politics was characterized by the hegemony of the Civilist regime. Founded in 1871, the Civilist Party represented the interests of the coast's commercial bourgeoisie and powerful landowners. The tenets of its political and economic programs were the articulation of the national territory through the construction of railways, as well as the reactivation of Peru's economy through the attraction of European immigrants and the promotion of export-oriented activities. Although during this period the Civilist Party alternated in power with the Constitutional and Democratic Parties (founded, respectively, in 1883 and 1889), the trio shared a positivist, liberal approach that emphasized the benefits of free trade and laissez-faire capitalism. The Civilist program for the country's Amazon territories was firmly supported by members of the Geographical Society of Lima; its bulletin became one of the main channels for the government's "modernizing" discourse (Martínez Riaza 1998b).

These policies were applied with some success in the *selva alta*, in areas such as Chanchamayo and Oxapampa (Santos-Granero and Barclay 1998). This was possible largely due to their proximity to Lima and Callao, the main Pacific Coast market and port, respectively. In contrast, the *selva baja* was too far away from the country's capital and main economic centers and could not be as easily integrated. Furthermore, when the demand for rubber in the international market soared during the 1880s, the *selva baja* became entirely devoted to rubber exploitation, giving rise to an economy oriented toward the Atlantic Ocean and largely independent of the rest of the country and its Pacific Coast elite.

The Civilist governments were unable to come to grips with the extractive, highly mobile economy of the *selva baja*, which was so different from the sedentary agropastoral economy characteristic of coastal and highland Peru. For this reason, they clung to their own model of integration; as a result, state intervention in Loreto was ambivalent. On the one hand, government authorities denounced what they saw as the shortcomings of the rubber economy, mainly its alleged inability to create permanent demographic and economic frontiers, its overspecialization and negative impact on other productive activities such as agriculture, and its extreme dependence on imports. On the other hand, confronted with an economy that had arisen thanks to previous state investments and was evidently flourishing, authorities adopted a pragmatist stance, attempting to regulate it in those aspects that they deemed strategic for the country.

War with Chile and prolonged occupation by Chilean troops left the country devastated. Already bankrupt before the war and with an exorbitant external debt, Peru was desperate for funds to reactivate the country's economy and to cover public expenditures. External credit would not become available until 1889, when Peru canceled its foreign debt through the transfer of a series of national assets and rights of exploitation of certain resources to the European holders of Peruvian bonds who were grouped in the British-controlled Peruvian Corporation Company (Barclay 1989: 29–33). Internal revenue was to be obtained through the promotion of an export economy, the reorganization of the system of taxation, and the creation of new customhouses and tariffs.

Beginning in 1872 the government had ceased transferring its monthly subsidy to Loreto. In 1877 it sold or leased most of its assets in Iquitos. The economic chaos brought about by war with Chile further restricted the government's capacity to pay the salaries of public servants and the military. To remedy this situation, in 1881 Loreto's prefect, David Arévalo, made a first attempt at establishing a customhouse in Iquitos. The decree, issued in Moyobamba—still Loreto's capital—was strongly opposed by the mercantile community. Invoking an 1832 law, which partially exempted Loreto from payment of import duties (Larrabure i Correa: I, 17), and an 1853 law, which exonerated the region from payment of import-export tariffs and personal contributions (Larrabure i Correa: II, 46), the merchants of Iquitos refused to pay tariffs. Later in 1881, the new president, Rear Adm. Lizardo Montero, appointed Col. Mauricio Rojas as prefect of Loreto and ordered him to levy newly established personal taxes. Local reaction against the measure was almost instantaneous. Shortly after Rojas's arrival in Moyobamba, the populace invaded the prefect's office, beat him, and forced him out of the city (Fuentes 1906: 458).

Col. Tadeo Terry, appointed prefect in 1882, was more successful. Instead of imposing personal contributions, Terry revived Arévalo's initiative of establishing a customhouse in Iquitos, but he was careful not to affront local merchants. Terry involved the Iquitos trading community in his actions by convening an ad hoc commission composed of some of its most prominent members, among them the Frenchman Charles Mourraille and the Peruvian Marcial A. Pinón, who had bought the state fluvial fleet in 1877. This inaugurated a brief period of cooperation between the local government and the region's economic elite.

The commission's goal was to propose what merchants considered to be fair import-export tariffs (Larrabure i Correa: I, 255). Terry appealed to the merchants' patriotism and referred to the distressing situation of the country and its finances. His arguments seem to have been effective, even with foreign merchants. In August 1882 Terry issued a decree that essentially implemented the taxes recommended by the ad hoc commission. The decree imposed a duty of 7.5 percent on imported merchandise, except for that bought in Brazil, which was taxed at only 3.75 percent. It also established a tariff of 0.43 *soles* per *arroba* (15 kilograms) of exported rubber, regardless of species or quality (Fuentes 1906: 499). Initially, the merchants of Iquitos agreed to pay the taxes; between August 1882 and December 1883 the new customhouse collected a total of 87,000 *soles* (Pennano 1988: 198), or roughly £13,000 (Bardella 1989: 77).

In Moyobamba, however, this measure was fiercely rejected. Led by Francisco del Aguila, who disavowed Terry and self-appointed himself prefect of Loreto, the Moyobambinos successfully refused to pay taxes (Fuentes 1906: 459). For more than a year the region had two prefects, one in Moyobamba and the other in Iquitos. In Iquitos things were not much better. Import tariffs led to price increases for subsistence goods, which in turn led to massive discontent with the local government. The merchants of Iquitos began to resist the measure (Palacios 1890b: 471); it is probable that they took advantage of popular unrest, even fueled it, to further their own interests. After several riots in late 1883, culminating in an attempt to burn the customhouse, Terry was forced to resign (Barletti 1992: 20). As a consequence of this uprising, Terry's successor was compelled to sign an act agreeing to reduce taxes. Although local merchants had forced Terry's resignation and succeeded in having taxes reduced, the central government scored an important concession by getting the traders to accept its right to levy taxes in the region.

In May 1885 David Arévalo, the founder of Iquitos's customhouse, again became prefect. Assuming office the second time, Arévalo raised the import-export tariffs to the level charged in Callao, the country's main Pacific port (Palacios 1890b: 472). Some authors (García Rosell 1905: 627) suggest that this measure did not last very long and that import duties were soon reduced to 50 percent of those charged in the rest of the country. Others (Palacios 1890b: 472) assert that "such an anomalous state" lasted from May 1885 to November 1887. Either way, even though tariff payments were still resisted by the commercial class, it had become a routine and accepted burden. Moreover, during this period confrontations between the government and citizens over payment of taxes were not particular to Loreto. After the 1879–1881 war with Chile resistance to taxation was common throughout Peru, not only because of the impoverished state of the population but also because of the resentment of regional elites to heavy taxation by the central government.

In partial response to this situation in 1886, Pres. Andrés Cáceres issued two related laws. The first raised customs tariffs countrywide and legalized the customhouse of Iquitos, which had been created by prefectural decree. The second law created departmental boards and treasuries in an effort to decentralize management of regional finances. As Loreto was thought to require special attention, it was the object of a more specific law in November 1887 (Larrabure i Correa: I, 260–3).

That law had several aims. First, it established a 15 percent tariff on the value of imported merchandise; this was lower than the countrywide tariff. Second, it attempted to promote the collection of hevea over castilloa by imposing a substantially higher export tariff on the latter. Third, it established that the revenue obtained was to be spent entirely in the region, with special emphasis on education, the promotion of fluvial navigation, and the construction of roads. In addition, the law called for the appointment of a special government commission to issue recommendations for reorganizing Loreto's administration. Traders did not oppose the law directly yet used indirect means to evade paying taxes. By 1890 the government commission, headed by Prefect Samuel Palacios, estimated that evasion of import duties was roughly 40 percent.

In the best Civilist tradition, Palacios believed firmly that most of the irregularities were due to administrative disorganization and institutional weakness. To improve the relation between regional authorities and traders, he suggested they organize a local chamber of commerce. Palacios expected such an institution to become not only a consultative body but also a moral authority within the trading community and the region. The chamber of commerce of Iquitos was created in 1890. Its foundation contributed to the consolidation of a lasting, though not always mutually trustful, relationship between the government and the merchant elite.

The tension underlying this relationship surfaced six years later. In May 1896 Col. Ricardo Seminario, who had been appointed by Pres. Nicolás de Piérola to command the police force in Iquitos, rose up in arms and proclaimed the creation of the State of Loreto within the "Federal Republic of Peru." Seminario's uprising can be characterized neither as a separatist movement nor as a classic coup d'etat. In a succinct telegram addressed to the government, Seminario declared: "In popular elections, Iquitos proclaimed the Federation. To ensure public order I had to accept this fact and assume the office of Provisional Governor. Piérola's government is recognized" (Palacios Rodríguez 1991: 411).

Little has been written about the motives behind Seminario's federalist movement. In recent years, three possible causal factors have been pointed out (Barletti 1992): (1) President Piérola's failure to institute a federalist system as promised; (2) Piérola's attempts to eliminate the departmental boards and treasuries, which were created in 1885 to provide greater financial autonomy to local governments; and (3) the pressures exerted by the merchants of Iquitos to obtain a reduction in taxes and tariffs. Although not much evidence is provided in support of this last point, the fact that central and local government authorities tightened the collection of taxes and tariffs between 1890 and 1896 suggests this could have been the case.

At least since 1890, the merchant houses of Iquitos were subject to payment not only of import and export tariffs but also of income taxes (Palacios 1890a: 420). In 1896 there was a spectacular increase in the collection of tariffs, which jumped from 175,308 *soles* the previous year to 322,953 *soles* (Maúrtua 1911: 147), or roughly £17,000 to £32,000 (see Bardella 1989: 119). As there was no increase in the value of imports and only a slight growth in the value of exports, we must conclude that the increase in revenue derived from stricter enforcement of the 1887 law. In effect, in 1896 the gathering of income and other taxes was put in the hands of the Compañía Nacional de Recaudación (National Collection Company), a private enterprise that depended on the sums it collected. Despite fierce local opposition, this arrangement improved tax collections (Izquierdo Ríos 1976: 126; Capelo 1900: 38).

Confirming the trading elite's involvement in the federalist movement is the fact that six days after the uprising a new chamber of commerce of the State of Loreto was created to substitute for the former chamber of Iquitos (Navarro Cáuper 1988a: 4). Charles Mourraille, the well-known French merchant, was the president of the board of directors. Board members included traders belonging to the four groups that controlled Loreto's commerce: Luis Felipe Morey, Guillermo de Souza, and Benjamín Dublé (Peruvians), Ferdinand Kahn and Louis Vatin (Europeans), Manuel Rocha (Portuguese-Brazilian), and Jaime Pinto and Theodore Schuler (Mediterranean Sephardim). The representation of each grouping seems proportionate to their respective shares in regional trade.

Unfortunately for it, the federalist government had a very short existence. So grave did the government consider the rebellion that at great expense it sent four military expeditions, three by land and one by sea, to suppress it (Memoria 1896: 4). To ensure victory and to send an unequivocal message to neighboring countries as to Peru's resolve to retain Loreto, President Piérola appointed his war minister, Gen. Juan Ibarra, as general commander of the government troops (ibidem). Colonel Seminario was unable to gain the support of other regional commanders and, isolated and threatened by the advance of the government troops, resigned in mid-July 1896.

The uprising had some positive results for the region and its elite. Following Colonel Seminario, who had declared Iquitos the capital of the State of Loreto, the central government moved the capital from Moyobamba to Iquitos in November 1896. This sanctioned Iquitos's unofficial position as the seat of power; from at least 1889 prefects had resided there (Ydiáquez 1890: 79). The government also ordered the reorganization of Loreto's administration, authorizing an increase in the annual budget (Larrabure i Correa: I, 477). However, although the federalist uprising drew government attention to the region, it did not have the desired effect of modifying the tax system, which not only remained unchanged but also was applied even more efficiently. As a consequence of this as well as the growth of the import-export trade, collection of tariffs increased steadily from £39,079 in 1897 to £62,004 in 1902 (Maúrtua 1911: 147).

The suppression of the federalist uprising did not mean that the government achieved complete political control of Loreto. In the following five years, local and central authorities had to confront several military rebellions—the most important was led by Col. Emilio Vizcarra—that responded to the climate of generalized political unrest characteristic of turn-of-the-century Peru. These turbulent years were followed by a prolonged period of political order. Between 1900 and 1921 the state managed not only to maintain the region under its control but also to increase regulation of the import-export trade and appropriation of the region's revenues. Before 1900 as much as two-thirds of Loreto's rubber production was smuggled into Brazil (Tizón y Bueno, in Larrabure i Correa: V, 404). A few years later, the generally overcritical navy officer Germán Stiglich (1904: 488) admitted that whereas before 1900 the customhouse of Iquitos had been "submissive" to the local merchants, who bribed its officers and engaged in large-scale smuggling, after that date it had become very effective in collecting taxes.

In 1903 the government passed new legislation to increase national revenue (Larrabure i Correa: I, 319–20). Instead of a flat 15 percent ad valorem import tariff, the new law established different tariffs for different categories of goods. By exonerating most subsistence goods, the government aimed to reducing the cost of living and, thus, indirectly, the cost of rubber extraction; by increasing tariffs on luxury goods it guaranteed a high level of income. Additionally, the law augmented tariffs on the exporting of rubber, establishing a scale in accordance with the price that each rubber quality achieved in the international market. The effect was immediate: from £54,658 in 1903, revenues increased to £135,807 in 1904 and to £142,931 in 1905 (Maúrtua 1911: 147). The merchant houses of Iquitos paid large tariffs and were also the largest payers of income taxes. By 1904 the fifty-one merchant houses of Iquitos paid £149,688 in tariffs and income taxes, which represented 8 percent of the country's total revenues of £1,990,568 (Fuentes 1906: 379; Matrícula 1910).

In 1906 the government yet again modified the tax system. A new law promoted local agriculture by exonerating the importing of assets and by taxing imported subsistence goods. It also stimulated extraction and cultivation of hevea, indirectly by imposing the same tariffs on hevea and lower-quality castilloa rubber, more directly by establishing some specific incentives for hevea cultivation. With these measures, the revenue of the Iquitos customhouse increased once more. Although the total value of the import-export trade did not vary substantially, revenues increased from £181,846 in 1906 to £249,038 in 1907 (Maúrtua 1911: 147).

To avoid paying the increased tariffs, many merchants turned to smuggling. Joseph Woodroffe (1914: 45) reported that during 1907–1909 smuggling was practiced on both sides of the Peru-Brazil border and that traders from both countries frequently joined forces to deceive customs officers. The 1906 law remained in force until the end of 1910, when Loreto's import duties were raised to the level of those prevalent in the rest of the country and rubber exports were taxed at 8 percent of market value (Ballón 1991: I, 207). This was the culmination of the government's efforts to integrate Loreto into the national tax system. These efforts were stalled by the 1910 drop in rubber prices, which resulted in a steady decrease in revenues at the Iquitos customhouse (Pennano 1988: 206). This, in turn, led Loreto's trading community to lobby for a reduction in the import-export tariffs (Ballón 1991: I, 224, 236, 242). Although that was granted in 1914, it did not prevent Loreto's rubber economy from collapsing.

Conflicts Over Land and Resources

The state was as exigent on the issue of land tenure as it was in collecting tariffs. During the rubber boom, Civilist governments attempted to integrate the Amazon with the rest of the country through European colonization and the development of modern agriculture. Laws passed in 1845 and 1853 allocated funds for the engagement, transportation, and establishment of European immigrants in Loreto and other areas (Larrabure i Correa: I, 229, 239). Under the law of 1853 two groups of European settlers were brought to Loreto to establish agricultural colonies near Nauta and Caballococha (Mattos 1854: 56, 71; Larrabure i Correa: V, 40–9). By 1854, however, most had abandoned the region because of isolation, bad sanitary conditions, and lack of economic opportunities.

Although the first experiments failed, they were continued unquestioningly by Civilist governments. In 1872 Manuel Pardo, the first Civilist president, created the Society for European Immigration. A year later he appropriated funds to stimulate foreign immigration (Fomento 1902: 121–3). Subsequent Civilist governments continued the policy.

By 1890 it became apparent that existing land laws were failing to adequately stimulate foreign colonization, promote development of regional agriculture, and regulate access to rubber resources. Prefect Samuel Palacios (1890b: 400, 526–9) denounced both the negative effects of the extractive economy on the region's agriculture, as well as the rapid depletion of rubber resources due to the tapping methods employed. Palacios asserted that the only way to stimulate agriculture and ensure a more rational management of rubber resources was to regulate the allocation of land. It took eight years for Palacios's recommendations to be partially enacted; in 1898 the government issued the first detailed law concerning land allocation in tropical areas (Fomento 1902: 148–51).

The new law promoted colonization, agriculture, and road construction while placing limits on land speculation. To achieve that aim, it established four ways to acquire public lands in Amazonia: (1) land grants; (2) concessions; (3) colonization contracts; and (4) purchase. Land grants (from the government to farmers at no charge) of up to two hectares could revert to the state if, within the first three years after the grant was made, at least half the land remained uncultivated. Grantees of concessions had to pay an annual rent of 1 *sol* per hectare during the first three years and, after that, 1 *sol* per cultivated hectare and 2 *soles* per uncultivated hectare. Concessions could be canceled for default in rent payments for two consecutive years. Contract colonists were subject to the same conditions, but had up to a five-year grace period to pay the rent. Land could be purchased outright for 5 *soles* per hectare; this was the only means to acquire perpetual ownership in tropical lands. Revenues from land allocations were to be used for road construction. The law aimed mainly at promoting agriculture and was actually little concerned with the situation in the rubber districts. Lands exploited for forest resources, such as timber or rubber, and not for agricultural purposes would become subject to a more specific law.

That law was issued in 1900 and was the first specifically designed to regulate access to rubber resources (Fomento 1902: 183–4). It established two ways to acquire rights in exploitation: (1) lease of lands, and (2) lease of rubber trails. Lands were leased for a ten-year period; leaseholders were forbidden to cut rubber trees and had to pay 2 *soles* per *quintal* (46 kilograms) of processed latex obtained. Payments were to be made at the customhouse and were in addition to export tariffs. The state also leased *estradas* (rubber trails) of 150 trees. Leaseholders had to pay in advance 0.20 *soles* per trail per year and an equal sum for each hectare occupied by the trails exploited. In addition, all leaseholders had to deposit a guarantee in domestic bonds of 1 *sol* per hectare, with interest accumulated going to the leaseholder.

It appears that the leasing of lands was designed to control castilloa extraction. Given the vastness of the region and the mobility of castilloa extractors, the state imposed a rent not on the land itself but on its produce. Payment of the 2 *soles* per *quintal* of rubber was made either by the extractor or was assumed by the merchant house that bought the rubber. The collection of rents on castilloa rubber by the customhouse of Iquitos seems to have been quite successful (Maúrtua 1911: 148). However, by 1908 the government abandoned the idea, arguing that supervising rubber extraction on leaseholds was so difficult that it led to the depletion of resources (Larrabure i Correa: XVIII, 119–20).

In contrast, the leasing of trails targeted hevea extraction, as that sedentary activity was thought to be more easily controlled by local authorities. However, collecting rents on hevea trails was difficult. Fuentes (1906: 442) reports that between 1900 and 1905 only 4,010 *soles* were collected; during two consecutive years (1901–1902) no rents were gathered at all.

The 1900 law and its 1901 bylaw (Fomento 1902: 189–190) were ill-regarded by rubber extractors and traders alike because they did not grant full property rights to rubber lands (Fuentes 1906: 434–5). Soon after passage, a group of hevea estate holders requested the government to repeal the 1901 bylaw, which authorized prefects to lease up to 500 hectares for rubber extraction. Instead, they demanded a law that allowed them to obtain title to lands they held (Larrabure i Correa: V, 417–8); that demand was rejected.

This, however, did not put an end to the issue of property titles. In 1905 members of the Loreto chamber of commerce petitioned the government to express concern over the depletion of rubber resources, pointing a finger at the existing land legislation (ibidem: 436–7). Merchants argued that leaseholders of state rubber trails extracted as much latex as they could, overexploiting hevea trees through methods that rapidly led to their demise. They further argued that the only way to end the noxious practices was to grant rubber trails as property, regulate latex-extracting methods, and penalize the cutting of trees. In addition, they encouraged the state to promote hevea cultivation through existing real estate taxes, granting bonuses to those who planted rubber trees.

This was in striking contrast to the reaction of the region's elite to a decree issued by the prefect of Loreto in 1888, which regulated hevea-extracting methods and penalized the cutting of castilloa trees (Larrabure i Correa: I, 278). On that occasion, the rubber elite appealed to the Peru Supreme Court, denouncing the decree as unconstitutional. Shortly thereafter, President Cáceres nullified the decree in the name of "the absolute liberty of industry" (ibidem). The reason for the radical change was the elite's sudden awareness that rubber resources were being irrevocably depleted, that the British were expanding their Southeast Asia rubber plantations, and that attempts were being made to find an artificial substitute for rubber (Pesce 1904: 32–7; Stiglich 1904b: 480).

Although the state shared in the worry over depletion of rubber resources, it could never be persuaded that granting property titles to rubber estates was the solution. However, in the 1906 law that increased import-export tariffs, the central government took heed of one of the recommendations made by the Loreto chamber of commerce. The law stipulated that 2 cents out of the 20-cent export tariff per kilo of rubber be applied to a fund to promote rubber cultivation (Larrabure i Correa: IX, 431); from 1906 to 1915 the government collected £49,472 on this account (Flores Marín 1987: 55–6). Although some large merchant houses, such as Wesche and Company, Israel and Company, and Barcia Brothers, started rubber plantations on the basis of such incentives, procedures for allocating funds were never specified and the money never reached the planters.

The 1898 land legislation had established procedures for purchasing land and obtaining absolute property rights, but the minimum price of 5 *soles* per hectare was considered too high not only by rubber extractors and traders but also by some former local authorities. Thus, Emilio Castre (1906: 158–9), Hildebrando Fuentes (1906: 434), and others supported the rubber elite's viewpoint that the government should grant property rights to rubber estates. Despite support from prominent figures for the idea, the government never gave in. Such stubbornness resulted from the Civilist model of frontier integration, which strongly favored agriculture over extraction. Even at the height of the rubber boom, many observers and former authorities continued to denounce the extractive economy as the root cause of stagnation in the agricultural sector (Herrera 1905: 130–1).

If the issue of property rights over rubber resources never produced a major confrontation between the government and rubber extractors, it was because, both before and after the 1900 law, the extractors managed to gain access to rubber resources without much expense. Rents on leased rubber estates were very low, and in Loreto the government was never very efficient at collecting them anyway; this suggests that the real issue for the state was not the collection of rents but the retention of land.

State Connivance in the Abuse of Indigenous Labor

Although Civilist governments were immovable in their decision to tax Loreto's import-export trade and to preserve state rights over regional natural resources, they were much less so in regulating labor relations. And even though conflicts did arise between rubber extractor-traders and local authorities over raids against tribal Indians, quasi-enslaving indebtedness, transfer of debts, and the removal of laborers into neighboring countries, they never culminated in an open confrontation. This was partly because some of these practices were common in the rest of the country, and partly because most local authorities were ambivalent in this regard.

The obligation of catechized Indians to provide services at the request by local authorities dated to colonial times. However, in 1825, almost immediately after independence from Spain, the Peruvian government forbade local authorities from forcing indigenous peoples to provide free personal services. The decree further established that Indian peoples could work only of their free will and that people interested in hiring indigenous peons had to furnish a contract specifying the work to be done and the salary to be paid (Mattos 1874: 68). The spirit of this decree was endorsed on several occasions in subsequent decades. In 1867 the central government issued a decree explicitly ratifying the 1825 law (Mattos 1874: 67). In 1870 the prefect of Loreto issued another decree urging local authorities to make sure that no Indians were forced to work against their will and that they were paid just wages (Mattos 1874: 73–4). However, despite these regulations, the central and regional governments had no means to enforce them. As a result, local authorities continued to abuse their positions and coerced indigenous peoples to extract rubber, whether for themselves or for other *patrones*.

Regional authorities also condemned *correrías* and trading in indigenous children. In 1869 the governor of Sarayacu on the Ucayali River denounced the existence of an active traffic in Ashaninka children that involved not only local *patrones* but also the children's parents, who exchanged them for iron tools (Mattos 1874: 70). To end such trafficking, the government allocated funds to buy and distribute for one time only iron tools among the "infidel," or nonreduced, Ashaninka population. That same year, the prefect of Loreto, Col. José Olaria, issued a decree reminding local authorities that slavery had been abolished in the country since 1854 and forbidding slave-raids as well as the selling, purchase, transfer, and "adoption" of indigenous children (ibidem: 71–3).

The indignation of regional authorities toward the exploitation of indigenous laborers and the enslavement of indigenous children seems to have melted away with the onset of the rubber boom. For more than three decades leading up to the 1900s, the subject was not a matter for serious concern; we know of no legislation on this problem during that period. It is as if the promise of rubber profits silenced even those who should have defended the interests of indigenous peoples. Thus, even Father Gabriel Sala, a renowned turn-of-the-century Franciscan missionary, saw the rubber extractors' methods of enslaving isolated indigenous peoples as a necessary step toward their evangelization. He claimed, "Once the rubber *patrón* has subjugated the ferocious Cashibo by the force of arms, it is time for the missionary to enter immediately onto the scene to offer them the services and consolation of our holy religion" (1896: 121).

However, by the beginning of the twentieth century the abuses and cruelties exerted upon tribal Indian peoples became so scandalous that few observers could escape from at least mentioning them in passing. A quick review of the prevalent opinions of the time shows that very few unequivocally condemned the practices, that most were ambivalent, and that such practices were subject to legislation only when they affected national interests.

Correrías were clearly condemned by two consecutive subprefects in the province of Ucayali: B. García Córdova and Estanislao Castañeda. The latter left no doubt as to what he thought about the rubber *patrones* who indulged in these practices: "Conquered by those who call themselves civilized, [Indians] become their slaves; and given the way they have been and are still treated [by their *patrones*], it is difficult to ascertain who are the savages; the infidels who defend themselves from the attacks of the so called *caucheros* or the *caucheros*, who knowing their duties engage in hunting their fellow men, killing many and enslaving others to sell them vilely for money" (in Fuentes 1906: 331). In a similar vein, von Hassel (1902c: 211–2) denounced the "profitable traffic of human flesh" and summoned Loreto's prefect to put an end to it, lest the indigenous populations disappear.

In contrast, Luis Pesce, an otherwise devoted medical researcher, asserted that "the steady and irresistible action of the rubber extractors, though not exempted of unjustness and abuses . . . has contributed the most to the civilization of those savages" (1904: 93). He added that because the subjugation of the indigenous peoples is of crucial interest for humankind and civilization "it is up to a certain point justified to apply the Machiavellian principle that 'the end justifies the means'" (ibidem: 95). Pesce even went so far as to quote the opinion of several contemporary missionaries and travelers who argued in favor of exterminating the indigenous peoples who resisted being "civilized" (ibidem: 97).

Most other authors, however, were not as candid or outspoken as Pesce. Germán Stiglich (1904b: 396, 436), for instance, praised the civilizing effect of the *correrías* yet suggested that "when *correrías* are inhuman, which they seldom are since their aim is to take prisoners, then they should be severely punished." Castre, condemning *correrías* as "barbarous acts," believed that if carried out by missionaries with the support of rubber *patrones* they could become the most effective way of "transforming Indians into useful beings instead of human beasts" (1906: 147). The ambivalence of most authorities and observers with respect to slave-raids can only be understood as a pragmatic awareness: The practice was indispensable both to clear the way for rubber extraction and to "produce" a disciplined labor force in the long term. By alluding to the benefits that indigenous peoples could accrue from the processes of civilization and Christianization, these authors stripped the *correrías* of their more pedestrian economic aspects and presented them almost as a moral imperative.

However, reference to the virtues of evangelization was mostly rhetorical; in the field, missionaries encountered strong opposition not only from rubber *patrones* but also from many officials. In 1898 President Piérola issued a law dividing the Amazon region into three Prefecturas Apostólicas (religious jurisdictions), each in charge of a different order (Larrabure i Correa: I, 207–10). One of them, San León del Amazonas, in charge of the Agustinian order, comprised a large portion of Loreto. The law's purported aim was to ensure "the reduction of the infidels to the Catholic faith and civilization" (García Jordán 1991: 299). However, its real goal, clear from the law's introductory clauses, was to pacify and reduce the numerous tribes that lived "in a state of barbarism . . . hindering the establishment of civilized settlers and the resulting industries and improvements" (Larrabure i Correa: I, 208).

Despite the fact that missionaries were given the task of clearing the way for rubber extractors, the latter mistrusted them, fearing that their indigenous peons would seek their protection. As a result, when the first Agustinian priests finally arrived in Iquitos to establish headquarters, they were strongly opposed by an alliance of rubber *patrones* and members of the town council (Gregorio y Alonso 1953: 28–35). Not until 1903 were the missionaries allowed to settle in Iquitos and start operating in the region.

In the following years, they founded a few mission posts in the larger riverine towns and frequently denounced the maltreatment of indigenous peons (Díaz 1903: 217). This aroused the protests of rubber *patrones*, who pressed the government to issue a law specifying that the missionaries' jurisdiction comprised only the territories inhabited by "savage" tribal Indians and that in no case could they extend their activities to "civilized" settlements (Gregorio y Alonso 1953: 31). In this way, rubber *patrones* clearly aimed to deprive missionaries of any power over indigenous peons. In 1907 the government passed a law supporting this stance, demonstrating its lack of determination to regulate labor relations between rubber *patrones* and their indigenous peons (Ballón 1991: I, 160).

Yet when the labor practices of the rubber *patrones* threatened perceived national interests, the government moved in to regulate them. This was the case in the early 1900s, when Peruvian rubber *patrones* started removing large numbers of indigenous peons from Peru to Brazil, and when the extermination of indigenous laborers on Arana's Putumayo rubber estates was denounced not only in Peru but internationally.

At the turn of the century, many indigenous peons were taken to the recently opened Yavari, Yurua, and Purus Basins to collect rubber. In many cases, engaged peons were passed along to Brazilian extractors through the system of transfer of debts (Fuentes 1905b: 30). Although the occasional selling of captives of slave-raids in Brazil had not aroused local authorities in the past, the massive removal of "civilized" laborers, the "capital" that sustained Loreto's economy, immediately raised economic and, occasionally, humanitarian concerns. In 1900 Joaquín Capelo, the government commissioner who later became an ardent defender of the country's indigenous peoples, issued a decree to prevent the exit of precious laborers. It established that rubber *patrones* could take peons out of the country only if they previously deposited a bail of 200 *soles* per laborer (Larrabure i Correa: I, 496), thereby ensuring that peons would be returned once their labor contracts expired. Shortly thereafter, Carrera i Raigada, the prefect of Loreto, increased the bail to 500 *soles* (Memorial 1904: 500). His successor, Col. Pedro Portillo, was adamant in enforcing this regulation, particularly among the rubber *patrones* working the Yurua and Purus Rivers.

Accusations of trafficking in human flesh and the measures taken to prevent it aroused protests not only among the large rubber *patrones* but also within the trading community in Iquitos. In a petition addressed to Hildebrando Fuentes, the new prefect of Loreto, rubber extractors and merchants demanded the repeal of Capelo's decree (Memorial 1904: 500–2). They argued it was unconstitutional, for it prevented the free movement of individuals; rather than benefiting the peons, it worsened their lot by forcing *patrones* to add the cost of the bail to their workers' debts. They also argued that there was no assurance that bails would be returned to the *patrones*. Finally, in order to demonstrate a measure of goodwill, the petitioners suggested that a commission of government authorities and representatives of the chamber of commerce be formed to draft a model contract that would regulate the temporary removal of peons from the country.

The commission presented its recommendations in 1905. The document, signed by well-known Peruvian merchant L.F. Morey, among others, made a clear distinction between literate and illiterate peons (Fuentes 1906: 439–40). Literate peons were free to leave the country if their contracts were signed in the presence of a subprefect. Illiterate peons had to first manifest, in the presence of a subprefect, their willingness to leave the country; additionally, their *patrones* had to deposit a 500-*soles* bail, to be returned upon the presentation of the worker in the subprefect's office at the end of his contract, or the submission of legal documents certifying his death. Finally, the regulation established that *patrones* who took peons out of the country without complying with these rules would be subject to a 1,000-*soles* fine. Such terms were very similar to those imposed by Capelo. This suggests that members of the rubber elite were aware that the government was determined to regulate the movement of indigenous peons across the border, and that this time it was better for them to support the government rather than oppose it.

Whereas local authorities were swift to react to denunciations that indigenous peons were being removed from the country, they were slow to investigate accusations about the labor situation in the Putumayo region. The first public denunciations of the maltreatment of indigenous laborers in Arana's rubber estates appeared in August 1907 in two small newspapers, *La Felpa* and *La Sanción*, published in Iquitos by journalist Benjamín Saldaña. As the charges did not prompt any official action, Saldaña accused Arana formally in court. According to Rómulo Paredes (1912: 190), a lawyer who was later commissioned to investigate the labor situation in the Putumayo, "The Arana Co. at that time was held in such fear that the act of Saldaña Roca was considered the limit of audacity." To avoid confronting Arana, the magistrates resorted to red tape and dilatory maneuvers. In the end, claiming they could not intervene in the Putumayo region because of the modus vivendi treaty signed in 1906 by Peru and Colombia (whereby the nations agreed to withdraw their respective authorities from the disputed region), the indictment was "pigeonholed indefinitely" (ibidem 1913: 190).

It was not until 1909 that new public denunciations were made, this time in London. Walter Hardenburg, a U.S. engineer who visited the Putumayo region, accused Arana and his section chiefs of cruel treatment of both indigenous and Colombian peons working on his estates. With the support of the Anti-Slavery Society, Hardenburg published in London his accusations in the newspaper *Truth*. His accounts aroused the indignation of the British public and eventually forced the British government to intervene. Taking as pretext the protection of its subjects— the Barbadian overseers hired by Arana—the British Foreign Office designated Roger Casement, the consul in Manaos, to visit Arana's estates and report on the labor situation. Casement visited the Putumayo region in 1910; in January 1911 he presented a preliminary report to the Foreign Office confirming Hardenburg's accusations (Collier 1981: 198).

In 1909 the British directors of the Peruvian Amazon Company sent a letter to Peruvian Pres. Augusto Leguía, informing the government of Hardenburg's grave accusations. Although Leguía never acknowledged receipt of this letter, it is known that the Peruvian Congress debated the matter in November 1909. Additional pressure from the British government forced Peru to initiate an investigation on the "Putumayo scandals." The situation in the Putumayo region was extremely delicate. Colombia and Peru claimed sovereignty over the region and several times had engaged in armed confrontations to ensure control over it. Arana's activities had tipped the balance in favor of Peru, and for that the government was very much indebted to him. However, if it was proved that the accusations were true and Peru was seen as condoning the atrocities committed by Arana's company, this would provide Colombia with extraordinary diplomatic leverage in its claims over the region. For that reason, in 1910 the attorney-general, Salvador Cavero, initiated judicial proceedings against the company. When Casement presented his report confirming Hardenburg's accusations, the British government put pressure on Peru to put a stop to the atrocities. Two months later, in March 1911, the government appointed Rómulo Paredes, judge of first instance in Iquitos, to head a judicial commission in charge of investigating the accusations in situ (House Documents 1913: 63).

The commission spent three and a half months in the Putumayo region; in the report to the prefect of Loreto, Paredes confirmed Hardenburg's and Casement's accusations in all their gruesome detail (House Documents 1913: 144–172). However, by the time Paredes arrived in the region most of the criminals had absconded, and the company had replaced almost all higher-rank employees and introduced changes to the organization of labor in an effort to save the firm from additional attacks and possible bankruptcy. As a result, the conditions of the indigenous laborers had improved (ibidem: 157). Back in Iquitos, Paredes issued warrants for the arrest of 215 company employees (ibidem: 63). These included overseers, section chiefs, and local managers as well as top executives, such as Pablo Zumaeta, Arana's brother-in-law, and even Arana himself. However, by the time the warrants were issued, most of the accused had escaped from Loreto; only 75 persons, mostly underlings, were arrested and imprisoned. Some claimed that most of the principal criminals were allowed to escape by corrupt local officers (ibidem: 56); others claimed that they escaped after hearing rumors that the government had appointed a judicial commission and that they were going to be prosecuted (ibidem: 186).

The judiciary was not much more efficient. Although Paredes found an important ally in Carlos Valcárcel, a judge of first instance in Iquitos, the superior court was reluctant to confront Arana and prosecute the indicted. Valcárcel confirmed the warrants issued by Paredes for the arrest of Zumaeta and Arana (Anonymous 1993a: 16). Arana was not in Iquitos and could not be captured. Zumaeta went into hiding but was eventually arrested by the prefect of Loreto (House Documents 1913: 129). However, through his attorney he succeeded in having the warrants dismissed by the superior court for lack of proof (ibidem: 135). In protest, Judge Valcárcel resigned (ibidem: 129). Those who had been arrested appealed all the way to the Supreme Court in Lima (ibidem: 20). This tactic was quite successful, for when Casement visited Loreto a second time, in October 1911, to assess what the government had done to improve labor conditions in the Putumayo region and punish those responsible for the atrocities, he found that only nine persons had been condemned (Collier 1981: 202). As Judge Paredes would assert later, "The efforts of the Government have not been as loyally supported as they should have been" (House Documents 1913: 193).

Casement's second report prompted the British government to put more pressure on Peru. As a result, in April 1912 President Leguía ordered the creation of a commission, headed by the attorney-general, to formulate a general plan for administrative, judicial, and political reforms in the Putumayo and other frontier regions. A month later he created an auxiliary commission, headed by Judge Paredes, to gather information in situ and issue recommendations to the Lima commission (ibidem: 32–33). After a second visit to the Putumayo, Paredes reported that the company had replaced the criminals with new personnel and that labor conditions had improved but that the situation of the indigenous workforce was far from satisfactory. As he put it: "The reform was not so thorough as we might wish, for if it is true that lives are not now sacrificed as wantonly as before, there still exists niggardliness and stinginess on the part of the 'bosses' and insufficient pay of the savages" (ibidem: 187–199).

The newly appointed U.S. consul in Iquitos, James Fuller, also visited the Putumayo region in 1912; he confirmed Paredes in that "the company [had] mended its ways to some extent" and labor conditions had improved. However, he asserted that it was "plain that, up to date, the Government has done nothing at all on the ground" (House Documents 1913: 46). By this he meant that the state had made no effort to increase the number of police and justices of the peace, although it did allow the Vatican to send a group of missionaries to establish themselves in the Putumayo region (García Jordán 1998: 16). Fuller thus concluded that the conditions that had given rise to the atrocities had not changed and that this "might bring a return to old conditions" (House Documents 1913: 1913: 59). Although Fuller was right, that did not happen. In June 1912 the British government published Casement's first report. By then Arana's company was in liquidation, rubber prices continued to go down, Loreto's economy was collapsing, and conditions were leading to the outbreak of World War I. As a result, the state lost interest in the region, and Arana's estates languished.

To summarize: During the rubber boom era the Civilist government policies regarding Loreto were not substantially different from those for the rest of the country. They reflected the liberal philosophy that the state should intervene as little as possible in the economic realm, confining itself to the building of basic infrastructure, the collection of taxes, and the defense of national sovereignty. Some authors have mistaken this general stance for an inherent incapacity of the state to perform its functions. As we have seen, however, the Civilist governments successfully enforced policies deemed to be vital to national interests. Far from having "precarious political control" over Loreto, as has been suggested, the state managed, despite the difficulties imposed by great distances and poor communications, to suppress all attempts at questioning its legitimacy. Moreover, revolts and insurrections were not confined to the region and took place all over Peru during this period.

It is also clear that the state did not play "a minor role in the rubber trade" (Walker 1987: 76). The local government not only promoted the organization of the rubber merchants; it also enforced, in the face of strong opposition, several laws regulating and taxing the import-export trade. The state was not entirely successful, however, in controlling such practices as smuggling goods and bribing customs authorities, just as in other important ports of the country (Palacios Rodríguez 1991: 626). Finally, although Loreto's administrative body was small relative to the size of the region, it could hardly be argued that it "was left in a state of vacancy by public authorities" (Roux 1994: 225). During this period Peru managed to establish military garrisons, police stations, and customhouses even in such remote places as the Yurua and Purus Basins.

If the state was thus able to impose policies considered vital to the country, it was largely the result of two factors: first, the ability of some prefects to involve the region's elite into the process of policymaking; and second, the decision not to intervene in the sensitive field of labor relations. By consulting members of the merchant elite on issues that most affected them, local authorities managed to overcome their resistance and to persuade them to comply with new policies that were frequently against their interests. But this sort of alliance was only possible because Civilist governments never attempted to meddle in the issues of recruitment, control, and retention of laborers, which in the context of the rubber economy constituted, as we have seen, the real source of wealth. The fact that Civilist governments never attempted to regulate labor should not be interpreted as a concession to the rubber extractors and traders or as a sign of weakness on its part; rather it should be seen as the consistent application of its liberal tenets. As we shall see, however, the refusal to put an end to the precapitalist labor relations prevalent in the region had lasting effects on its later economic development.

*   *   *

The period between 1851 and 1914 was a formative stage in Loreto's economy. During those sixty years the region was opened to international trade; it was also explored, occupied, and effectively linked to the market. That does not mean, however, that the region became immersed in capitalist relationships. Outwardly, Loreto's economy functioned according to the logic of nineteenth-century capitalism; inwardly, it lacked a domestic market and was based on precapitalist forms of labor and exchange. This was not exceptional in Peru and other Latin American countries. In fact, except for urban economies and a few "modern" regions, such as São Paulo, most rural areas were articulated externally and internally in a similar fashion.

What distinguished Loreto's economy from other rural areas during this stage was its "frontier" character: a dependence on external demand and capital; the predominance of extractive over productive activities; poor internal articulation and communications with the rest of the country; an absence of stable demographic and economic fronts; transient and selfish elites; the weak presence of the state; governmental actions subservient to the interests of the economically powerful; and a general situation of lawlessness. These general conditions, however, were neither fixed nor stationary. Some were not as clear-cut as in other frontier settings; others were true for a certain time—but not afterward.

Thus, as indicated, at the outset of the rubber boom the region's native elite had been able to capitalize, avoiding complete dependence on foreign capital. Although the extraction of rubber displaced export agriculture and the Panama hat trade as the region's most important mercantile activity, commercial agriculture was not eliminated. It was still practiced on specialized landholdings that catered to rubber extractors. Moreover, whereas Loreto's economy in the initial years of the boom was based on the highly itinerant exploitation of castilloa rubber, which discouraged permanent occupation of the land, it experienced a process of heveaization beginning in the late nineteenth century. This eventually led to the creation of stable settlements along the larger navigable rivers.

Initially foreigners who had settled in the region with the aim of becoming rich and returning to their countries of origin, trading elites in the end became deeply involved in regional politics through participation in the chamber of commerce. They also integrated into local high society via marriage. In fact, although many left Loreto after the rubber bust, many others stayed and settled permanently in the region.

As to government presence and action during the 1851–1914 period, we argue that rather than being weak it would be more precise to say that it was not uniformly felt throughout the region. In effect, the state established, at great cost, a string of small military garrisons, police stations, and customhouses along the frontiers with Ecuador, Brazil, and Colombia. It also appointed a large number of functionaries. In the early 1870s, the region's politico-administrative system included a prefect, who was the department's highest authority, four subprefects at the province level, twenty-five governors at the district level, and dozens of deputy governors in towns with populations more than 300 (Mattos 1874: 54). Additionally, there were four judicial territories, each with its judge and forty-nine justices of the peace (ibidem). In contrast, in remote, mostly interior fronts there were few or no state representatives, whether military, political, or judicial. It would also be inappropriate to assert that state intervention in the region served mostly the interests of its elite. As we have seen, although the government was very lenient on the issue of indigenous labor—thereby favoring rubber extractors and traders—it did not hesitate to confront them resolutely to impose taxes and tariffs and to preserve as public property the regional lands and forest resources.

As a result of its uneven presence and incapacity to adequately supervise local authorities, the state was unable to enforce legislation protecting indigenous peoples. By law, Indians had the same rights as every other Peruvian citizen. In fact, however, their rights were not respected, or even recognized, by local authorities. Catechized Indians were treated as second-class citizens; tribal Indians were treated as if they were almost subhuman. Given that these two groups represented roughly two-thirds of the Loreto population, most of the region's citizens were thus denied their civil rights. The mestizo population may have been better off economically than the indigenous population, but most of them could not exercise full citizen rights, either; only literate, propertied males over twenty-five years could vote or be elected. Thus, the election of regional representatives—which by the end of the period consisted of two senators and six house representatives—and the administration of public affairs rested in the hands of a very small minority. Moreover, despite the expansion of the judiciary, it was common knowledge that the administration of justice was far from satisfactory. This was attributed to the "enormous distances," the "absence of justices of the peace with independent incomes," and a "lack of titular judges sufficiently remunerated to be able to dedicate themselves to the full of their mission" (House Documents 1913: 21). In the last analysis, the state had little or no capacity to enforce its laws in certain areas. In remote fronts, violence was the principal means for resolving conflicts, and most of the population was deprived of civil rights. Without a doubt, during this period Loreto's economy was a frontier economy.

Despite its shortcomings, however, the rubber economy had an important integrating effect. Rubber extraction and trade promoted the consolidation of important urban centers. It also led to the establishment of vast fluvial trading networks, to the appearance of permanent demographic and economic fronts along the larger rivers, to the integration into the marketplace of previously isolated tribal Indians, and to the reinforcement of a state presence in the region. A small hamlet of only 234 inhabitants in 1850, Iquitos had become, by 1913, a burgeoning town of 12,498 (Rodríguez Achung 1986: 23). Using their own steamboats and outfitting smaller fluvial traders, the region's large merchant houses successfully connected Iquitos with the most remote rubber fronts. Many towns, villages, and hamlets sprouted along the region's larger navigable rivers, as did numerous rubber estates and rubber posts.

Almost all the indigenous peoples who until then had avoided direct contact with the national society were persuaded, or forced, to engage in rubber extraction. Even those groups who managed to escape that fate were deeply affected by processes triggered by the rubber economy. After the rubber bust, some of these peoples reverted to an isolated life, but most became dependent on the market for the acquisition of manufactured goods and were thus forced to maintain links with the marketplace. By the end of this period the state had attained the two objectives it had set itself to accomplish by the mid-nineteenth century, namely, to assert its sovereignty over the upper portion of the Amazon River and to create the material conditions for the economic integration of the region. Partly by design, partly by chance, the state established the conditions for the political integration of the region and the gradual taming of the frontier.

Naval Workshop Built in Iquitos in 1864, circa 1903
(Junta de Vías Fluviales 1907:199).

Dock Built by The Booth Steamship Co. in the Port of Iquitos, 1904
(Junta de Vías Fluviales 1907:126).

Government Commission Exploring the Headwaters of the Purus River, 1904 (León 1905).

Extractors Weighing Castilloa Rubber Balls in Puerro Portillo, Yurua River, circa 1903 (Junta de Vías Fluviales 1907:274).

Police Station in the Frontier with Brazil, Breu River, circa 1904 (León 1905).

Iñapari Indian Peons in the Rubber Post of Carlos Scharff, Purus River, circa 1903
(Junta de Vías Fluviales 1907:75).

Steamlaunch Loading Firewood in Puerto Waltibori, Yurua River, circa 1904 (León 1905).

Gentlemen Promenading in the Main Plaza of Iquitos, circa 1903
(Junta de Vías Fluviales 1907:88).

Women Packing Barbasco Roots for Export in the Baling Yard of Israel and Company, circa 1947 (Higbee 1949:13).

PART TWO

In Search of a New Economic Identity, 1915–1962

The 1914 collapse of rubber prices—a result of the startup of British-controlled Southeast Asia rubber plantations and World War I (1914–1918)—led to a deep recession. The price collapse also had important effects on patterns of territorial settlement, the distribution of the population, and the organization of rural production. However, we contend that the crisis did not paralyze Loreto's mercantile community and did not sever the region's links with the international market. Furthermore, the rubber crisis did not alter either the fluvial trading network that revolved around Iquitos or the *habilitación* system on which it was based. Although it is true that the region's economy experienced several ups and downs during this time, this period cannot be characterized as one of economic stagnation.

In Part 2 of this book we examine the efforts of Loreto's elite to find new economic options after the rubber bust; we also analyze the economy that gradually took shape as a result of such efforts. We begin our analysis with an examination of the 1914 crisis and its effects on Loreto's economic, social, and political life and end it with an inquiry into the set of events that caused the decline of the region's agroextractive export economy during the early 1960s.

In Chapter 6 we analyze Loreto's political economy in the context of the 1914 rubber crisis. The discussion focuses on three aspects: (1) the reaction of the government and the rubber elite to the signals that the rubber economy was about to break down; (2) the effects of the crisis on the region's economy and its main economic agents; and (3) the political reactions to the state's indifference to the region's plight. The impact of the rubber crisis was particularly noticeable in the shrinking of the import-export trade, the constriction of credit, the loss of property values, and the crisis in fluvial-maritime transportation. These factors coalesced to produce a grave economic recession that affected rubber traders, extractors, and tappers. We conclude that the state did little to mitigate the effects of the rubber crisis because the country as a whole had been experiencing a severe fiscal crisis since at least 1910. The polarization of local politics into "regionalists" and "centralists," beginning in

1913, gave rise to a regionalist ideology that was to mark local politics in subsequent decades and fuel several multiclass political movements and uprisings.

In Chapter 7 we analyze Loreto's new agroextractive export economy from the perspective of commerce, placing particular emphasis on the import-export trade, the sequence and combination of export cycles, the recomposition of the "grand commerce," and the integrating role played by merchant houses. We begin our analysis by questioning the assertion that Loreto's economy during the 1915–1962 period was a "survival economy" characterized by a series of self-contained and consecutive extractive minibooms. We maintain that the different export booms overlapped in time and involved different areas; thus, unlike the rubber bust, they did not affect the economy as a whole when they came to an end. After 1921 Loreto's grand commerce experienced a radical recomposition. Although merchant houses continued to rely on precapitalist modes of operation, we suggest that they were very effective in coping with the problems of long distances, weak regional integration, and the lack of a domestic market.

In Chapter 8 we study Loreto's agroextractive export economy from the perspective of rural production, in particular the transformations experienced by the region's rural landscape, the development of new means of control of the rural labor force, and the organization of the riverine *fundos* that emerged during this time. Loreto's landscape changed significantly as a result of a general move from the eastern to the western sections of the region, the abandonment of interfluvial areas for the banks of large rivers, and the resurgence of agriculture to compensate for the scarcity and high prices of imported foodstuffs. After the 1914 rubber bust the *habilitación* system not only continued but acquired its "classical" form. *Fundo* owners managed to retain and increase their workforce through the combination of old and new economic, political, and ideological mechanisms. Due to their special relationship with the merchant houses of Iquitos, *fundo* owners kept remote rural areas connected to the marketplace. More importantly, the expansion of *fundos* contributed to the consolidation of riverine demographic fronts and, thus, to the sedentarization and stabilization of the region's economy.

In Chapter 9 we analyze the decline of Loreto's agroextractive export economy in the early 1960s and the disappearance of both merchant houses and riverine *fundos*. Although several factors affected the region's economy, in our opinion all of them can be traced to two events: (1) the outbreak of World War II (1939–1945), which generated new interest in the region's products; and (2) the 1941 war with Ecuador, which revealed how isolated the region was from the rest of the country. Both events stimulated the state to renew efforts not only to integrate the region but also to modernize its economy. Better communications reoriented the region's production and flow of trade from the Atlantic Ocean to the Pacific Ocean, from the international market to the domestic market. We contend that the region's merchant houses could not adapt to these changes and were excluded from the new trading networks. In addition, the state implemented a series of policies that gradually eroded the power of merchant houses and *fundo* owners. A decrease in the demand for tropical products in the international market further contributed to their decline.

To summarize, from 1915 to 1962 Loreto, far from being dormant, became involved in an active search for economic opportunities. Whereas we can conceive of the 1851–1914 period as the formative stage of Loreto's political economy, the 1915–1962 period was one of transition. It was characterized as much by the persistence of economic traits associated with frontier settings as by important transformations in the region's social and political landscapes. These changes eventually brought about the elimination or diminution of the worst "frontier" traits. Nonetheless, the region continued to lack a domestic market; its economy was still very much dependent on precapitalist relations of production and exchange. Although the worst aspects of these relations disappeared, the *habilitación* system persisted and, with it, many of its coercive traits.

Furthermore, despite a much greater state presence, including an extended judicial apparatus, the appointment of a greater number of local authorities, and the expansion of state services, most authorities and state functionaries in the rural areas were subservient to the landed and trading elites. The tension between continuity and change is thus a dominant theme.

6

"Kept in the Cruelest Oblivion": Rubber Crisis, State Indifference, and Private Gambles

After the 1907–1908 price drop, the cost of rubber rose gradually and steadily until January 1910, when it increased abruptly (Weinstein 1983: 213). By June 1910 prices had increased between 48 percent and 87 percent, with the lesser-quality rubber experiencing the higher rise (Bonilla 1974: Cuadro 2). International orders for rubber increased spectacularly. So did the amount of credit provided by foreign firms to the merchant houses of Iquitos and, thus, to rubber extractors participating in the *habilitación* network. This rubber craze was the last to sweep the Amazon Basin. Expecting a rise in customs tariffs, local import firms overstocked (Mitchell 1911: 232). When prices started falling in June, few merchants realized it would be an irreversible trend. The brief recovery of rubber prices at the beginning of 1911 obscured the imminent collapse of the rubber economy. This took place in 1914, with the beginning of World War I, and although the region continued to export rubber until 1921, that year marked the beginning of a new period in the development of Loreto's economy.

In this chapter we analyze three aspects of the rubber crisis: (1) the actions of the government and of the rubber elite vis-à-vis events signaling the impending collapse of the rubber economy; (2) the effects of the crisis on the region's economy and its main agents; and (3) the political response of the region's population to state indifference concerning their critical situation. Unquestionably, members of the government and the rubber elite were aware of the danger to local rubber extractors posed by the rubber plantations that the British were promoting in their Southeast Asia colonies. Contrary to the prevailing view, however, we believe that if the government and rubber elite failed to take adequate measures to counteract the peril it was not because of shortsightedness or greed. If the government did little to avert the crisis it was because it continued to cling, following the Civilist tradition, to an agriculture-based model of colonization and economic integration. Local rubber extractors and traders did not engage massively in rubber cultivation, partly because they lacked the kind of massive financial and technical support that Great Britain provided its Southeast Asia colonists. Above all, however, they were convinced that cultivated rubber would not be as productive as wild rubber, mainly as a result of pests. They believed that the flexibility inherent to Amazonian rubber economies would allow them to remain competitive by reducing payments to tappers, by accepting lower margins of profit, and by decreasing or even eliminating export taxes.

The crisis had ramifications. It led to the reduction of the import-export trade, the contraction of credit, the loss in value of real and movable property, and a crisis in fluvial-maritime transportation. We analyze these different aspects in turn, emphasizing the various ways in which they aggravated the economic recession for rubber traders, extractors, and tappers. Although the crisis affected commerce immediately, only small traders were forced to close shop. Large and medium-sized merchant houses continued doing business, displaying a remarkable capacity to adapt to bad times while searching for new economic alternatives. Small rubber extractors were equally affected by the crisis. Many had to part with their peons, being no longer able to maintain them. Others, however, retained enough capital to keep their peons while moving to riverine areas, where they settled and established *fundos*. These landholdings became the main productive units of the agroextractive export economy that emerged after the rubber bust. The crisis, in turn, allowed many indigenous tappers to emancipate themselves from their bankrupt *patrones*. In some of the more remote rubber fronts many Indian peons were able to revert to a tribal way of life.

In the years after the 1914 rubber bust, the people of Loreto expected the government to alleviate the effects of recession. Foremost among their demands was a reduction in tariffs and duties. The fact that the state was slow in taking measures to counteract the crisis has been interpreted as one more instance of the central government's alleged indifference toward the region and its inhabitants. Although this view contains some truth, we contend that if the government was slow to react it was because it was convinced that the 1914 price drop was simply another episode in a constantly fluctuating economy.

The fact remains, however, that the government did little to mitigate the crisis, thereby generating much discontent among Loreto's population. Politically, such dissatisfaction manifested in the polarization of the ruling classes. The urban middle and upper classes segregated into centralists and regionalists. In the early 1910s two political parties were created and reflected these two positions. The confrontations between defenders and opponents of political centralism culminated with the uprising of Capt. Guillermo Cervantes in 1921, which was based on a loose federalist ideology and counted on widespread popular support. The defeat of Cervantes coincided with the definitive breakdown of the rubber economy. In search of a new economic identity, the rubber elite experienced a radical recomposition in the aftermath. The agroextractive export economy that took shape after the rubber bust was, to a large extent, an achievement of the new trading and landed elites. With little or no support from the government, they managed single-handedly to keep the region's economy alive.

Signals of the Impending Rubber Bust

From at least 1903, several voices in Loreto were warning about the impending threat of cultivated rubber. In his extensive monograph on Loreto, Luis Pesce (1904: 32–44) warned that the depletion of castilloa due to the felling of the trees, the inadequate methods applied in the tapping of hevea, and the exhaustion of the older hevea stands were jeopardizing the future of Loreto's economy. Pesce asserted that to counter these trends other rubber-producing countries had started promoting rubber cultivation. He strongly suggested that Peru should follow suit by offering incentives and premiums such as those being provided by Brazil.

Though Pesce (1904: 43) mentioned the saving advantages of plantation rubber in time, money, land, and labor, he was little aware of the overwhelming superiority that plantation systems had for lowering costs of production and boosting output. Moreover, though worried about the disappearance of natural rubber, Pesce (1904: 44) did not agree with contemporaries who were claiming that Amazonia was on the verge of an immediate collapse in rubber yields.

Local authorities were also aware of the problem. In his 1905 annual report, Prefect Hildebrando Fuentes shared Pesce's concerns (1906: 427). He mentioned the successful British attempts to cultivate rubber in Southeast Asia and warned the central government about the threats posed thereby. Quoting Jorge von Hassel, he reminded authorities how in the recent past the cultivation of quinine in British Ceylon had all but excluded Peru from this lucrative trade.

Through the reading of such specialized periodicals as *Indian Rubber Journal*, quoted by Fuentes, or *Journal d'Agriculture Tropicale*, quoted by Pesce, local authorities and contemporary observers were well-informed as to the progress being made in rubber cultivation in Southeast Asia. Large rubber extractors and traders were also aware of the increasing disappearance of natural rubber sources, attempts to establish rubber plantations, and the need to promote cultivation in the region. Thus, in a 1905 document submitted to the government, the chamber of commerce of Iquitos argued that the only way to preserve the rubber industry was to promote cultivation. They warned, however, that this was possible only if the state granted free property rights over rubber estates and premiums to those starting rubber plantations (in Fuentes 1906: 436–7).

Despite the growing awareness of the depletion of natural rubber sources, the exhaustion of the old hevea estates, and the success of the Southeast Asia rubber plantations, no effective steps were taken by the private or public sectors to counteract them, either in Peru or in Brazil. In Peru the government refused to grant free title to lands and never allocated the scarce funds collected to promote rubber cultivation. As a result, very few extractors and traders undertook rubber cultivation. This seeming apathy in the face of known danger has been explained by the parasitic attitude, lack of foresight, and greed of the rubber elite (San Román 1975: 161). Barbara Weinstein has challenged this viewpoint with reference to the case in Brazil. She contends that extractors and traders, given the natural and economic constraints, could not have developed a rubber plantation system on their own, as it would have required similar decisive and massive technical and economic support that the British government provided the Southeast Asia colonists.

Weinstein (1983: 221–4) suggests that in Brazil this kind of support was not available for two reasons. First, Amazonia was peripheral to the southern-centered national economy and was thus not deemed of sufficient strategic importance by the federal government. Second, the *aviador* houses that controlled the chamber of commerce were not interested in developing a plantation system that would have eliminated their roles as middlemen. The first reason—that the Amazon was peripheral to the national economy—was also true in Peru. Civilist governments since coming to power in the early 1870s followed an economic model based on the promotion of colonization and agriculture. Unable to implement that model and confronted with an extractive and highly mobile economy oriented toward the Atlantic Ocean rather than the Pacific Ocean, Civilists opted to promote export agriculture (mainly for the production of cotton and sugarcane) in the more accessible valleys along the Pacific Coast.

The second reason, however, did not apply to Peru. The largest merchant houses in Iquitos were multifunctional importers, exporters, and outfitters, which explains why the chamber of commerce did not feel threatened by plans to develop a plantation system but, indeed, supported such plans. This raises a question: Why were the merchant houses not determined to put a plantation system into practice? From our point of view, this can be explained only as the result of a generalized and deep conviction throughout Amazonia that the region's wild rubber had natural and economic advantages over cultivated rubber. Peruvian extractors believed that the Malaysian and Sinhalese rubber plantations were not going to be competitive. They were convinced that the exotic rubber trees were prone to acquire local diseases and that the Malaysian and Tamil laborers were not as strong and experienced as the Amazonian tappers (Mitchell 1911: 228, 234). This underestimating of the competition had deadly consequences for Loreto's rubber economy.

N.H. Witt (1908: 43–5), a knowledgeable British merchant appointed by the chamber of commerce of Manaus as representative to the First International Rubber Exhibition Conference held in London in 1908, summarized in his talk most of the prevalent views on the superiority of wild over cultivated rubber. Witt contended that the quality of wild rubber could not be equaled by cultivated rubber and that, given the organization of production in Brazil's rubber estates, extractors could always cut costs to match those of rubber plantations. This could be achieved by stimulating rubber peons to combine rubber tapping with subsistence agriculture, hunting, and fishing, so as to avoid the expenses entailed by costly imported foodstuffs. Additionally, Witt argued, in case of a price drop the government would always be willing to cut export duties to ensure that Amazonian rubber remained competitive in the international market. Finally, almost as an afterthought, he added that even if the output of rubber plantations increased substantially the market would always be able to absorb the kind of high-quality rubber produced in Amazonia. On the basis of these and other considerations, Witt concluded that "the increase of plantation rubber will be considerably slower than most people want to have it. Therefore, Brazil will have plenty of time to improve on its way of working" (1908: 45).

In this he was wrong. The rubber crisis was only two years hence, and when it did arrive little could be done. Moreover, in Loreto the global rubber crisis was aggravated by several internal factors. Excessive rains in 1910 and 1911 shortened the rubber-collecting season and thus reduced output (Mitchell 1911: 227–8). Skirmishes between Peruvian and Ecuadorian military forces on the Napo River during the 1910 tapping season affected rubber collection and diminished the stock of exportable rubber while prices were particularly high (ibidem). New confrontations in 1911—between Peruvian and Colombian forces along the Caqueta River—had similar effects on rubber production; matters became even worse thanks to an almost 50 percent drop in prices and the persistence of high export tariffs (Mitchell 1911: 234).

Nevertheless, as Witt foresaw, rubber extractors were able to remain competitive for a time by cutting costs of production and continuously reducing profit margins. They attempted to maintain previous levels of income by increasing production. All of these strategies explain why—even though London prices per ton of rubber dropped from £965 in 1910 to £333 in 1913 (Santos 1980: 236)—Loreto's rubber exports did not diminish but actually slightly increased, from 2,294 tons in 1910 to 2,349 tons in 1913 (see Table 4.6).

Nevertheless, the beginning of World War I in 1914 and the consequent disruption of transatlantic navigation added new strains to regional trade (Huckin 1914: 286). The result was a substantial reduction in rubber production and exports, which plummeted to 1,570 tons. The export trade also reoriented toward the United States, which in 1914 came to absorb 40 percent of the region's rubber exports versus 9 percent in 1913 (see Table 4.5). Although rubber prices would rise as a result of the war demand (Wolf and Wolf 1936: 180), they continued to fall steadily until 1925. By 1920 it was clear that the crisis initiated in 1910 was not temporary and that despite the strategies to remain competitive and cut export taxes rubber producers were no longer able to meet costs of production. As a result, Peru's rubber exports plunged from 1,478 tons in 1920 to 208 tons in 1921 (see Table 4.6). Rubber production would never recover.

The crisis affected rubber traders differently. The brief 1910 rubber frenzy raised the economic expectations of the entire rubber industry. This and the widespread belief that the government was about to rise import duties led merchant houses to substantially increase overseas orders, producing an overstock. In the wake of high rubber prices, smaller traders and extractors also increased demands for credit in goods and, especially, in luxury items. Thus, by the end of 1910 most large merchant houses had placed credits for some £20,000–100,000 (Huckin 1913: 259). On a smaller scale, second-rank merchant houses and traders followed suit. In 1911, when prices fell farther, all these firms found it difficult to recover their investments. By 1912 British consul David Brown reported that "many small importers have gone bankrupt" (1912: 248). In 1913—"one of the most disastrous years"—an additional number of small merchant houses were forced to close (Huckin 1913: 258). As many as 60 percent of the Jewish traders that had settled in Loreto at the onset of the rubber boom left the region during this time (Rosenzweig 1967: 27).

Large foreign merchant houses were able to survive thanks to support from their European offices, agents, and associates, many of whom were unwilling to withdraw from the region altogether because of the large sums they had invested. Other large merchant houses also relied on commercial connections with overseas firms. This led British consul V. Huckin (1913: 284) to assert that it seemed that the region's commerce could remain in a state of animated suspension even if the war was prolonged and the prices of rubber did not experience a permanent recovery. However, the steady drop in rubber prices prevented many clients of merchant houses in Iquitos from paying accounts; thus much of the region's capital was in uncollectable debt.

This and the existence of a cheaper and more regular source of rubber from Southeast Asia led large European and North American companies to cut credit for goods and orders for rubber and to put pressure on Loreto's trading firms to recover their investments. This situation was reproduced up and down the *habilitación* chain, with the merchant houses putting pressure on the smaller traders and extractors and so on. However, the *habilitación* chain ended with the highly indebted and cash-poor peons—who could pay only in low-priced rubber—and so very soon the credit system started falling apart.

Attempts to restrict the supply of credit had been made even as early as 1912 (Brown 1912: 248). By 1913 the leading merchant houses were trying to modify the nonmonetary dimension of the *habilitación* system, whereby rubber was paid for with additional credit in goods to be repaid with rubber, by instead making payments in cash. But as British consul Huckin put it, "Any attempt at introducing a system of payment in cash for the extant stocks of rubber would be impossible, partly because many of these firms are too involved financially to risk producing in their desperate clients a disavowal of their debts, but also because of the acute misery this would cause in the rubber estates" (Huckin 1913: 258). Thus, merchants were trapped: They could not recover their investments and leave the region and were thus forced to make additional investments lest the system collapse—and their firms with it.

The establishment of branches of the Bank of Peru and London and of the Commercial Bank of Spanish America Ltd. by the end of 1911 brought some welcome relief to Iquitos's trading community. The former had been incorporated in Lima with Peruvian capital and carried out general commercial transactions; the latter was a subsidiary of the London-based Anglo–South American Bank and combined banking business with mercantile activities (Brown 1912: 252). Why these two banks decided to establish branches in Iquitos at this very critical time is not clear, but their presence was considered highly beneficial, because they granted credit at fixed, fair rates and introduced the current-account system, with the use of personal checks (ibidem). However, World War I soon forced banks to restrict their activities. In order to hinder the exit of capital, provide relief to the merchants and entrepreneurs, and ensure the circulation of money, the government prohibited the export of gold, declared a moratorium on payments of external debts and bank loans until October 1914, and allowed banks to print their own bills (Huckin 1914: 284–5).

In the Wake of the 1914 Crisis

The economic situation by late 1914 was untenable; merchant houses were forced to reduce imports, stop granting credits, and foreclose on client assets. The value of imports dramatically decreased from US$4,518,500 in 1910 to US$697,000 in 1914 (Appendix 2). Although this was partly a consequence of the outbreak of World War I, which interrupted maritime trade and permitted only one ship to enter the port of Iquitos in 1914, the main cause was economic recession. The reduction in the import trade affected not only luxury goods but also basic commodities such as foodstuffs, textiles, and medicines. By the end of 1914 many imported foodstuffs had become scarce in Iquitos (Huckin 1914: 284). This was especially grave given the fact that the region produced very little of what it consumed.

The shortage of imported foodstuffs together with further credit restrictions created severe problems in the rubber fronts, particularly those located on the periphery. By 1913 there was evidence that in general terms peons were working "less energetically" due to the diminished flow of goods they were receiving from their *patrones* (Huckin 1913: 256). Insofar as *patrones* were not able to cover all the subsistence needs of peons, workers were forced to fish and hunt for food and "made no rounds of the *estradas* save when the overseers were upon them" (Wolf and Wolf 1936: 179–80). It became more and more difficult for *patrones* to retain their labor forces, and many peons started abandoning the rubber camps and estates (Rumrrill et al. 1986: 161).

Even tribal Indian *habilitado* peons were reluctant to extract rubber under these restrictive conditions, opting to abandon *patrones* who, weakened by the economic crisis, could not retrieve them by force. Bernardino Izaguirre (1922–1929: XII, 351) reported that in 1914 the Ashaninka of the Apurucayali River did not accept the reasons offered by their *patrones* as to why they were not being remunerated as highly as in the recent past. Such reactions were common. Thus, as the rubber crisis became more acute, in areas such as the upper Ucayali indigenous peons started leaving *patrones* and disbanding (Ortiz 1974: II, 568). In more peripheral fronts, such as those along the Purus, Yurua, and Galvez Rivers, tribal Indians displaced by *caucheros* took advantage of the latter's sudden vulnerability, attacking, pillaging, and destroying their posts (Rumrrill et al. 1986: 153; Lamb 1974: 171, 176).

Without means of subsistence and facing mounting hostility from indigenous peoples eager to recover lost territories, many *patrones* left the peripheral rubber fronts and retreated to safer, more integrated areas. Thus, one of the most visible effects of the collapse of Loreto's rubber economy was the dislocation of many of the remote rubber fronts from the regional economic center and, as a consequence, there was a shrinking of the sphere of the mercantile economy. Peripheral areas remained closed to any white-mestizo presence for many years and reverted to a subsistence economy. This provided a respite to some tribal Indian peoples, who were able to regroup and recover from the decimation and disarticulation they experienced after being subjected by rubber extractors.

In the wake of credit restrictions and the loss of their labor forces, many small *patrones* were unable to continue extracting rubber or to cover debts with outfitters, local traders, and large extractors. This was especially true for owners of hevea estates, where costs of production were higher compared to castilloa (Huckin 1914: 286). In turn, local traders and extractors were not able to pay creditors—the merchant houses of Iquitos. After 1914, when the crisis deepened, some of these firms attempted to recover as much of their investments as they could by foreclosing on clients' assets. However, as Weinstein (1983) and Bradford Barham and Oliver Coomes (1994a: 91) have argued, "investments in rubber extraction and infrastructure rapidly lost value."

In the new context of recession, indebted peons were no longer the valuable commodity they were at the height of the rubber boom. Given the low price for rubber, the transfer of peons in payment for debts was not good business. And because it was not feasible to put them to work, for lack of profitable economic alternatives, or to transfer them to other extractors, for lack of labor demand, accepting peons in payment became an economic burden.

The only other assets that could be seized were hevea estates, urban properties, and steamboats; merchant houses seized these whenever possible, but none were of much value. Many of the foreclosed hevea holdings were auctioned, but as there were no buyers, they ended up in a state of total abandonment (Rumrrill et al. 1986: 161). Steamboats were not a better option. Although shipping had constituted a highly profitable activity during the rubber boom, given the decreasing production and exports the local fleet largely exceeded the volume of available cargo. As in Brazil (Weinstein 1983: 236), many shipowners in Loreto opted to drydock their vessels rather than operate them at a loss (Rumrrill et al. 1986: 161).

Contrary to the British consul's assertion that the commercial system was "not flexible enough to allow a rapid adaptation to confront the present crisis" (Huckin 1913: 256), the merchant houses of Iquitos did react to the crisis with remarkable speed, immediately searching for alternative economic opportunities. As early as 1911, efforts were being made to stimulate the export of *tagua*, or ivory nuts, to Italy and Germany (Mitchell 1911: 234). Small quantities of *tagua*, the fruit of the *yarina* palm (*Phytelephas macrocarpa*), had been exported before the rubber crisis for the manufacture of buttons. However, it was only after 1910 that merchant houses saw *tagua* as an alternative export product and promoted its collection with extraordinary success, as shown by the sudden increase in the export figures (Appendix 14). Unfortunately, in 1913 international prices experienced a sharp drop, and by 1914 they were so low that it was no longer worthwhile to ship ivory nuts (Huckin 1914: 261, 287).

Also in 1911, local merchants promoted cotton cultivation, this time through the chamber of commerce (Mitchell 1911: 235). Samples were shipped to Europe, and some fetched good prices, but lack of capital amid the crisis hindered development of this crop on a larger scale, at least during the early years of the bust era (Huckin 1913: 264). Merchant houses not only attempted to renew the export of traditional local products such as hides, sarsaparilla, and tobacco; they also searched for markets for new products, such as fine timber, palm fibers, and oil nuts (Huckin 1914: 287).

Despite the efforts of the mercantile community, the region's economy continued shrinking. Extraregional transportation was also strongly affected. By the end of 1911 the Amazon Steam Navigation Company, one of the two companies that operated along the Amazon route, changed hands and was renamed Amazon River Company. The new company stopped making trips from Manaus to Iquitos (Mitchell 1911: 239). For a while, the rival Iquitos Steam Ship Company Ltd. monopolized extraregional fluvial transport from Iquitos, but with the decreasing volume of import-export trade the firm was absorbed in 1913 by its parent company, the Booth Steamship Company. This company had been exclusively devoted to maritime navigation between Belém and European and North American ports (Huckin 1913: 264). After the merger the new company drastically reduced the number of steamship calls on Iquitos, which dropped from fifty-four in 1907 to nine in 1914 (Bonilla 1976: III). Transportation services were also restricted by the onset of World War I. In 1915, to solve the transport crisis, the prefect of Loreto asked the government to establish a navigation line connecting the Pacific port of Callao with Iquitos via the Panama Canal, which had been inaugurated the previous year (Romero 1983: 125). His proposal was ignored.

When World War I ended the worst fears of local authorities and merchant elites were realized: The British Booth Steamship Company withdrew, leaving the region almost totally isolated and without means of transportation for its exports. Traders and authorities asked the government to negotiate with the Peruvian Steamship Company an extension to Iquitos of its Callao-Manaus route (Sotomayor et al. 1949: 27). This company, which had been incorporated in 1906 with private and public Peruvian capital, operated along the Pacific Coast; sometime after the opening of the Panama Canal it started making trips to the Brazilian port of Manaus. The proposed route change also went unheeded, and it was not until the 1930s that the Peruvian Steamship Company began calling regularly on the port of Iquitos. The only state response to the transportation problem was to assign one of its old steamlaunches and a large scow to make trips from Iquitos to Manaus carrying commercial cargo (Romero 1983: 127).

Relief finally came from the private sector. In 1918 Adolfo Morey, by then the region's largest shipowner, took advantage of the opening of the Panama Canal to establish a permanent navigation line between Iquitos and the port of Callao (Anonymous 1992: 6). Although that line was served by a fluvial steamer, the 200-ton *Yurimaguas*, and not by a proper maritime vessel, for many years it was the only connection between Iquitos and Lima. By 1919 Morey's company started regular trips between Iquitos and the Brazilian ports of Belém and Manaus with one 120-ton and two 300-ton steamships (Navarro Cáuper 1988b: 19). In Belém, passengers and cargo destined to European and North American ports were transshipped to the vessels of the New York–based Lamport and Holt Line, for which Morey acted as agent (Sotomayor et al. 1949: 168). Morey's vessels also made internal trips, connecting Iquitos with Yurimaguas on the Huallaga River and intermediate ports.

The reestablishment of fluvial navigation ensured greater stability for Loreto's import-export trade, but recession greatly reduced its scale. Given the region's much lower consumption capacity, imported foodstuffs were out of reach for a large proportion of the urban and rural populations. In 1914 it was reported that many Iquitos inhabitants had moved to riverine properties, where they began producing local staples for the urban market (Huckin 1914: 284). This local agricultural production prevented food scarcity in Iquitos from becoming even worse.

In the rural areas there was also an important shift from extraction to cultivation. Taking along their peons, many former rubber *patrones* left peripheral areas and established agricultural operations along the rivers more frequently visited by steamships, such as the Ucayali, Napo, and Urubamba (Ortiz 1974: II, 574; Gow 1992: 44). Together with converted hevea estates and a few traditional *fundos* that had been established during the rubber boom, the new agricultural properties became the central productive units of the economic system that emerged after the rubber crisis and lasted until the early 1960s.

As a result of the rubber bust, the region's economic and demographic landscape experienced an important transformation. Whereas during the rubber boom there was a gradual move from west to east toward the Colombian and Brazilian borders, and from north to south toward the Bolivian border, during the years following the rubber bust traders, extractors, and their families returned westward and northward. And though in the recent past rubber extractors, particularly castilloa collectors, had established camps in the most remote interfluvial areas, the tendency now was to settle along the region's largest and more accessible rivers. The Amazon-Napo, Amazon-Ucayali and Amazon-Marañon-Huallaga axes became the region's main commercial arteries and the core of the new *fundo*-based agroextractive economy. In contrast, the Yavari, Putumayo, Yurua, Purus, and upper Madre de Dios Rivers—which during the last two decades of the rubber boom had supplied a large proportion of the region's rubber production—were virtually abandoned and became more or less detached from the central productive and trading areas.

The rubber crisis stimulated the migration of many who had come to the region attracted by the prospects of rubber-tapping (San Román 1975: 168). Though it is true that some abandoned Loreto forever, it is apparent that in contrast to the Brazilian case (Petey 1972: 120–1) most people stayed on in the region. Thus, rather than experiencing a significant out-migration, the region experienced a massive redistribution of the resident population (Rodríguez Achung 1986: 24).

State Apathy and the Irruption of Regionalism

In the years following the rubber bust, the government was indifferent to the plight of the region, at first because it failed to recognize that the crisis was irreversible. Taking the 1910 upsurge in rubber prices as a sign of even more prosperous times to come, the government, in October of that year, raised the import and export tariffs to the levels imposed for the rest of the country (Cazes 1910: 223). Even when rubber prices plunged during 1911, the tariffs remained in force, aggravating considerably the effects of the crisis on the regional economy. Not until the end of 1911 did the government reduce export tariffs, and then only to their previous level of 8 percent ad valorem, still considered to be too high (Mitchell 1911: 231). In the words of G.B. Mitchell, the British consul: "Peruvian rubber, which has the world's highest cost of production and experiences the greatest difficulties to reach the market, is being destroyed by a heavy export tax" (ibidem: 236).

Through a spokesperson in the local *El Oriente* newspaper, rubber extractors and traders requested a 50–75 percent reduction of the export taxes for the various qualities of rubber (Mitchell 1911: 236). Even government officials such as Col. Pedro Portillo (1914: 176), the former prefect of and then-senator for Loreto and minister of development, were of the opinion that rubber export tariffs should be reduced. Unfortunately, the government was very slow to respond. When it finally did respond in 1914, the effective reduction was a mere 25 percent (Huckin 1914: 291). Only in 1919, when the rubber economy was collapsing, did the government exclude the rubber exported through Iquitos from tariffs (Ballón 1991: II, 25).

The state was equally slow to react to the problem in extraregional fluvial transport. The only occasion when the government acted more or less swiftly to guarantee the continuity of Loreto's commerce was when the import trade ran the risk of coming to a complete halt. In 1911 the Booth Company threatened to stop warehousing incoming merchandise. According to its agreement with Peru for the construction of Iquitos's dock, it was the state's obligation to cover expenses for storage (Mitchell 1911: 240). If the government did not assume those costs, the Booth Company threatened to forbid the next arriving vessel from unloading its cargo. To resolve the impasse, the government allowed Booth to charge an extra fee for its storage services. Although this measure allowed the port to continue operating, it did very little to relieve traders and extractors from high freights and heavy taxes.

Other measures, such as the moratorium on bank loans decreed in 1914 at the onset of World War I, were of national scope; they were not designed specifically to alleviate Loreto's economy. The few actions undertaken by the government in Loreto after the 1910 rubber crisis were intended to mitigate the recession rather than promote new economic alternatives being explored by merchant houses. The only exception was a lukewarm decree issued in 1915 that exempted agricultural export products from tariffs. This measure was intended to orient the region's economy toward farming (Ballón 1991: I, 315). Even so, the government was not consistent. Once the cultivation and exportation of cotton and coffee became significant, in the following decade, the government soon revoked the measure.

The government's scant attention to the region during the 1910–1920 period was the result of the general crisis that affected Peru rather than an expression of centralist policies. The 1910 reforms of the customs system and tariffs were largely a response to a growing public deficit. State rents had diminished once more as a consequence of World War I; that affected the import-export trade and promoted the transfer abroad of large volumes of gold currency. The moratorium on payments of external debt, as well as the ban on the export of gold decreed by Pres. Oscar Benavides in 1914, helped stabilize the economy but not revitalize it. Few large-scale public works projects were undertaken during the war years. The government directed its efforts to promoting the cultivation of export crops such as cotton and sugar in the Pacific Coast valleys. Thus, although the government restricted its actions in the Loreto region to the defense of national sovereignty, doing little to protect or stimulate the economy, it acted much the same way in the rest of the country.

The resentment of the local population toward the central government for its recurrent insensitivity festered with the rubber crisis (El Comercio 1917). In the early 1910s, local politics in Loreto was marked by a confrontation between two political factions: La Cueva (The Cave) and La Liga Loretana (The Loretan League). The first references to La Cueva appear in December 1912 (Anonymous 1993a: 16), and it seems obvious that this was not a self-title but rather a derogatory term applied by political enemies. Its members did not constitute a formal political group; opponents saw them as individuals sharing and defending common "oligarchic" interests (Torres Videla 1923: 20). In effect, La Cueva was made up mainly of outsiders: public officials, professionals, and intellectuals from the coastal provinces who controlled not only the regional government and armed forces but also the region's delegation to the National Congress (Dávila 1994: 6). Two local newspapers backed La Cueva: *El Oriente*, the region's most prestigious daily, and *La Razón* (Torres Videla 1923: 30).

In contrast, middle-class and upper-class native Loretans supported La Liga, founded in January 1913. This category included people born in the Huallaga basin, which later became the department of San Martín. Members of La Liga adhered to a loose regionalist ideology. They struggled to end the hegemonic control of La Cueva and to gain greater autonomy for the region (Anonymous 1938: 69). Its leaders seem to have been influenced by Jenaro Herrera, a writer and lawyer born in Moyobamba who had organized Unión Loretana, a study group devoted to analyzing the region's problems (ibidem).

Unlike La Cueva, La Liga constituted a formal political association. It had a board of directors and an internally elected secretary, and it held regular meetings. The opinions of La Liga members were voiced in local newspapers, *La Mañana* and *La Región* (Torres Videla 1923: 30; Empresa 1938: 70). Its partisans resented the discrimination exercised by authorities appointed by the central government. In turn, they were accused by the regional government of promoting separatist, federalist, and regionalist ideals. Often, La Liga members compared their situation to that of blacks in the United States (Torres Videla 1923: 20).

Little is known as to the finer points of the ideologies, allegiances, and actions of these two groups. We do know, however, that one of the first issues centered on Julio C. Arana, the controversial rubber baron of the Putumayo. Prominent Loretans (who later founded La Liga) viewed Arana as a patriot, a defender of the national sovereignty in a region increasingly threatened by Colombians. In contrast, members of La Cueva regarded him as a criminal whose cruel treatment of Indian peons had stained the national reputation. Two of the most prominent members of La Cueva were Rómulo Paredes, the lawyer, journalist, and owner of *El Oriente* who denounced Arana publicly, and judge Carlos Valcárcel, who in 1912 condemned Arana to prison (Anonymous 1993a: 16; House Documents 1913: 20). To counter these accusations, Arana's brother-in-law, Pablo Zumaeta, wrote a pamphlet blaming these two, plus Judge Eduardo Lanatta, the leader of La Cueva, of conspiring to ruin Arana's company for personal profit (1913: 5–13). When Judge Valcárcel ordered Arana's imprisonment, Zumaeta and other Arana supporters helped to organize popular riots. At the end, Arana escaped imprisonment; in 1920 he was even elected senator for Loreto (Pennano 1988: 168).

Additional confrontations took place in 1913, after La Liga was founded. That year, Pres. Guillermo Billinghurst ordered the deportation of his predecessor, Augusto Leguía (1908–1912), and dissolved Congress, by then dominated by Civilists and Leguía's followers. La Liga backed up the Civilist Party and Leguía, whereas local authorities belonging to La Cueva supported Billinghurst. When Billinghurst convoked parliamentary elections, La Liga presented Enrique Llosa, former mayor of Iquitos, as its senatorial candidate. Soon thereafter, the public forces shot followers of La Liga in street confrontations; Llosa was assassinated at a public meeting (Torres Videla 1923: 20). These events marked the debut of La Liga as a regional force in national politics.

The controversial 1919 presidential elections (Antero Aspíllaga, a member of the party in power, and the opposition's candidate, Augusto Leguía, accused each other of electoral fraud) provided fertile ground for additional clashes between La Liga and La Cueva. Although Leguía won the election, Pres. José Pardo threatened to annul them. In Iquitos, members of La Liga, who had campaigned in support of Leguía, attacked public buildings as well as the residences of Eduardo Lanatta, leader of La Cueva, and the chief of police (Anonymous 1938: 70; Anonymous 1988: 25). Local army forces repressed the protesters. In July 1919 Leguía, with the support of the army, deposed President Pardo, assuming power for a second term that lasted until 1930. In Iquitos, members of La Liga celebrated Leguía's accession to power with public demonstrations (ibidem). In response, the Pardo-appointed prefect of Loreto imprisoned several of Leguía's local supporters (Torres Videla 1923: 21). Meanwhile, Leguía called for elections for a national assembly, which would be responsible for drafting a new constitution.

Why the regionalist La Liga originally supported Leguía remains unclear. During his first presidency (1908–1912), Leguía had done very little to help the region recover from the rubber crisis. Immediately after deposing Pardo, Leguía did reward Loreto by suspending indefinitely the collection of rubber export tariffs. Members of La Liga, however, perceived his subsequent policies as treacherous. What would finally trigger La Liga's opposition to Leguía was the behavior of César Ruiz y Pastor, the prefect he appointed for Loreto. Although the latter was an old supporter of La Liga, he soon accommodated the demands of La Cueva and the merchant elite. He even tried to neutralize La Liga by founding a parallel organization (Torres Videla 1923: 22–3). As a result of these machinations, La Liga's support for Leguía turned into radical opposition. When the new constitution was finally promulgated in October 1919, La Liga urged its followers to protest through the pages of *La Mañana* (ibidem). From then on, conditions worsened; a major confrontation was only a matter of time.

Members of La Liga criticized Leguía on several fronts: betraying Civilist ideals, increasing the country's foreign debt, imposing heavy taxes, and allowing the spread of political corruption (Torres Videla 1923: 19). Discontent with Leguía's government deepened thanks to its reorientation of foreign policy. During the early 1920s Peru initiated talks with Colombia to solve their border conflicts in the Putumayo-Caqueta area. In 1906 and again in 1909 the countries had signed agreements to withdraw troops and functionaries from disputed territories (San Román 1975: 183–4). However, in 1911 a military clash broke out in the environs of the old rubber post of La Pedrera on the Caqueta River. Although Peru emerged victorious, the battle did not resolve the conflict; in fact, it exacerbated tensions. When word reached Loreto that Leguía was willing to make territorial concessions to end the conflict, there was widespread discontent.

Adding to the discontent was a general feeling that the government had kept Loreto in the "cruelest oblivion" (Rumrrill 1986: 229). Such sentiments led Capt. Guillermo Cervantes, in August 1921, to rise in arms against President Leguía with the support of La Liga. The rebels gave three additional reasons to justify the insurrection: (1) the complicity between the Leguía-appointed prefect and the largest merchant houses of Iquitos had resulted in the latter obtaining juicy contracts, tax exemptions, and impunity for their commercial practices; (2) the scarcity of cash, artificially aggravated by the merchant houses, allowed large traders who still had credit abroad to force their clients to continue accepting credit in merchandise; and (3) since 1920, a delay in the transfer of funds to the region, as well as the government's decision in 1921 to suspend such transfers altogether, had left most public servants unpaid for well longer than a year (Torres Videla 1923: 35–70).

Capitalizing on previous conflicts between the prefect, who was supported by the police, and the army, Captain Cervantes persuaded his unit—Colonization Regiment No. 17, known as the Cazadores del Oriente—to rise in arms, crush police opposition, and take military and political control of Iquitos. La Liga took part in the rebellion from its inception. In fact, Juan Olórtegui Villacorta, La Liga's president since its foundation, was a member of the executive committee of the revolutionary movement (Anonymous 1938: 70). When Cervantes took power, he appointed Olórtegui to be subprefect and chief of police. Such was the intimacy between the president of La Liga and the rebel leader that when the latter had to leave Iquitos to confront the advancing government troops he entrusted Olórtegui with the direction of the revolutionary government.

Cervantes attempted to gain support from the region's population, including the military and public servants, by issuing three public manifestos. In them he denounced the government's position with regard to the Peru-Colombia border dispute, the poor administration of the region, and indifference in face of Loreto's crisis (Ortiz 1974: II, 497). Endorsements were not difficult to obtain.

By 1921 the value of imports had dropped even farther to US$458,738 (Appendix 3), reducing fiscal income to a negligible sum. The government's 1919 decision to exclude rubber exports from tariffs came as a relief for exporters, yet it affected regional revenue adversely. As a result of the fiscal crisis, the state stopped paying the salaries of Loreto's military and public servants for several months. Understandably, Cervantes's promise to pay outstanding salaries generated wide sympathy for his movement. Operating as Movimiento Pro-Patria Amazónica (Pro-Amazonian Fatherland Movement), the Cervantes coalition aimed not to separate Loreto from Peru but to oust Leguía and obtain greater political and economic autonomy for the region (Bendayán 1993: 26). Not surprisingly, the government quickly labeled the movement as separatist and treated it accordingly. Leguía ordered the immediate closure of the border with Brazil, dispatching two military contingents to crush the insurrection. This was achieved in January 1922 following several armed clashes along the Ucayali and the Huallaga Rivers.

In contrast to previous uprisings, such as those of Seminario and Vizcarra, Cervantes's movement benefited from widespread support, not only in Iquitos but also in the smaller riverine towns, where many joined his forces (Ortiz 1984: 266). Although he was successful in attracting army supporters, civil servants, and the urban population, he was unable to obtain the allegiance of the navy. To neutralize it, Cervantes seized most of its vessels (Romero 1983: 129). Cervantes was also unable to gain the support of the merchant elite. In fact, his actions seem to have alienated merchants early on. In order to pay overdue salaries, Cervantes seized £23,300 from the Bank of Peru and London (Torres Videla 1923: 118). But that was insufficient to finance the insurrection, so in October 1921 he ordered the issuance of "provisional checks of compulsory circulation" (Ortiz 1984: 265). This measure was strongly resisted by local merchants, who immediately closed their stores. Cervantes's detractors assert that the populace was invited to loot the establishments of merchants who refused to accept the "revolutionary" bills (Rumrrill et al. 1986: 230). In contrast, followers of Cervantes claim that he impeded the ransacking of stores by paying civil servants with sterling pounds instead of the new notes (Torres Videla 1923: 174).

In smaller towns such as Moyobamba, Tarapoto, and Lamas, the forces imposed levies on local merchants and other affluent neighbors (Izquierdo Ríos 1976: 92). Additionally, Cervantes confiscated several vessels from the private fleets of such merchant houses as Israel and Company and A. Morey and Company. The demands imposed on traders were aggravated by Cervantes's closure of the port at Iquitos to commercial navigation (Romero 1983: 129). He also imposed tariffs on the region's new export products (ivory nuts, cotton, balata, and fine timber), as well as imported goods that could be produced locally. These measures triggered protests from the chamber of commerce, whose members argued that no profits would be left after paying the tariffs (Torres Videla 1923). Despite the protests, the measures were enforced.

Cervantes directed his regionalist discourse not only against the central government but also against the commercial elite, whom he saw as selfish, opportunistic, and unresponsive to Loreto's difficulties. The rebels' view of the trading community was not only contemptuous but carried overtones of racism and anti-Semitism. After criticizing the commercial practices of Loreto's grand commerce, Samuel Torres Videla (1923: 63), secretary of the revolutionary government, asserted that "unfortunately Jewish commerce prevails here and Peruvians and foreigners adopt its ways with admirable ease." With similar vitriol, he referred to Chinese retail traders as "that odious plague" (ibidem: 175). Nonetheless, Cervantes managed to obtain public support from a few (mostly Peruvian) merchants and entrepreneurs. Among them were Luis Felipe Morey, Otoniel Vela, Juan Abelardo Morey, and the Pinto brothers (Menacho Morey n.d.: 8; Proceso 1972, No. 16; Torres Videla 1923: 239).

Despite enjoying widespread popular support, being well armed, and controlling fluvial navigation, Cervantes was easily defeated. The leaders of the opposition movement, including Olórtegui, escaped to Ecuador. This apparently brought La Liga to an end, for no evidence of its activities exists thereafter. This fact notwithstanding, Cervantes's insurrection became a milestone in the shaping of Loreto's regionalist ideology. During the long 1915–1962 period, regionalist sentiment continued to grow, even though it did not find expression in concrete actions or political struggles. It would resurface in 1932, when the people of Iquitos attempted to recapture Leticia (the region President Leguía ceded to Colombia during his second term in an effort to settle the border conflicts).

If 1910 marked the beginning of the rubber crisis and 1914 the inevitability of its demise, 1921 signaled the death of the rubber economy in Loreto. However, the search for new economic alternatives leading to the radical recomposition of Loreto's grand commerce, and to the emergence of a new landed elite, had actually begun several years earlier. By the onset of World War I it had become clear that Amazonia had little chance of competing with the colonial rubber plantations in Southeast Asia.

7

"Buyers of All Sorts of Regional Products": Merchant Houses and Export Cycles

It has been claimed that Loreto's economy merely "survived" between 1914, when the rubber economy collapsed, and 1962, when Peru renewed efforts to incorporate the Amazon region, thanks to "brief periods of export of any plant or animal product for which there was an international demand" (Haring 1986b: 72). The so-called minibooms that characterized this new period have been represented as if they were sequential, in such a way that "each product had its own fad" (San Román 1975: 174; Haring 1986a: 35). By concentrating on individual export fads, conceived of as small-scale replicas of the original rubber boom, previous studies have not taken into account the dynamics of the economy as whole, losing sight of how the various export cycles overlapped each other. Following the rubber crisis, the scale of Loreto's economy certainly diminished. We maintain, however, that it was not reduced to a state of mere survival, as many have suggested. Also, it did not evolve in a fluctuating manner characterized by repetitive self-contained, boom-and-bust extractive cycles.

In this chapter we analyze the commercial dimension of Loreto's new agroextractive export economy. Particular emphasis is placed on the following aspects: the structure and evolution of the import-export trade, the sequence and combination of export cycles, the recomposition of the "grand commerce," and the integrating role played by the merchant houses of Iquitos. We suggest that the import-export commerce during the 1915–1962 period can be conveniently divided into three phases. Of these, only the second (1928–1942) corresponds to the image of economic stagnation and negative commercial balance that traditionally has been attributed to the entire period. In fact, the third phase was one of extreme prosperity, one in which the volume of regional external commerce reached levels similar to the best years of the rubber boom and the commercial balance was mostly positive.

The analysis of the structure and flow of the region's exports allows us to question the widespread notion that during this period Loreto's economy continued to be mainly extractive. Export agriculture, combined with other productive and extractive activities, contributed to the expansion of the demographic and economic fronts that were established in fluvial areas during the rubber era. In addition, our analysis of the several agricultural and extractive export cycles that took place during this half-century allows us to question the ideas that these were sequential and that at the end of each the region's economy collapsed, as it did during the rubber bust. We suggest that these export cycles, because they overlapped in time and involved different areas within the region, did not affect the economy as a whole when they ended.

During the 1915–1962 period, Loreto's grand commerce experienced a radical recomposition. This did not take place immediately after the 1914 rubber bust, however, but after 1921, when the region stopped exporting rubber altogether. By 1929 only 14 percent of the merchant houses that operated during the rubber era were still active. Among them were a majority of the large Peruvian merchant houses, some of the large foreign-owned but Peruvian-based companies, and some of the small and medium-sized firms that were able to expand thanks to the closure of larger rivals. With the disappearance of most firms that acted as agents for large European and U.S. companies, the region's grand commerce became even more autonomous.

Despite greater autonomy, the merchant houses of Iquitos continued to rely on foreign credit. They also continued to be multifunctional and to operate on the basis of the *habilitación* system, the largest firms carrying out all functions typical of merchant houses during the rubber era, that is, import, export, outfitting, whole-sale-retail commerce, shipping, and banking. The only important organizational innovation that merchant houses undertook during this period was to develop small-scale industrial activities related to the processing of key export products.

The chapter ends with an analysis of the relationship between merchant houses and agroextractive *fundos*. Merchant houses played an important integrating role, just as they did in the past, articulating the region externally, with the international markets, and internally, between urban centers and rural areas. Following our argument, in the new agroextractive economy large *fundo* owners became the main partners of the merchant houses in the rural areas. By providing credit to *fundo* owners and channeling their products, trading firms continued to link the region's most remote areas with the international market. Together, large *fundo* owners and merchant houses controlled much of the regional economy throughout this period. Their relationship, however, varied over time depending on the requirements that different extractive and agricultural products placed upon export procedures. To underscore this variation, we analyze the modes through which trading firms promoted, financed, and organized the production and marketing of four of the region's most important export commodities: cotton, barbasco, rosewood oil, and fine timber. We demonstrate that merchant houses were extremely flexible vis-à-vis the changing demands of the international market and the requirements of the various export products.

The New Agroextractive Export Economy

An analysis of the evolution of Loreto's export trade during the 1915–1962 period allows us to identify three distinct phases (Appendix 3; Table 7.1). During the first phase (1915–1927) the export trade clearly reflected the traumatic effects of the rubber bust, although the region's economy was far from paralyzed. During this phase the annual average value of exports decreased roughly by half (48 percent) from US$3,618,310 for 1900–1914 to US$1,889,806. Although the import trade also experienced a sharp fall during 1914–1915 and again during 1921–1922, on average it decreased less than the export commerce. Despite the economic depression during these years, the region's commercial balance remained generally positive.

In this first phase the export trade was based on the almost contemporaneous production and extraction of four products: ivory nuts, cotton, fine timber, and balata rubber (*Manilkaria sp.*). Some of them were being commercially exploited even before the 1914 rubber bust (see Figure 7.1). By the end of this phase, the exported volume of all of these products had experienced an abrupt fall (see Appendixes 14–17). In the case of ivory nuts, mainly used for the manufacturing of buttons, the fall was due to the discovery of an artificial substitute (Villarejo 1988: 136). In the case of fine timber it was due to the decreasing quality of the logs exported. The export of balata, a nonflexible, waterproof rubber used for, among other things, the manufacture of submarine cable coatings and machine belts, began in 1919. Exports of this product fell sharply after the 1925 speculative rise of prices promoted by British importers and did not recover until World War II (Lausent-Herrera 1986). Lastly, the 50 percent reduction in cotton exports between 1925 and 1928 was the result of the recovery in 1925 of U.S. cotton production after several years of severe weevil plagues (Thorp and Bertram 1978: 79). The reduction in demand for these four export products coincided with the strong devaluation in 1927 of the Peruvian currency (from 2.06 to 4.00 *soles* per dollar), which affected the import trade. The 1929 international economic crisis also had profound and lasting effects on Loreto's external commerce, as in the rest of Peru.

Table 7.1   Annual Average Value of the Import-Export Trade by Period, 1900–1962

	Annual average value (in US$)		
Year	*Imports*	*Exports*	*Total*
1900–1914	2,221,665	3,618,310	5,839,975
1915–1927	1,367,625	1,889,806	3,257,431
1928–1942	924,491	685,134	1,609,625
1943–1962	2,517,752	3,203,793	7,221,545

SOURCES: Appendixes 2 and 3.

Figure 7.1   Evolution of Loreto's Post–Rubber Era Export Cycles

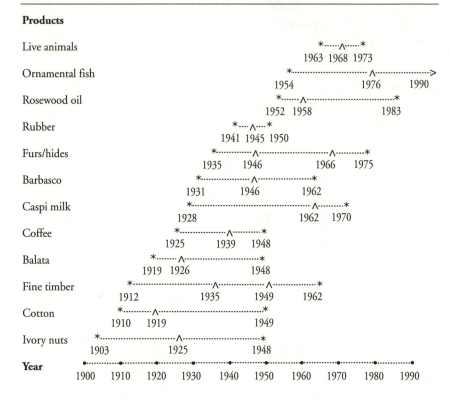

Products

Live animals

Ornamental fish

Rosewood oil

Rubber

Furs/hides

Barbasco

Caspi milk

Coffee

Balata

Fine timber

Cotton

Ivory nuts

Year

SOURCES: Annexes 14–24
* = beginning or end of export boom
^ = peaks in terms of volume (or units) exported
> = ongoing export boom

Although most authors have assumed that the region fell into economic chaos immediately following the rubber bust (San Román 1975: 168), it was not during the rubber bust's aftermath but rather during 1928–1942 that Loreto's export trade experienced its nadir. During this second phase, the annual average value of exports dropped more than 60 percent, and that of imports fell about 30 percent. As a result, during this phase the commercial balance of payment was almost permanently negative. Hence, the portrayal of Loreto's post–rubber era economy as "stagnated" is only true for the period between 1928 and 1942.

Paradoxically during this time, the region's export trade achieved its highest degree of diversification, with merchant houses in Iquitos proclaiming themselves "buyers of all sorts of regional products." The overlapping of export booms also found its maximum expression during this time. Not only did the region continue exporting ivory nuts, fine timber, cotton, and balata rubber; it also started exporting coffee, caspi milk (*Couma macrocarpa*), barbasco (*Lonchocarpus nicou*), furs, and hides (see Figure 7.1). Nevertheless, this was a time of transition during which the old export products were bringing very low prices and their volume was in decline while new products were not yet well established, either in the regional or international markets. The only export boom exclusively associated with this transition period was coffee, which fetched high prices during the 1920s. However, because of its inferior quality and low volume, Loretan coffee was never very significant in the export structure (Appendixes 5, 6). In 1948 Loreto stopped exporting coffee (Appendix 7). Renewed coffee exportation in the 1950s was mostly based on the production of the department of San Martín (Appendix 18).

The third economic phase (1943–1962) witnessed spectacular growth in exports. The annual average value of US$3,203,793 almost equaled that of the rubber boom (see Table 7.1). The import trade experienced a similar increase, with an annual average value that surpassed even that of the mythically prosperous rubber era. As a result, the region attained for the first time in many years a positive balance of payment. The flourishing of Loreto's economy during this third phase was very much linked to World War II demand, particularly to the U.S. geopolitical interest in Amazonia as a source of raw materials and a point of passage. The Japanese invasion of Southeast Asia had cut off the supply of several strategic products such as hevea, balata rubber, and derris, a plant used as a powerful insecticide. During the wartime world order, the Amazon Basin became the provider of these and other products, such as caspi milk, used for the manufacture of maritime paints, and barbasco, a substitute for derris. Most of these export booms ended shortly after the war. Of the earlier export products, only two continued to have importance: fine timber and caspi milk. Exports of fine timber, however, declined gradually until 1962 (Appendix 18). In contrast, the export of caspi milk peaked during the 1950s and early 1960s (Appendix 19). During this third phase, two new products achieved importance: rosewood oil (*Aniba rosaeodora*) and ornamental fish. By 1962 the value of the export trade reached its highest level since 1900. However, as we shall see, the export-oriented agroextractive economy was already collapsing.

Loreto's economy was based on production of commercial crops and extraction of many forest products for the international market. Although several authors point out the resurgence of agricultural activities during this period, even those who stress the importance of commercial agriculture contend that Loreto's economy continued to be basically extractive (San Román 1975: 168). Yet as the figures in Table 7.2 indicate, at least for part of this period this was not true. During the 1915–1962 period, agricultural products represented on average roughly 38 percent of the value of Loreto's exports; in some decades, however, they represented more than 60 percent. Cotton and coffee constituted most of the region's agricultural exports. Much of the cotton and coffee exported was cultivated in the central Huallaga valley, in the neighboring department of San Martín. However, insofar as it was financed, transported,

Table 7.2   Relative Weight of Agricultural and Extractive Products in the Structure of
Loreto's Export Trade, 1928–1962

	Percentage of value of exports				
Products	*1928*	*1939*	*1948*	*1955*	*1962*
Agricultural	37.9	62.3	42.6	32.6	14.1
Extractive	62.1	37.7	57.4	67.4	85.9
Total	100.0	100.0	100.0	100.0	100.0

SOURCES: Appendixes 5–9.

and marketed through the commercial network controlled by the merchant houses of
Iquitos, this production can be considered as part of Loreto's economy. The cultivation of barbasco constituted the third pillar of Loreto's export agriculture during this
period. With the decline of the *fundo* economy, the consolidation of an independent
peasant sector, and the implementation of new agrarian policies by the government,
Loreto's export agriculture disappeared by the end of this period. It was replaced by
an agriculture oriented to fulfill the needs of the regional and national markets.

Recomposition of the Region's Grand Commerce

Most of the large merchant houses of the rubber era continued doing business until
at least 1921. Cervantes's uprising and the ensuing paralysis of the external commerce for almost a year, however, represented the straw that broke the camel's back.
In subsequent years Loreto's grand commerce underwent a radical process of recomposition. Of the sixty-two merchant houses operating in Iquitos in 1908, only
nine were still active in 1929 (Guzmán Rivera 1929). Among the firms that had
ceased operating by 1929 were many of those that acted as agents for overseas companies, including the three largest: Wesche and Company, Marius, Lévy, and
Schuler, and Kahn and Polack.

As a result, until the 1940s, when the import-export trade recovered, Peruvian-
based companies monopolized Loreto's grand commerce. The only exception was
the U.S.-based Astoria Importing and Manufacturing Company, which opened
shop in the region in 1929 and was originally specialized in the extraction, processing, and export of fine timber. The Peruvian Amazon Company, Arana's British-reg-
istered enterprise, also ceased when its credibility collapsed after the long inquiry
carried out by the British Parliament on the crimes perpetrated against indigenous
peons on the Putumayo estates. In 1911 Lloyd's Bank stopped providing credit, and
Arana's company went bankrupt (Pennano 1988: 168). Arana was appointed liq-
uidator, but he continued operating in the region through his firm, J.C. Arana and
Company. In 1920 the Peruvian Amazon Company was finally liquidated, and
sometime before 1929 Arana's Iquitos-based firm ceased operating altogether.

Most of the large Peruvian-owned merchant houses survived the crisis and were instrumental in the conversion of Loreto's economy. A. Morey, L.F. Morey, and C. Hernández continued to be among the region's leading merchants. The first two continued to control much of Loreto's fluvial transport. Adolfo Morey even ventured into maritime navigation, providing an outlet for the region's products during the crisis of the British navigation companies. In addition, L.F. Morey's firm became one of the region's largest landholders. Between 1915 and 1928 it acquired fourteen *fundos*, mostly along the Marañon and Ucayali Rivers, with a total area of 167,225 hectares (Padrón 1939). In turn, C. Hernández continued his tradition of associating with foreign firms and was one of the first Peruvian merchants to get involved in the nascent fine timber export business.

Among the other survivors were some medium-sized, foreign-owned, Peruvian-based merchant houses that filled the void left by the larger companies; some became versatile and powerful firms. Kahn and Company, which had specialized in the import-export trade, diversified after the rubber bust, taking on shipping, wholesale-retail trade, and industry, activities that were characteristic of larger companies (Rodríguez 1928; Guzmán Rivera 1929). Although Kahn and Company was already among the ten top Iquitos firms during the rubber era, during this period it became one of the three leading merchant houses together with Israel and Company and Strassberger and Company.

Israel and Company, which had engaged exclusively in the import trade, during the late 1920s grew to become the region's most powerful merchant house, carrying out the gamut of commercial activities and operating on almost every large river. In addition, after 1921 V. Israel managed to acquire a large number of small *fundos* along the Ucayali River and three large rubber concessions along the Yavari and Morona Rivers (Padrón 1939).

Strassberger and Company, the third leading firm, is a special case. During the rubber boom Emilio Strassberger acted as administrator of the Iquitos agency for the powerful Wesche and Company. He was an active member of the mercantile and social community of Iquitos. Given his experience as a shipper, in 1905 he was asked, together with A. Morey and L.F. Morey, to advise the local government on which steamboats to buy in order to upgrade the state fluvial fleet (Fuentes 1908: 67). He was also a prominent member of the chamber of commerce of Iquitos. When Wesche and Company closed down in the early 1920s, Strassberger purchased its assets; his new company continued to carry out all the activities of the original firm. In addition, it engaged in banking activities as representative of the Transatlantic German Bank. Strassberger and Company was based in Iquitos and had branch offices in Manaus and Zurich (Anonymous 1938: 220). He was twice mayor of Iquitos, in 1912 and 1924 (Treceño 1989: 265). In the post–rubber boom years, Strassberger was appointed consul of Germany. He continued to officiate as such until at least 1940 (Guía 1940). However, after Peru joined the Allies in World War II, Strassberger, who sympathized with the Nazi regime, was deported and his assets confiscated (Rojas Vela 1991).

Of the thirty-seven merchant houses that appeared after the rubber crisis, many were founded by minor Peruvian and foreign traders who during the rubber era were dedicated to urban retail commerce, petty manufacturing, and services; others were established by newly arrived immigrants. Among the foreign traders who prospered in this period, the Chinese constitute the most outstanding case. Although in 1903 the Chinese formed the largest foreign colony in Iquitos (Maúrtua 1911: 132; Lausent-Herrera 1996), by 1908 there were only two Chinese-owned merchant houses (Matrícula 1910). Two decades later there were seven, two owned by small manufacturers of the rubber era and five by newcomers. However, in contrast to other immigrant groups, the Chinese tended to confine themselves to the import and wholesale-retail trade, almost never venturing into the export trade (see Rodríguez 1928; Guzmán Rivera 1929). For this reason, Chinese merchants had very little impact in the financing and shaping of Loreto's agroextractive economy.

The radical recomposition experienced by Loreto's grand commerce in the wake of the rubber bust was followed by additional changes during subsequent decades. Change affected it not only in terms of the number of merchant houses but also in their membership. Thus, the number of merchant houses progressively decreased, from sixty-two in 1908 to thirty-nine in 1940, when the region's import-export trade was submerged in its worst crisis. In turn, the renewed prosperity of the 1940s was accompanied by an increase in the number of firms, which in 1949 totaled forty-seven. Table 7.3 shows the number of houses operating by year, distinguishing between those that survived from previous years and those that appear in a given year. Thus, in 1940 there were a total of thirty-nine firms, six of which had been already listed in 1908 and twelve in 1929, with twenty-one appearing registered for the first time.

Most of the merchant houses that appeared and disappeared during this period were small firms, suggesting that they were the most vulnerable to the constant fluc-

Table 7.3   Evolution of Loreto's Grand Commerce by Period of Opening and Closing of Its Merchant Houses, 1908–1963

Year	1908	1929	1940	1949	1963
1908	62	9	6	5	2
1929	—	37	12	6	2
1940	—	—	21	10	3
1949	—	—	—	26	3
1963	—	—	—	—	nd
Total	62	46	39	47	10

SOURCES: Matrícula 1910; Rodríguez 1928; Guzmán Rivera 1929; Guía 1940; Sotomayor et al. 1949; DNEC 1964a.

NOTE: A complete list of merchant houses for 1963 could not be found. Data for that year only refers to firms engaged in wholesale-retail trade or industrial activities and not to other activities such as import or export trade. Thus, the number of houses established in previous years but still operating in 1963 was probably higher.

tuations of the international market and the changing scenarios brought forth by the export booms. In contrast, the larger and medium-sized firms showed remarkable continuity and retained their leading roles within the merchants' guild, which by then was renamed the Chamber of Commerce and Agriculture (Guzmán Rivera 1929). The continuity of these firms and of the Chamber conferred a certain stability to Loreto's otherwise changing economy.

The Chamber actively promoted promising new export products through the dissemination of information, the granting of credit to producers and extractors, and lobbying activities to keep tariffs and other taxes low. Sometimes it also adopted measures to avoid possible overstocking and the subsequent fall in prices of the region's main export products. This was the case in 1929, when in the face of falling balata prices one of the recently established houses, the Moch Peruvian Export Company, proposed to introduce quality controls and assign export quotas among the exporters so as to keep prices high (Guzmán Rivera 1929: 130). In addition, the Chamber offered a forum for its different interest groups to discuss specific matters. Thus, in 1929 it was through the Chamber that merchant shippers and independent shippers reached an agreement on common freight and travel fares (Guzmán Rivera 1929: 139).

Despite recurrent changes in its composition, Loreto's grand commerce maintained several of the characteristics it had developed during the rubber era. Among them was the strategy of integrating functions rather than specializing. From Table 7.4 it becomes apparent that the number of functions performed by merchant houses did not change immediately after the rubber crisis. Both in 1908 and 1929, about 55 percent of the merchant houses carried out two or three functions, generally import and export activities plus either shipping, wholesale-retail commerce, or industry, whereas about 15 percent performed four or five activities. Among them were the largest trading firms. As during the rubber era, the integration of the maximum number of functions continued to be synonymous with economic power. The remaining merchant houses were exclusively devoted to the import trade.

This structure underwent a radical transformation during the 1928–1942 economic period, when the region's external trade contracted. During those critical

Table 7.4   Percentage Distribution of the Merchant Houses of Iquitos According to Number of Functions Performed, 1904–1949

Number of Functions	1904	1908	1929	1940	1949
4–5	15.7	16.1	15.2	7.7	12.8
2–3	27.5	53.3	58.7	92.3	78.7
1	56.8	30.6	26.1	—	8.5
Total	100.0	100.0	100.0	100.0	100.0

SOURCES: Fuentes 1908:29–30; Maúrtua 1911:156; Matrícula 1910; Rodríguez 1928; Guzmán Rivera 1929; Guía 1940; Sotomayor et al. 1949.

years the tendency was for all monofunction firms to engage in additional activities, whereas many of the larger, multifunction companies reduced the number of activities they once performed. As a result, 92 percent of the merchant houses came to perform two to three activities. Only the larger firms—Israel and Company, Kahn and Company, and Strassberger and Company—continued to carry out more.

Although multifunctionality continued to be the strategy favored by merchant houses in Iquitos, the actual performance of the different functions changed over time. Between 1908 and 1949, for example, the percentage of houses devoted to export activities diminished, reaching its lowest point in 1940, the tail end of the most depressed phase. In contrast, the percentage of firms engaged in wholesale-retail commerce increased more than twofold in the same interval (see Table 7.5). In 1949, this kind of trade was mainly based on imported goods and oriented toward supplying Iquitos's growing urban market. It involved hardware and appliance stores, groceries, and general stores selling all kinds of novelties (Sotomayor et al. 1949).

Although many merchant houses were engaged simultaneously in the export and wholesale-retail trades, Table 7.5 suggests that during years in which the export trade was high the wholesale-retail trade was low, and vice-versa. This shift from one activity to the other, which entailed a transfer of capital, seems to have been associated with the degree of vitality and profitability of the export trade. Thus, in 1908 and 1949, when export prices were high, the proportion of houses engaged in exports increased, whereas that of import firms also dedicated to wholesale-retail commerce tended to diminish. During such junctures much of the wholesale-retail trade was left in the hands of smaller firms, which were not involved in the import-export trade and thus were not part of the region's grand commerce. The contrary occurred in 1929 and 1940, when the export economy was either in decline or already depressed, and the wholesale-retail trade became a sort of refuge for the merchant houses of Iquitos. Concomitantly, by the end of the 1915–1962 period, when Loreto's export economy was no longer profitable and all but collapsed, the combi-

Table 7.5   Incidence in the Performance of Functions by the Merchant Houses of Iquitos, 1904–1949

	Incidence in percentage				
Functions	*1904*	*1908*	*1929*	*1940*	*1949*
Import	100.0	100.0	100.0	100.0	100.0
Export	43.1	64.5	39.1	38.5	48.9
Shipping	27.5	35.5	17.4	28.2	12.8
Commerce[a]	15.7	21.0	47.8	66.7	55.3
Industry	—	8.1	26.1	25.6	23.4

SOURCES: Fuentes 1908:29–30; Maúrtua 1911:156; Matrícula 1910; Rodriguez 1928; Guzmán Rivera 1929; Guía 1940; Sotomayor et al. 1949.
NOTE: Wholesale-retail trade.

nation of import trade and wholesale-retail commerce became the merchant elites' major source of profits.

A second important change took place with regard to industrial activities. In 1908 only 8 percent of the merchant houses of Iquitos were engaged in any kind of industrial activity, most of it being in the hands of other agents. During the following decades the proportion of merchant houses carrying out manufacturing activities increased to about 25 percent, and the nature of their industries changed. In 1908 the few houses engaged in manufacturing owned workshops, shipyards, or light industries, such as factories for the production of soda water. After the rubber bust, the merchant houses began a timid process of diversification of their light industrial activities by manufacturing a broader range of consumer goods, such as brooms, ice, bread, hardtacks, noodles, soap, and paving tiles (Guía 1940). In the small-scale economy of Loreto some of these industries had important effects by reducing the need for imports.

But the most important change was that to increase profit margins some of the larger merchant houses began to develop new factories for the primary processing of agricultural and extractive export products. These industries were very much affected by the hazards of the export booms. In the 1920s several merchant houses established ivory nut shelling plants, cotton gins, cotton baling plants, cottonseed paste and oil production mills, steam-powered sawmills, and balata laminating yards. The 1930s saw the appearance of caspi milk washing facilities, as well as barbasco drying and grinding plants, and in the 1940s and 1950s tanneries and rosewood oil distilleries were established.

These industries demanded little technological infrastructure and skilled labor and were scarcely above the handicraft level, as was true of the rest of the industrial sector. Although this was not a true process of industrialization, it introduced an important dimension into the workings of the merchant houses and the urban economy of Iquitos. By the end of the period, Eduardo Watson (1964: 10) even characterized Iquitos as a "factory city." The demise of Loreto's export economy by the early 1960s, together with the disappearance of the traditional merchant houses, put an end to such light industry. From then on, the only industrial activity linked to extractive resources that managed to survive and even thrive was timber.

Traders, Export Booms, and Diversification

Although between 1915 and 1962 merchant houses experienced several changes in the number, membership, and type of functions performed, their relationships with both extractors and producers were based on the *habilitación* system. In the new agroextractive economy large *fundo* owners became the merchant houses' main partners in the rural area. Together they controlled much of the region's economy. However, because each agricultural and extractive activity had specific requirements, merchant houses were forced to adopt different strategies. We will analyze the role of merchant houses in promoting, financing, collecting, processing, and marketing four of the products that gave rise to some of the region's most significant export cycles: cotton, barbasco, rosewood oil, and fine timber.

Cotton Export Cycle

Cotton was one of the first products to be exported during the post–rubber boom era. It had already caught the attention of local authorities in the early 1900s, when it fetched high prices in the international market. Both Germán Stiglich (1904: 222) and Hildebrando Fuentes (1906: 397) asserted that cotton was destined to become the basis "of a new and powerful industry in the region." However, given the high profitability of the rubber trade, it was not until the 1910 rubber crisis that local merchants decided to try their luck with this product. In 1911 samples of local varieties (mostly *Gasipaes raimondii* and *Gasipaes barbadensis*) were sent to London, where they were well received. A year later, C. Hernández and Son imported cottonseeds to distribute among the region's landholders (Anonymous 1938: 44). The turmoil during the first years of the rubber crisis prevented cotton production from immediately taking off. However, by 1919, thanks to the active promotion of cotton cultivation by the chamber of commerce and the increased demand due to World War I, cotton exports reached a high of 2,345 tons (Appendix 15).

Cotton had already been an important commercial crop in the central Huallaga Basin prior to the rubber boom, when spun cotton and cotton cloth were used as currency in local economic transactions. After the rubber crisis, this area, part of the department of San Martín, once again became a major cotton supplier (Rumrrill et al. 1986: 154). However, cotton cultivation extended to the lower Huallaga, in Yurimaguas within the department of Loreto, as well as to the upper Marañon, the Ucayali, and the Napo Rivers. In San Martín cotton was grown in small mestizo, or indigenous, landholdings, whereas in Loreto it was mostly cultivated in large, market-oriented *fundos*. In both departments, however, cotton was marketed through the *habilitación* network controlled by the merchant houses of Iquitos. In the Huallaga Basin these firms outfitted producers directly, either through branch offices established in the larger towns, like Yurimaguas, Tarapoto, Moyobamba, Rioja, and Lamas, or through the designation of buyers in smaller hamlets, like Picota and Bellavista (Maskrey et al. 1991: 116).

In other cases they operated indirectly through the *habilitación* system of local traders. For example, Kahn and Company provided merchandise to at least two such traders who, in the early 1910s, had established cotton gins in Shapaja (Maskrey et al. 1991: 110). Yurimaguas became the most important collecting center in the Huallaga Basin because it was the highest navigable point of the river and the larger traders had established themselves there. They had large warehouses where they stored, burled, and packed the cotton that was brought downriver on balsa rafts by producers and minor traders they outfitted. Cotton bales were transported to Iquitos, where they were handed to the merchants' creditors. Kahn and Company and Israel and Company were among the largest buyers of Huallaga cotton (ibidem: 136).

In the 1920s most of the post–rubber era *fundos* along the Ucayali were dedicated, among other activities, to cotton cultivation (Gómez Perea 1991). Israel and Company was one of the most important cotton outfitters in this area (Ortiz 1974: II, 573). Kahn and Company and Strassberger and Company also had important interests in the area. In contrast with the Huallaga Basin, in this area the merchant houses of Iquitos relied on fluvial fleets to gather the annual cotton production. *Melita*, Israel and Company's largest steamboat, and *Manco Cápac*, which steamed for Delgado and Company, navigated the length of the Ucayali River, calling in *fundo* and town ports to collect cotton from *habilitados* and associated traders.

Most of Ucayali's cotton production was shipped unburled to Iquitos, where it was processed in one of five existing cotton gins (Gómez Perea 1991). Three gins belonged to the above-mentioned large merchant houses. The only cotton gin that existed within the Ucayali area was located in Contamana and belonged to a local trader; he operated as an outfitter of smaller producers and as a provider of burling services for owners of large *fundos* who, though outfitted by the merchant houses of Iquitos, preferred to burl the cotton in situ and then transport it to Iquitos to obtain better prices. In the towns of Requena and Pucallpa, where there were no cotton gins, local traders stored their clients' cotton production in large warehouses. Once a year they transported the cotton stocks to Iquitos to cancel their old debts and obtain new credits in goods from outfitters. Thus, the commercialization of cotton was similar to that of rubber.

About 1925 the exportation of cottonseed oil and paste became profitable, and in both the Huallaga and Ucayali Basins merchant houses started buying cottonseed. By 1928 close to 1,500 tons of cottonseed were exported from Iquitos (Appendix 5). Although never comprising more than 2 percent of the value of Loreto's exports, cottonseed became an important ingredient for the local production of soap (Watson 1964: 35).

As cotton was one of the few agricultural products with commercial value, the Peruvian government imposed several taxes on the cotton trade between 1920 and 1930 (Ballón 1991: II, 32–5, 46–63, 200). Cotton exports diminished throughout the 1920s, but even in 1928 cotton and cottonseeds still represented 30 percent of the value of Loreto's total exports (Appendix 5). By 1939 cotton's share of the export trade had dropped to 18 percent, but in the context of the general economic contraction that the region was suffering contemporary observers still asserted that cotton was the one product that "contributes to sustain Loreto's anemic economy" (Coriat 1943: 213). This was no longer true by 1948, when cotton only accounted for 2 percent of the value of the region's exports.

In Loreto cotton production never recovered. Cotton exported through Iquitos from the late 1950s onward was mainly produced in San Martín. Thus, whereas in 1962 San Martín produced 1,667 tons, Loreto produced a mere thirty-three tons (Watson 1964: 33). Furthermore, cotton produced in San Martín from the 1950s onward was no longer financed by the merchant houses of Iquitos but by Lima-based firms such as Anderson, Clayton, and Company, Somerecs, and Bronsky.

Barbasco Export Cycle

In contrast to its marginal role as a cotton producer and exporter, Loreto became one of the world's largest exporters of barbasco. Barbasco is a generic Spanish term for a wide variety of plants of the genera *Verbascum* that were used as fish poison since ancient times in Europe (Wille et al. 1939: 12). In South America there are also a variety of plants belonging to different families that contain similar poisons. In 1917, W.J. Dennis, a U.S. trader residing in Peru, saw the commercial possibilities of barbasco, also known as *cube*, and its active principle, rotenone. In 1927 he requested and was granted a North American patent for a compound "of his invention" based on ground barbasco roots that could be used as vermifuge and insecticide and, more particularly, as a cattle tick killer (ibidem: 106–8; Killip and Smyth 1930: 75).

In 1929 a scientific expedition was organized by the Smithsonian Institution and the New York Botanical Garden to gather information on the geographical distribution of barbasco in both Peru and Brazil. Members of the expedition concluded that *Lonchocarpus nicou* was the most powerful of the barbasco plants as well as the most widely cultivated, especially along the upper Amazon River in the environs of Iquitos (Killip and Smyth: 75–9). This species was also attractive because it contained eight times as much rotenone as did derris, a similar plant cultivated in Southeast Asia. From then on there was a frenzy to develop the commercial potential of barbasco.

Kahn and Company was quick to react to international demand, and even though by 1929 it was deeply involved in the cotton export trade, only a few years later it became renowned as an important "dealer in *cube* roots" (Wille et al. 1939: 14–5). Promoted initially by Kahn and Company and from 1934 onward by Loreto's chamber of commerce, the cultivation of barbasco increased spectacularly, particularly in the lower Huallaga and upper Marañon Rivers, but also along the Amazon and the Ucayali (Higbee 1949: 6; Ortiz 1974: II, 649). Barbasco had a broad range of applications. It was used as insecticide in horticulture, as sheep and cattle tick killer, as mosquito killer in tropical areas, and even for the production of antifouling ship paints during World War II. As a result, barbasco demand increased and Loreto's exports swelled from little more than 1 ton in 1931 to 245 tons in 1934 and to 1,105 tons in 1939 (Appendix 20).

To ensure that barbasco plants would not be smuggled out of the country and reproduced abroad, as had happened with hevea, in 1933 the government forbade the exit of fresh barbasco roots and stalks. In addition, it decreed that only dry barbasco roots with up to 10 percent humidity could be exported (Wille et al. 1939: 116–7). From then on, barbasco roots were dried and exported either whole or chopped.

As Watson (1964: 10) has pointed out, barbasco was produced and marketed through the traditional *habilitación* network. In the Huallaga area barbasco was either cultivated in *fundos* on the basis of the *habilitado* indigenous workforce or by independent mestizo and indigenous peasants. The old colonial mission towns of the Huallaga Basin—Santa Cruz, Cahuapanas, Jeberos, and Lagunas—became important centers of barbasco production and places of residence for the larger *fundo* owners (Higbee 1949: 6). Within two hours' walk around the town of Lagunas, all available land was devoted to barbasco cultivation (Anonymous 1944c: 733–8). With a total of 1,000 hectares in barbasco and an average production of 50 *quintales* of dried roots per hectare, Lagunas was hailed as the "barbasco capital of the world" (ibidem). Through the *habilitación* system, the Huallaga *patrones* engaged the local Cocamilla, Jebero, and Chayahuita peoples to work the barbasco plantations, which in a few cases were as large as 100 hectares (Stocks 1981: 95; Dradi 1987: 40). There were also a large number of smaller autonomous producers who cultivated barbasco in plots of a dozen or so hectares (Maskrey et al. 1991: 130).

The merchant houses of Iquitos provided credit in goods to the Huallaga *fundo* owners, as well as to a large number of agent-buyers and small traders, who in turn outfitted the mestizo and indigenous peasants. In the early 1940s Kahn and Company had several agents located in small towns along the Huallaga River. They were in charge of providing credit and buying barbasco for the firm (Rumrrill et al. 1986: 166). One of the company's steamboats made regular trips to Yurimaguas to collect the barbasco loads remitted by these agents, as well as those remitted by the company's clients (ibidem). The existence of such an extensive network of middlemen affected small producers, who were sometimes paid as much as 250 percent less per kilogram of barbasco than was paid in Iquitos (Maskrey et al. 1991: 130).

Given that barbasco roots become harvestable three to five years after being planted, the granting of credit for the cultivation of barbasco, as well as the activity of growing it, entailed important risks for outfitter-exporters and producers. However, despite these risks as well as volatile market prices, barbasco rapidly displaced other products as the region's main export. Thus, whereas in 1939 cotton still represented an important 18 percent of the value of the region's exports, barbasco accounted for 35 percent (Appendix 6). With the outbreak of World War II and the Japanese occupation of derris-producing Southeast Asia, the demand for Peruvian barbasco soared. The United States and Peru signed a bilateral commercial accord whereby Peru agreed to sell all production to the United States, whereas the latter agreed to pay maximum international prices (Sotomayor et al. 1949: 8). Peru further secured the barbasco export trade through the regulation of freight fares for the product (Ballón 1991: II, 306).

The renewed demand for barbasco during the 1940s, together with other factors discussed below, attracted a new generation of merchant houses: Compañía Importadora Exportadora, Compañía Industrial de Loreto, and Compañía Comercial Suramérica S.A. (Guía 1940; Sotomayor et al. 1949). The most important of these was Suramérica, established in Iquitos in 1943. The company acted as agent for Hecht, Levis, and Kahn of London, a former rubber-buying company that also had branch offices in Hamburg, Tangier, and New York (Lequerica 1991; Spence 1908: 7). The Iquitos branch specialized in selling hardware and exporting regional products. It had a Peruvian board of directors, which between 1943 and 1962 was headed by Luis Arana Zumaeta, the son of rubber baron Julio C. Arana. In later years, the board included important national entrepreneurs (Rodríguez Ramírez 1968: 65). The managerial abilities of Luis Arana, who had obtained a degree in engineering in the United States, were crucial to the rapid expansion of the company and its involvement in the barbasco export business (Rumrrill et al. 1986: 166).

In contrast with more traditional merchant houses, Suramérica did not operate through the *habilitación* system (Lequerica 1991). Instead, at a time when there were no banks in the region that offered credit for the promotion of agricultural activities, Suramérica became the first merchant house to grant credit in cash for the cultivation of barbasco. In addition, it bought barbasco from other producers, either directly when they brought their production to Iquitos, or through local agent-buyers, as in the case of the town of Lagunas. On occasion it also bought barbasco from large and small river traders. Again, in contrast with firms such as Kahn and Company, transactions were cash.

The barbasco export trade was so profitable that even firms specializing in lumber exporting, like the Astoria Importing and Manufacturing Company, ventured into the market (Lequerica 1991). By 1946 the volume of barbasco exports peaked at almost 5,500 tons (Appendix 20). However, with the end of World War II and the recovery of derris-producing Southeast Asia, the United States ended its agreement with Peru, and barbasco prices experienced a marked fall (Sotomayor et al. 1949: 8). Barbasco exports fell to slightly more than 1,500 tons in 1948; however, barbasco still represented 41 percent of the value of Loreto's exports (Appendix 7).

About this time, barbasco began to be ground in order to cut freight costs and maintain profit margins. For this purpose several merchant houses, among them Astoria and its subsidiary, the Paranapura Cube Export Company, established barbasco mills in Iquitos. The latter company had two large mills imported from the United States for the production of chopped and pulverized barbasco, its own power plant, water reservoirs, and a bagging plant (Treceño 1991: 10). It also operated a laboratory to analyze the rotenone content of barbasco lots it purchased and to ensure that the mix of exported barbasco contained the standard content of rotenone of no less than 5 percent.

Contrasted to the prior case of Peruvian exports, where the main market was Europe, particularly Great Britain, France, and Germany, Peru's barbasco exports were linked from the beginning to the U.S. market. During the 1930s no less than 50 percent of barbasco exports was destined for the United States; during World War II it absorbed Peru's entire barbasco production (Wille et al. 1939: 112). Even after the bilateral agreement, the United States bought 96 percent of Peru's barbasco exports; Peru was its main supplier of barbasco (Sotomayor et al. 1949: 110; Higbee 1949: 4).

In the late 1930s and much of the 1940s barbasco production and exports were so profitable for producers, traders, and the local government that some thought the rubber-boom prosperity had returned (Sotomayor et al. 1949: 8). However, from 1949 through the 1950s, with some ups and downs, prices tended to decline. By the end of the 1950s large-scale production of DDT, patented in Switzerland in 1941, had displaced barbasco almost entirely from the market (Anonymous 1945: 287). In 1959, in only six months, barbasco prices collapsed from US$0.14 to US$0.03 per kilogram (Rumrrill et al. 1986: 166). Though barbasco continued to be produced and exported during the following decades, from 1962 on it never regained a significant share of regional exports (see Appendixes 9–13).

Rosewood Oil Export Cycle

Whereas barbasco was declining as an export product, the age of rosewood oil was just setting in. Cut into pieces, then ground and distilled, timber from rosewood trees (*Aniba rosaeodora*) produces an oily essence that was used as a fixer in the perfume industry (Watson 1964: 16). Samuel Roggeroni, the owner of Fundo Pucabarranca on the Napo River, was the first to send samples of rosewood to Europe in 1941 (Treceño 1992: 11). But it was not until the 1950s that it began to be commercially exploited in Peru and Brazil, the two countries that attained a virtual monopoly over rosewood oil production and trade (Watson 1964: 77). Rosewood extraction was located north of the Marañon-Amazon axis, along the Tigre, Napo, and Putumayo Rivers, where the tree was more abundant. However, rosewood was also extracted south of that axis, along sections of the Ucayali and Yavari Rivers.

Rosewood oil production gave rise to one of the last important export booms in Loreto. By then, most of the pre–rubber era merchant houses had disappeared; the processing and export of rosewood oil was mostly in the hands of companies established in Loreto since the early 1940s. Of the four rosewood oil distilleries working in Iquitos by 1962, none belonged to traditional trading firms (DNEC 1964b). Compañía Peruana Astoria, the former Astoria Importing and Manufacturing Company, a timber-exporting U.S. firm that opened shop in the late 1920s, owned one of them. The other three belonged to companies established in Loreto after 1940: Compañía Industrial de Loreto, Amazon Trading Company (AMTRA), and Compañía Loretana de Oleos Esenciales, a latecomer incorporated to profit from the rosewood oil boom. These were the largest rosewood factories in the region, employing an average of forty workers each (ibidem).

However, there were other distilleries in Loreto. Given that a kilogram of oil required processing an average of 125 kilograms of wood (Watson 1964: 16), and given the region's high freight costs, some large merchant houses preferred to establish factories at the extractive fronts themselves. Israel and Company, one of the few surviving traditional merchant houses, set up a remote distillery along the Putumayo River (DNEC 1964b). Menezes and Company, a firm established in Loreto in the 1930s, operated three factories along the Putumayo, Yavari, and Napo Rivers, and Destilería Amazónica S.A. had a distillery on the Tamaya River in the middle Ucayali (ibidem). These riverine factories were smaller, employing an average of sixteen workers each. In addition, Watson (1964: 16) mentions the existence of a distillery mounted on a tugboat, which was hauled to different extraction sites to process rosewood in situ.

Little is known about the functioning of the large foreign companies dedicated to the processing and exporting of rosewood oil, such as Astoria or AMTRA. However, it is probable that they obtained much of the raw material by granting credit to other merchant houses more knowledgeable of the region's trading habits. As we shall see, this was the modus operandi of Astoria to obtain fine timber for its sawmill. It was also that of AMTRA for obtaining caspi milk for its processing plant (Lequerica 1991). In both cases, river-wise trading firms acted as outfitters of *fundo* owners, small traders, and independent extractors on their behalf. However, foreign firms occasionally dealt directly with some large extractors, such as Alfonso Cárdenas Rengifo (see Box 13). Cárdenas owned Negro Urco, one of the largest *fundos* located on the Napo River, and operated a rosewood oil distillery on the Algodon River, a tributary of the Putumayo. He started working with Suramérica but later switched to AMTRA, selling all his rosewood oil production to the latter company.

Other large firms that did not own distilleries in Iquitos, such as Menezes and Company, combined different strategies to obtain as much of the precious rosewood oil as possible. On the one hand, the company outfitted large *fundo* owners who had their own distilleries to obtain already processed rosewood oil. This was the case of Oscar Peñafiel, owner of Monterrico, another large *fundo* on the Napo River (see Box 11). Peñafiel was outfitted by Menezes and Company. Each month the firm sent one of its boats to collect the *fundo*'s production, which at the height of the rosewood export boom amounted to fifteen to twenty barrels of forty-two gallons each (Herrera 1991). On the other hand, the company outfitted local *fundo* owners and indigenous extractors to obtain rosewood logs for its Yavari and Putumayo distilleries. Finally, in 1957 the firm bought Pucabarranca, the important *fundo* in a rich rosewood-producing area along the Napo River, which already had several small distilleries and a large number of *habilitado* indigenous peons (Abensur 1991).

Contrasted to the other export cycles that of rosewood oil was very brief. In 1952, Loreto's rosewood oil exports amounted to a mere thirteen tons. In only three years of intense exploitation that increased more than tenfold, accounting for 26 percent of the value of the region's export trade (Appendixes 22, 8). To avoid the depletion of rosewood trees, the government in 1955 established a minimum diameter, under which trees could not be felled (Anonymous 1955). In 1958 rosewood oil exports peaked at 262 tons, but prices had gone down from US$7.10 per kilogram in 1955 to US$3.40 (Watson 1964: 17). Prices recovered briefly in 1962, when the United States absorbed 73 percent of Loreto's rosewood oil exports and France 13 percent (ibidem). Such price fluctuations were partly due to overproduction, partly to the adulteration of the product once rosewood trees became scarce in the environs of the larger rivers. By the mid-1960s a chemical substitute for rosewood oil was discovered, causing a price collapse. By 1967 exports had dwindled to fifty-five tons, and in 1972 many of the merchant houses of Iquitos still could not sell their old stocks of rosewood oil (Appendix 22; Banco de Crédito 1972: 150).

Though rosewood oil continued to be exported in small quantities as late as 1983, it never recovered its past importance.

Fine Timber Export Cycle

Loreto's first timber exports took place in 1912, when the first samples of fine hardwoods were sent to New York (Brown 1912: 254; Huckin 1913: 262). Trade in fine timber was originally in the hands of small *fundo* sawmills and was mostly based in the extraction of mahogany (*Swietenia macrophylla*) and cedar (*Cedrela odorata*). The first entrepreneur to venture into this trade was Otoniel Vela, the son of a Spanish immigrant; since at least 1890 he owned a *fundo* and sawmill on the left bank of the Amazon River, near the port of Nauta, known as Puritania (Navarro Cauper 1988b: 19). In 1902 Puritania mainly produced construction lumber and wooden crates for rubber (Mavila 1902: 556). In 1914, however, Vela incorporated the Puritania Timber Company, which was to be devoted to the processing and exporting of fine timber (Huckin 1914: 287). Vela worked with his own capital and did not depend on merchant houses for credit or fluvial transport (Rojas Vela 1991). His first attempts to export cedar lumber were not very profitable because of low market prices and high transportation costs to Iquitos (Huckin 1914: 28). However, as a result of the increasing demand for fine timber during the 1920s (Appendix 16), Vela's sawmill and export firm became very profitable until his death in 1934.

The case of Paraíso, a smaller lumber-producing *fundo*, is quite different from that of Puritania in its relation to the merchant houses of Iquitos. Located downriver from Puritania, Paraíso was founded during the rubber boom. In the early 1910s the *fundo* began producing lumber for the local market. It was not until the 1920s, however, that the *fundo*, under a new owner, Francisco Riera, began to produce fine timber for the national and international markets. Riera was not as economically powerful as Otoniel Vela. As his sawmill required 3,000 logs per year to work at maximum capacity, he resorted to Luis F. Morey and Sons for credit. He worked with that firm for ten years, until it reduced its activities in the aftermath of the 1929 world economic crisis. Riera then worked with Israel and Company. Both merchant houses provided Riera with timber they obtained from *fundo* owners and other extractors they had outfitted. Under this arrangement, Riera sold his sawing services to these export firms in exchange for payments in cash and merchandise for his *fundo*'s store. The lumber was collected in Paraíso's port by Morey's or Israel's boats and shipped to Lima via the Panama Canal (Riera Vásquez 1991).

Sometime in the early 1930s Riera founded the Compañía Maderera Loretana. In 1935 this company imported, free from taxes, new equipment for Paraíso's sawmill (Ballón 1994: II, 244). Three years later Riera ended his relationship with Israel and Company and started working with Banco Popular, which had opened a branch in Iquitos that same year (Riera Vásquez 1991). From then on he began to market Paraíso's production directly through his company, avoiding the mediation of the merchant houses in Iquitos. By then Paraíso was producing about 1 million board feet per year (Anonymous 1938: 165). Most of the production was shipped to Lima through the Peruvian Steamship Company. Riera's firm continued to be active in the timber business until the 1950s, when he died.

Until 1918 local sawmill owners controlled Loreto's fine timber export trade. In that year, however, Peruvian merchant Cecilio Hernández associated with the Boston-based Aguna Mahogany and Timber Company to form Nanay Mills (Aguna) Ltd. (Rodríguez 1928: 113). The new company established premises close to Iquitos, on the confluence of the Nanay and Amazon Rivers. Despite rudimentary conditions for extraction and sawing, the company managed to export almost 2 million board feet of fine lumber between 1926 and 1928 (Rodríguez 1928: 114). In 1929 the company was taken over by another U.S.-based firm, Astoria Importing and Manufacturing Company, which also operated in Brazil, Mexico, and Belize (Zegarra 1945: 163). Shortly thereafter, Astoria became the region's largest lumber producer and exporter.

Astoria obtained timber for its sawmill through the direct granting of credit to *fundo* owners and independent contractors or through the mediation of some of the larger merchant houses of Iquitos (Rumrrill et al. 1986: 163). An example of the first type of relationship is that of Berlín, a large *fundo* established around 1920 on the Ucayali River. The owner of this *fundo* was outfitted by Astoria, as well as by other Iquitos-based sawmill owners such as Bartens or López, to extract cedar and mahogany from the Roaboya, Pisqui, and Sharamasho Basins (Gómez Perea 1991). In this case, credits received from the company were always in cash and amounted to 100,000 *soles*. Berlín's owner transported the *fundo's* timber production to Astoria's sawmill, where its volume was determined and accounts settled.

The second type of relationship is illustrated by Israel and Company and Kahn and Company (Rumrrill et al. 1986: 163). Astoria granted credit to those large merchant houses, which in turn outfitted timber extractors with imported merchandise and sometimes small amounts of cash. Credit in merchandise was canceled in timber, which these firms collected and transported to Astoria's mill. Although in all of these instances the merchant houses of Iquitos had a subordinate role in financial terms, they retained a certain amount of power, insofar as the timber-extraction companies depended on their network of clients for raw material. When in 1937 Congress approved the regulation for timber-extraction permits (Ballón 1991: II, 258), Astoria was quick to request six concessions along the Ucayali River. These were granted that same year, with a total area of 105,254 hectares (Padrón 1939). This move was aimed at eliminating the brokerage of the traditional merchant houses. From then on Astoria furnished its sawmill with timber extracted from its concessions through the granting of credit in cash to independent contractors.

Unlike other contemporaneous export cycles, that of fine timber was much longer and yet never attained a dominant position within the region's export economy. Thus, even in 1948, when fine timber exports came to represent an all-time high of 13 percent of the value of Loreto's exports, they still occupied the third position behind barbasco (41 percent) and caspi milk (31 percent). What distinguishes the fine timber export boom is that the end was not determined by an abrupt fall in demand or a drop in prices but by the depletion of resources.

This was already evident in the early 1940s, when several contemporary observers warned that Loreto's stock of accessible cedar and mahogany would soon be exhausted (Delboy 1952: 16; Villarejo 1988: 134). By that time, fine timber extraction was carried out only in the vicinity of large rivers, which constituted the only cheap way to transport the felled logs. As a solution to the increasing scarcity of fine hardwoods, some recommended the initiation of massive reforestation programs (Sotomayor et al. 1940: 84; Delboy 1952: 16). With a few exceptions, such as Astoria, which in 1941 had a plantation of several thousand mahogany trees (Anonymous 1941: 809), and Compañía Maderera Loretana S.A., which had large mahogany plantations along the Ucayali River (Delboy 1938: 220), most companies failed to heed the warnings. The government was also aware of the dangers of resource depletion. In 1937 it had established in Iquitos the Intendencia Forestal del Oriente, which in 1949 and again in 1956 attempted to regulate the extraction of hardwoods by setting the minimum diameter of exploitable trees (Mensaje 1939; Ballón 1994: II, 547). Although cedar and mahogany were becoming scarcer, timber companies not only continued felling as many logs as possible but exploited trees of increasingly smaller diameters (Ortiz 1986: 196).

Export figures show that the production of hardwoods was extremely erratic, depending on such factors as the discovery of unexploited, accessible areas and the height of annual river flood tides (Appendix 16). This explains why the fine timber export cycle does not have a "peak" in terms of volume exported but rather several points of high production. It also explains why during 1939–1940 and again during 1948–1949 one year of very low timber exports was followed by one year of spectacular increase in volume. However, after 1949, when the export of hardwoods reached another peak, the timber trade entered a period of gradual but irreversible decline. By 1960 the volume of fine timber exports had dropped to almost the same level as that of 1923, when the fine timber cycle was taking off. If Loreto's timber industry did not collapse altogether, it was mainly because since 1943 it gradually reoriented its activities toward the fulfillment of the domestic market's demand for other hardwoods and softwoods. As we shall see, this gave rise to a completely different timber-extraction boom, which experienced a formidable boost during the early 1960s when new companies, mainly dedicated to the extraction and processing of softwoods, started business in Iquitos.

$$* \quad * \quad *$$

The protracted rubber crisis brought forth important changes in the composition of Loreto's grand commerce. By 1929 all old merchant houses that had acted as agents for European firms had disappeared. Eighty percent of the merchant houses were new, having opened shop after the rubber bust. Among them were some important companies that acted as agents for U.S. firms and were organized along more modern lines. However, despite these changes the leadership of the region's grand commerce remained in the hands of a few powerful merchant houses established during the rubber boom. Among them were the larger Peruvian firms. For most of the period, they controlled the chamber of commerce and handled a large portion of the region's financial services and external commerce.

The mode of operation for merchant houses in Iquitos was similar to that of the rubber era. The *habilitación* system continued to rule the region's economic life. The only change in the *habilitación* network was that *fundo* owners replaced rubber *patrones* as the merchant houses' major partners in rural areas. As in the past, the new merchant houses supplied credit in goods to *fundo* owners and to a variety of local merchants, fluvial traders, and agent-buyers. In exchange, they received commercially valuable extractive and agricultural products. In turn, *fundo* owners outfitted mestizo and indigenous peons as well as a range of smaller independent producers and extractors. All these people remained in a state of indebtedness. The socioeconomic hierarchy, reinforced by the *habilitación* network, thus remained basically unchanged: A minuscule commercial elite dominated the region's economy, a mass of rural laborers occupied the bottom of the ladder, and a small, landed elite composed of large *fundo* owners acted as brokers.

During this period the merchant houses of Iquitos proved to be highly flexible vis-à-vis the changing demands of the international market. An expression of this adaptability was their increasing involvement in industrial activities. However, their manufacturing activities never rose above the level of light industries, namely, the primary processing of agroextractive export products, which required little investment in technology and labor. The merchant houses depended on the input of commercial capital; their profits were not reinvested in the industrial sector but were rechanneled into commercial activity. Moreover, the industrial activities of the merchant houses were totally subordinated to the needs of the export commerce and were thus unstable. Restricted by their owners to the basic processing of raw materials, these fragile industries did not provide the conditions for a radical transformation of the way trading firms, or the region's economy, functioned.

Even new commercial firms possessing modern capitalist structures were unable to escape involvement with the *habilitación* system. Both Astoria in the 1930s and Suramérica in the 1940s attempted, and failed, to establish more modern and efficient relations with their clients and purveyors by demanding that all transactions be made in cash. Both firms were eventually forced to enter, albeit indirectly, into *habilitado* relationships. Astoria did so by granting credit to the large, rubber era merchant houses; Suramérica by working in association with various traditional traders and agent-buyers, who in turn outfitted extractors and producers with goods.

Their exclusive access to the international market, and their virtual monopoly over fluvial navigation, wholesale commerce, and credit, placed the merchant houses of Iquitos in a unique position. They were the main pillars of the region's economy as well as its principal beneficiaries. However, as we shall see, the conditions that granted them such a privileged position began to change in the early 1940s. The outbreak of World War II brought new economic opportunities. War with Ecuador in 1941 over disputed Amazon territories forced the government to pay renewed attention to Loreto. Finally, the inauguration of the Lima-Pucallpa Road in 1943 opened a new outlet for the region's production. But these changes constituted a mixed blessing for Loreto's grand commerce. Whereas on the one hand the merchant houses of Iquitos prospered to an extent not seen since the rubber boom years, on the other hand their various monopolies started breaking down, forcing them out of business one by one.

8

"Purveyors of All Sorts of Regional Products": The Workings of the *Fundo/Patrón* System

In the wake of the rubber bust, Loreto's rural landscape experienced important transformations. New patterns of population distribution, types of economic units, and dominant productive activities emerged. These changes led to the formation of a new economic system based on *fundos*, or landholdings, centered around a *patrón* and devoted to agroextractive activities. In this chapter we analyze Loreto's agroextractive export economy in the post–rubber bust era from the perspective of rural production and the *fundo/patrón* system. We focus our discussion on three aspects: (1) transformations in the rural landscape and characteristics of the new land tenure structure; (2) development of new forms of control and retention of rural workers; and (3) organization of the riverine *fundos* that proliferated during this period.

The most important effects of the rubber boom on rural Loreto were the shift from agriculture to extraction, the massive migration of people from west to east, and the move from riverine to interfluvial areas. After the rubber bust, these trends reversed. There was a general move from the east to the west and from the interfluvial to the riverine areas. There was also a resurgence in agricultural activities to compensate for the decrease in the import of foodstuffs caused by the economic crisis. Together with the demand for new tropical products in the international market, these factors encouraged the formation of a new kind of productive unit combining the features of the old agricultural *fundos* with those of the rubber posts. Integrating agriculture with forest resource extraction primarily for commercial purposes, but also for subsistence purposes, the new *fundos* became the dominant economic units of the region's riverine areas. Closely associated with the merchant houses of Iquitos, which financed their operations, *fundo* owners replaced rubber *patrones* as the new rural elite.

We contend that the formation of these new economic units was not a uniform process. In fact, our historical analysis of nine *fundos* reveals at least four different ways in which they came into being. Similarly, our analysis of the evolution of land grants and sales confirms our suspicion that interest in acquiring land was not uniform throughout this period. When export trade expanded, requests for land and purchases of land increased; when external commerce contracted, interest in land decreased significantly. The new land-tenure structure that emerged was not, as has been assumed, based on the consolidation of vast tracts. Our analysis of Loreto's land registries shows that almost 80 percent of the *fundos*, despite the existence of some very large, mostly unexploited concessions, were less than 50 hectares. These small to medium-sized units provided most of the region's agroextractive production.

After the 1914 rubber bust played out, the use of force to recruit and retain labor diminished, and *correrías*, the slave-raids, stopped being a common practice. In our opinion, this was partly due to the abandonment of the most remote fronts, where the majority of tribal Indians lived. But it was mostly due to the emergence of a mixed-blood social stratum that became a new source of "civilized," disciplined workers, thereby mitigating the problem of labor scarcity. However, *habilitación* continued to be the basis of the region's economy, so long as the conditions that gave rise to this system—namely, the lack of a free labor market—persisted.

In fact, we argue that it was during this period that the *habilitación* system acquired its classic form. Through a combination of old and new economic, political, and ideological forms of coercion, *fundo patrones* managed to retain and even increase their labor forces. In the past, we saw that monopoly over trade in manufactured goods provided rubber *patrones* a powerful instrument to persuade indigenous peoples to work for them. During the 1915–1962 period the *patrones'* monopoly over land became yet another important economic hold over the workforce. White and mestizo *patrones* occupied most of the nonfloodable terraces along navigable rivers, displacing indigenous inhabitants or simply filling the void left by the removal of indigenous peoples from those lands during the rubber era. Given the fact that trade by then was confined to larger navigable rivers, indigenous peoples who had become highly dependent on manufactured goods were forced to work for the owners of the new riverine *fundos*. In addition, control over the appointment of local authorities provided *fundo* patrones with a political hold over their peons.

However, if the system persisted unchallenged for nearly a half-century, it was because of two important ideological holds. First, the establishment of *compadrazgo* and *padrinazgo* ties—ritual links of coparenthood and godparenthood—between *fundo* owners and their peons disguised the exploitative character of their relationship. Second, the *patrones'* adoption of cultural traits characteristic of traditional indigenous leaders legitimized their authority. The combination of these different holds on the population were far more effective, in our opinion, than was the past indiscriminate physical violence in more remote rubber fronts. This effectiveness accounts for the almost total absence of overt violent resistance on the part of *fundo* peons during this period.

We close our discussion of the regional rural economy with an analysis of the new *fundos'* spatial and economic organizations. Despite the different ways in which they came into existence, agroextractive *fundos* showed remarkable uniformity in organization and the way they operated, differing only with respect to location and scale of operation. In our opinion, *fundos* cannot be defined solely as territorial units or as aggregates of *habilitado* peons. *Fundos* were more than the legal area they possessed, more than the group of *habilitado* peons living within the legal boundaries. This is because *fundo* owners exploited not only their riverine lands but also adjacent (generally vacant) interior areas, neighboring areas occupied and exploited by indigenous or mestizo settlements, and even remote, sparsely settled extractive fronts. In addition, to carry out productive activities they relied not only on *fundo* peons but also on temporary *habilitado* laborers from adjacent villages as well as small independent extractors and even specialized wage laborers.

Our conclusion is that *fundos* acted as economic constellations with very fluid physical and social boundaries centered on a *patrón* and devoted to a range of agroextractive, subsistence, and commercial activities. Through their ramifying economic and social ties, large *fundos* contributed to the internal integration of the rural areas. In association with the trading elite, the new landed elite kept the region's rural areas closely linked to the principal urban centers and to the international market. As we shall see, this interdependence proved fatal; changes affecting one sphere in the partnership had immediate effects on the other. When the prevalent socioeconomic and sociopolitical conditions began to change, beginning in the 1940s, the system started falling apart.

Changes in the Rural Landscape

During the rubber era the region's rural space was dominated by three types of economic unit: castilloa rubber posts established on tributaries and headwaters; hevea rubber *fundos* located on larger rivers; and small agricultural *fundos* mainly on Loreto's western fringe. Castilloa rubber extractors moved between their centers of operation—*fundos* dedicated to small agricultural production run by a wife or concubine and temporary camps along the constantly expanding rubber fronts. Hevea *fundos* combined rubber extraction with subsistence agriculture carried out by *patrones* and peons. *Fundos* dedicated to commercial agriculture and cattle-raising provided rubber *patrones*, fluvial merchants, and shipowners with foodstuffs (plantains, beans, maize, manioc, manioc flour, and salted fish and meat), *aguardiente*, and firewood. Agricultural *fundos* were adapted to the needs of the rubber economy; thus their production was consumed either in situ or distributed through local markets. The predominance of one or other type of economic unit varied according to river basin. This becomes apparent by comparing the situation in the Huallaga-Marañon, Napo, Ucayali, and Amazon-Yavari Basins.

In his 1902 inspection trip along the lower Huallaga and upper Marañon, Subprefect César Derteano (1903: 601–10) reported the existence of twenty-nine *fundos* and posts, describing the activities of twenty-one. Nineteen of those were dedicated to agropastoral activities: More than half had sugarcane as its main crop and produced molasses cakes, sugar, and, particularly, *aguardiente*, an important item for outfitting peons. The rest combined the production of foodstuffs for the local market with a second mercantile activity, such as cattle-raising, production of firewood for passing steamboats, and brick manufacturing. All of these *fundos* functioned on the basis of a *habilitado* workforce (generally, catechized Indians). Although on average they employed fifteen peons, the size of each workforce varied and could range from three to seventy-seven peons.

On the Napo River, the situation was mixed. In 1906, for half of the thirty-three existing *fundos* and posts (excluding those abandoned or belonging to the state), rubber extraction (castilloa or weak hevea) was the main activity. This was combined with agriculture, cattle-raising, the production of manioc flour, or the distillation of *aguardiente* (Fuentes 1908: 169). The other half combined agricultural activities with cattle-raising, the breeding of domestic fowl, or the production of salted fish for the local market.

Information for the Ucayali River is less detailed. In 1904 Germán Stiglich (1904: 290–326) provided information on the activities of nineteen *fundos* along the Ucayali River. Half were mainly devoted to agropastoral activities, whereas the rest were hevea producers. In addition, Subprefect Darío Urmeneta (1905: 71) reported the existence along the Ucayali of fifty-one sugarcane mills for the production of *aguardiente* distributed in both small and large landholdings. Thus, in the Ucayali Basin there was a combination of hevea estates and agricultural *fundos*, the latter being dedicated mostly to the production of *aguardiente*, salted fish, and manioc flour for the local market and the Yavari, Yurua, and Purus peripheral rubber fronts.

In contrast, the Amazon River (that is, from Iquitos downriver) and the Yavari River were clearly dominated by hevea-producing *fundos*. Hildebrando Fuentes (1908: 81–3, 147–8) reported the existence of ninety-three hevea estates in the Amazon, with a total of 1,960 rubber trails, and of fifty-five in the Yavari, with a total of 1,368 trails. The size of these *fundos* varied from two to 179 trails. All combined rubber-tapping with some kind of subsistence agriculture. However, Fuentes underscored the fact that in the lower Amazon agricultural and cattle-raising activities were minimal and that in the Yavari they were virtually nonexistent, for in both areas most of the riverine lands flooded periodically. The same can be said of the peripheral rubber fronts, such as those in the Tigre, Pastaza, Yurua, and Purus Rivers, where there were no agricultural *fundos* and itinerant castilloa-rubber posts predominated.

The region's larger *fundos*, whether rubber-producing or agricultural, were few and mostly owned by foreigners or Peruvians from outside the region (Fuentes 1906: 269). Some of them had fine houses, and many owners enjoyed the comforts of urban life. In addition, smaller landholdings (*chacras*) scattered along the riverbanks were predominantly devoted to subsistence production. However, they were not numerous, as most of the rural population had abandoned agricultural activities and were engaged in rubber extraction in the interfluvial areas.

After the 1914 rubber crisis, previous settlement patterns reversed. Peripheral fronts were abandoned and people tended to move back west and to settle once again along the larger rivers. Given that larger rivers constituted the region's only means of communication and transport, riverine lands became the most sought-after. In addition, there was a resurgence of agriculture both to supply the depressed local market, which could not afford the high prices of imported foodstuffs as in previous times, and to respond to new demands in the international market. In time this commercial agriculture was combined with new extractive activities. This combination of commercial agriculture and forest extraction, for both the regional and international markets, bestowed on the *fundo* economy of the post–rubber bust period its particular identity.

In general terms the new agroextractive *fundos*, sometimes known as *haciendas*, developed as a result of four major processes: (1) the conversion of old rubber *fundos* and posts (see Box 8.1); (2) the transformation of traditional agricultural *fundos* (see Box 8.2); (3) the establishment of new *fundos* by rubber *patrones* who, after the crisis, managed to retain their peons (see Box 8.3); and (4) the opening of *fundos* by a new generation of *patrones* that had not been engaged in rubber extraction and was able to co-opt the population of old mission towns and independent indigenous settlements (see Box 8.4 and Map 8.1).

Box 8.1   Fundos Monterrico, Yanayacu, and Panguana

The process of conversion of old rubber *fundos* and posts is well illustrated by the examples of Monterrico, Yanayacu, and Panguana. Monterrico, located on the upper Napo River, was founded in the late nineteenth century as the rubber post Angoteros by Ecuadorian Daniel Peñafiel (Herrera 1991). Its workforce was composed of *habilitado* Quichua-speaking Naporuna peons brought from Ecuador. In 1904 Angoteros was mainly dedicated to the collection of castilloa rubber, but its owner also carried out some agricultural activities and produced manioc flour (Fuentes 1908: 169).

D. Peñafiel survived the rubber crisis but died sometime thereafter. Following his death the administration of the *fundo* was taken over by his son, Oscar Peñafiel, who changed the *fundo*'s name to Monterrico and converted it to adapt to the new demands of the international market. In 1928 he founded a second *fundo* on the Napo River, San Martín (Padrón 1939), and sometime later he founded Villa Luisa (Sotomayor et al. 1949: 51).

Under Peñafiel's administration these three *fundos* were organized as commercial enterprises, producing foodstuffs, raising cattle, and becoming involved in almost all of the region's export booms. In the 1930s and 1940s Peñafiel's peons were sent to the Curaray River for extended periods to extract caspi milk (Mercier 1979: 305). In the 1950s he began to extract rosewood and produce essence in his own distillery in Monterrico (ibidem; San Román 1974: I, 67). He also operated a small sawmill. As a result, Peñafiel became one of the most powerful *patrones* on the Napo River. He was also abusive and feared, and when inspecting the *fundo*'s operations he was carried in a litter by his men (Mercier 1979: 307).

(continues)

Box 8.1   *(continued)*

In contrast with most of Loreto's *fundo* owners, Peñafiel maintained control over his indigenous workforce until well into the 1970s. By 1961 Monterrico still had a labor force of forty-three peon families (DNEC 1966: 297). In the early 1970s it continued to be organized as a *hacienda* and had a peon population of 395 distributed in sixty-six households (San Román 1974: I, 67). By then the *fundo* produced timber, ojé resin (*Ficus insipida*), furs, and hides, but it was not as prosperous as it had been in the past. The social reforms initiated by the 1968 military government of Gral. Velasco Alvarado contributed to the fundo's demise. In 1975 Monterrico was recognized as a native community, and Peñafiel was forced to move out (AIDESEP 1992: 34).

* * *

Yanayacu, originally located at the confluence of the Sucusari and lower Napo Rivers, belonged to Corsino Ríos. That *patrón* started operating in the region about 1876, when he managed to engage several Mai Huna families from the Tutapishco River in the extraction of castilloa rubber (Espinosa 1955: 165; Girard 1963: 131). About 1887 he moved with his peon families to the mouth of the Sucusari River, where he established his *fundo* (Girard 1963: 131). Its area of influence extended from the Sucusari to the Yanayacu Rivers. According to Fuentes (1908: 169), in 1904 the *fundo*'s only activity was agriculture. This is, however, difficult to believe, since Ríos had been gathering rubber in the area for at least thirty years. The *fundo* continued operating after the 1914 rubber crisis but changed its activities, combining agriculture for the local market with the extraction of ivory nuts for export (Bellier 1994: 42).

In the late 1930s Ríos died, and the twenty-seven Mai Huna peon families who were still under his control were divided between his daughter and his son José (Girard 1963: 131). José moved to the Yanayacu River with nineteen of these families. In those years he resumed rubber extraction and ventured into the cultivation of barbasco (Bellier 1994: 42). He must have been quite successful in expanding his business, for in 1940 it was reported that Yanayacu included thirty-nine peon families and a total population of 185 (DNE 1949: IX, 66). In the 1950s he increased his labor force, buying the debts of several Mai Huna peons who had worked for a neighboring *patrón* (Bellier 1994: 40). About 1957 his peons were mostly engaged in the extraction of caspi milk, furs, and hides, as well as in the raising of cattle and the cultivation of sugarcane (Girard 1963: 131; Bellier 1994: 42).

In later years J. Ríos started losing control over his laborers, presumably as a result of reduced profits and an inability to provide for his peons. By 1961 there were only thirteen families with a total of seventy-six people living in Yanayacu (DNEC 1966: 293). Sometime in the late 1960s or early 1970s J. Ríos moved to Iquitos. By 1973 the *fundo* had stopped operating as such, but J. Ríos continued outfitting some of the ten remaining peon families through his young wife, who regularly visited the area (San Román 1974: I, 93, 114). In 1975 the Mai Huna of Yanayacu sought and obtained official recognition of their settlement as a "native community" under the name of Puerto Huamán (AIDESEP 1992: 37).

* * *

(continues)

Box 8.1   *(continued)*

Panguana was a hevea rubber *fundo* established at the turn of the century on the right bank of the Amazon River, upstream from Iquitos, by Matías Shapiama, an immigrant from Moyobamba (Dávila Shapiama 1997). Shapiama legalized his possession of the *fundo* in 1911, obtaining title over thirty-eight hectares (Padrón 1939). Shortly thereafter the fundo was inherited by one of her daughters, Elena Shapiama, and her husband, Ezequiel Dávila. Dávila, also from Moyobamba, had settled on the Amazon River about 1891 (Atarama 1994: 59). In 1904 he owned a hevea rubber *fundo* in the environs of the town of Caballococha with a total of ten trails (San Román 1975: 134). And by 1908 he was registered as a small importer in Iquitos (Matrícula 1910: 45). After the rubber bust, Dávila sold his Caballococha *fundo* and acquired three other *fundos* along the Amazon River: San Guillermo (1920), San Carlos (1922), and Tres de Mayo (1923). Of these, San Guillermo was the largest at fifty hectares. It was located on the left bank of the Amazon River across from the site of Panguana. The family house was in San Guillermo, most of the *habilitado* workforce lived in Panguana. These two *fundos* became known as Hacienda Dávila.

In the 1920s the *hacienda* diversified its agricultural and extractive activities. It produced rice, corn, and manioc, from which fariña flour was made. It had sugarcane plantations and produced *aguardiente* and molasses. The owners also raised cattle, pigs, and poultry, and produced jerked beef, and preserved pork meat. They also produced firewood. These products were used to outfit the *fundo*'s peons or were traded with the numerous steamboats that called in the *fundo*'s port. In addition, the owners extracted fine timber, mainly cedar and mahogany, and balata.

When Dávila died in 1928, his widow took the reins of the *fundo*. In the 1930s, she ventured into large-scale cultivation of barbasco in the *fundo*'s interior uplands, started extracting caspi milk, and increased the *fundo*'s herd to 200 head of cattle. In 1940 the *fundo* had become one of the largest in the area, having a resident workforce of ninety-three peon families and a total of 637 inhabitants (DNE 1949: IX, 71). By then the owner had the *fundo*'s old rubber trails cleared and resumed rubber extraction encouraged by high wartime rubber prices.

E. Shapiama moved to Iquitos in 1943. The administration of Panguana was taken over by Ezequiel, one of her sons; San Guillermo remained in the hands of one of her daughters, Jovita. Ezequiel lacked the skills demanded from a *patrón*. Furthermore, he did not provide for his peons as expected. As a result, he gradually lost hold over his laborers, and the *fundo* entered a period of decline. About 1951 he started selling the cattle and portions of the *fundo*. By the early 1960s he had sold most of it and retained only the core of the original *fundo*. In 1966 he moved to Iquitos, leaving what little remained of the *fundo* to one of his younger sons.

The renewed interest in land and agriculture after the rubber bust is manifested by the evolution of land grants after the passing of the Ley de Terrenos de Montaña (1898), which promoted agricultural activities. That law established three modes of land allocation: sale, concession, and free allotment. In a period of twelve years, until 1910, only 174 landholdings were legally granted (see Table 8.1). This was

Box 8.2   Fundos Sanango and Santa Rosa

Sanango and Santa Rosa are good examples of the second process by which pre–rubber bust traditional agricultural *fundos* became engaged in agroextractive production for the export market. Located on the lower Huallaga River, upstream from the town of Yurimaguas, Sanango was already active in 1902, when it belonged to Juan Abelardo Morey, an important trader and shipper from Yurimaguas (Derteano 1903: 609; see Box 4.1). At that time the *fundo* was run by an administrator and employed twenty *habilitado* indigenous peons. It was mainly devoted to cattle-raising and *aguardiente* production, though it also had some rubber trails. Fuentes (1905: 273) reports that Morey owned a steam sawmill and that most of the *fundo's* cattle and *aguardiente* production was shipped to the Iquitos market.

Amid the 1910 crisis, Morey sought legal titles for his property and obtained a concession of 414 hectares (Padrón 1939). After the rubber crisis Sanango was converted to produce cotton and coffee for export (Rumrrill et al. 1986: 154). It also expanded its sawmill facilities and became one of the most important producers of fine export timber together with the *fundos* of Puritania, Paraíso, and Porvenir in the upper Amazon. By 1940 Sanango had become one of the largest *fundos* in the lower Huallaga region; within its boundaries were 101 peon families totaling 439 individuals (DNE 1949: IX, 78–9). However, in the following decade the *fundo* must have declined and been abandoned by its legal owner, for in 1961 it was not listed among the *fundos* located in the lower Huallaga Basin (DNEC 1966). This assumption is confirmed by the fact that in 1965 Sanango reverted to the state under legislation passed in 1963, which established that property of Amazonian lands would only be recognized provided these were effectively occupied and under production (Ballón 1992: II, 633, 703).

* * *

Santa Rosa was by far the richest *fundo* in the lower Huallaga Basin in 1902. It belonged to Lucas Meza and Brothers, a Yurimaguas-based trading firm, and was valued at the time at £4,000 (Derteano 1903: 601). Located close to Yurimaguas, the *fundo* was run by an administrator, an accountant, and a foreman. It had a workforce of seventy-seven indigenous and mestizo laborers: forty-nine adult men, fifteen adult women, ten boys, and three female cooks. Its total population, however, was much larger. The *fundo's* sugarcane mills and distillery produced fifty molasses cakes and fifteen demijohns of *aguardiente* per day. Santa Rosa also had pastures and cattle.

In 1913, after the death of Lucas Meza, his widow obtained legal title to the 859 hectares of the *fundo* (Padrón 1939). In the 1920s Alcibíades Weninger acquired Santa Rosa, adding to the *fundo's* traditional activities the cultivation of cotton and coffee for export (Rumrrill et al. 1986: 154). By 1940 the *fundo's* workforce had decreased to twenty-three families and 122 individuals (DNE 1949: IX, 79), suggesting that it was not prospering. The particular reasons for the decay of this *fundo* are not clear. However, its decline continued throughout the 1940s and 1950s. By 1961 Santa Rosa did not operate as a *fundo* anymore and was listed as a *chacra,* or "small landholding," containing only seven households (DNEC 1966: 301).

Box 8.3   Fundos Negro Urco and Monte Carmelo

The process by which new *fundos* were established by former rubber *patrones* who had managed to retain their peons is well illustrated by the histories of Negro Urco and Monte Carmelo. These two *fundos* were founded by former rubber *patrones* who re-settled with their indigenous peons and shifted to agriculture and other extractive ex-port activities. Located on the right bank of the lower Napo River, Negro Urco was founded by Clímaco Arbeláez, a Colombian rubber *patrón* who in the early 1900s resided in the upper portion of the Peruvian Napo but extracted rubber from its Ecuadorian portion (Cárdenas 1991; Barclay 1995b).

Arbeláez had a large *habilitado* workforce of Naporuna families from Ecuador. After the rubber crisis he took his peons downriver, resettling in Negro Urco. By 1925 he augmented his workforce by engaging local Mai Huna people from neighboring Zapotecocha (Bellier 1991: 75; Mercier 1979: 316). In 1927 Arbeláez legalized his possession of Negro Urco, buying sixty hectares from the state (Padrón 1939). That same year he bought a 286-hectare *fundo*, named La Floresta, also located on the left bank of the lower Napo (Ballón 1991: II, 98). During the 1920s and 1930s, Negro Urco was devoted to agriculture, as well as to the extraction of export products such as ivory nuts and caspi milk (Bellier 1991: 75).

As a result of the 1933 war between Peru and Colombia over the possession of the Putumayo Basin, many of the Peruvian *patrones* established there were forced to move to the Napo River. In 1934 Alfonso Cárdenas, an immigrant from Yurimaguas who had worked for Julio César Arana exploring Brazilian rivers for balata and had lived in his Putumayo estates, settled in Negro Urco. With permission of Arbeláez, he estab-lished a *fundo* called Alianza, bringing along twelve families of Huitoto-Murui indige-nous peons (San Román 1974: I, 89; Treceño 1990). Shortly thereafter, Arbeláez transferred his own *fundo* to Cárdenas (Mercier 1979: 316), though it is not known under which circumstances. Under Cárdenas's direction the *fundo* became involved in the extraction of balata, tagua, and caspi milk (Atarama 1992: 74). He increased the *fundo*'s workforce by engaging some Mai Huna families from the Algodon River in the Putumayo Basin (Bellier 1991: I, 75).

By 1940 the *fundo* had fifteen peon families and a total of 149 inhabitants (DNE 1949: IX, 65). In the 1950s Cárdenas ventured into rosewood extraction in the Algo-don River, a tributary of the Putumayo, where in 1952 he established a mill for pro-ducing rosewood essence. He was renowned for the maltreatment of his peons, and in the 1950s many of his Mai Huna peons abandoned him (Mercier 1979: 316; Bellier 1994: 40). By 1961 the *fundo*'s workforce had decreased considerably, amounting to ten families and seventy-three inhabitants (DNEC 1966: 293). In the following years the *fundo* continued to decline. In 1972 most of his peons had abandoned Cárdenas, and he was able to retain only three families (Atarama 1992: 74). By 1973 he was al-most ruined (San Román 1974: I, 89). Two years later Negro Urco was recognized and titled as a native community, and Cárdenas was forced to abandon it (AIDESEP 1992: 33, 67; Cárdenas 1991).

* * *

(continues)

Box 8.3   *(continued)*

Monte Carmelo was founded on the lower Ucayali River sometime in the early 1920s by José Enrique Urresti. An immigrant from the coastal town of Chiclayo, Urresti had worked during the rubber boom in the upper Ucayali area, where he operated several rubber posts (Padoch and de Jong 1990). After the rubber crisis he moved downriver with a workforce mainly composed of Ashaninka peons, which he had engaged in the area of the Sepa River. He settled in Monte Carmelo, a choice site on the right bank of the Ucayali River, not far downstream from the town of Requena. In 1927 Urresti legalized his possession of the *fundo*, obtaining a concession of 5,560 hectares from the government (Padrón 1939). Through the outfitting of Cocama and mestizo laborers living in independent neighboring settlements he augmented his workforce to a total of around fifty peons and their families.

At the beginning Urresti became involved in large-scale cattle-raising and the production of *aguardiente* and sugar. In addition, he extracted fine export timber and collected furs and hides. In the 1930s and 1940s Urresti turned to barbasco production, making important investments and devoting a large extension of his *fundo* to the cultivation of that crop (Padoch and de Jong 1990). By 1940 the population living within the *fundo* was composed of nine peon families and fifty-nine individuals (DNE 1949: IX, 76). However, it is very probable that Urresti continued his practice of outfitting peons from nearby villages.

The decrease of barbasco prices beginning in 1948, the increasing competition from fluvial traders, and the death of its owner gravely affected the *fundo*'s economy (Padoch and de Jong 1990). His son, Víctor Urresti, who took over the administration of Monte Carmelo, ventured into the extraction of caspi milk. However, given the scarcity of caspi trees in the *fundo*'s lands, about 1951 he moved to the Putumayo Basin with his peons. For a while the wives and children of his peons remained in the *fundo*, but a year later they were also taken to the Putumayo. This marked the disintegration of Monte Carmelo as a *fundo*. In 1971 the *fundo* reverted to the state (Ballón 1991: II, 99).

Box 8.4   Fundos Berlín and Jibacoa

The establishment of *fundos* by a new generation of *patrones* not related to the rubber economy but who, after the rubber bust, were able to co-opt indigenous settlements composed by former peons is well represented by the cases of Fundos Berlín and Jibacoa. Teodosia Gómez founded Berlín around 1920 (Gómez Perea 1991). It was located on the right bank of the central Ucayali River, upstream from the town of Contamana, at the mouth of the Roaboya River. Its possession was legalized in 1928, when its owner purchased 40 hectares from the state (Padrón 1939). The work force of Berlín was composed of local Shipibo peons, whom the owner and her son, José Estanislao, were able to recruit through the *habilitación* system. The most trusted Ship-

(continues)

Box 8.4 *(continued)*

ibo workers, ten to twelve families, lived in the *fundo* close to the owners' house. The rest were regrouped in three nearby settlements: Colonia Chama, Roaboya, and Paococha. In addition, the owners of Berlín outfitted mestizo peons from neighboring riverine villages.

From the beginning the *fundo* had a strong mercantile orientation. In the 1920s and 1930s its commercial activities included the raising of cattle and the production of vegetables, *aguardiente,* manioc flour, salted fish, conserved pork, rice, and beans for the local market. It also included the extraction of cedar and mahogany and the cultivation of cotton and coffee for the export market. In the late 1920s the owner established a 15,000 tree cedar plantation. By the late 1930s, when Berlín was flourishing, high floods and riverbank erosion resulted in the loss of the cedar plantation. That and the imposition of taxes on rural properties in 1940 led José Estanislao, who by then had inherited the *fundo,* to gradually sell the cattle and the *fundo*'s facilities. About 1943 the owner abandoned Berlín and moved to Iquitos. The *fundo* was divided among its former overseers and Shipibo peons; in 1974 it was recognized as the native community Roaboya (AIDESEP 1992: 50).

* * *

Jibacoa was established by Manuel Antonio Navarro sometime after the 1910 rubber crisis. Navarro settled on the left bank of the Marañon River, close to the town of Nauta, in the vicinity of the Cocama settlement of Santa Fé. Shortly thereafter, its owner claimed rights over the lands occupied by the Cocama and by 1915 obtained legal property over 802 hectares (Padrón 1939). Although the strategy of co-option of indigenous peons was not novel in the Marañon area (Agüero 1994: 215), the resulting *fundos* differed from previous ones in that they were adapted to Loreto's new agroextractive export economy. In effect, Jibacoa combined the cultivation of sugar cane for the production of aguardiente with cattle-raising and the extraction of fine export timber (Agüero 1994: 216). In the following decades, its owner also became engaged in the extraction of caspi milk and the gathering of hides. In addition, Jibacoa produced fine hevea rubber intermittently, according to price fluctuation in the international market.

Between its foundation and its disintegration, Jibacoa changed hands two times (Agüero 1994: 216). Jibacoa was not one of the largest *fundos* of this area. By 1940 the fundo had only seven resident families and a total of forty-seven individuals; the hamlet of Santa Fe, belonging to the *fundo,* had a population of nineteen peon families (DNE 1949: 75–76). In the first half of the 1940s, when the Amazon Peruvian Corporation stimulated rubber production through promotional credit, Jibacoa resumed hevea tapping. During the 1950s the *fundo*'s population increased. By 1961 Jibacoa had 171 inhabitants; Santa Fé had 218 (DNEC 1966: 322–323). However, by then the *fundo* was in decline, and its Cocama peons began to question the authority of the *fundo* owner (Agüero 1994: 216, 221). That and increased competition from fluvial traders led the last *patrón* of Jibacoa to abandon the *fundo* in 1965 and move to Nauta (Agüero 1994: 215, 220). In 1972 Jibacoa reverted to the public domain (Ballón 1991: II, 204).

Agroextractive Fundos Mentioned in the Text, 1915–1962

partly because under this law hevea-rich lands could only be leased. However, the low number of land grants during the rubber era also reveals the scant interest in the acquisition of agricultural land at this time.

This attitude changed after the 1910 rubber crisis. In the following ten years the number of land grants jumped to 962. Of these, two-thirds was granted after 1915, demonstrating the close correlation between the collapse of the rubber economy and the growing interest in the acquisition of agricultural lands. This was tightly linked to the reorientation of Loreto's export economy that also started at this time. It should be underscored that the increase in land grants during the 1911–1920 period resulted both from the establishment of new *fundos* and the legalization of already existing rubber and agricultural *fundos*. This sudden growth also reflects increasing competition for riverine lands as a result of the general move from the interfluvial areas toward the region's larger rivers.

The growth in demand for such export crops as cotton and coffee generated interest in the acquisition of land during the 1920s, when the number of land grants peaked. In the following decade interest in landownership subsided. This was clearly related to the general depression that the region's export trade experienced between 1928 and 1942 (see Table 7.1). The price of cotton had collapsed, coffee was mostly produced outside Loreto, and the cultivation of barbasco was only beginning (see Appendix 20). The prosperity brought about by the outbreak of World War II, especially the barbasco boom, immediately and dramatically increased land requests and grants during the 1940s and 1950s.

Interest in agricultural land varied according to river basin and period (see Table 8.2). There were also some important variations between river basins in terms of their land-tenure structure (see Table 8.3). On the whole, however, we can assert that 77 percent of Loreto's *fundos* were small to medium-sized, having an area of less than 50 hectares (though many exploited areas much larger than they legally owned). Another 22 percent were large *fundos*, ranging between 50 and 500 hectares. Finally, 1

Table 8.1   Land Grants by Period, 1898–1970

Year	No. of grants[a]	%
1898–1910	174	3.1
1911–1920	962	17.3
1921–1930	1,020	18.3
1931–1940	196	3.5
1941–1950	645	11.5
1951–1960	979	17.5
1961–1970	1,609	28.8
Total	5,585	100.0

SOURCES: Padrón 1939; Ministerio de Agricultura 1973.
NOTE: [a] Land grants include sales, concessions, and free allotments. Timber concessions and temporary use permits are excluded.

Table 8.2   Land Grants by Period and River Basin, 1898–1937

Year[a]	Huallaga	Marañon	Ucayali	Amazon/Napo	Total Loreto
1898–1910	24	6	57	87	174
1911–1920	236	74	124	528	962
1921–1930	56	64	405	495	1,020
1931–1937	19	12	30	86	147
Total	335	156	616	1,196	2,303

SOURCE: Padrón 1939; elaborated by the authors.
NOTE: [a] Land grants include sales, concessions, and free allotments. Timber concessions are excluded.

Table 8.3   Percentage Distribution of Land Grants by Size, Class of Holding, and River Basin, 1898–1937

Size class of holding (hectares)[a]	Huallaga	Marañon	Ucayali	Amazon/Napo	Total Loreto
0 < 10	25.4	6.6	13.7	29.6	23.3
10 < 50	56.2	61.2	55.6	50.8	53.4
50 < 100	12.0	13.9	17.4	10.0	12.6
100 < 500	6.4	17.4	12.3	8.6	9.8
500 + more	0.0	1.9	1.0	1.0	0.9
Total	100.0	100.0	100.0	100.0	100.0

SOURCE: Padrón 1939; elaborated by the authors.
NOTE: [a] Only includes lands acquired from the state through purchase.

percent of the region's holdings was made up of very large land concessions of more than 500 hectares. These, however, were mostly unexploited. Thus, although owners of large *fundos* composed the rural elite, it was the small to medium-sized *fundos* that furnished the bulk of the region's agroextractive production.

Labor Control in the *Fundo* Economy

It has been argued (San Román 1975: 176) that after the rubber crisis there was a general amelioration of the situation of the indigenous peoples, who managed to regain a large margin of independence and freedom. Other authors (Stocks 1981: 94) have countered that this was not true in all cases and that many indigenous groups remained subjected to local *patrones*. Both viewpoints are correct to some degree. As we have seen, withdrawal from many of the peripheral rubber fronts effectively meant liberation for many tribal Indians who had been forcibly engaged in the rubber economy; in some cases it even meant violent retaliation by previously oppressed indigenous peons.

However, this was not always the case. Quite often rubber *patrones* moved out of the remoter fronts, taking along their indigenous peons. Ashaninka engaged in the upper Ucayali, Huitoto-Murui from the Putumayo, and Quichua from the upper Napo were moved to new locations on the lower Ucayali, the Napo-Amazon, and the lower Napo, respectively (Padoch and de Jong 1990; Atarama 1992; San Román 1974: I). In turn, Piro peons who had been taken to the Purus and Yurua, Shipibo-Conibo who had been transferred to the Madre de Dios area, and Cocama-Cocamilla who had been driven to the lower Amazon were returned by their *patrones* to their respective places of origin, on the Urubamba, Ucayali, and Huallaga-Marañon Rivers (Gow 1991; Mercier and Villeneuve 1974; Agüero 1994).

After the rubber bust, there was a significant decline in the forced recruitment of indigenous peons, and *correrías* were no longer a common practice. This was a consequence of the withdrawal of the *patrones* from the peripheral interfluvial areas, where most of the tribal Indian peoples resided, and of the increased pool of "civilized" peons. In effect, the abandoning of the interfluves diminished the possibilities of confrontation between tribal Indians and *patrones*, making raids to "clear the land" and "punitive" attacks unnecessary. In turn, the emergence of a large stratum of mixed-blood civilized rural dwellers—which will be analyzed in more detail in Chapter 12—reduced the problem of labor scarcity and rendered violent means of labor recruitment and control unnecessary.

One of the most important consequences of the rubber boom was the conformation of the *ribereño* peasant stratum—the native mixed-blood population that came to characterize the region's social and cultural profile. The process of configuration of this sector took place mainly in the rural areas but also in the region's urban centers. Punitive *correrías*, slave-raids, engagement of indigenous leaders in rubber extraction, and recurrent dislocation and relocation of tribal Indians contributed to the integration of entire or partial segments of indigenous peoples. Some maintained an indigenous identity but no longer led a communal tribal life. Others had mixed indigenous identities but did not feel part of any specific Amerindian people, whereas still others became part of the increasingly larger mixed-blood stratum.

Rooted out from their past tribal life but unable to become independent, market-oriented producers, most rural inhabitants remained attached to their *patrones* or were co-opted by the new generation of *patrones* to work in *fundos* as *habilitado* peons. Only a small number of rural dwellers managed to escape this fate and settle as independent producers of foodstuffs for neighboring towns. This was the case in the environs of Iquitos and along the lower Huallaga River.

Although the terror-inducing and indiscriminate physical violence characteristic in Arana's Putumayo estates became a thing of the past, the *habilitación* system continued to be the basis of Loreto's economy. In fact, with the proliferation of *fundos* and the sedentarization of production, the system was adjusted and consolidated, acquiring what could be called its classic form. In this context, new means to control the rural labor force were devised. Thus, the *habilitación* system practiced in the new agroextractive *fundos* was based on a combination of economic, political, and ideological controls; some had existed in previous times, whereas others were developed after the rubber bust.

After the end of the rubber boom the main condition that gave rise to the *habilitación* system—the lack of a labor market—remained unchanged. Other factors, however, changed significantly. First, tribal Indian populations had dwindled as a result of the *correrías* and the punishments and cruelties inflicted on them during the rubber era. Second, the region's economy was no longer based on an export product with such a high demand and margin of profit as rubber. Subsequent booms consisted of multiple, shifting, overlapping, rather short-lived export surges. Lastly, with the appearance of *fundos* production became more sedentary.

The first factor demanded the preservation of the existing workforce to avoid the risk of being left without laborers and, thus, without the possibility of profits. The second made it necessary to ensure the continuity of the labor relationship, so as to have a stable and cheap labor pool that could be tapped whenever a market opportunity appeared. The third factor required the concentration and fixation of the labor force in the vicinity of the *fundos'* headquarters in order to ensure better control and administration. These requirements explain the modifications introduced into the *habilitación* system after the rubber bust. As we shall see, however, control over land and local authorities provided *fundo* owners with additional means to coerce poor mestizo and indigenous rural dwellers to toil on the *fundos*.

Previously, the *patrones'* main economic hold over catechized and tribal indigenous populations was their monopoly over local commerce and highly valued manufactured products. Given the remoteness and the absence of a domestic market, *patrones* became the sole intermediaries between indigenous populations and the market. The rural population became even more dependent after the rubber bust. By the 1920s many indigenous peoples had lost their ability to carry out some of their traditional manufacturing activities. In 1922 it was reported that in the Ucayali River indigenous women who had been civilized under the tutelage of *patrones* had forgotten how to spin and weave and were no longer able to make their own clothes (Ortiz 1984: 257). This situation was aggravated by the fact that bankrupt rubber *patrones* were not able to provide *habilitado* peons with manufactured fabrics. Similar reports indicate that not only spinning and weaving techniques were lost but also the knowledge of the art of pottery and the manufacturing of weapons and utensils.

Despite having been heavily affected by the collapse of the rubber economy, former rubber *patrones* managed to retain their monopoly over credit and commerce, mostly because of their alliance with the merchant houses of Iquitos and their control of local fluvial transport. Industrial goods continued to be the primary form of advance payment to peons. However, after the rubber bust the system of in-kind payments became more sophisticated. Most large *fundos* established their own general stores where peons could acquire a range of goods in exchange for future services. Goods included basic necessities like textiles, mosquito nets, tools, pots, shotguns, and even sewing machines. They also included imported as well as local foodstuffs processed within the *fundo*: salted fish, jerked meat, conserved pork, manioc flour, vegetables, preserves, molasses cakes, and, particularly, *aguardiente*. Negro Urco, Monterrico, and Pucabarranca on the Napo River (Cárdenas 1991; Herrera 1991; Abensur 1991; see Boxes 8.1 and 8.3), Panguana on the Amazon (Dávila Shapiama 1997; see Box 8.1), and Arica on the Ucayali (Llerena Rengifo 1991) had these kinds of stores. In some *fundos*, for example, Puritania on the Amazon River, peons were paid with chips that had fixed nominal values and could be redeemed only in the *fundo*'s store (Rojas Vela 1991).

In this new context the state of permanent indebtedness continued to enforce the retention of peons. As in the past, the values of services rendered, products gathered, and goods provided were arbitrarily set, with services and forest products always being undervalued and manufactured goods overvalued. According to a former peon of Fundo Jibacoa, "*Patrones* charged us twice the value of the things they gave us and peons had to pay with their labor so we never had money and, thus, remained bound to them forever" (Agüero 1994: 227; see also Box 8.4). However, the worst aspects of these debt ties seem to have softened. There is evidence, for instance, that although the so-called transfer of debts (whereby *patrones* could sell their peons' debts to obtain cash or pay a debt) was not completely eradicated, the practice was mainly confined to the remoter areas such as the upper Napo River and the interior lands of the Putumayo Basin (Barclay 1998; Chaumeil 1981: 72).

It has been argued (Gow 1991: 46) that "the Ucayali *hacienda* was not based on the expropriation of native land but rather on the control of native labor through ties of debt." This is only partly true. Although the *patrones*' monopoly over commerce and credit continued to guarantee a strong hold over their peons under the guise of accumulated debts, monopoly over land became the key to retaining rural laborers during this period. In such a vast and sparsely populated region as Loreto, it is difficult to imagine that land could be considered a scarce resource and that landownership could become a means to subject native inhabitants. To understand how this became possible, it is necessary to take into account the local economic geography.

Although there was plenty of land in the region, especially in the peripheral areas and the interfluves, the most valuable land—located along the commercial waterways—was scarce. Large tracts along the banks of major rivers were underwater for most of the year. High, nonfloodable terraces, known as *alturas* and *restingas* in Loreto, were few and scattered. These were the first places to be occupied by former rubber *patrones* and new *patrones* during the post–rubber era land rush. This phenomenon has been well reported for the Ucayali (Villeneuve 1974: 164–5) and the Napo Rivers (Domínguez 1988: 90), but it probably took place along all of Loreto's larger rivers. In some cases, former indigenous inhabitants, who had been forcibly engaged in rubber collection or had fled to avoid being subjected, had abandoned the high terraces. In other cases, indigenous families were displaced by incoming *patrones* who claimed legal title to the lands being occupied.

Indigenous peoples could certainly have retreated to the interfluvial areas, and some did. The Cashinhua, Amahuaca, Matses, Uni, as well as segments of the

Ashaninka, Ticuna, Yagua, and Urarina, opted to seclude themselves in out-of-the-way headwater or terra firme areas. But most of the indigenous peoples that had become voluntarily or forcibly engaged in mercantile relations during the rubber era and were dependent on market goods opted to remain close to the region's fluvial trading routes. To do so they had to attach themselves to a *fundo* owner, given the absence of suitable free riverine lands. Regardless of whether a *patrón* had legal title to the land he claimed, the argument that he was allowing peons to live on his lands as a "favor" provided a second and very important hold over laborers.

In fact, many *patrones* did not have legal title to their lands. Others had title, but to much smaller areas than those that were claimed. As the son of the founder of Fundo Berlín put it: "The interior lands had no owner, and as the *fundo* limits were not officially fixed and there was no control of the lands being used, *fundo* owners occupied whatever lands they required" (Gómez Perea 1991; see Box 8.4). Thus, Fundo Berlín legally covered only 40 hectares, but its owner had large plantations of sugarcane, cotton, coffee, and staples, as well as more than 100 head of cattle. In addition, she was involved in large-scale extraction of timber. All these activities required an area that far surpassed what was legally held. A similar, more extreme case was that of Mario Pezo, who transformed San Antonio, founded in 1926, into one of the largest cattle-raising and timber-producing *fundos* of the upper Ucayali while legally possessing only a single hectare (Padrón 1939; Gow 1991: 109).

In a few cases, however, *patrones* held vast concessions from the government. Alfonso Cárdenas, who in the 1940s bought Negro Urco, which had an original extension of 60 hectares, later obtained a timber-extraction concession of 10,000 hectares. He was thus able to control not only the Huitoto-Murui peons he brought with him from the Putumayo River but also many of the Quichua and Mai Huna families who lived in the area and who had managed, until then, to retain a certain degree of freedom.

In exchange for rights to live on their lands, which included the planting of gardens and use of local resources, *patrones* demanded exclusive access to peons' labor and produce. Peons ascribed to a *fundo* could not work for other *patrones* or trade with other merchants. In addition, by allowing peons to farm within the *fundo*, *patrones* were freed from the obligation to feed their laborers. This was particularly convenient during times when prices for commercial agricultural or extractive products dropped and *fundo* owners thus saw profits diminish radically. However, in some cases, such as that of Fundo Panguana, peons had little time to plant their own gardens and depended almost entirely on their *patrón* for their livelihoods (Dávila Shapiama 1997). Thus, through real or fictional ownership of lands, *patrones* were able to retain laborers within their domains, maintain exclusive access to their labor, and cut down the costs for maintaining them.

In some extreme cases, *patrones* even demanded rent from their peons. This was the case of Cocama peons in Fundo Jibacoa who had to work for the *patrón* six days each year without pay or even meals to discharge what he called the "payment of lease" (Agüero 1994: 220). Payment for the right to live on *fundo* lands was also common along the Amazon River. In some cases, as in Santa Otilia, payment was in free work; in others, as in Alfaro, *fundo* owners charged a monthly cash rent or its equivalent in produce (San Román 1974: I, 24, 45).

Monopoly of land became the major innovation in the Loretan patron-client system after the rubber bust. As a result, during much of the 1915–1962 period the region's rural landscape was dominated by strings of *fundos* and *haciendas* located along larger rivers, interspersed by very few independent indigenous or mestizo settlements and towns. A similar process took place in Brazilian Amazonia, where, according to Eugene Parker (1985b: xxv), ownership of land by trading-post operators (the Brazilian equivalent of Loreto's *fundo* owners) allowed the *aviamento* (*habilitación*) system to persist well beyond the rubber bust. As we shall learn below, indigenous peons interpreted landownership claims by *patrones* in terms of their own cultures—frequently with unfortunate consequences.

The economic hold that *fundo* owners had over peons was reinforced through the control of the authority system at the rural level. Local authorities were frequently chosen from the pool of *fundo* owners. This was especially true of the *tenientes gobernadores* (deputy governors), local authorities who were subordinate to district governors, provincial subprefects, and departmental prefects. Although at the bottom of the hierarchy of authorities appointed directly by the central government, deputy governors constituted the main authority at the rural level, acting both as police and judiciary, and thus had considerable power. Alfonso Cárdenas, the infamous owner of Negro Urco, acted for many years as deputy governor of the lower Napo River (Cárdenas 1991). As commander of the local Guardia Civil (rural police), *fundo* owners who acted as deputy governors held another powerful mechanism to coerce peons. There are several accounts of Cárdenas maltreating peons, locking them in the *fundo*'s jail whenever they disobeyed his orders and, together with the local guards, raping their wives (Mercier 1979: 316). The owner of Fundo Jibacoa was also deputy governor of his area (Agüero 1994: 220), and the owner of Fundo Arica was appointed governor of the district of Emilio San Martín on the Ucayali River (Llerena Rengifo 1991).

Most powerful *patrones* held local political offices at one time or another during their lifetimes. Sometimes, however, they preferred to exert political control indirectly through the designation of loyal subordinates as local authorities. In fact, some *fundos* became the seat of government within a given river tract, with the owners unofficially holding the prerogative to designate civil servants and local authorities. This was the case in Fundo Berlín, on the lower Ucayali; it had a schoolhouse, a post office, and a police station and was the seat of the local deputy governor (Gómez Perea 1991). It was also the case in Fundo Panguana during the 1930s; it too had a school and was the seat of the deputy governor and the municipal agent (Dávila Shapiama 1997).

Even if they were not authorities themselves, or not influential enough to appoint them, *fundo* owners could always count on the support of local authorities to settle disputes with their peons, force peons to work, and capture fugitives. There are numerous eyewitness accounts of *patrones* obtaining the complicity of deputy governors and the Guardia Civil to further their interests. On the Huallaga River, the police would help the *patrones* of Santa Cruz draft Cocama men in the independent indigenous settlement of Tipishca who were considered to be "their" peons as a result of indebtedness (Stocks 1981: 95–6). On the Napo River, Oscar Peñafiel enlisted the help of the Guardia Civil to interrupt Easter celebrations being held by peons without permission and to return them to work (Mercier 1979: 316).

Through their control of local authorities, some *fundo* owners committed acts against peons that were as atrocious as those during the rubber era. It was reported that Samuel Roggeroni, the original owner of Fundo Pucabarranca on the Napo River, ordered his foremen to whip and spread salt on the wounds of peons who refused to work for him (Mercier 1979: 316). It should be stressed, however, that *fundo* owners were not totally above the law. Thus, there are several examples of *fundo* owners being punished for crimes committed against their peons. The infamous Roggeroni was such a case: After killing one of his peons, he was arrested and imprisoned by the Guardia Civil of Iquitos (Mercier 1979: 316). This was also the fate of two other Napo *patrones* renowned for their cruelty (Bellier 1991: 75). This does not mean that the rule of law prevailed in Loreto, but it indicates some important changes with respect to the total impunity enjoyed by *patrones* during the rubber era.

However, violence alone does not account for the successful and generally quite smooth reproduction of the *fundo/patrón* system for almost a half-century. In contrast to the rubber era, when indigenous peoples ambushed and killed incoming teams of rubber tappers, attacked their camps in retaliation for previous grievances, and rose up in arms in the wake of the rubber crisis, there were no instances of active resistance in the post-rubber bust decades. At most, resistance was passive: Peons ran away, were intentionally less productive, arranged for debts to be transferred to another *patrón*, and sold their produce clandestinely to fluvial traders.

In our opinion, if *patrones* were able to retain peons over long periods without serious resistance, it was because two ideological constructs helped legitimate the system and made it acceptable. The first, based on the Catholic ritual practices of *compadrazgo* and *padrinazgo*, gave rise to a paternalistic relationship between *fundo* owners and peons; it has been the object of considerable attention since San Román's (1975: 104–5, 175–6) seminal remarks on the subject. In contrast, the second construct, in which *fundo patrones* were equated with traditional indigenous leaders by their indigenous peons, has only been hinted at (Gow 1991: 67–8, 214).

Compadrazgo is the spiritual bond established between the parents of a child and the man and woman chosen to become the child's godparents in the Catholic baptismal ritual. *Padrinazgo* is the spiritual bond established between the baptized child and the godparents. *Compadrazgo* and *padrinazgo* are thus two faces of the same coin. Godparents are expected to contribute to the spiritual and material welfare of their godchildren and, if the need arises, to take the place of the parents. In turn, godchildren have to respect and help godparents upon request.

Given these obligations, many parents choose godparents of higher economic and/or social standings. Parents and godparents conceive of themselves as "coparents" of the child, *compadres* and *comadres*, as both have the duty to ensure the child's welfare. By extension, coparents have obligations of mutual support. However, as co-parents have generally different economic and social statuses, the obligations tend to be vertical and asymmetrical. When status differences are substantial, as in the case of *fundo* owners and peons, *compadrazgo* and *padrinazgo* may disguise, beneath the cloak of paternalistic concern, highly inegalitarian and exploitative relationships.

In Loreto, *fundo* owners and their spouses were frequently asked to become god-parents of the children of peons (Stocks 1981: 100; Mercier 1979: 316; Gow 1991: 214). The mutual obligations entailed by the *compadrazgo* and *padrinazgo* ties had a hierarchical character: *Fundo patrones* acted as fatherly providers and protectors, whereas peons were obliged to play the role of submissive child-servants. *Patrones* provided certain goods and services to *compadres* and godchildren: medicines for an ill godchild, a free boat ride for a *comadre* visiting a nearby town, or intervention on behalf of a *compadre* imprisoned by local authorities for a minor offense. This re-duced potential conflict inherent in the *patrón*-peon relationship. Organizing feasts for peons, participating in their celebrations, and speaking their language were also mechanisms to disguise the exploitative character of the *patrón*-peon link as a rela-tionship of sharing and reciprocity. The usefulness of these ritual links is illustrated by the fact that they survived the demise of the *fundo* economy; at present, they continue to provide a basis for relationships between hierarchically different peoples in rural Amazonia (Zarzar 1985: 84–5).

Whereas the *compadrazgo-padrinazgo* system disguised the exploitative nature of the relationship, the equating of *fundo* owners with traditional indigenous leaders legitimized it. Among Amazonian indigenous peoples there is a general tendency for founders of longhouses (*malocas*) or plurihouse settlements to be considered "own-ers of the house" or "owners of the land." Settlement founders are also considered to be leaders of their people, defined as a group of men and women related by kinship and affinal ties. The clearest example is that of the Piaroa of Venezuela, described by Overing Kaplan (1975: 53–5). In the upper Amazon, these elements, present in varying degrees, can be found, for instance, among the Achuar (Descola 1982: 304), the Ticuna (Goulard 1994: 345–6, 368–9), the Mai Huna (Bellier 1994: 98–9, 108–9), and the Yagua (Chaumeil 1994: 259). It should be stressed, however, that in all cases "ownership" of the land is nominal and does not entitle leaders to ap-propriate it to the detriment of other settlement members. However, given their po-sition as settlement founders and nominal owners of the land, indigenous headmen were sometimes granted the prerogative of determining the sites where followers could plant gardens. In addition, people who wanted to live within the boundaries of a headman's territory but did not belong to his following had to formally request his permission (Descola 1982: 304).

We contend that in the wake of disrupted traditional social and political net-works that resulted from the raiding, killing, displacement, and multiple relocation of indigenous peoples during the rubber era, many *patrones* came to be seen by in-digenous peons as equivalent to the leaders of old. This was especially true when a *patrón* started a *fundo* with his workers in a new territory. In that situation *patrones* acted, albeit unknowingly, like indigenous leaders, who in the past were the ones who took the initiative to abandon a settlement site to begin the construction of a new longhouse or group of houses (Goulard 1994: 345; Frank 1994: 176). The *patrones*' claim that they were "owners of the land" was, therefore, not totally alien to indigenous peons and coincided with the traditional concept of settlement leadership.

Similarly, the *patrones*' were father figures. The Ticuna refer to settlement leaders as "owner of the house" or "father of the house," adding a paternal dimension. This is also true of the Mai Huna leader, who is known as "the one who guides as a father" (Bellier 1994: 108). The remarks of a Cocama man about the former *patrón* of Jibacoa express how indigenous peons also conceived of *patrones* as authoritarian father figures: "He was like a father, like a man who dominated everybody in the hamlet. . . . When we did not obey him, he threatened to punish us, asserting he was a 'big authority'" (Agüero 1994: 221). The case of the Huitoto constitutes one of the best examples of how indigenous concepts of leadership worked in favor of *fundo* owners. In the past, and in the context of ritual celebrations, the Huitoto referred to their longhouse politico-religious leaders as "father" (Gasché 1982: 12). Men or women who had lost their leader due to inter- or intratribal warfare were considered, and conceived of themselves, as "orphans." As such they could request to be admitted, that is, "adopted," by the leader of another longhouse. In these cases, however, adopted orphans were considered to have a lower social status than did the core members of the longhouse.

Following the social chaos brought about by the death of traditional leaders and the relocation and dispersal of longhouse members as a result of the rubber boom, there was widespread feeling among the Huitoto that they constituted, as a whole, an "orphan people" (Gasché 1982: 12). In this context, *patrones* came to be seen as substitutes for the disappeared longhouse leaders. This in turn led the Huitoto to find the tutelage of *patrones* as convenient and even desirable and help make *patrones*' authoritarian ways more acceptable.

The Piro of the Urubamba River explicitly equated *patrones* with traditional leaders, a view that was endorsed by the *patrones* themselves. For example, Francisco Vargas, owner of Fundos La Huaira, La Providencia, and Sepa, was considered by his peons to be both *gran patrón* (big boss) and *curaca* (chief) of the Piro people (Gow 1991: 67, 214). He actively assumed a role not only in organizing labor but as ceremonial leader of the community, arranging marriages, leading initiation rites of young women, and baptizing children. Many *patrones* carried out such roles, though less consciously, throughout the region. It should be noted, however, that the role of the *patrones* was not identical to that of indigenous chiefs, insofar as in precontact times chiefs had little power, never had the prerogative of commanding the labor of their followers, and lacked the means to enforce their orders and requests. Despite these more authoritarian traits, many peons still likened *patrones* to the leaders of old, a fact that bestowed a certain legitimacy to what was otherwise a highly vertical and exploitative relationship.

In summary, the *correrías*, which in some contexts had been a constitutive element in the clearing of the land, punishment of hostile indigenous peoples, and in the "production" of peons during the rubber era, stopped being practiced. Likewise, overt physical violence, which had been used to retain indigenous laborers, force them to work harder, and produce "disciplined" laborers, became the exception rather than the rule. Instead, *fundo* owners controlled laborers with a combination of two or more of the following factors: monopoly of the trade in foreign goods, exclusive access to the land, control of local authority, manipulation of *compadrazgo-padrinazgo* ties, and the assumption of some of the functions of traditional indigenous leaders. These elements coalesced to provide *fundo* owners with formidable power, which rendered overt violence unnecessary. It is therefore not surprising that there was no escape from the domination of *fundo patrones*, that the state of indebtedness was lifelong, and that the *patrón*-peon link was transmitted from parents to children.

The Spatial and Economic Organization of *Fundos*

Fundo life revolved around the pivotal figure of the *patrón* and his house, generally a two-story structure built of fine materials. This was usually located on a high terrace, close to the *fundo*'s port, where the *fundo*'s fleet was anchored and where passing vessels called to buy firewood, deliver merchandise, and collect the *fundo*'s produce. Together with the general store and several storage facilities, the *casa grande* (big house) constituted the core of the *fundo*. All of these buildings surrounded a large open patio, where in some cases a stocks for punishing rebellious peons was prominently displayed. Along its periphery, the compound might also include such facilities as sugarcane mills, *aguardiente* or rosewood oil distilleries, sawmills, and open or covered drying yards. Some also included a schoolhouse.

On both sides of the central compound and following closely the bank of the river, there was a string of houses occupied by workers and employees. These were frequently arranged in a hierarchical order, with those of the higher white-mestizo employees (managers, accountants, stewards, foremen, etc.) closer to the big house and built of lumber, those of the indigenous or mestizo peons, mostly palm-thatched huts, located at the extremes. *Fundo* peons lived with their families; often, their wives and children also worked for the *patrón* carrying out household and menial chores.

Not all *fundo* workers lived close to the *patrón*'s house. The largest *fundos* usually included one or more hamlets inhabited by peons and their families, located at varying distances from the *fundo* center and close to pasturelands and plantations (i.e., wherever a large labor force was required on a daily basis). In addition, many *fundos* had close links to nearby independent indigenous or mestizo settlements and towns. Examples along the Amazon River were the hamlets of San Fernando and San Juan, as well as the former colonial mission of San Joaquín de Omaguas, whose members worked as *habilitado* peons for the sawmill *fundos* of Puritania and Paraíso, respectively (Rojas Vela 1991; Riera Vásquez 1991). Similarly, the inhabitants of the Co-camilla settlement of Arahuante on the Huallaga River worked regularly as *habilitado* peons for the owner of Hacienda Montero (Stocks 1981: 94).

Analysts of the 1940 census (DNE 1949: IX, ii) pointed out how difficult it was to distinguish between those riverine hamlets established within *fundo* boundaries and those independent settlements linked to a *fundo* through *habilitado* ties. However, there was an important difference between the two. Although in both cases peons were bound to a *patrón* or *fundo* owner by *habilitado* ties, those living outside the *fundo* boundaries had a larger degree of autonomy. They were not obliged to work exclusively for him and could, therefore, search for the best deal among a variety of local *patrones* and river traders. In addition, as they lived on their own lands, their families were not subjected to the authority and demands of the *fundo* owner. From a peon's standpoint, this made a world of a difference.

Most agricultural activities were carried out within or close to the *fundos'* titled area. The most important commercial crops, such as sugarcane, cotton, coffee, and barbasco, were grown on the higher terraces. Pasturelands were also opened in these areas. Rice was sown in the alluvial lands along the river shores, known as *barrizales* (muddy flats), while peanuts and a variety of vegetables were grown along the *playas* (sandy beaches and bars). In addition, at the back of the *patrón's* big house there were orchards, pigpens, and henhouses.

In contrast, extractive activities were mostly carried out in interior lands, which generally were not included in the *fundo's* legal area but lay within its area of influence. Groups of peons, supervised by a foreman, were designated to carry out specific extractive activities (lumbering, collection of ivory nuts, tapping of balata, etc.) in specific areas, where they frequently settled for extended periods. In some cases extractive activities were even carried out in areas located far away from the *fundo* center. Thus, the owner of Fundo Arica used to designate six or seven Cocama peons and their families to go to the Pacaya River, upriver from the *fundo* along the Ucayali River, in order to fish *paiche* (*Arapaima gigas*)(Llerena Rengifo 1991). These peons were exclusively dedicated to this activity. Every six months they delivered the bundles of dried, salted *paiche* to the *patrón's* house, at which time they were replaced by another team.

Additionally, *fundo* owners outfitted indigenous or mestizo men from independent satellite settlements to extract specific products in distant areas. In the 1930s and 1940s many Cocamilla men were engaged in the production of salted fish for the *fundos* of the Huallaga Basin (Stocks 1983: 242). The owner of Puritania, on the Amazon River, outfitted the inhabitants of neighboring independent settlements to extract rosewood from a faraway area on the Tigre River, where it was collected by one of his three boats (Rojas Vela 1991). The owner of Monterrico, on the Napo River, established similar relations to obtain timber for his sawmill and rosewood for his distillery (Herrera 1991).

Thus, a *fundo* was much more than the legal area it possessed, and in the case of the larger ones its layout could include a central compound, various attached or associated hamlets, as well as several temporary extractive posts, some of which could be in very distant zones. Given the changing demands of the international market and the need to exploit a variety of products located in different habitats, the areas effectively used by any given *fundo* could vary radically over time. A *fundo* was also much more than the *habilitado* personnel living within its boundaries. Its workforce could also include *habilitado* indigenous and mestizo laborers from neighboring settlements and towns, smaller independent extractors with their own *habilitado* teams of workers, and even some wage laborers, such as administrative employees and specialized operators.

More than just a territorial unit or an aggregate of laborers, *fundos* constituted versatile economic constellations with extremely fluid geographical and social boundaries centered on a *patrón*. Because of their spatial and social ramifications, *fundos* had an important integrating role in rural areas; in addition, due to their special relationship with the merchant houses of Iquitos, they played an important role in connecting remote rural areas to the region's urban-centered market economy.

Despite their similarity in organization and operation, Loretan *fundos* were not homogeneous. *Fundos* differed both in terms of the scale of operations, which depended on area, workforce, infrastructure, and availability of capital, and in terms of location—and thus their access to commercially valuable resources. Most of the *fundos* discussed above were among the largest and therefore were the most visible in the region. With the renewed export prosperity of the 1940s, many increased their operations and became extremely profitable.

Thus, during the 1940s some *fundo* owners incorporated commercial firms, which had as their main asset one or more large landholdings. Agroextractive units forming part of a commercial firm began to be referred to as *haciendas*. Internally, the organization of these landholdings did not differ substantially from that of the *fundos*. They continued to operate on the basis of the *habilitación* system, to have diversified production, and to use resources within and without their boundaries. The main differences were the larger scale of their operations and a greater emphasis on production for regional urban markets, but, especially, because they tended to replace merchant houses as outfitters at the local level.

Villa Luisa, located on the Napo River and belonging to the firm Oscar Peñafiel and Sons, constitutes an outstanding example of this new trend in rural Loreto (Sotomayor et al. 1949: 51). Together with two other *fundos*, Monterrico and San Martín, Villa Luisa became the center of a vast agroextractive operation along the Napo Basin. It produced foodstuffs, especially rice, for the Iquitos market and extracted a range of forest products: timber, caspi milk, *ojé* resin (*Ficus insipida*), rubber, furs, and hides. For the gathering of these products the firm not only counted on its own labor force but also outfitted many small extractors and bought the produce of smaller *patrones*. Thus, it began to perform some of the functions that until then had been characteristic of the merchant houses. The firm owned a large steam-launch and two scows and operated several smaller motorboats along the Napo-Iquitos route. In addition, it had offices in Iquitos. Although by owning its own fleet the firm managed to cut transport costs and thus increase profit margin, it could not altogether avoid its dependence on merchant houses (in this case, Casa Menezes) for credit and for the marketing of its export production (Herrera 1991).

By 1949 owners of large agroextractive units had organized the Asociación de Productores de Loreto, with offices in Iquitos (Sotomayor et al. 1949: 144–6). An analysis of the location of *haciendas* reveals that the new model was particularly successful in the Ucayali Basin. In effect, 67 percent of the association's eighty-one members maintained *haciendas* on that river; 12 percent were on the Amazon and the rest were on the Napo, Marañon, Huallaga, and Yavari. This is not surprising, as we shall see, because the inauguration in 1943 of the Lima-Pucallpa Road had opened an outlet for the production of the *fundos* of the Ucayali Basin.

Arnaldo Collazos, son of the most important rubber *patrón* of the Purus River, was one of the Ucayali *fundo* owners who, taking advantage of the new opportunities, transformed his landholdings into a large-scale agroextractive operation. This included a large *hacienda*, Santa Isabel, three smaller agropastoral *fundos*, La Industria, San Leopoldo, and Aumento de San Leopoldo, and four rubber and timber *fundos*, Ipururo, Moena Cocha, Santa María de Shiari, and Aumento de Santa María de Shiari (Sotomayor et al. 1949: 97). The production of these *fundos* and *haciendas* prefigures the shift from the international toward the domestic market that was to become the hallmark of the Ucayali *haciendas* established after 1960. Thus, Collazos's firm was mainly devoted to general agriculture, cattle-raising, commercial fishing, and timber extraction for regional and national markets; the only export activity was the collection of rubber, which flourished for a brief period as a result of World War II.

Large *fundos* and *haciendas* constituted the most conspicuous landmarks on Loreto's rural landscape during the 1940s. It would be a gross error, however, to assume that they were representative of all the region's *fundos*. Most of Loreto's landholdings were much smaller. They often covered less than 10 hectares, had a workforce of only a handful of peons, possessed little infrastructure, and enjoyed limited access to credit. In the smaller *fundos* the standard of living of the *patrones* differed little from that of their peons, as in Brazil (Parker 1985b: xxvi). The only elements that distinguished *patrones* from peons were ethnic backgrounds and family ties. Unlike the *haciendas*, which because of their scale and diversity of operations could accommodate the changing demands of the international market, thereby preserving certain stability, the fate of the smaller *fundos* fluctuated according to location and time.

Given that commercially valuable forest resources were not evenly distributed throughout the region, all *fundos* could not profit equally from any given export boom. Thus, whereas the 1920s ivory nut boom and the 1950s rosewood oil trade mostly benefited *fundos* located north of the Marañon-Amazon axis, the 1920s cotton boom and 1940s barbasco export cycle mainly favored *fundos* to the south. Some activities, such as timber extraction, could in theory be carried out all across the region. But not all *fundos* had access to such resources or had the credit and workforce necessary to exploit them. The ups and downs of the region's export economy had different effects on the various *fundos*.

It is commonly assumed that the end of each export boom had devastating effects on Loreto's economy. But this perception derives more from a narrow focus on the *fundo* owners who were most affected rather than a broader assessment of the shape of the regional economy. Periodic crises hit specific sectors of Loreto's *fundos*. Moreover, given the overlapping nature of the export cycles involving different resources and, thus, different parts of Loreto's territory, what constituted a time of crisis for some *fundos* meant prosperity for others. However, during certain periods the entire region fell on hard times. Thus, for instance, during the 1928–1942 transition phase, when the demise of several exports coincided with the beginning of new export surges, the region was trapped in a sort of economic limbo. In general, however, the heterogeneous character of the environment and the peculiarities of each area lessened the effects of specific export busts.

Despite the renewed prosperity that *fundos* and *haciendas* experienced during the 1940s, new conditions were building up at the regional, national, and international levels. These were to have a serious impact on the functioning and perpetuation of Loreto's agroextractive export economy.

9

"Ensuring the Region's Future": State Action and the End of *Fundo*/Merchant House Dominance

Loreto's economy prospered between 1943 and 1962, so much so that in 1962 the value of the import-export trade equaled that of the best years of the rubber era. Unfortunately, this was the swan song: The agroextractive export economy was in decline by then, and *fundos* and merchant houses no longer exerted hegemonic control over the regional economy. In this chapter we analyze the causes of this decline and detail the effects that improved communications with the Pacific Coast markets and government modernizing policies had on the regional economy.

It is difficult to pinpoint a single cause for the decline in Loreto's agroextractive export economy. The disappearance of *fundos* and merchant houses in the early 1960s had multiple causes. However, in our opinion, their decline can be traced in one way or another to two principal events: the outbreak of World War II and the 1941 war with Ecuador. These almost parallel events had a single effect: to revive Peru's interest in integrating its Amazon region with the rest of the national territory, incorporating it into the nascent modernization process initiated a few years earlier. World War II had the effect of increasing demand for tropical forest products vital to the Allied war effort. War with Ecuador was hastened by the prospect of finding oil in the upper Amazon. Although Peru won the conflict, the difficulties encountered in transporting troops and stores constituted for the government a reminder of the region's isolation. Thus, the government's renewed interest in Loreto did not differ essentially from past efforts (1851–1872 and 1890–1910). It obeyed geopolitical objectives, namely, the defense of national sovereignty, and economic goals, namely, the possibility of enhancing fiscal revenues by increasing exports and oil exploration.

To achieve regional integration and economic modernization, the government promoted better communications with the Pacific Coast. It encouraged the gradual transformation of the regional economy into a producer of foodstuffs for the domestic market. It advocated the elimination of precapitalist relations of labor and exchange. By 1943 the government had finished building the road between Lima and Pucallpa, a small port on the Ucayali River. With support from the United States, it also built two airports, one in Iquitos and the other in Tarapoto, in the Huallaga River basin. We argue that the effect of these events was to reorient the region's production and commercial flows from the Atlantic to the Pacific and from the external market to the domestic market.

In addition, the new road stimulated the economy of the Ucayali River basin. Tiny Pucallpa grew rapidly; soon it became an important economic center rivaling Iquitos. Reacting to the centralist tendencies of Iquitos's economic and political elite, the nascent elite of Pucallpa presently demanded the separation of Ucayali from Loreto as a new department; they attained that objective in 1981. All of these changes, we contend, constituted a blow to the merchant houses of Iquitos. Unable to adapt to the new conditions, they became excluded from the new productive activities and trading networks, as well as from Ucayali's blossoming economy. Gradually, commercial firms from Lima replaced the old import-export companies.

Economic intervention by the state also played an important role in transforming Loreto's economy. The state's regional economic model during this period did not differ much from the old Civilist model at the turn of the century. In both cases, the objective was to transform the region into a producer of foodstuffs for the domestic market. Whereas Civilist governments adhered to a liberal stance, calling for little state intervention in economic affairs, the postwar governments recognized that some state intervention was necessary to modernize Peru's economy. With these objectives in mind, the government provided promotional agricultural credits and technological assistance. It also invested to extend education, attempted to eliminate deeply entrenched, anachronistic relations of production and exchange, and tried to improve the lot of the working classes, particularly in rural areas.

The state was cautious in implementing the new policies; it avoided direct confrontations with local elites. However, through a series of indirect measures, it contributed to the erosion of the power of *fundo* owners and large merchants. It favored small producers over large *fundo* owners in granting promotional credit. It democratized access to important resources such as timber and alluvial lands, which in the past had been virtually monopolized by *fundo* owners and merchant houses. Lastly, it enforced existing legislation that taxed uncultivated lands, seeking to impede land concentration, eliminate large, unproductive concessions, and stimulate agricultural production.

All these measures—together with the reorientation of the region's trading flows—helped to break the empowering monopolies held by merchant houses and *fundo* owners over trade, credit, land, and resources. They might have survived the crisis, but a decrease in the international demand for tropical products in the late 1950s drove *fundos* and merchant houses out of business. By the early 1960s most of the merchant houses that had opened after the rubber bust had closed (see Table 7.3). Similarly, the number of *fundos* decreased. The trading and landed elites openly opposed the state's new policies for the region. But, as we contend, they were unable to reverse the trends beginning in the 1940s that eventually led to their demise.

The International Context

World War II generated a large demand for strategic raw materials such as rubber, derris, and quinine, most of which had been previously supplied by producers in Southeast Asia. However, the Japanese invasion of that region cut off Allied access to such resources. As a result, the Allies turned to the Amazon Basin to ensure a steady flow of these strategic materials. Rubber was used mainly in the manufacture of tires and other parts for war vehicles. Barbasco, commercially exploited beginning around 1934, substituted for derris as an effective insecticide and as an ingredient in marine antifouling paints. Finally, quinine was distributed among soldiers fighting in tropical areas to prevent malaria.

Given the importance of rubber, the United States started negotiating with Brazil well before the war. By October 1940 the two countries signed an agreement to, among other things, promote the cultivation of hevea (Delboy 1952: 15). However, there was a concern that Brazil might side with the Axis due to its large and influential colony of German immigrants, so the United States approached the Andean-Amazon countries, especially Peru; this proved premature. In January 1942, a month after the United States entered the war, Brazil declared war on the Axis (Dean 1987: 93). In March 1942 the United States signed an agreement to buy Brazil's entire export rubber production at fixed prices. A similar agreement was signed with Peru in May and, later, with other Andean-Amazon countries (Zegarra 1945). A second agreement was signed with Peru in October regulating the acquisition of quinine (Ballón 1991: II, 352). With the acquiescence of Peru, the United States also financed the construction of airports and hospitals in Loreto and neighboring San Martín. All of these activities required Peru to play a more active role in Loreto.

In July 1941, when the United States was negotiating important trade agreements with the Amazon countries, war broke out between Peru and Ecuador. It is unclear as to who was responsible for beginning the conflict (Yepes del Castillo 1996). What matters here, however, is not the development of the military events that ended with the defeat of the Ecuadorian army but the circumstances that led to war and the governmental actions they engendered for Loreto. Many historical reasons have led Ecuador and Peru to lay claim to Loreto—or Maynas, as the region was called during colonial times—but in the 1930s a new powerful reason was added: the prospect of oil as a source of national income.

Ecuador had began prospecting for oil in its Amazon territories in 1921, when it granted the Leonard Exploration Company, a subsidiary of Standard Oil of New Jersey, a 250,000-hectare concession along the upper Pastaza River (Muratorio 1987: 204–5). This pioneer exploration found nothing. In 1937 the contract with Leonard was canceled, and a larger concession of 10 million hectares was granted to Anglo Saxon Petroleum, a subsidiary of Royal Dutch Shell Company.

As for Peru, surface oil had been discovered in Loreto in 1920, close to the town of Contamana on the Ucayali River (Ordeloreto 1980: 60). Beginning in 1922 Standard Oil, registered as the Standard Oil Company of Peru and taking advantage of an oil law passed that year, made several unsuccessful explorations along the Ucayali Basin; it withdrew around 1930 (ibidem: 61). In 1934 oil was discovered superficially in the area of Aguas Calientes near the confluence of the Pachitea and the Ucayali Rivers (Ortiz 1974: II, 557). Three years later, when Ecuador signed its contract with Shell, Peru passed a new law promoting oil exploration throughout the country, granting special benefits to companies working the Amazon (Pontoni 1981a). Under this law, in 1939 the Ganso Azul Company, a subsidiary of U.S.-based Sinclair Oil Company, began small-scale oil production in Aguas Calientes.

Several authors (including Galarza, Delgado, and Deler; see Muratorio 1987: 205; Tamariz 1991: 64) have argued that the border conflict prompted by the promise of oil in the Amazon was aggravated by the showdown between Standard Oil and Shell. These companies ultimately represented the interests of the United States and Great Britain, respectively. In effect, the companies had clashed during the 1920s over oil concessions along Peru's northern coast close to the border with Ecuador, an area that was already under dispute. On that occasion Standard Oil managed to retain control through a secret agreement with Shell (Thorp and Bertram 1985: 150).

The 1937 replacement of Standard Oil by Shell in Ecuador sparked a new episode in the corporate rivalry. According to Jaime Galarza (in Muratorio 1987: 205), Standard Oil supported Peru's territorial claims in North American government circles during the 1941 war. If that was the case, it was mainly because Standard Oil was defending its investments along Peru's northern coast and not because it had vested interests in fields in the Peruvian Amazon, from where it had withdrawn in 1930.

In any event, by the late 1930s both Peru and Ecuador were moving toward ensuring their sovereignty over territories believed to be rich in oil deposits. The signing of the Rio de Janeiro Protocol in 1942, after the war's end, formalized what in fact had been the *uti possidetis* (actual possession) border between them during the rubber era. The only exception was the Napo and Pastaza Rivers, where, as a result of the war, Peru was able to push the border upriver a few tens of kilometers (Bustamante 1991: 94). Many years later, after several failed explorations by foreign companies, and even after a joint declaration by Standard and Shell that there was no oil in Amazonia, oil was discovered on both sides of the border (Muratorio 1987: 205). Paradoxically, Ecuador, which had a smaller portion of Amazon territory, possessed much larger and richer oil fields than did Peru.

The important point is that war with Ecuador had the unexpected effect of prompting a more active presence of the Peruvian government in its northern Amazon territories, particularly Loreto. This, in turn, had short- and long-term effects on the external and internal articulation of the region, on the structure, organization, and orientation of its economy, and on its social profile. As we shall see, the changes brought forth by the new governmental policies and actions in the end impaired the development of Loretan merchant houses and agroextractive *fundos.*

Integration Policies and the Reorientation of Trade

Throughout the 1930s, in its attempts to integrate the economy, the government initiated a national program to improve internal communications. The emphasis was no longer railways but rather the expansion of the meager national road network. The building of roads connecting Lima with important coastal and highland cities began in 1931. So did the opening of a few "penetration" roads to the *selva alta.* Road-building gained momentum during the second half of the decade; between 1935 and 1940 the government built 3,756 kilometers of main roads and 1,500 kilometers of secondary roads (Guerra 1984: 149). Despite winning its 1941 war with Ecuador, Peru's hold over the northern section of its Amazon territories could be ensured only by improving connections between Loreto and the rest of the country.

After its reorganization in 1935, the Peruvian Steamship Company started making trips between Lima and Iquitos via the Panama Canal. However, communication via ship was slow and irregular. Construction of a road linking Lima with the Ucayali River had been undertaken in 1933. Progress was slow and the road did not have a predetermined route, so much so that its intersection with the Ucayali River had not even been established when construction began. After the 1941 war construction speeded up, and the small port of Pucallpa was selected as the terminus. This was no coincidence; just to the north were the oil fields of Aguas Calientes–Ganso Azul.

The 843-kilometer road was officially inaugurated in September 1943. In a publication commemorating the event, the government proclaimed that the new road was to become the means to incorporate the Amazon into civilization, to bring progress to the region, and to better extract its abundant riches (in Ortiz 1984: 443–46). The rhetoric of civilization, progress, and wealth did not differ substantially from that prevalent in turn-of-the-century Civilist discourse. However, this time the measures implemented were much more successful in connecting the region to the rest of the country. As we shall see, the construction of the Lima-Pucallpa Road had economic impacts that far surpassed its immediate area of influence.

Less conspicuous but equally influential was the construction of airports at Iquitos and Tarapoto under the auspices of the United States. Beginning in 1927 small airplanes flew from Lima to San Ramón, in the *selva central,* and from there either to Pucallpa or Maquía on the Ucayali River, where passengers and cargo were transferred to hydroplanes for the last stretch to Iquitos, which had no landing strip. When the United States declared war in December 1941, Peru was one of the first Latin American countries to follow suit. The United States was interested in northern Peruvian Amazonia as a possible stopover for transcontinental trips. It was not long before both countries signed a treaty whereby Peru allowed the United States to build two airports for military purposes. At Iquitos and Tarapoto (San Martín), the airports provided a faster connection between Lima and the Amazon River basin and allowed the landing of larger aircraft, thereby greatly increasing the flow of products to and from the capital city.

The new road and air connections dramatically affected regional commercial activity. Providing access to the domestic market, the Lima-Pucallpa Road stimulated the economy of the upper Ucayali region, which until then had been entirely subordinated to Iquitos. Easier accesses to the Lima market, together with a series of governmental policies intended to promote food production, stimulated large-scale cattle-raising and rice production, thus providing new economic opportunities for the larger *fundos* in the area. As we learned in Chapter 8, during the 1940s the *fundos* in the upper Ucayali flourished, providing the bulk of Loreto's agropastoral production. The road also boosted the lumber industry. Until then upper Ucayali had been a minor supplier of fine timber, as the costs to transport logs downriver to the sawmills at Iquitos were too high. With the opening of the road, several sawmills were established in Pucallpa, and timber production in the area grew exponentially. In 1944 Iquitos produced ten times as much lumber as did Pucallpa; only eight years after the inauguration of the road Pucallpa managed to surpass Iquitos as Loreto's main lumber producer, and by 1962 it produced twice as much as Iquitos (Appendix 26).

Providing an easy outlet for regional produce, the Lima-Pucallpa Road reoriented Loreto's trade flow from the Atlantic to the Pacific and from the overseas international markets to the domestic market revolving around Lima. Timber is a case in point. After the Peruvian Steamship Company established regular trips between Iquitos and Lima, part of Loreto's timber production was exported to the capital via the Panama Canal. The opening of the road increased the volume of timber destined to Lima almost threefold between 1944 and 1948 (see Table 9.1). It also affected the trading circuits. Scarcely one year after the opening of the road, 21 percent of Loretan timber production for Lima was being transported over road. In 1948 it was 46 percent, and by the early 1960s all timber and lumber destined for Lima was transported over the road through Pucallpa.

The reorientation of the timber trade routes was not just the result of lower transport costs. During the 1940s Loreto's timber exports were subjected to a 10 percent ad valorem tariff. In 1954 the government exempted from this tariff export lumber sent by road to the coastal port of Callao, but it maintained the tariff for timber exported through the port of Iquitos (Ballón 1994: II, 518). This had the effect of increasing the export of lumber by road. The road also opened the region to migration from the highland and coastal regions. As a result, the population of Pucallpa grew from 2,368 inhabitants in 1940 to 26,391 in 1961 (Rodríguez Achung 1991: 153). The boomtown also attracted a new generation of entrepreneurs that invested mainly in commerce, the lumber industry, and fluvial and overland transportation. As a consequence, in the following decade Pucallpa became an important economic

Table 9.1   Percentage of Loreto's Timber Production Destined to Lima by Transport Route, 1944–1948

	Maritime route		Land route		Total
Year	Vol. (sq. ft)	%	Vol. (sq. ft)	%	Vol. (sq. ft)
1944	1,898,873	79.2	500,024	20.8	2,398,897
1945	2,835,845	73.8	1,005,104	26.2	3,840,949
1946	2,416,371	72.2	932,282	27.8	3,348,653
1947	3,105,121	48.9	3,248,782	51.1	6,353,903
1948	4,138,651	53.8	3,558,064	46.2	7,696,715

SOURCE: Sotomayor et al. 1949.

center, breaking Iquitos's monopoly over certain industries, including lumber, and developing economic and political dynamics all its own.

The increasing economic independence of Pucallpa found expression at political and administrative levels. At the time of the opening of the Lima-Pucallpa Road, Congress passed a law dividing the old province of Ucayali into three new provinces: Requena, comprising the lower Ucayali River; Ucayali, comprising the middle Ucayali; and Coronel Portillo, with Pucallpa as its capital, comprising the upper Ucayali. However, since 1942 some reformers went even farther, suggesting that Ucayali be detached from Loreto as a new department (Delboy 1952: 45). This proposal was ardently supported by Pucallpa's nascent economic elite, which as early as 1946 voiced their "separatist" intentions through the newly formed Committee for the Creation of the Department of Ucayali (Proceso 1979, No. 37). The struggle for separation from Loreto was strongly resisted by Iquitos's commercial elite, which saw its interests menaced by their Pucallpa peers.

The owners of the merchant houses of Iquitos were right to feel threatened. The building of the road provided an outlet for the region's produce, which was beyond their control. Many of the new products destined to the domestic market, such as cattle, rice, and jute, were produced without resort to the *habilitación* network controlled by the merchant houses. In addition, if in the past the merchant houses of Iquitos had not been directly involved in the lumber industry, under the new conditions they were completely excluded from it (San Román 1975: 197). This was a strong blow to the traditional mercantile elite, especially considering that the contribution of timber to the region's export trade rose from 9 percent in 1939 to 13 percent in 1948 and to 20 percent in 1950 (Appendixes 6, 7; Ordeoriente n.d.: 236). As the trading houses of Iquitos were excluded from production for the domestic market, particularly from fine timber extraction and lumbering, the power they derived from their mediatory role as outfitters, processors, and exporters was eroded.

The construction of the Lima-Pucallpa Road and of the airport at Iquitos not only opened a new outlet for Loreto's products but also provided an alternative source of foodstuffs and manufactured goods produced domestically and abroad. A new generation of traders from within and without the region took advantage of these new commercial opportunities, further weakening the merchant houses' control over the import trade. In addition, faster communications with the capital granted Lima's large importing firms, such as E. Ferreyros, A. Lulli, and G. Berckemeyer, an advantage over Iquitos's importers. Local publications in the 1950s are filled with their advertisements (e.g. Misiones Agustinianas 1953). By 1949 more than half the trading firms extant in Iquitos were new, having been established after 1940 (see Table 7.3). Many of these were small import-export firms very much dependent on their Liman business associates. Likewise, in Pucallpa most of the new import commerce was, from the very beginning, out of the hands of the merchant houses of Iquitos.

Many of the products brought from Lima by the new traders were considerably cheaper than those that the traditional merchant houses once imported from Europe and the United States via the Amazon River. This was especially true during and immediately after World War II, when many previously imported industrial products began to be produced in Peru (Guerra 1984: 157). After the end of the war, improvements in the size and speed of aircraft made it even cheaper to transport imports from Lima to Iquitos by air than from Belém to Iquitos by river. This too constituted a blow to the Iquitos-based merchant elite, which until then had carried out its import-export trade across the Atlantic. Additionally, postwar Europe's economic prostration deprived the more traditional firms from what until then had been their main market. Thus, by 1949 97 percent of Loreto's exports were sold to the United States, whereas Great Britain and Brazil absorbed a meager 1.7 percent and 1.6 percent, respectively (Sotomayor et al. 1949: 110).

Attempts to Modernize the Rural Economy

Taking advantage of the opportunities opened by World War II and responding to the urgent geopolitical demands that arose from the 1941 war with Ecuador, Peru designed a series of policies aimed at ensuring the economic and social development of its Amazon territories. The integration and economic model was not radically different from that of prior Civilist governments. The main tenets were that the Amazonian economy should be based on agriculture and cattle-raising and that production should be mainly oriented toward supplying the growing coastal urban markets. The idea that Amazonia should become the "pantry of Peru"—an expression popularized at the end of this period by Fernando Belaúnde, the future president, in his 1959 book, *Peru's Own Conquest* (1994)—started taking shape in the 1940s. However, the economic policies themselves differed substantially from Civilist policies. Forgotten was the idea that the economic takeoff of the Amazon region required colonization by white European immigrants. The 1940s witnessed an unprecedented demographic explosion in the coastal and highland provinces. As a result, pressure on land increased, creating a sector of landless and land-hungry peasants who could easily be persuaded to colonize Peru's vast Amazon territories.

Also absent was the Civilists' laissez-faire attitude that economic development of interior regions could be achieved simply by building a better transportation network without additional state intervention. Though not denying the urgency of improving the country's internal communications, the new official discourse stressed the importance of more active state intervention to ensure economic and social development. Under the new political paradigm the need for the construction of railroads, central to the Civilist model, was replaced by the need to provide credit, technology, and education as well as to regulate access to land and resources. In both cases, the final goal was to modernize the economies of the interior regions.

However, unlike the Civilists—who believed that modernization would naturally follow the construction of railroads—the postwar governments were aware that in order to achieve modernization, and, with it, social stability and economic prosperity, it would be necessary to eliminate anachronistic labor relations and to improve the lot of the labor classes. But rather than attack the problem directly the government opted to gradually implement a series of policies to remove the conditions that sustained such labor relations and to benefit small landholders rather than large *fundo* owners. In the late 1960s, with the ascension to power of the reformist Gen. Juan Velasco Alvarado, the government would take a more decisive stance on these issues, yet the policies implemented during the 1940s and 1950s weakened large *fundos* and traditional merchant houses and led to their final disappearance.

The creation of alternative sources of credit was one of the government's priorities. After the 1929 international financial crisis, Peru founded Banco Agrícola to replace bankrupt commercial banks in providing agricultural credit. During its first years of existence, the bank's services in the Amazon region never went beyond the granting of credit to large coffee-growers in the *selva central* (Santos-Granero and Barclay 1998: 89). And though in 1937 the bank announced plans to extend its services to the *selva baja*, it was not until 1943 that it granted its first loan in Loreto. This was clearly no coincidence. However, in following years Banco Agrícola had very little impact in the region (see Table 9.3). This was due to the founding in 1942 of the Amazon Peruvian Corporation (Corporación Peruana del Amazonas, or APC) under the auspices of the U.S.-Peru trade agreement on rubber.

In the context of the war effort the U.S. Rubber Reserve Company (RRC), which until then had been responsible for the development of synthetic rubber, was entrusted the task of establishing partnerships with Panama and the Amazon countries to ensure a steady supply of raw material. With the sponsorship of the RRC several rubber trade agreements were signed between the United States and rubber-producing countries. Under the terms of these agreements, the United States committed itself to provide economic and technical support to finance rubber-gathering, storage, and commercialization, as well as to promote rubber cultivation. To this effect, in February 1943 the United States government created the Rubber Development Corporation (RDC).

Pursuant to its agreement with the United States, Peru agreed to sell its entire rubber production to the RDC for a period of five years at fixed prices (Zegarra 1945). In June 1942 Peru created the Amazon Peruvian Corporation, a government agency with a considerable autonomy that became the Peruvian counterpart of the RDC. The APC monopolized the financing and handling of rubber exports to the United States. To promote rubber production, the RDC and the Peruvian government capitalized it with some $1 million (ibidem). The United States supplied most of this sum (94 percent) (Corporación n/d: 6).

The APC began by establishing offices in strategic rubber-producing areas in Peruvian Amazonia. Of the fourteen offices established, eleven were located in the department of Loreto; the other three were in Madre de Dios and the Pichis Valley. In Loreto, the APC's offices were distributed as follows: two on the Amazon River (Iquitos and Caballococha), five on the Ucayali (Pucallpa, Requena, Contamana, Puinahua, and 2 de Mayo), two on the Huallaga (Yurimaguas and Yurac), one on the Marañon (Nauta), and one on the Napo (Santa Clotilde). The offices acted as bank branches, providing cash credit to local extractors who wanted to reopen old hevea trails, open new ones, or exploit castilloa stands. They also acted as general stores, supplying basic necessities, such as tools, shotguns, foodstuffs, and medicines; in contrast to the traditional local traders, the items were sold at reasonable prices (Rumrrill et al. 1985: 155). Finally, the APC offices acted as gathering and storage points for local rubber production. The APC operated a fluvial and air fleet to collect the rubber produced by clients, very much like the traditional merchant houses (Anonymous 1944a: 39). The offices in Iquitos, Caballococha, and Pucallpa were in charge of collecting the rubber bought by minor offices and shipping it to the United States either by boat through Brazil to the Atlantic or by truck or airplane to the Pacific Coast.

The APC not only was in charge of promoting rubber production but also gathered and channeled other tropical products, such as barbasco, vital to the Allied war effort. In May 1942 Peru signed an agreement to sell to the United States and the United Kingdom a minimum of 2.5 million pounds and a maximum of 6 million pounds of barbasco per year at fixed prices (Extracto 1942: 75–76). Peru also granted those two countries priority in purchasing any barbasco production in excess of 6 million pounds. It is not clear whether the APC had a legal monopoly over the barbasco trade, as was the case with rubber. It is clear, however, that the APC marketed part of the production; even after 1947, when the U.S.-Peru agreement ended, it continued to be one of the main barbasco buyers (Sotomayor et al. 1949: 76).

The APC had to face innumerable problems to increase rubber production, not the least of which was the firm control that the trading establishment held over regional production and commerce. The government was keenly aware that the "old trading system" worked against a rapid increase in production (Anonymous 1944a: 37–41). It thus entrusted the APC with the task of "establishing a new form of *habilitación* which would eliminate the old system" (Zegarra 1945). This was to be achieved by supplying extractors with credit in cash, foodstuffs, and basic working materials at lower interest rates than those available from the merchant houses. This policy was only partially successful.

In a very short period, the APC managed to establish a huge network of offices, gathering points, and transportation channels, which in scale far surpassed the individual networks of even the largest merchant houses of Iquitos. The credit advanced amounted to about US$538,000 during 1942–1943 and to US$692,000 during 1943–1944 (Anonymous 1944a: 37–41; 1944b: 632). The results were spectacular. In only three years (1942–1945), the APC managed to increase Loreto's rubber production tenfold and boosted national production to the level it had attained during the most productive years of the rubber boom (see Table 9.2; Appendix 2).

However, the new prosperity never reached the rubber tappers whom the government expected to benefit. Official sources indicate that during the 1943–1944 tapping season the APC granted a total of only 232 loans and that the recipients operated with a workforce of 5,800 tappers (Anonymous 1944a: 37–41). This clearly indicates that the beneficiaries of APC loans were not small rubber tappers but large extractors: rubber *patrones, fundo* owners, and local merchants. Although the APC was unable to dismantle the exploitative *habilitación* network that linked peons to *patrones,* thanks to its monopoly over rubber exports it was quite successful in excluding the merchant houses of Iquitos from the rubber business. In addition, by providing cheaper basic supplies and credit at lower interest rates, it also limited their control over the trade of other important regional products. As a result, in 1947 it was reported in the local newspaper *Eco* that the merchant houses of Iquitos were extremely impaired by the competition of the APC (Kanatari 1997, No. 667: 14).

The establishment in Iquitos of branches of Banco Popular (1937) and Banco de Crédito (1943) further eroded the role of the traditional merchant houses by broadening sources of commercial credit. Excluded from the burgeoning timber export trade due to the inauguration of the Lima-Pucallpa Road, and from the rubber and barbasco trade because of the activities of the APC, Iquitos's merchant houses were

Table 9.2   Loreto's Share of Peru's Rubber Production, 1941–1950 (in metric tons)

Year	Rubber production		
	Loreto (tons)	Peru (tons)	Loreto/Peru (%)
1941	55	nd	nd
1942	182	185	98.4
1943	480	641	74.9
1944	650	1,414	46.0
1945	1,933	2,453	78.8
1946	1,694	2,836	59.7
1947	1,251	2,099	59.6
1948	341	1,443	23.6
1949	709	1,457	48.7
1950	739	1,522	48.6

SOURCES: Anuario 1950: 217; BA 1942–1952.

unable to fully profit from the economic opportunities offered by the war. This did not cause their immediate fall, but it weakened them, rendering them increasingly unfit to adapt to the postwar economy.

Shortly after Peru's involvement in the war effort, a prominent Loretan politician warned that the government should not only take advantage of the new economic opportunities but also aim at "ensuring the region's future" after the war's end (Delboy 1952: 5–6). The government was aware that the war-induced prosperity would not last forever, and in 1944 the minister of development asserted that the APC might become the institutional framework that could ensure the prosperity of the Amazon region after the end of the war (Caravedo 1981: 103). Thus, after the United States ended its bilateral agreement with Peru in 1947, the government retained the corporation and even endowed it with new funds. The reformed APC was entrusted with promoting agrarian, mining, and industrial activities in Amazonia, as well as building and administering basic infrastructures (Corporación n.d.: 5). The means to achieve this were not radically different from those applied in the past: (1) grant credit in cash and/or basic goods; and (2) monopolize the marketing of regional production.

Despite its efforts, the APC still was unable to break the *habilitación* system. In 1951 its administrator addressed a memorandum to the International Labor Organization in Geneva, denouncing the unjust labor conditions to which "jungle Indians" were subjected through the *habilitación* system (Villeneuve 1974: 145). He concluded that "escape is the only means of liberation, but they do not always achieve this goal, for affected *patrones* call on the authorities to chase the fugitives and force them back to work" (ibidem.). In doing so, he implicitly recognized the APC's failure to eliminate such labor relations.

Decline and Decay of *Fundos* and Merchant Houses

In the early 1950s the government decided to change its credit policies for the Amazon region. In 1952 it merged the APC with Banco Agrícola, forming Banco de Fomento Agropecuario (BFA). In Loreto, the new bank promoted agropastoral activities through subsidized credit to ensure food self-reliance, reduce expensive food imports, and stimulate the production of a surplus to be exported to the coastal urban centers. In addition, instead of favoring large and medium-sized *fundo* owners, as the APC had in previous years, the bank prioritized the granting of credit to small producers (see Table 9.3). In the long run this introduced important transformations to rural Loreto, particularly at the *fundo* level.

The new government's policies for the region profited from a decade-long experiment with and promotion of new crops and breeds of cattle at state-run farms and scientific stations. In 1943, with the technical and financial support of the United States, the government founded Servicio Cooperativo Interamericano de Producción de Alimentos (SCIPA) to boost agropastoral production (Sotomayor et al. 1949: 94). In the Amazon region SCIPA concentrated on promoting the cultivation

Table 9.3   Agricultural Loans Granted by Banco Agrícola and Banco de Fomento
Agropecuario in Loreto by Type of Farmers, 1943–1962

| | | | Percentage granted | |
Year	No. loans[a]	Credit (US$)	L & M farmers[b]	Small farmers
1943	4	5,508	nd	nd
1944	15	18,123	nd	nd
1945	19	21,462	62.6	37.4
1946	5	7,585	81.1	18.9
1947	nd	nd	nd	nd
1948	1	7,846	100.0	—
1949	2	56,350	100.0	—
1950	2	18,577	100.0	—
1951	1	8,717	100.0	—
1952	16	7,095	—	100.0
1953	229	109,644	—	100.0
1954	203	72,002	5.7	94.3
1955	228	197,724	79.8	20.2
1956	172	65,058	—	100.0
1957	223	63,132	—	100.0
1958	642	233,475	1.1	98.9
1959	832	304,696	6.1	93.9
1960	1,031	405,828	13.9	86.1
1961	2,006	643,981	8.7	91.3
1962	3,304	1,195,061	34.1	65.9

SOURCES: BA 1942–1952; BFA 1953–1962.
NOTES: [a] Loans were granted by mid-year at the beginning of the agricultural season.
[b] L & M farmers = large and medium-sized farmers.

of rice and jute and the raising of cattle resistant to tropical climates. Not only did the government grant credit through the BFA and provide technical assistance through agencies such as SCIPA; it also guaranteed fixed prices and a market for some of the products it sponsored. Thus, from at least 1952 the government assigned the Caja de Depósitos y Consignaciones, the tax-collecting agency, the task of buying the region's rice production (Ballón 1994: II, 499).

To ensure the success of its Amazonian development plans, the government also designed new policies for access to land and natural resources. Jute and new strains of rice can be cultivated only in annually flooded alluvial lands, which until then were in the hands of the rural elite. In 1953 the government passed legislation declaring such lands state property and regulating the granting of permits for temporary use (Banco de Crédito 1972: 113). This not only allowed small farmers to gain access to these rich lands but also provided them with the legal backing required to obtain credit from the BFA. All of these measures had almost an immediate effect on the area devoted to rice production (Appendix 25). By 1960 Loreto had not only satisfied its own demand for rice but also began selling its surplus in neighboring departments (Villarejo 1988: 138).

These government policies also had an important impact on the viability of traditional *fundos*. Not only did *fundo* owners lose direct control of lands that had suddenly become valuable for the production of marketable crops; they were no longer the favored subjects of credit. Still, many *fundo* owners ventured into extensive rice cultivation and cattle-raising. However, only those in the Ucayali area, who had more direct communications with Lima, were able to make the profits they were accustomed to in previous decades by combining extractive and agricultural activities. In fact, it seems that only the large Ucayali *fundos* were able to obtain credit from the BFA (see Table 9.4).

Rather than relying on the Asociación de Productores de Loreto, which grouped the region's largest producers, SCIPA opted to promote the organization of committees of small *fundo* owners residing in riverine settlements close to the region's larger towns. This provided further proof that the government's plans for Loreto were not aimed at supporting large *fundo* owners. By 1949 SCIPA had formed twenty-six such committees, totaling 400 associates, in the provinces of Maynas, Loreto, and Requena (Sotomayor et al. 1949: 95). They were grouped in the Asociación Departamental de Agricultores de Loreto, the counterpart of the large *fundo* owners' organization.

Intentionally or not, two additional government measures further impaired the profitability of traditional agroextractive large *fundos*. The first measure related to *fundo* taxation. Around 1940 the government decided to enforce the collection of taxes that had been established in the 1909 land legislation. Under this law purchasers or grantees of public lands were required to pay an annual tax of one cent per hectare of uncultivated land. In 1941 the Chamber of Commerce and Agriculture complained that the Caja de Depósitos y Consignaciones had not only begun collecting this tax but was demanding retroactive payment (Legislatura 1943: 65–71). Additionally, in the early 1940s the government started enforcing Law

Table 9.4   Loans for Rice Cultivation Granted by Banco de Fomento Agropecuario in Loreto by River Basin and Type of Farmers, 1953

	Credit (US$)	
Basin[a]	Small farmers	L & M farmers[b]
Amazon/Napo	57,940	—
Ucayali	24,766	13,574
Marañon	4,988	—
Huallaga	247	—

SOURCE: Anuario 1954: 155; elaborated by the authors.
NOTES: [a] The four river basins were served respectively by the BFA's offices in Iquitos, Pucallpa, Nauta, and Yurimaguas.
[b] L & M farmers = large and medium-sized farmers.

7904 of 1934 in Loreto; it imposed a tax on rural properties equivalent to 7 percent of annual net income (CIDA 1963: 386). The tax was also applied retroactively and mostly affected large *fundos* (Gómez Perea 1991). As a result of the tax burdens, some *fundo* owners sold their properties and abandoned the area; others remained but saw their gains diminished.

The second measure was the government's attempt to regulate access to timber resources. In the past, *fundo* owners had been largely free to exploit forests located beyond the legal boundaries of their properties, within what was considered their area of influence. This privileged them over the logging companies of Iquitos and their sometimes agents the merchant houses. In 1947, the government issued a decree whereby timber extractors were required to obtain an official permit to carry out logging activities; those who did not comply were subject to fines and/or seizure of timber production. The new legislation broke the de facto monopoly *fundo* owners held over state forests, allowing independent extractors and logging companies to obtain logging permits. Though this did not totally exclude *fundo* owners from extracting timber, it certainly curtailed their control over forest resources. This was no small loss, as timber extraction and lumber production were in the process of becoming one of the region's most dynamic and profitable activities.

In 1942 Emilio Delboy (1952: 52), former prefect and future house representative for Loreto, claimed that "Amazonia deserves the state's resolute protection." Delboy was echoing the regional elites' demands for a more active state role in regional development. However, not long afterward, when the government started implementing its new development policies, the landed and trading elites were swift to voice dissent.

Landed elites and trading elites were tightly associated. By 1917 the Iquitos chamber of commerce had become the Chamber of Commerce and Agriculture of Loreto so as to incorporate the interests of the emerging landed elite. In the 1940s large *fundo* owners were grouped in the Asociación de Productores de Loreto, an elitist organization with only eighty-one associates, affiliated with the chamber of commerce (Sotomayor et al. 1949: 144–6). The landed and trading elites opposed what could be considered as the three pillars of the government's development strategy for the region: (1) the reorientation of the regional economy from extraction to agriculture; (2) the shifting of trade from the Atlantic to the Pacific and thus from the international market to the domestic market; and (3) the modernization of labor relations.

As for the first point, a 1949 article by Günther Schaper ("Is Amazonia a Promising Agricultural Area?") contains the main arguments wielded by both merchants and *fundo* owners. Schaper, an important Iquitos merchant of German origin, argued that Amazonia, given its natural and human limitations, would never achieve more than subsistence-level agriculture. In support he pointed out the low fertility of the high interior lands, the constant threat of inundation of the richer riverine lowlands, and Loretans' apathy for agricultural work vis-à-vis their enthusiasm for extractive activities. He went on, asserting that "the future of Peruvian Amazonia lies in the exploitation of the forest itself and not in its disappearance [due to agricultural expansion]. Rubber, timber, oil nuts, resins, ivory nuts, and chemical and medicinal products constitute the real wealth of these forests" (1949: 81). Schaper concluded that instead of promoting agriculture the government should foster silviculture or "the rational management of the forest."

Enrique Zegarra, former prefect of Loreto and former director of the APC, expressed the elite's point of view with respect to the second point (shifting trade from east to west). Although congratulating the government for planning to build several railroads connecting the coast with the Amazon region, Zegarra (1949: 27) argued against government attempts to convert Loreto's economy to serve coastal markets. Without dismissing the importance of the domestic market, Zegarra stressed that "to the north of the Caribbean Sea and across the Atlantic Ocean there are many consumers for Peru's tropical products," concluding that "the future of Amazonia lies in the sea, or more exactly, in its interoceanic communications." He asserted that "the life of the Amazonian departments languishes as the transatlantic ships move away from its ports" and complained that the lack of a regular fluvial-maritime service in the region was impairing the export trade and causing a general shortage of food. Zegarra concluded that the only way to end this situation was for the government to order the state-subsidized Peruvian Steamship Company to make regular trips along the Iquitos–New York–Callao route (ibidem: 25).

The reaction of Loreto's elite to the third point (modernizing labor relations) was not as direct or explicit. Rather than openly confront government attempts to modernize Loreto's economy and improve living conditions for regional workers, elites indirectly referred to the need to accommodate time-tested mechanisms for recruiting labor. To support this point of view, they underscored past failures to change the traditional *habilitación* system. For example, the editors of *Guía de Loreto* (Sotomayor et al. 1949: 3) demanded "an intensive official action that is adapted to the region's methods and conditions, in order to provide its inhabitants with reasonable means of living." And although they called for national capitalists to invest in Loreto, they warned that this should be done "carefully and on the basis of the knowledge of local people, who are better acquainted with the region's special conditions" (ibidem: 4). In a veiled condemnation of the Amazon Peruvian Corporation's attempts to replace the *habilitación* system with a more modern and fair credit system, Schaper (1949: 81) criticized capitalist enterprises that in recent years had failed "for lack of discernment and the stoic pursuit of erroneous principles which were born in other lands and could not adapt to the jungle's conditions."

This time, however, the regional elite was unable to counter the factors leading to the progressive exhaustion of Loreto's agroextractive economy and that, presently, would cause the ruin of merchant houses as well as large *fundos*: (1) the improvement of communications with the highland and coastal markets; (2) the appearance of alternative sources of credit and trading networks for the region's agroextractive export products; (3) the promotion of agricultural production for the local and domestic markets through state-subsidized credit to small producers; (4) the democratization of access to natural resources; and (5) the tax reforms that affected *fundo* production and exonerated exports through Lima from tariffs. No policy by itself accounted for the decline of the trading and landed elites. Combined, however, they had an enormous impact on merchant and rural establishments.

This situation was aggravated by a decrease in international demand for tropical products. The early 1960s witnessed the ends of the region's last major export booms: caspi milk, barbasco, rosewood oil, and fine timber (see Figure 7.1). In the ensuing years Loreto's export trade would be based mainly on processed softwoods and a few minor, highly destructive export booms: ornamental fish, live animals, furs, and hides. The end of this era was also associated with a generational change (Chibnik 1994: 46; Barclay 1995: 263–4). Many owners of traditional merchant houses and *fundos* died at this time, and their more educated, urbanized descendants were reluctant to take the reins of declining enterprises, preferring instead to move from rural Loreto to the region's growing cities.

The monopolies that the merchant houses once held over fluvial transport, credit, the import-export trade, and internal commerce were severely eroded. As a result, by the beginning of the 1960s most of the large merchant houses of Iquitos had disappeared; the few that survived were only shadows of their former selves (see Table 7.3). A new generation of merchants gradually replaced them, combining, as we shall see, elements of the old and new systems. Likewise, the control that large *fundo* owners exerted over land, natural resources, and access to the market had been considerably weakened. Although governmental policies and actions proved unable to transform the traditional labor system, other forces at play, which will be discussed in Chapter 12, would lead to the emancipation of the region's rural laborers from *patrones* and debt-peonage ties—and thus to the demise of the *fundo* system itself.

* * *

The 1915–1962 period was not, as has been assumed, one of economic stagnation, state indifference, and general backwardness. In fact, it was a very dynamic period in which the region's main economic agents undertook the search for a new economic identity. The agroextractive export economy that took shape, flourished, and then declined during this period was not a small-scale replica of the rubber economy. The new economy was not purely extractive or based on a linear sequence of minibooms. Export agriculture played an important role in the new economy, providing more than 60 percent of the value of the region's exports during some decades. The various agricultural and extractive export cycles overlapped in time but not necessarily in space. As a result of such unevenness, whenever one cycle ended it did not affect the entire economy, as in the case of the rubber bust.

Although the agroextractive export economy was different in many respects from the rubber economy, it can nevertheless be characterized as a transitional economy with a frontier flair. *Correrías* were eliminated as a long-term means of "producing" peons; generally, open violence and physical punishments were no longer central to retaining and controlling rural laborers. This phenomenon was closely associated with the formation of a new social segment of mixed-blood people—we will analyze this process in greater detail in Chapter 12—which provided *fundo* owners with a new source of disciplined laborers, rendering unnecessary the more violent means of labor control.

Nevertheless, the *habilitación* system continued to be the basis of the region's economy, both in terms of exchange (commercial credit) and in terms of production (debt-peonage). It involved all economic agents in a pyramid that went from the most powerful merchant houses of Iquitos down to the humblest peons, passing through a long chain of trading agents, fluvial peddlers, local merchants, independent extractors, and *fundo* owners. This happened despite attempts by some of the most modern merchant houses to grant credit in cash rather than in merchandise and, contrary to postwar efforts by the government to eliminate *habilitado* relationships, by creating alternative sources of credit. Yet most merchant houses and *fundo* owners strongly opposed the elimination of precapitalist relations of production. They were convinced that the *habilitación* system was the institution best adapted to the region's geographic, social, and economic conditions. The failure of such a vast and powerful state agency as the Amazon Peruvian Corporation to eradicate *habilitado* relationships merely confirmed the beliefs of the trading and landed elites.

Even though the government was unable to eliminate the *habilitación* system, it contributed to its erosion by curtailing monopolies traditionally held by large merchant houses and *fundo* owners. By improving communications with coastal markets, promoting the reorientation of the region's economy from the export to the domestic market, and exonerating from taxes Loreto's exports through the Pacific port of Callao, the government severely undermined the power of the Atlantic-oriented merchant elite. In turn, by favoring small producers in granting promotional credit and technical assistance, by democratizing access to key resources such as alluvial lands and timber, and by taxing uncultivated lands and large producers, it weakened the landed elite. Finally, by enlarging the judicial apparatus, by appointing a greater number of local-level authorities, and by expanding such services as education and health, the government helped extend civil rights to a larger proportion of the region's population, particularly in rural areas. All these factors created conditions for the appearance of a new, more capitalist generation of entrepreneurs and to the emancipation of *fundo* peons from debt-bondage. We will analyze these processes in Part 3.

PART THREE

The Taming of the Frontier, 1963–1990

If the 1851–1914 period marked the coming of age of Loreto's frontier economy and the 1915–1962 period marked a transition characterized by the persistence of attenuated frontier traits, then the period beginning in 1963, with the accession of Pres. Fernando Belaúnde, and ending in 1990, with the election of Pres. Alberto Fujimori, can be defined as the taming of the frontier. It witnessed a passage, from the doctrine of development to the triumph of neoliberalism. The *habilitación* system was severely undermined; capitalist relations of production and exchange expanded; and the violent features generally associated with frontier economies were eradicated. More importantly, civil rights were extended to previously disenfranchised populations who now became empowered. Mestizo regional identity and culture were consolidated, reinforcing the cross-class regionalist ideology that originated in the late nineteenth century. In Part 3, we analyze the radical political, economic, and social changes that led to the transformation of Loreto into a tamed frontier.

In Chapter 10 we examine the policies designed to achieve the modernization and greater integration of the Amazon region, particularly Loreto, by the first two administrations of this period: the democratically elected government of architect Fernando Belaúnde (1963–1968) and the "revolutionary" military government (1968–1980). We maintain that there were three central factors at play during this period. First was the integrating role now assumed by the state and its constant experimenting with development. Second was the instigation of new policies on taxation, credit, price subsidies, land allocation, resource exploitation, social spending, and politico-administrative demarcation. Third was the availability of abundant financial resources derived from large-scale oil extraction beginning in the early 1970s. These three factors, which led to a most dramatic transformation of regional economic and social orders, are explored in Chapters 11, 12, and 13.

In Chapter 11 we analyze the changes experienced by the region's economy since the early 1960s: how these shaped, and were shaped by, a new generation of entrepreneurs filling the vacuum created by the disappearance of traditional merchant houses. Loreto's economy ceased to be an export economy during this period. This led to a shift from the export to the import trade and from the international to the regional and domestic markets. More importantly, it resulted in a shift from extractive enterprises (agriculture and mining) to the transformation sector (industry and construction). We maintain that the new entrepreneurial elite acquired some of the traits characteristic of regional bourgeoisies during this period, namely, greater emphasis on manufacturing rather than commercial activities, capitalist modes of operation, investment of profits in the region, adherence to regionalist political proposals, and greater attachment to the region. However, despite the efforts of its most progressive members, the new economic elite has been unable to dispense completely with the precapitalist aspects so as to shift toward sustained investment in the manufacturing sector. These shortcomings prevented Loreto's elite from becoming a fully modern entrepreneurial class.

Chapter 12 is devoted to the analysis of the important transformations that took place in Loreto's rural areas as a consequence of the collapse of the agroextractive export economy and the disappearance of *fundos*. We argue that a deteriorating regional economy, accessible fluvial transportation, and increased literacy weakened the economic and political holds that *fundo* owners had over peons and allowed many peons to free themselves during the 1950s and 1960s. As a result, there was a marked increase in the number of *caseríos*, or "independent settlements," which became the dominant feature of the region's rural landscape beginning in the 1960s. There was also an increase in the number of indigenous settlements—"native communities" that were legally recognized and titled by the state. The emancipation of *fundo* peons and their transformation into independent peasants went hand in hand with their consolidation as a new social stratum—the *ribereño*, or "riverine," mixed-blood population—which after the breakdown of the *fundo* economy became dominant in Loreto's rural areas, both demographically and culturally.

The last chapter is devoted to an investigation of the organization of Loreto's popular sectors—the classes, class segments, and other social groups occupying a subordinated economic and political position—and the emergence of a multiclass movement with a regionalist ideology and political platform. We argue that during the first phase of the military government (1968–1975), when the mobilization of the country's popular sectors was considered crucial to the success of the government's economic and social reforms, the state actively promoted the organization of those sectors. After analyzing the process of organization and mobilization of each sector, we conclude that although most of the political activity was concentrated in the region's two largest cities—Iquitos and Pucallpa—and their areas of influence, the need to organize reached the region's remotest areas. This generated a greater awareness of rights among the region's poorest and most disenfranchised sectors and encouraged them to mobilize in defense of those rights.

In summary, during the 1963–1990 period Loreto ceased being a frontier in the economic and political senses. Increased government intervention helped to modernize the region's economy, expanding the sphere of capitalist relations and confining production and exchange based on the *habilitación* system to the remoter areas. The transformation of *fundo* peons into independent peasants, as well as the replacement of traditional merchant houses by a new, more modern generation of entrepreneurs willing to invest in the production sector and take root in the region, contributed in turn to the development of a regional market. Although it is still not fully developed and does not yet include the whole region, it has accelerated internal articulation and national integration.

Greater government influence in the region through the increase of the state apparatus and the extension of public services has helped to eliminate the violence and lawlessness characteristic of frontier economies. But if greater state intervention has been fundamental in the taming of the Loretan frontier, so has the political organization and mobilization of the region's popular sectors. In combination, this led to the empowerment of previously disenfranchised segments of the population, the extension of civil rights throughout Loreto, and the general strengthening of the region's civil society.

10

"Amazonia Will Become a Joyous Region": State Planning and Oil Exploration

The evolution of Loreto's economy from the early 1960s on resulted, to a large extent, from a change in the state's perception of its role in economic development. It also derived from a change in the role that the Amazon region was supposed to play in the development of Peru. To understand these changes, we must consider the transformations taking place at the international, national, and regional levels. In the late 1950s, Peru entered a new phase of modernization tightly linked to the expansion of industrial activities in previous years. Unlike the enclave-type economy of the previous period (1915–1962), the new industrial sector required free labor for its functioning (Cotler 1978: 286–7). This resulted in the confrontation between, on the one hand, the nascent industrial bourgeoisie and the progressive segments of the middle classes and, on the other hand, the oligarchic bourgeoisie associated with foreign capital and traditional large landowners. The former were represented by the national daily *El Comercio*, which promoted greater state intervention, structural reforms, and a more nationalistic stance; the latter were represented by the national daily *La Prensa*, which advocated unrestricted economic freedom.

The progressives demanded the suppression of feudal labor relations in the countryside and greater autonomy with respect to foreign capital. They called for agrarian reforms that would eliminate *latifundia* and *minifundia* (extremely large and extremely small landholdings) and promote the emergence of a land market, the creation of a group of modern and productive farmers, and the formation of a sector of salaried workers. The reforms were expected to foster expansion of the domestic market, viewed as a precondition to industrialization. The progressives also demanded greater state control over economic sectors considered to be strategic for the country's development, together with the adoption of centralized planning to reorganize and expand production (Cotler 1978: 304).

So that the state would have the necessary resources to promote economic development, progressives also called for fiscal reforms. This reformist, progressive ideology soon gained important adherents in the army and the Catholic Church. Like modern segments of the bourgeoisie, these institutions came to see imperialism and traditional oligarchy as a common enemy, creating conditions for social unrest and the dissemination of communist ideologies. The Cuban revolution in 1959 confirmed their fears and conferred greater urgency upon their demands.

The implementation of social and economic reforms that would achieve development in Latin America was a top priority in the agenda of international agencies and institutions. Most important among them was the Economic Commission for Latin America (ECLA), created by the United Nations in 1948. On the recommendations of several European economists who were widely read and discussed in Latin America, Raúl Prebisch, ECLA's main theorist, shaped the doctrine of industrialization through the substitution of imports. This economic philosophy was to have an enormous influence on the economic programs of Latin American countries during the 1950s (FitzGerald 1991). The ECLA also played an important role in promoting agrarian reform, public expenditure, and centralized planning. Its underlying premise was that the state should play a more active role in promoting economic development. Thus, in 1962, the ECLA and the Organization of American States (OAS), which by then were fiscal advisers to the Peruvian government, encouraged the creation of the National Planning Institute (Kuczynski 1977: 47).

In Amazon countries, the notion that industrial development required the elimination of precapitalist labor relations and the creation of a domestic market went hand in hand with the perception that those goals could be achieved only by geographical, social, and economic integration. Not surprisingly, during the 1950s and early 1960s all these countries renewed efforts to integrate and develop their relatively isolated Amazon territories. They attempted this by constructing pioneer roads, by advancing programs of colonization, and by promoting economic growth through low-interest loans as well as tax exemptions. Several international organizations linked to the United States, the OAS, and the UN played a decisive role in planning and/or financing these activities. Among the most important were the Agency for International Development, the Inter-American Development Bank, and the ECLA. The policies taken by the Peruvian government with respect to its Amazon territories, and to Loreto in particular, were similar to those implemented throughout the Amazon Basin. Sometimes Peru took the lead; other times it followed in the steps of Amazonian neighbors.

In this chapter we analyze the policies of integration and modernization taken by the first two governments of this period: the democratically elected government of architect Fernando Belaúnde (1963–1968), and the "revolutionary" government of the armed forces, led in its first phase by Gen. Juan Velasco Alvarado (1968–1975), and in its second phase by Gen. Francisco Morales Bermúdez (1975–1980). We contend that these governments, despite their many differences, shared two important notions about the Amazon. First, to ensure the country's development and territorial integrity, it was necessary to integrate the region. Second, given its relative isolation and great distance from the market, the Amazon required special treatment, or at least special status. The two administrations also shared the idea that some degree of state intervention was necessary to attain those objectives.

However, important differences existed as to policy. Depending on their political bent, policies expressed different notions about the extent of state intervention necessary. Another difference centered on which social segments were the most appropriate to carry out the required transformations and which deserved support. The liberal administration of President Belaúnde called for moderate state intervention through state incentives and corrective measures. In other words, the state should not attempt to become an active economic agent but should leave the economy in the hands of the private sector. In contrast, the nationalistic, reformist, antiimperialist military government of President Velasco Alvarado accused the private sector of repeatedly failing to modernize the country and to accomplish development efforts. Given the situation, he argued, the state should step in and assume a more active economic role. Whereas Belaúnde relied on the progressive sectors of the bourgeoisie and the middle classes to further his reforms, the military contended it was necessary to mobilize support from the popular sectors to implement its reforms. The organization and empowerment of subordinated, disenfranchised sectors brought repercussions for the country as a whole and for Amazonia in particular.

During this period, the government was very active in regulating the region's economy; it was constantly experimenting with development. That reformist agenda was expressed in numerous policies changes on taxation, credit, price subsidies, land allocation, resource exploitation, social spending, and politico-administrative demarcation. We contend, however, that the new policies, despite constant changes, led to a drastic transformation of the region's economic and social orders and to the taming of the frontier. The availability of abundant fiscal resources derived from oil extraction beginning in the early 1970s accelerated this process.

Belaúnde and the Subsidizing State

The 1963 election of Fernando Belaúnde, leader of the populist Acción Popular Party, expressed the increasing consensus among political forces and the electorate on the need to implement social and economic reforms. Belaúnde believed that the state should be active in modernizing the country and creating conditions for development. He also thought the state should regulate society so as to harmonize the interests of its different sectors (Cotler 1978: 345). To achieve these objectives, Belaúnde's political platform included: (1) the implementation of an agrarian reform that would eliminate large unproductive landholdings and the anachronistic labor relations on which these were based; (2) the promotion of industrialization through tax incentives; (3) the activation of the agrarian sector through the granting of low-interest credit; and (4) the improvement of the standard of living and capacities of the poorer social sectors through an increase in social spending and the expansion of basic public services such as education, health, and housing.

The integration of the Amazon was a key element in Belaúnde's development strategy, as manifested in *Peru's Own Conquest* (1994), which was originally published in 1959. It is clear, however, that Belaúnde assigned different roles to the *selva alta* and *selva baja*. Because of its proximity, the *selva alta* should provide an outlet for the thousands of landless highlands peasants, become a supplier of foodstuffs for the growing coastal urban markets, and contribute its abundant resources to national development. Thus, his government designed an ambitious, 2,400-kilometer road-building plan; the Carretera Marginal, as it was called, aimed at connecting the important colonist towns along the Andean piedmont. In addition, through the Institute of Agrarian Reform and Colonization, founded in 1960, Belaúnde launched several large colonization programs in the *selva alta*, granting free lands and promotional credit and extending public services. The moderate Law of Agrarian Reform passed in 1964 was instrumental in furthering his colonization projects; it not only regulated the expropriation of unproductive landholdings in the Andean highlands but also expedited the mechanisms to acquire land in the Amazon.

In contrast, the integration of the *selva baja*, especially Loreto with its larger urban centers, was to be achieved by promoting industrial activity. To attain this, Belaúnde passed a series of laws intended to hasten industrialization in the *selva baja*, particularly Loreto (though the laws applied to the entire Peruvian Amazon). In early 1964 the government issued Supreme Decree 04, arguing that the 1959 general Law for Industrial Promotion (Law 13270) had proved insufficient to foster industrialization in the Amazon, which required new incentives to overcome its "state of economic prostration" (Ortiz 1986: 485). Existing Law 13270 had exempted commercial and industrial activities from payment of profit taxes (Ocampo 1983: 503); in contrast, the new law exempted those who owned or established industries in the region, as well as those who rendered direct or indirect services to these industries, from payment of all taxes, including income taxes and import-export tariffs, for a period of ten years.

By granting Loreto special status, the law aimed to induce regional elites, such as those residing in Iquitos and Pucallpa, to shift investments from the commercial to the industrial sector. It also attempted to attract external capital, both national and international. In the exulted words of the minister of finance: "Amazonia will become a joyous region, where nobody will pay taxes to the state and everybody will receive all kinds of benefits. It will, thus, turn into a place of world attraction" (Ortiz 1986: 192).

Supreme Decree 04 was complementary to the Peruvian-Colombian Customs Agreement, signed in 1938, whereby Peru and Colombia agreed to exempt bilateral trade from taxes and to establish a common external tariff for goods imported into the area covered by the agreement. In addition, it contemplated exempting from import duties a series of items considered of basic importance (Ocampo 1983: 498). In Peru, the agreement originally applied to the portion of the Amazon River from Iquitos to the frontier, as well as the tract of the Putumayo River shared by both countries. By 1964, however, Peru and Colombia agreed to extend the area to include the departments of Loreto and San Martín (Banco de Crédito 1972: 230).

Although the incentives provided by these two legal instruments (i.e., Supreme Decree 04 and the 1938 customs agreement) did not have an immediate effect in promoting investment in the industrial sector, they stimulated Loreto's external commerce, particularly its import trade (Appendix 4). But they also stimulated a series of fraudulent trading operations. As a result, by the end of 1964 Congress ordered the revision of all the exoneration permits granted by the government (Banco de Crédito 1972: 229).

In 1965 Belaúnde replaced Supreme Decree 04 by Law 15600, which exempted all sectors within the Amazon from profit and income taxes for a fifteen-year period. It also exonerated exports from the payment of all tariffs, except for those imposed for local purposes. The law benefited not only the industrial sector, which was purportedly its main objective, but also the commercial, agricultural, and transport sectors (Ocampo 1983: 504–5). Law 15600 introduced two innovations: (1) It established that the exemption from import duties was only valid for that portion of the Amazon not included within the area of application of the Peruvian-Colombian Customs Agreement; and (2) it excluded the mining sector from tax exemptions. These innovations were aimed at harmonizing Law 15600 and the Peruvian-Colombian Customs Agreement and maintaining revenues from the region's oil industry.

The incentives applied to merchandise entered through the port of Iquitos, as well as to that imported through cities along the Pacific Coast (Banco de Crédito 1972: 230). Capital and consumer goods imported under these laws were meant for the exclusive benefit of the areas where they applied. However, smuggling of exempted imports into areas not exonerated became rampant, as some took advantage of the possibility of importing goods through the Pacific Coast. To curtail smuggling, which had become a national issue, in 1966 (Law 16231) and again in 1967 (Supreme Decree 134-H) the government decreed that only merchandise entered through the port of Iquitos would be exempted from payment of duties (Banco de Crédito 1972: 231). These measures generated widespread rejection, as they led to a rise in prices of imports coming from Pacific countries and, as a result, to a sharp decrease of the import trade. In 1968, at the end of his administration and following a 44 percent devaluation of the national currency, Belaúnde was forced to pass Law 16900, which cut by 50 percent the tax exemptions established by Law 15600. This measure applied to all but the industrial sector. It affected commerce in general and, particularly, the import-export trade.

The tax exemptions in Law 15600 included agricultural activities. These incentives had little impact in most of Loreto, where large *fundos* had all but disappeared. However, near Ucayali, better connected to the coastal markets, it stimulated the establishment of large cattle ranches. Members of Pucallpa's trading elite owned most such ranches. Belaúnde's policies promoting agriculture in the *selva baja* did not differ substantially from those of previous governments. The government continued to grant low-interest credit through the Banco de Fomento Agropecuario (BFA) for the cultivation of rice in an attempt to ensure Loreto's self-sufficiency and the production of a surplus to be marketed in neighboring Andean markets.

In addition, since 1963 the BFA had been granting credit for the cultivation of jute, a crop introduced in 1951 in response to the demand for jute sacks for the coast's growing fish-meal industry (Cha 1969: 96). The amount of agricultural credit granted in Loreto during Belaúnde's administration more than quadrupled between 1963 and 1967 (see Table 10.1). Priority was given to small operations over large and medium-sized businesses, with around 77 percent of all loans being granted to small farmers. To further stimulate rice cultivation, the government continued the policy of buying rice through the Banco de la Nación at guaranteed prices, ensuring a market for the region's rice production (Ballón 1994: II, 641, 810). Similar incentives were applied to jute cultivation.

Belaúnde's development policies were based on the political paradigm that the state should support the private sector through subsidies, rather than attempt to replace it (Alvarez 1994: 71). In other words, the state should intervene in the economy only to correct distortions resulting from extraeconomic factors and to stimulate development; but it should allow economic agents to fend for themselves, and in no way should it attempt to become an economic agent itself. The strategy of granting tax exemptions and imposing higher duties for the importing of consumer goods to promote investment in the industrial sector and diminish the reliance on imports did not, however, fully accomplish its objectives. Most of the new industries that sprang up as a result continued to be linked to the export sector, were financed by foreign rather than national entrepreneurs, and were heavily dependent on foreign technology (Thorp and Bertram 1985: 420).

Despite these shortcomings, state incentives induced a rapid diversification of the economy, an expansion of the modern sector of the economy, and an increase of capital investment in the production sector (ibidem: 418). In Loreto, the potential effects of tax exemptions on industrial activities were curtailed by the simultaneous incentives given to the import-export trade and by the constant and erratic changes in the rules of the game. Although direct incentives to the industrial sector were never subject to radical change, the constant modifications regarding the import trade negatively affected industries that depended on foreign inputs. As we shall see, despite such obstacles, the number of industries established in Iquitos and Pucallpa, particularly in the food and timber sectors, increased significantly (see Table 11.3).

Belaúnde's agrarian policies for the *selva baja* were, at least in quantitative terms, similarly effective. Thus, rice production increased from 14,480 tons in 1963 to 29,545 tons in 1968 (Appendix 25). The increase in rice production and the tax exemptions granted to the industrial sector induced the establishment of private rice mills in most of the large towns of the region. During this stage, however, these promotional policies mainly reached rural areas closest to the larger towns and mostly benefited small rural *patrones*. Only during the following decades did state subsidies became massive, resulting in widespread engagement of the *ribereño* peasant sector in commercial agriculture.

Table 10.1   Agricultural Loans Granted by Banco de Fomento Agropecuario and Banco Agrario in Loreto by Type of Farmers, 1963–1989

			Percentage granted	
Year	*No. loans*	*Credit (US$)*[a]	*L & M farmers*[b]	*Small farmers*
1963	1,962	398,732	17.2	82.8
1964	1,147	355,875	24.2	75.8
1965	1,463	551,667	19.7	80.3
1966	2,025	925,172	27.5	72.5
1967	2,780	1,793,886	nd	nd
1968	nd	nd	nd	nd
1969	nd	nd	nd	nd
1970	5,386	2,550,219	nd	nd
1971	nd	nd	nd	nd
1972	2,958	nd	nd	nd
1973	3,854	1,972,937	nd	nd
1974	3,518	2,430,290	20.0	80.0
1975	6,581	5,471,533	19.4	80.6
1976	nd	nd	nd	nd
1977	13,310	10,134,097	nd	nd
1978	nd	10,319,693	nd	nd
1979	nd	14,103,248	nd	nd
1980[c]	nd	11,813,811	nd	nd
1981	nd	11,420,187	nd	nd
1982	7,532	17,384,724	nd	nd
1983	5,895	12,101,510	nd	nd
1984	12,429	13,196,331	nd	nd
1985	13,039	11,546,000	nd	nd
1986	25,327	31,547,833	nd	nd
1987	26,258	26,974,558	nd	nd
1988	21,225	9,769,188	nd	nd
1989	32,267	29,333,974	nd	nd

SOURCES: BFA 1963–1969; BAP 1970–1984; INEI 1990a, 1990b.
NOTES: [a] Conversion of Peruvian currency into U.S. dollars is based on average exchange rates provided by Haring (1986a: 192) for 1963–1980, and Cuánto (1993) for 1981–1989.
[b] L & M farmers = large and medium-size farmers.
[c] From 1980 onward figures do not include loans granted in the area of Yurimaguas, which began to be served by the Tarapoto (San Martín) branch. In 1984, after the separation of Ucayali from Loreto, the bank opened a branch in Pucallpa. To maintain the consistency of the information from 1984 onward we have aggregated the data for both departments.

Belaúnde's government was unable to bring about the reforms that most progressive segments of the bourgeoisie and middle classes considered necessary for development. Constant congressional opposition hindered the passing of important reformist legislation or stripped it of its more radical aspects. This was the case for the 1964 Law of Agrarian Reform. Industrial incentives did not contribute to the emergence of a national industrial sector, which mostly remained in the hands of foreign capital. Increased public spending, including the granting of promotional credit, and decreasing revenues, due to the tax-exoneration policies, generated fiscal deficits and skyrocketing foreign debt (Cotler 1978: 368). This, in turn, led to galloping inflation and, in 1967, to a major devaluation of the national currency.

The government's inability to transform the land-tenure structure led Andean peasants to invade and repossess large *haciendas*. The deepening of the economic crisis led to widespread discontent in the cities. In 1965 the military's worse fears came true: Guerrillas began operating in central and southern Peru, both in the Andes and the Amazon. Although they were defeated in less than six months, they confirmed the diagnosis of the more progressive military and demonstrated the urgent need for structural reforms. The government's ineptitude in implementing reforms and the scandal concerning government negotiations for the expropriation of International Petroleum Company, a subsidiary of Standard Oil of New Jersey, were the last straws. In October 1968 the military ousted Belaúnde, inaugurating the Revolutionary Government of the Armed Forces under the leadership of Gen. Juan Velasco Alvarado (who ruled during 1968–1975).

The Military Government and the State Economy

The new government differed from past military governments in that it did not reflect the personal interests of a particular commander but involved the armed forces as an institution. Most of the officers involved in the government had been heavily influenced by the nationalistic, reformist, antiimperialist ideology that had taken shape within the Center of Higher Military Studies (CAEM), founded in 1953. Based on CAEM's assessment of the country's problems, the government designed a political platform, its main objectives being to reduce social and economic inequalities, eliminate foreign economic control, ensure national sovereignty and reinforce national identity while maintaining a strong anticommunist stance. In order to overcome what it considered the "dependent capitalist model," the military proposed to reform access to property in all economic sectors (agrarian, industrial, and mining), nationalize strategic enterprises and financial institutions, establish alliances with other Third World developing countries, and reform the education system. The ideological foundations of the revolution, its political and economic objectives, as well as the measures to accomplish them were expounded in a master plan known as Plan Inca.

Under the new political paradigm, the state, representing society as a whole, was to have a "leading role" in the "promotion, change and redistribution of resources and social roles which until then had been imposed . . . by the dominant class" (in Alvarez 1994: 73). Having witnessed the failure of the state subsidy scheme to the private sector, and blaming the country's propertied class for failing to lead the national development effort, the military concluded that the state should replace the dominant class and assume many of its economic functions. From the government's point of view the state should intervene more actively in the regulation of the national economy. Thus throughout the 1970s and the 1980s Peru's economy became largely a state economy.

The military also concluded that the government had to enlist the support of the popular sectors to guarantee the success of the proposed reforms. They thought that the progressive sectors of the bourgeoisie on which Belaúnde had relied to further his reforms had not been up to the challenge. By engaging the popular sectors in its reformist program, the military sought to ensure that the reforms were implemented as well as to defuse the more radical political platforms of the leftist parties. The orderly engagement of popular sectors was to be achieved by fostering organization according to a corporate model. In the words of President Velasco Alvarado, the ultimate goal of the military government was "to complete the transfer of all the dimensions of power to the autonomous grassroots organizations created by the Peruvians so as to lay the foundations of a fully participatory social democracy" (in Anonymous 1974: 82). To this effect, in 1972 the government created the National System of Social Mobilization (SINAMOS, a play on words meaning "without masters").

The military government had a special interest in the Amazon region because of its isolation, which made it vulnerable to feared expansionist drives by neighbors, and its backwardness relative to other regions, which demanded more decisive state action. In 1967 Texaco and Gulf Company found exploitable oil reserves in Lago Agrio, in Ecuador's northeastern Amazon. That same year, Brazil established a free-trade zone in Manaus; soon thereafter it launched its National Integration Plan, which included the construction of the Transamazon Highway (Schmink and Wood 1992: 60, 70). In 1970 Brazil's foreign minister declared, "No country will be able to maintain indefinitely its sovereignty over vast unproductive regions" (in Relaciones 1972: 2), making a scarcely veiled reference to the Amazon. This did not go unnoticed in the Peruvian Ministry of Foreign Affairs. Commenting on this statement in a confidential document, the ministry outlined a plan it had elaborated with the Joint Command of the Armed Forces and the National Planning Institute for the integration and development of the country's frontier areas, particularly those adjacent to Brazil and Colombia (ibidem).

The document also quoted a 1971 secret report by the Joint Command. In it, the Joint Command acknowledged that the country did not have the human and military resources to defend its frontiers and stated that the only way to do so was to organize "a civilian army that will take effective possession of its territory with full rights, duties and obligations" (ibidem). In other words, only by ensuring full civil rights to the Amazonian population could the state engage it in a wholehearted defense of the national territory. As we shall see, this belief became one of the cornerstones of the government's platform for the Amazon.

The government's plan for Loreto included six major objectives: (1) rationalization of land tenure; (2) regulation of access to renewable and nonrenewable resources; (3) promotion of commercial agriculture; (4) expansion of the industrial sector; (5) development of the oil industry; and (6) organization of the rural and urban populations. In the following sections we examine the measures taken to achieve the first five objectives. The sixth objective will be discussed separately.

Land Tenure

In 1969 the military passed a new and radical Law of Agrarian Reform. The law applied to the coast, the Andean highlands, and the *selva alta*; the *selva baja* was to be the object of special legislation to be passed in the near future. The law established that peons in areas where the agrarian reform was not applicable could request the property of the plots they had been permanently occupying if they did not exceed fifteen hectares (Ballón 1994: III, 36). In Loreto, the law fostered the rationalization of land tenure, insofar as it also established that land concessions and properties not under production should revert to the state. This norm was also present in the 1909 land legislation but had not been systematically enforced due to lack of political will.

Under the military, the process of reversion began almost immediately (Ballón 1994: III, 48). A large number of reverted properties had been originally granted to, or acquired by, rubber-era merchant houses and *patrones*, many of whom had ceased operating decades before. Some of the largest were Venecia and Líbano (9,921 hectares) belonging to Luis F. Morey and Sons, Aumento de Parinari (3,782 hectares) owned by Strassberger and Company, and five *fundos* located along the Yavari River (6,829 hectares) owned by Israel and Company (Ballón 1994: III, 458, 461, 473, 239). Reverted lands were put up for sale or granted freely to former peons living on them. The new land policies liberated large tracts, making them legally available to the *ribereño* peasants, who since the 1950s had been occupying abandoned *fundos*. In turn, this contributed to the strengthening of the peasant sector and the proliferation of independent *caseríos*.

In 1974 the government issued Decree-Law 20653 (Law of Native Communities and Agrarian Promotion of the Selva Alta and Selva Baja Regions), specifically designed to regulate access to land in the Amazon (Chirif 1985). Among other things, the law recognized the rights of indigenous settlements to hold legal title to their lands. It constituted a significant advance with respect to its antecedent, Supreme Decree 03, issued in 1957. That decree, which established the mechanisms for creating indigenous "reserves," granted land "for use" and not in property. In contrast, Decree-Law 20653 declared indigenous communal lands to be "inalienable, imprescriptible and unseizable." However, that law recognized the land rights only of "native communities" and not of indigenous peoples as ethnic groups.

Decree-Law 20653 also established a model of organization for the new communities and recognized their inhabitants' right to solve minor civil disputes under customary law and through elected authorities. It also assigned community authorities the task of keeping local civil registers and issuing birth and death certificates, which were necessary to obtain personal identity documents. This was a radical transformation, insofar as in the past indigenous people rarely had the opportunity to obtain personal documents and thus could not vote, sign contracts, and apply for credit. Between 1974 and 1991 334 native communities were officially recognized in Loreto. Of these, 257 were granted land titles. Among the indigenous people that benefited from this law were the peons of some of the agroextractive *fundos* consolidated during the post–rubber boom era, such as Pucabarranca, Negro Urco, and Tempestad (Ballón 1994: III, 326–7). As we shall learn in Chapter 13, the effects of Decree-Law 20653 went far beyond its stated aims as a land law, insofar as it made indigenous peoples visible, acknowledged for the first time their rights as citizens, and indirectly promoted their (modern) political organization.

Natural Resources

Regulation of access to and exploitation of natural resources was also a high priority of the military government. In 1973 it imposed through Supreme Decree 934 an indefinite ban on the hunting of tropical animals for commercial purposes. Two years later Peru signed the Convention on International Trade of Endangered Species (CITES) and issued Decree-Law 21147 (Law of Forestry and Wildlife), which was aimed at ensuring the rational use of forests and wildlife while contributing to the country's social and economic development.

The law had an immediate effect on Loreto's burgeoning trade in furs and hides. That sort of trade, begun during the 1930s, by 1939 had already accounted for 16.3 percent of the value of exports (Appendix 6). Although hunting and export permits were required, there were no limits on the number of animals that could be taken. This led several contemporary observers to warn the government about the risk of extinction of the region's most valuable animals and to demand the regulation of the activity (Delboy 1952: 24). These warnings went unheeded, and during the 1960s an average of 270,000 pelts were being exported annually through Iquitos. Decree-Law 21147 put an end to this trade by forbidding altogether the commercial hunting of wild animals (a prohibition that continues today). The law also regulated the commerce of live wild animals, which, with the exception of ornamental aquarium fish, could be exported only for scientific purposes. Lastly, it amended legislation on the exploitation of timber, giving priority to native and peasant communities, cooperatives, and public enterprises in granting timber extraction permits (d'Ans 1982: 220).

Additionally, Decree-Law 21147 attempted to eliminate debt-peonage relations upon which extraction of forest products was based by nulling all debts acquired under the *habilitación* system. Passage of this law aroused the protests of entrepreneurs involved in the export of furs and hides and in the extraction and processing of timber (Proceso 1975, No. 28). Unfortunately, although the government was very effective in enforcing regulations regarding the exploitation of forest resources, it was unable to eradicate debt-peonage.

Commercial Agriculture

In the field of agriculture, the military government continued the policy of granting credit for the cultivation of basic staples, such as rice, and agroindustrial crops, such as jute and yellow corn. It also promoted large-scale cattle-raising in an attempt to make the country self-sufficient in beef production (Chirif 1985: 188). Under the new administration, promotional credit grew dramatically both in scope and value. Despite some fluctuations, from 1967 to 1977 the number of loans increased from 2,780 to 13,310, whereas credit jumped from US$1.8 million to US$10 million (see Table 10.1). However, most of the credit went to producers living near the largest urban centers and still benefited a small proportion of the region's rural households. In effect, if we consider that in 1972 the Banco Agrario—the successor of Banco de Fomento Agropecuario—granted 2,958 loans, and that the number of rural households in Loreto according to the 1972 census was 27,073, we can conclude that promotional agricultural credit reached roughly 11 percent of the region's rural households (Table 12.3).

The military government's main difference from previous administrations in regard to agriculture was a more direct and aggressive intervention in the marketing of staple agricultural produce in an attempt to bypass traditional intermediaries and to benefit producers as well as urban consumers. In 1970 the government tasked the National Service for Agricultural Commerce with buying Amazonia's production of rice (Ballón 1994: III, 71). Soon, that agency was replaced by the Empresa Comercializadora de Arroz S.A. (ECASA), the government's rice-marketing agency. ECASA operated through buying centers located in Iquitos and smaller riverine towns. Except for Iquitos, where it contracted the services of private mills, ECASA's buying centers maintained their own storehouses and mills (Chibnik 1994: 60).

The number of buying centers increased steadily beginning in the 1970s. Shortly before it was dissolved in 1992, ECASA had a network of eighteen storehouses, six of which ran their own mills (Nauta, Requena, Yanashi, Lagunas, San Lorenzo, Contamana, and Pucallpa). The establishment of ECASA facilities throughout Loreto allowed a significant number of peasant families, whether or not on promotional credit, to count on a guaranteed market for their produce at fixed prices, which were generally one-and-a-half times higher than those paid on the open market. Thus, government incentives benefited far more than the 11 percent of rural households that received low-interest credit.

The government also sought to benefit urban consumers by setting artificially low prices for rice. As the difference between the price ECASA paid to the producers and that charged to wholesalers did not allow the agency to cover its operating costs, over the years the state enterprise accumulated great losses (Chibnik 1994: 61). A similar system was established to promote the cultivation and marketing of the region's corn production, which was mainly used as feed for Iquitos's poultry industry. Subsidized through promotional credit, fixed prices, and guaranteed markets, Loreto's commercial agriculture experienced an artificial boost during the 1970s.

This is reflected in the region's rice output, which from 1968 to 1979 increased from 29,545 tons to a record 51,800 tons (Appendix 25), turning Loreto into a national supplier of rice. It should be noted, however, that productivity was low and that the quality of the rice produced in the region was second-rate.

Industrial Sector

The military government considered industrialization to be crucial to development. In the words of the minister of energy: "We have in our hands a revolutionary project which necessarily has to lead us to accelerated industrial development" (Fernández Maldonado 1974: 16). In 1970 the government passed a new general law promoting industrial activities; Decree-Law 18350 established tax incentives to industries created outside the Lima-Callao region: reduction of tariffs for the import of capital goods and industrial inputs, as well as reduction of profit taxes.

Loretan entrepreneurs and technocrats firmly opposed this law. They argued that in granting all regions other than Lima-Callao similar incentives to those established by Laws 15600 and 16900, and in ignoring the greater disadvantages of the Amazon region, it would discourage new investments in Loreto (Banco de Crédito 1972: 224). Among the disadvantages mentioned were higher transportation costs, insufficient supply of electric energy, lack of a qualified labor force, and a smaller regional market. This led the government to issue in 1971 Decree-Law 18977, which granted additional exemptions to industries established in the Amazon and frontier areas (ibidem: 223–4). Such incentives attracted new investments and promoted the establishment of some new industries. However, the evolution of the gross product of Loreto's industrial sector (in 1979 constant prices) shows that after an initial period of gradual growth between 1970 and 1976 it stagnated until 1982, when it started experiencing a sharp decrease (INE 1988b: Cuadro 226).

From the beginning the military government realized that tariff exemptions to promote industrial activity should be consistent with policies for other productive sectors if they were to contribute to the development of the Amazon. However, the constant legislative changes bear witness to their failure. One of the first measures taken by President Velasco Alvarado in this regard was the reestablishment of exemptions for the import of foodstuffs granted by Law 15600, which had been temporarily eliminated by Belaúnde through Supreme Decree 053–68 shortly before he was deposed. This prohibition had aroused popular protests and the opposition of the import traders of Iquitos through the chamber of commerce (Proceso 1968, No. 8).

In 1970 the military government updated the Peruvian-Colombian Customs Agreement, and in 1971 the list of exempted imports was revised and enlarged (Banco de Crédito 1972: 231). That same year, the director of the National Planning Institute sent a memorandum to the minister of industry and commerce recommending that the existing legislation on tariff exemptions be revised and rationalized to ensure the "satisfaction of the majority's basic needs and the promotion of industry" (INP 1971: 1). He also called for the establishment of controls that would impede "the excesses in the import of consumer goods to the detriment of capital goods" (ibidem). In the following years, up to eight different decree-laws reducing or increasing import duties were issued (Ocampo 1983: 506–10).

The discovery of important oil deposits in 1971, the needs of the nascent oil industry, and the economic bonanza it brought forth conspired to distort the region's economy even more. Demand for imports greatly increased, making it difficult for the state to harmonize its interest in promoting industrial development of the region while avoiding superfluous imports and enhancing fiscal revenues.

Oil Industry

Under Belaúnde, oil exploration was not a government priority. However, given the promise of the 1956 discovery of oil in Maquía in the Ucayali Basin, and the opportunities provided by a new oil law passed in 1952, a significant number of companies requested oil concessions. During Belaúnde's term twelve oil companies operated in Loreto (Ballón 1994: II). Most of them were U.S.-based companies. However, two were owned by Peruvian capitalists: Compañía Peruana de Petróleo El Oriente, operator of the Maquía oil field, which was controlled by the Gildemeister family, and Petróleo Sullana and Compañía, owned by the Wiese brothers (Thorp and Bertram 1985: 339–40).

Of these twelve companies, four were granted concessions for the first time under Belaúnde's administration. They concentrated on the Ucayali and Huallaga Basins. Only two were actually extracting oil: Ganso Azul, a subsidiary of Atlantic Richfield Company, in Aguas Calientes, and Compañía Peruana de Petróleo, which since 1966 was associated with Deutsche Erdöl, in Maquía. Oil extracted in these two fields was exported as crude to Brazil or processed at Ganso Azul's Pucallpa refinery or at the state-owned Empresa Petrolera Fiscal, established in Iquitos in 1954 (Watson 1964: 86). Loreto's production during these years stagnated at about 1,100 barrels per year (Appendix 28), and despite much prospecting and drilling no new oil wells were discovered.

The 1967 discovery of oil in the Ecuadorian Amazon was seen as a possible threat to Peru's hold over the portion of Loreto north of the Marañon-Amazon axis. As a result, in 1970 the military government passed a new law to stimulate oil exploration. Although the law applied to all Peru, it was mainly aimed at attracting investment to the Peruvian Amazon. The government also wanted to avoid the kind of quasimonopoly of oil production that the International Petroleum Company had enjoyed up to that time.

In accordance with the government's nationalistic stance and its struggle to curtail foreign economic control, the law established a new scheme for the relationship with foreign oil companies. This became known as Modelo Perú, or "Peruvian Model." Whereas under previous legislation foreign companies were obliged to pay taxes on oil production as well as profits, under the new scheme they were exempted from paying taxes but had to share half of total production with the government. In 1971 the government also exempted the oil companies from paying duties on imports of capital goods for a period of eight years (Ballón 1994: III, 137). However, what triggered the oil rush was the discovery of oil by Petro-Perú, the new state oil company created in 1969 to replace Empresa Petrolera Fiscal.

In contrast to the old company, which operated only a few old wells on the Pacific Coast, Petro-Perú was directly involved in oil exploration and exploitation. One of its first tasks was to administer the oil fields operated by the International Petroleum Company, which the military expropriated in 1968 shortly after taking power. In addition, under the 1970 oil law Petro-Perú reserved for itself a large block in northern Loreto, in the area of the Tigre and Corrientes Rivers. Exploration began in 1970. This encouraged three companies, notably Occidental Petroleum Corporation, to follow suit.

However, it was only after November 1971, when Petro-Perú found oil in Trompeteros in the Corrientes River basin, that numerous companies rushed to apply for oil concessions in the region. Excitement increased when the Occidental Petroleum Corporation soon discovered oil to the north of Petro-Perú's block. In only two years (1972–1973), eleven foreign companies or consortiums applied for and obtained oil concessions in Loreto. Most of the fourteen private oil companies that settled in the region were based in the United States (Caller 1974; Pontoni 1981a: Cuadro 9). A small number of companies that had been operating in the region before 1970 continued to do so for a brief period after the new legislation was passed.

It is worth noting that most of the capital invested in the oil industry during the military government, despite the large number of private companies operating in Loreto, came from the public sector. Thus, whereas private oil companies invested a total of $632.1 million between 1971 and 1979, Petro-Perú invested $1.09 billion. Most of Petro-Perú's investment (75 percent) was destined for the construction of a 1,313-kilometer pipeline that would pump oil across the Andes from Loreto to the northern coast (Pontoni 1981b: 3). This was inaugurated in 1977. The rest was invested in exploration and extraction activities.

The companies established in Loreto were not as successful as Petro-Perú and Occidental, and no major discoveries were made after 1971. As a consequence, between 1975 and 1976 most of the oil companies left the region. Thus, Petro-Perú and Occidental remained as the major producers, with the latter extracting roughly 70 percent of the region's oil. The impacts of oil exploration and, later, of oil extraction were pervasive. Oil production stimulated Loreto's economy. It benefited the region's trading elite by stimulating external trade and the fluvial transport sector. It also had a great impact on the rural area, creating new labor opportunities, inducing migrations, and increasing consumption.

Due to its heavy participation in the oil industry and its investments in other sectors, the state assumed a pivotal role in Loreto's economic life. The impact of oil extraction on Loreto's economy further increased after the government granted Loreto in 1976 an oil canon (a share of the oil revenues) of 10 percent ad valorem of the region's annual production. Given that oil production grew from 606 barrels in 1973 to 47,066 barrels in 1979 (Appendix 28), funds derived from this source became a significant component of Loreto's annual budget.

*   *   *

In order to coordinate development efforts in Loreto and San Martín and to promote a certain degree of decentralization, the military government created the Comité de Desarrollo Regional del Oriente (CDRO) in 1972. CDRO members were presided over by the commander of the Fifth Military Region, based in Iquitos (Proceso 1972, No. 16). The main objective of the organization was to promote regional development by coordinating the efforts of the various government agencies, supervising their functions. Ordeoriente, a branch of the National Planning Institute operating within CDRO, was in charge of preparing a regional development plan (Mora 1974: 65). However, CDRO lacked the authority to approve development policies and investment plans. This led many to demand that it be granted greater autonomy and power of decision (ibidem).

As a result of those demands, the government in 1977 created the Organismo Regional de Desarrollo de Loreto (Ordeloreto), a more autonomous regional administrative entity (Ordeloreto 1980: 72). The aim of this organization was "to promote the integral development of the region in accordance with the objectives and policies of national development" (ibidem: 72). The creation of a regional development corporation increased the state's presence in Loreto. Ordeloreto, which in 1980 became the Corporación de Desarrollo de Loreto (Cordelor), was in charge of implementing the investment plan elaborated by the central government. Its most important attribute, however, was being entrusted in 1979 with the administration of the resources derived from the oil canon. Such fiscal resources were supposed to be used to promote industrial development in the region. Unfortunately, they were not always invested wisely or honestly, and once more Loreto lost the opportunity to build its economy on more solid ground (Cordelor 1982: 371; INE 1988a: 182; INE 1989: 124).

The policies and projects implemented by the Belaúnde government and the military regimes had a profound effect on Loreto's economic and social profiles during the 1963–1990 period. Each of the policies benefited a particular social sector to the detriment of other sectors. Nonetheless, taken as whole, they energized the region's economy, helping to organize the region's popular sectors.

11

"Attempting to Change the Phoenician Mentality": From Trading Elite to Regional Bourgeoisie

By the early 1960s most merchant houses of the rubber boom and post–rubber bust eras had closed shop. Much of the region's internal and external trade had fallen into the hands of an emerging group of traders from within and without the region. In this chapter we examine the important changes in the regional economy during the 1963–1990 period, focusing on how they shaped and were shaped by a new generation of entrepreneurs. Throughout this period Loreto's economy underwent marked ups and downs, with brief phases of prosperity followed by inflation and scarcity of foodstuffs. These oscillations were very much linked to ever-changing governmental policies and to the distortions introduced by sudden bursts of legal or illegal economic activities, such as oil exploration, smuggling, and drug-trafficking. During this period Loreto's economy ceased to be an export economy; trade experienced a shift in orientation, from exports to imports and from international to regional and domestic markets.

Thanks to tax incentives, it also experienced a more important shift, one away from the extractive sector of the economy (agriculture and mining) and toward the transformation sector (industry and construction). By 1990 Loreto's economy was more diversified and monetarized, less dependent on the import-export trade, and more connected to the national economy than ever. Yet it was also to a large extent an artificial economy, highly dependent on state subsidies and incentives. Many of the transformations to Loreto's economy during this period proved irreversible.

The changes in the regional economy were closely linked to the appearance of a new generation of entrepreneurs. The biographies of three of these new entrepreneurs reveal that they were able to accumulate capital very rapidly in the mid-1960s, either by profiting from minor export booms (which for a while sustained the region's economy) or by the import of exonerated, cheap consumer goods such as foodstuffs and textiles (see Boxes 11.1, 11.2, and 11.3). The greater availability of capital and state incentives during the second half of the 1960s encouraged many entrepreneurs to invest in the industrial sector, particularly timber. In the 1970s members of the new elite ventured into shipping, benefiting from the opportunities offered by intensive oil exploration and exploitation.

The new entrepreneurs differed markedly from their predecessors. The president of Loreto's Chamber of Commerce and Industry made this clear in the early 1970s: "Throughout the history of Iquitos and of the people of the Amazonia, we have always had a Phoenician mentality. . . . We have always been merchants and extractors of raw materials, and it could be said that only in the past years have we attempted to change this mentality" (Banco de Crédito 1972: 27). Although the Phoenician mentality was never completely overcome, during the 1963–1990 period, we argue, Loreto's trading elite acquired the traits of a regional bourgeoisie. This is expressed in greater emphasis on productive rather than commercial activities, capitalist modes of operation, investment of profits in the region, adherence to regionalist stances, and, in general, greater rootedness and attachment to the region. We conclude, however, that the new elite was unable to dispense with the precapitalist aspects of some of its economic endeavors and failed to shift completely to a course of investment in the production sector. These failures prevented Loreto's elite from becoming a fully modern bourgeoisie capable of generating wealth not only for itself but also for the region.

Changing Economic Trends

In previous periods, the import and export trades were tightly associated. During the rubber era foreign buyers pumped money into Loreto's economy by providing credit for the import of merchandise in an attempt to increase the number of *habilitado* workers and thus augment production and exports. In turn, larger exports increased profits, enhancing the region's purchasing capacity and boosting the import trade. Whenever the volume of foreign credit contracted, so did the export trade. Likewise, whenever exports diminished, the import trade decreased. To a lesser extent, this was also the case during the 1915–1962 period, the main difference being that most of the capital and credit available was regional or national (e.g., that provided by the Amazon Rubber Corporation) rather than foreign.

From 1963 onward Loreto's economy diversified and became increasingly oriented toward the domestic rather than the international market. Export production and commerce ceased to be the region's main source of wealth. Moreover, the export trade did not necessarily generate the capital that financed import commerce. In fact, with the decline of the agroextractive export economy capital in the region became scarcer. As a result, the dynamics of the import and export trades became increasingly independent, their distinct rhythms being the consequence of the response to different factors or of different responses to the same factor. In this context, the only constants were that the balance of payment was negative and that the general trend of the export trade was to contract while imports expanded. Thus, the deficit became larger every year.

The analysis of Loreto's exports during this period reveals three phases within this general declining trend (Appendix 4). The first phase (1963–1971) was characterized by a gradual reduction in the value of exports, which in 1971 had dropped by 40 percent. This was associated with the fact that most of the export cycles that had sustained Loreto's economy during the 1940s and 1950s came to and end in the early 1960s, or dragged along throughout the following decades having an insignificant weight. As a result, during this first phase the region's export trade was mainly confined to three minor products: furs and hides, ornamental fish, and live wild animals.

The second phase in the evolution of the export trade, from 1972 to 1981, was one of growth resulting partly from new developments in the timber industry, but mostly from the temporary export of crude oil to Brazil. The transformation of Loreto's traditional timber industry took place in 1962, with the establishment of the first plant for the production of plywood cores. With the proliferation, in later years, of new factories for the sawing of hardwoods other than mahogany and cedar, the manufacturing of plywood out of softwoods, and the elaboration of veneers of fine woods, the export of timber and timber-derived products soared. Whereas in 1962 timber represented only 4 percent of the value of Loreto's exports, in 1974 it accounted for 58 percent (Appendixes 9, 11). After the government banned the export of live animals, furs, and hides in 1975, timber and timber-derived products became the region's dominant export, representing 83 percent of regional exports by 1981 (Appendix 12). In addition, between 1973 and 1976 the region's export trade experienced a boost when crude oil discovered in northern Loreto started to be exported to Brazil while the pipeline to the Pacific Coast was being completed.

The last phase began in 1982, with a sharp reduction in the value of the region's exports of almost 40 percent, in 1981–1982, and by almost 50 percent, in 1982–1983. This fall continued for the rest of the period. By 1990 the value of Loreto's exports had dropped to slightly more than US$1 million, even less than in 1914, when the prices of rubber collapsed. The decline of the export trade was mainly associated with the stagnation of the timber industry. Decreasing demand, scarcity of raw materials, increasing costs of production, and stationary prices seriously affected that industry (Banco Amazónico 1982). Between 1981 and 1986 the proportion of timber in the region's export structure fell from 83 percent to 67 percent, and its value dropped from US$11 million to US$1.2 million (Appendixes 12, 13). The decrease of timber exports, which during much of the 1963–1990 period had dominated the export scene, constituted the final blow to Loreto's already ailing export economy.

As the decline of the export commerce deepened, the import trade became increasingly attractive. This tendency was accentuated by both the tax exemptions established in the early 1960s, as well as the demands of the nascent oil industry from 1971 onward. As a result, throughout this period Loreto's import trade flourished— sometimes beyond control. Although the general trend was one of growth, the analysis of its evolution shows the existence of four phases of booming imports followed by brief periods of acute contraction (Appendix 4).

The first of these phases took place between 1964 and 1968. Before 1964, imports had been exempt from tariffs or were subject to low tariffs thanks to the 1938 Peruvian-Colombian Customs Agreement. Supreme Decree 04 of 1964 and Law 15600 of 1965 provided new incentives by exempting importers from payment of income and profit taxes. This had an immediate effect on the volume of imports, which in only three years more than tripled. Law 16900 of 1968, which cut tax exemptions by 50 percent, put an abrupt halt to this first phase.

The discovery of oil in 1971 gave rise to a second phase of growth of imports, which began in 1972 and lasted until 1976. The fifteen national and foreign companies looking for oil in Loreto depended heavily for their operation on the import of capital and consumer goods. By 1975 the value of imports had increased 40 percent compared to 1966, when the region's import trade achieved its first peak. However, two years later, after most of the oil companies left the region, the import trade dropped sharply once more.

Imports recovered briefly between 1979 and 1982, when the government began transferring to Loreto's administration a canon equivalent to 10 percent of the value of the region's oil production. This annual injection of money activated the local economy; together with the trade liberalization established by President Belaúnde at the beginning of his second term (1980–1985), it had the effect of boosting imports to unprecedented levels. Belaúnde's liberal measures produced a large deficit in the country's balance of payment. Pressured by the International Monetary Fund, Belaúnde backed down in 1983, and imports plummeted (ibidem: 28).

The last boom phase of Loreto's import trade began shortly after Pres. Alan García took office in 1985 (he served until 1990) and liberalized the import of foodstuffs in an attempt to reduce the cost of living and improve the lot of the poorer segments of Peruvian society. As a result, in 1986 the value of imports attained a record high for the 1963–1990 period of US$60 million. This last phase came to an end in 1988, amid a generalized economic crisis; the region's import trade remained depressed for the rest of the period.

Loreto's new elite was deeply involved in the import trade and profited from all four of these booms. However, as we shall see, many of its members took advantage of the tax exemptions not only to expand their trading activities but also to venture into other economic sectors. In effect, with the gradual decline of the export economy, the new elite was forced to diversify and reorient its activities from export to import, from the commercial to the production and service sectors. In the past such diversification had been a function of the elite's main activity: the export trade. For this reason, the agricultural, industrial, and transportation activities were totally subordinated and highly dependent on the requirements of this trade. In contrast, during the 1963–1990 period these activities gradually emancipated from the export trade and attained a dynamic all their own as they became increasingly oriented to the regional and national markets.

Economic Structure

The demise of the export economy together with the growth of the production and service sectors transformed Loreto's economy. Hence, to determine the size and performance of Loreto's economy after 1963, it is not possible anymore to rely on the volume of its import-export commerce; it requires other indicators, such as the gross domestic product (GDP). Unfortunately, in Peru GDP figures by department were produced and published only since 1970. Nevertheless, the analysis of the evolution of Loreto's GDP by economic activity between 1970 and 1990 is quite telling (see Table 11.1). The most striking feature is the enormous influence of the mining activity (mainly oil extraction) between 1978 and 1986, when it represented about 60 percent of Loreto's GDP and transformed the region into the second largest contributor to the country's GDP. No less remarkable is the accelerated rise and fall of mining activity, which endowed oil extraction with the character of an economic boom similar to the extractive booms of previous periods.

Although in absolute terms all economic activities experienced some growth, a second interesting feature is that the most spectacular growth (excluding mining) was registered in construction, nongovernmental services, and trade. This was mostly linked to the oil boom and the pumping of resources from the oil canon into the regional economy. The effects of this in the import-export trade have already been explored. The flourishing of construction derived initially from the building of the pipeline to the Pacific. It was also associated with the fact that a large proportion of the oil canon administered by Cordelor and the municipalities was invested in the construction of much needed infrastructure, such as schools, hospitals, paving, running water systems, roads, and so on (Cordelor 1982: 371; INE 1988a: 182; INE 1989a: 124). In turn, the increase of Loreto's GDP in the category of "other services" or nongovernmental services reflects the expansion of the shipping sector associated with the emerging oil industry, as well as the accelerated growth of Loreto's urban population, especially in Iquitos. In contrast, agriculture and industry fared poorly; their GDPs did not grow in proportion to the incentives and subsidies received from the state since the early 1960s.

As has been argued (Haring 1986a: 72), the boomlike character of oil extraction generated ephemeral and artificial economic growth. The artificiality lies mainly in the fact that revenues from oil production as well as profits made from oil-related economic activities, such as commerce and transport, were not invested in strengthening the region's production sector. Thus, when in the 1980s the existing oil wells began to dry up and no new oil deposits were discovered, the region's economy experienced an acute contraction. However, even if we were to exclude the direct contribution of the mining activity, between 1970 and 1990 Loreto's GDP increased almost seven times. Moreover, the structure of the region's GDP experienced some important changes during those years, reflecting the transformation and greater diversification of its economy.

Table 11.1 Percentage Distribution of Loreto's GDP by Economic Activity, 1970–1995

Year	Agric.[a]	Mining[b]	Indust.	Constr.	Trade[c]	Govern. serv.	Other serv.[d]	Total %	Total (US$ million)[e]
1970	22.4	1.4	10.3	7.4	20.5	11.1	26.9	100	182.6
1975	12.6	2.9	10.0	24.5	18.8	8.7	22.5	100	521.6
1980	4.2	66.0	3.4	6.8	7.6	2.8	9.2	100	2,366.9
1985	3.7	64.3	3.3	8.7	6.0	3.1	10.9	100	1,244.3
1990	6.0	11.9	5.9	27.3	14.3	3.8	30.8	100	1,420.6
1995	5.2	9.5	8.6	19.8	13.9	4.9	38.1	100	2,195.2

SOURCE: INEI 1996c: 149.
NOTES: [a] Includes hunting, fishing, and extraction of forest resources.
[b] Mainly oil extraction.
[c] Includes restaurants and hotels.
[d] Non governmental services; includes house rental.
[e] Original figures in soles were converted into U. S. dollars according to the average exchange rates presented by Haring (1986a: 192), Cuánto (1993) and newspaper quotations for 1995.

Between 1970 and 1990 the weight of the primary or extractive sector (agriculture, forestry, and mining) diminished considerably, from 24 percent to 18 percent. That of the tertiary or service sector (trade and services) also decreased, from 59 percent to 49 percent. In contrast, the weight of the secondary or transformation sector (industry and construction) almost doubled, from 18 percent to 33 percent (see Table 11.1). The greater importance of the transformation in the extractive sector contradicts those who claim that Loreto's economy has not changed since the rubber boom and continues to be basically an extractive economy.

The resulting structure, characterized by a hefty tertiary sector (trade and services), a trait that has been harshly denounced by the critics of the region's entrepreneurs as a proof of their "Phoenician" mentality and their resistance to investing in the production sector (Rumrrill and Zutter 1976), is not, however, particular to Loreto. In fact, by 1990 the weight of the tertiary sector in GDP was greater in the country as a whole (61 percent) than in Loreto (49 percent), whereas that of the secondary sector (industry and construction) was very similar (33 percent and 30 percent, respectively)(INEI 1996c). To better understand how this came to be, we must analyze the modes of capital accumulation of the region's elite, as well as its economic strategies.

The New Entrepreneurs

The 1950s and 1960s witnessed the transition from an export-oriented economy dominated by merchant houses to a more diversified economy oriented toward regional and national markets and controlled by a new group of entrepreneurs. In her pioneering study, Maria Margaretha (Rita) Haring (1986b: 75–7) argues that Loreto's contemporary regional bourgeoisie is composed of three groups: (1) the heirs of the rubber barons; (2) the merchants that profited from the "survival booms" of the post–rubber bust era; and (3) the entrepreneurs that emerged in the 1970s. According to Haring, those in the first group have lost their economic base and power but are considered to be part of the bourgeoisie because of the prestige associated with their social station. The second group is composed of a new class of merchants that emerged in the late 1940s and 1950s; their "activities expanded especially during the second half of the 1960s, when Iquitos became a free port" (ibidem: 76). The third group is made up of a younger generation of entrepreneurs; its capital, according to Haring, derives from smuggling activities in the 1960s and was subsequently increased as a result of their involvement in drug-trafficking.

The characterization of Loreto's present-day economic elite (i.e., the last two groups) is loosely based on the criteria of age and origin of capital. Yet a closer analysis shows that these two elements are not good defining features. In the first place, as Haring (1986b: 77) herself admits, despite their generational differences members of both groups acquired their capital assets in the mid-1960s, taking advantage of the same economic opportunities, namely, tax exemptions. Second, the two groups do not differ in their strategy of diversification, both having opted for the establishment of "small conglomerates" (ibidem). Lastly, though there are hints that some of Loreto's entrepreneurs have made their fortunes through smuggling and there are rumors that some have enriched themselves through money-laundering, these accusations have been made equally to entrepreneurs belonging to both groups. Moreover, even if these rumors were true, it would be unjustifiable to indict the whole 1970s generation of entrepreneurs as drug traffickers.

Given that there are no significant differences among the members of the new generation of entrepreneurs, we find that it is more useful to focus on their common traits. We argue that the new entrepreneurs, regardless of how long they had been operating in the region, whether locals or outsiders, capitalized during the mid-1960s thanks to the tax exemptions established by the Belaúnde government. With few exceptions, these merchants were able to accumulate capital through the export and/or import trades. We further argue that in a second stage they diversified their activities by investing the proceeds from commerce into industry, transportation, and financing. This diversification took place within a very brief period and was stimulated by the oil and timber booms of the 1970s. Lastly, we contend that the most significant difference among Loreto's entrepreneurs is the degree to which they have shifted from commercial to industrial activities. In Boxes 11.1, 11.2, and 11.3 we include the commercial biographies of three of the best known and more successful of the region's entrepreneurs. The biographies show that despite their differences of origin, family backgrounds, and initial economic activities, all of them followed a similar economic trajectory.

Box 11.1   The Entrepreneur Joaquín Abensur Araujo

Joaquín Abensur Araujo is the best known among the entrepreneurs who started out as employees of well-established merchant houses. Of Sephardic origin, his father and uncle, Alberto and David Abensur, operated as merchants and rubber extractors in the Yavari River basin. After the collapse of the rubber economy, they moved to the environs of the small town of Orellana, in the Ucayali Basin, where they prospered as traders and *fundo* owners and, later on, as timber extractors (Padrón 1939: 111; Guía 1940; Sotomayor et al. 1949: 135).

In the late 1940s or early 1950s J. Abensur started working as a fluvial buyer of furs and hides for Comercial Menezes and Company, an import-export firm that opened shop in Iquitos in the 1930s. By the time Abensur joined the company it had become an important exporter of regional products, mainly furs and hides, caspi milk, and rosewood oil (Gregorio y Alonso 1953: 157). In later years Abensur became a partner, and by 1957, after the company's Portuguese founder, Viriato de Menezes, died, he took over the reins and became its main shareholder. That year Abensur acquired *Fundo* Pucabarranca on the Napo River, which was devoted to the distillation of rosewood oil, rice cultivation, and cattle-raising (San Román 1974: 85). Prior to its expropriation in 1969 under the Law of Agrarian Reform, he had increased the *fundo*'s stock to 2,000 head of cattle (Abensur 1991).

(continues)

Box 11.1   *(continued)*

After taking over Comercial Menezes, Abensur enhanced its import-export activities by consolidating a large fluvial network of agents (*apoderados*) who were in charge of buying furs, hides, and other regional products for the company. By 1963, when the price of rosewood oil briefly recovered, Comercial Menezes expanded its activities, operating three refineries in the districts of Napo, Putumayo, and Yavari.

Through Comercial Menezes, Abensur was also involved in the import trade. Sometime before 1968 he increased his import activities by investing in Loreto Importaciones S.A., an import company founded by Artemio Saavedra to break the monopoly that foreign firms, such as the German-owned Comercial Suramérica, had over the import trade in hardware and construction materials (Proceso 1970, No. 12; Rodríguez Ramírez 1968: 22–3). In later years, taking advantage of tax exemptions, he expanded his interests in the import-export trade by founding a new firm, Joaquín Abensur Araujo EIRL, which had its own wholesale store and specialized in the import of foodstuffs (Malpica 1989: 811).

Having capitalized through his export and import activities, Abensur ventured into the timber industry, establishing an important sawmill in Petrópolis on the Yavari River. Registered in 1963 by Comercial Menezes (DNEC 1964b: 160), it later changed its name to Industrial Maderera Yavarí S.A. Strategically located on the Peruvian-Brazilian border, its production was mainly oriented toward the export market. By 1980 the firm contributed 6 percent of the value of Loreto's timber exports, making Abensur the fourth largest timber exporter of the region (Durand 1980). In 1967 Abensur diversified his investments in the industrial sector, associating with the Lima-based Lindley family to establish in Iquitos Embotelladora La Selva S.A., which produced Inka Kola, one of Peru's most popular soda waters. This was one of the companies in which incorporation was directly related to the incentives granted by Law 15600 (Banco Amazónico 1967).

In 1962, together with a small group of local entrepreneurs, Abensur incorporated Banco Amazónico, a regional bank that aimed at attracting local savings in order to invest them "in and for the region." President of the bank between 1964 and 1969 and twice member of its board of directors (in 1962–1963 and 1970–1973), Abensur had great influence not only on the bank's foundation but also on its credit policies. Abensur's venture into financing was crucial for his own economic expansion, as he became one of the bank's major credit recipients. In addition, in 1963 he founded Mutual Loreto, a savings-and-loan mutual-aid society, the first of its kind in the region.

Abensur had also been involved in shipping since his takeover of Comercial Menezes, which like most merchant houses had its own fluvial fleet. In 1963 Abensur was instrumental in the creation of the Asociación de Armadores de Loreto, a guild that grouped the region's largest shippers in an effort to overcome the crisis in the fluvial transport of the early 1960s. By the early 1970s Comercial Menezes had become Loreto's third largest fluvial transport company (INP 1972: Cuadros 1–2) and had accumulated enough capital to venture into oceanic shipping. In 1970, when oil exploration was in its infancy, he associated with Lizardo Alzamora, a prominent entrepreneur and banker from Lima, and, with the financial support of the Banco Amazónico,

(continues)

Box 11.1   *(continued)*

---

formed Naviera Amazónica Peruana S.A. (NAPSA), a fluvial-maritime shipping company (Banco Amazónico 1971, 1973).

The timing was perfect. Between 1972 and 1973 eleven oil companies began operating in the region, increasing the demand for fluvial and maritime transport. Under new legislation passed by the military government 50 percent of the country's external trade had to be transported by Peruvian vessels (Rumrrill and Zutter 1976: 256). Being the only Peruvian oceanic company in Loreto and having as competitors only Booth Peru S.A. and Línea Amazónica S.A., both subsidiaries of the Booth Steamship Company of Liverpool, NAPSA grew spectacularly. By 1973 it owned three oceanic vessels, was about to buy a fourth ship, and made regular trips between Iquitos and U.S. ports in the Gulf of Mexico. The construction of the oil pipeline to the coast, begun in 1974, further contributed to the company's expansion.

Part of the company's success was due to the excellent relationship between Abensur's partner, L. Alzamora, and Pres. Juan Velasco Alvarado. This allowed the partners to obstruct and finally block the 1975 initiative of the state-owned Peruvian Steamship Company to operate along the Iquitos-Lima and Iquitos–Gulf of Mexico routes, which would have broken NAPSA's monopoly over fluvial-maritime navigation between Iquitos and the United States (Rumrrill and Zutter 1976: 258–9). In effect, when earlier in 1975 the Booth Steamship Company sold Línea Amazónica and ceased operating along its Iquitos–New York route, NAPSA became the only shipping firm to travel to the United States. At the time NAPSA was accused of taking advantage of its monopoly to impose arbitrary tariffs on oil companies and timber exporters alike (ibidem: 255). In later years Abensur founded a second shipping company, Sociedad Anónima de Navegación Amazónica, devoted to fluvial transport services for the oil industry.

Abensur has not only been a successful businessman but also an active community leader. He was president of the chamber of commerce three times, and in the 1970s it was said that he and the Lindley family almost totally controlled it (Rumrrill and Zutter 1976: 157). In 1958 he was elected deputy mayor of Iquitos (Trahtemberg n.d.: 190). A follower of Pres. Fernando Belaúnde, he was elected mayor of Iquitos in 1967. A year later, however, he was impeached and removed from office for allegedly misappropriating funds destined for the construction of the Punchana-Bellavista periurban road. In the early 1970s Abensur was one of the first to raise the issue of Loreto's right to benefit from its oil production, demanding from the government that revenues from oil taxes be transferred to its municipal councils (Banco de Crédito 1972: 203). In spite of his 1968 impeachment, he was once more elected mayor of Iquitos in 1993. In the meantime, he was thrice president of Centro Social Iquitos, a social club that includes the most prominent families of Iquitos, and four times he was president of Centro Social Internacional, another prestigious club. In contrast to other descendants of Jewish immigrants, Abensur continues to acknowledge his Jewish ancestry and has been president of Sociedad de Beneficencia Israelita de Iquitos (Trahtemberg n.d.: 188, 192). Until his death in 1997, Joaquín Abensur was referred to as the "patriarch of Iquitos," an informal title that attested not only to his acumen as a businessman but also to his active participation in the region's political and institutional life.

Box 11.2   The Entrepreneur Luis Valdez Villacorta

Luis Valdez Villacorta is representative of the kind of local entrepreneurs who began their activities as small independent traders. Valdez Villacorta was of very humble origins. He began his career in the 1950s as a small fluvial trader in furs and hides along the Ucayali River selling to Comercial Menezes in Iquitos. Having accumulated some capital, he associated with an Argentine to found his own company, Exportadora Perú, in the 1960s. He began exporting furs and hides as well as live animals, and by 1973 he had become one of the three largest exporters of such products (Rumrrill and Zutter 1976: 58).

Taking advantage of the 1964 liberalization of the import trade, Valdez Villacorta diversified his commercial activities by importing textile remnants directly from the United States. This trade, which fulfilled the demands of a growing urban market, where most clothes were still homemade, was initiated in Pucallpa by the Levy family. By 1967, however, Valdez Villacorta completely monopolized the Pucallpa market in textile remnants through his enterprise Textil Universal S.A., which was located in one of the most modern buildings of Pucallpa and was considered to be the city's best-supplied wholesale store (Rodríguez Ramírez 1967: 8).

Capitalization through the import-export trade allowed Valdez Villacorta to enhance the range of his activities and invest in land and the timber industry. By 1969 he had acquired a large cattle *fundo* in the environs of Pucallpa. That year he associated with Joaquín Planas and the Scavino Levy brothers to incorporate Industrial Loreto S.A. (ILSA), a sawmill located in Iquitos that became the largest exporter of cured lumber to the United States (Proceso 1975, No. 28).

In the early 1970s Valdez Villacorta expanded by importing chainsaws, outboard motors, and motorcycles, which he sold through two large stores he established in Iquitos, as well as electrical appliances which he marketed in Pucallpa through Textil Universal. By 1973 he had become Loreto's largest importer, controlling 12 percent of the value of the region's imports (Mora 1974: 79). He had also entered financing, founding Créditos Pucallpa, a personal credit firm; he became one of the main shareholders of Banco Amazónico (Malpica 1989: 809). As a result of his multiple economic activities, he was the country's twelfth largest individual income-tax payer in 1973, although thanks to the tax exonerations that benefitted the Amazon region he did not have to pay the full amount he owed (Rumrrill and Zutter 1976: 157).

By 1974 Valdez Villacorta had settled in Pucallpa but also had large investments in Iquitos. That year, in a 50–50 association with the Scavino Levy brothers, who by then owned Pucallpa's largest sawmill, he founded in Iquitos Triplay y Enchapes S.A. (TRENSA), an enterprise devoted to the production of plywood and fine timber veneers (Proceso 1975, No. 28). The partners' investment amounted to almost US$3.5 million. In 1976 TRENSA contributed 30 percent of the country's plywood production (Proceso 1976, No. 32), and by 1980 it had become Loreto's largest timber exporter, contributing 15 percent of the total value of timber exports (Durand 1980).

Like other large entrepreneurs, Valdez Villacorta ventured into shipping to profit from the increasing demand for fluvial transportation triggered by the 1970s oil

(continues)

Box 11.2   *(continued)*

exploration. In association with other local entrepreneurs, he founded Servicios Fluviales del Oriente S.A. a fluvial-maritime company that became one of the largest in the region and that for a while acted as agent for the Peruvian Steamship Company. In addition, his two timber factories had their own fluvial fleets.

Under the industrial incentives provided by Law 18350 of 1970, Valdez Villacorta expanded his activities in this sector, investing in industries other than those linked to timber extraction and processing. In the 1970s he established Ensambladora Amazónica S.A. in Pucallpa, which assembled motorcycles from parts provided by Suzuki (Malpica 1989: 824). This was no mean feat, as this broke the monopoly that Octavio Mavila, an outstanding Lima entrepreneur, held over the production of motorcycles in the country through his Honda assembly plant.

In 1978 Valdez Villacorta once more took the lead in the timber industry by establishing a modern floating factory for the production of plywood on the Yavari River (Proceso 1979, No. 36). The only one of its kind in the region, Laminadora Amazónica S.A. (LASA) employed 200 workers. Through state-of-the-art techniques LASA was able to use a wide variety of softwoods previously discarded for plywood production. LASA's entire output was exported to the United States, Europe, and Colombia. By 1980, through the combined productions of ILSA, TRENSA, and LASA, Valdez Villacorta and his associates came to control close to 25 percent of the region's timber exports (Durand 1980).

Though it has been rumored that part of Valdez Villacorta's capital derived from drug-related activities, he was never formally accused (Rumrrill and Zutter 1976: 54; Rumrrill 1982: 142–43; Haring 1986a: 74). In contrast to J. Abensur, he has not participated directly in the region's political or institutional life. This has made him less visible and popular. Nevertheless, like Abensur, he is considered to be one of Loreto's most resourceful businessmen and an outstanding example of Pucallpa's new generation of entrepreneurs.

Box 11.3   The Entrepreneur Arquímedes Lázaro

Arquímedes Lázaro represents the kind of outside entrepreneur who settled in Loreto as a small trader and made fortune in the region. Of Sephardic descent and humble origins, Lázaro was born in Trujillo, on the northern coast of Peru, and migrated to Iquitos in the first half of the 1960s. With small capital of his own he began a career as an importer, buying and selling cheap textiles under the tax exemptions granted by Belaúnde during his first government. A few years later he increased his import activities after obtaining a concession to administer the general stores of the armed forces. It has been said that he made his fortune through large-scale smuggling, taking advantage of his military concession, which he held for almost two decades, until the end of Belaúnde's second term (Malpica 1989: 826).

In spite of the 50 percent cut in tax exemptions decreed in 1968, Lázaro continued a very successful career in the import trade. In 1972 he became the region's largest im-

(continues)

Box 11.3 *(continued)*

---

porter, controlling 10 percent of the value of its imports, rivaled only by L. Valdez Villacorta (Rumrrill and Zutter 1976: 74). By then he owned three import firms, Importaciones Lima S.A., Lago S.A., and Importaciones Santa Rosa, which were devoted to the import of consumer goods, namely, textiles and foodstuffs (Mora 1974: 79). This gained him the title "king of the textiles import trade."

In addition, he founded the firm Arquímedes Lázaro S.A., which acted as an agent of National Peruana S.A., a subsidiary of Matsushita Electric Industrial, which imported and distributed electrical appliances. During these years Lázaro also became an important wholesale trader in foodstuffs produced on the coast, controlling 22 percent of the trade in evaporated milk, 18 percent of butter, 19 percent of cheese, and 18 percent of canned fish (Rumrrill and Zutter 1976: 75). By 1973 Lázaro came to be the country's sixth largest individual payer of income tax (ibidem.: 157).

While J. Abensur and L. Valdez Villacorta made their fortunes through a combination of import and export activities, Lázaro concentrated on the import trade, never becoming involved in the export of extractive products. Like the other two, however, after capitalizing through external commerce, he diversified his activities. In the early 1970s he invested in the industrial sector, founding Textil Iquitos S.A., and manufacturing school uniforms, which by then were compulsory for students of both private and public schools (ibidem.: 61). He also invested in a radio assembly plant (ibidem.: 75). In 1974 he ventured into the timber industry, founding Industria Maderera Peruana S.A. in Iquitos, a sawmill specialized in the production of lumber for the domestic market.

In 1979 he further diversified his activities by entering into fluvial shipping. Though his company, Transportes Lázaro, was not one of the largest and did not benefit from the extremely prosperous years of oil exploration, it made good profits by rendering services to the Occidental Petroleum Company. It also served his other enterprises.

Like most of the region's large entrepreneurs, Lázaro ventured into regional financing, acquiring shares in Banco Amazónico. He was not, however, a major shareholder. Instead, he invested in Banco de Crédito, Peru's largest private bank, becoming in 1989 the largest shareholder after the seven Lima-based families that controlled it (Malpica 1989: 826). In addition, in the early 1980s he established a foreign-exchange firm, Lázaro Casa de Cambios, which became the largest of its kind (ibidem.: 827).

Despite his enormous economic success, Lázaro has remained very much an outsider, participating neither in local politics nor in the social institutions of the region's bourgeoisie. However, until at least the mid-1980s he had considerable influence over local authorities due to his links with the armed forces. In more recent times, he has become more actively involved in the chamber of commerce and was elected as a member of its Board of Directors for 1990–1991.

Capital Accumulation

The export trade was an important means of capital accumulation for a segment of the new class of merchants. Although in the early 1960s the region's exports had started to decline, some of the new traders found a niche in three minor extractive export cycles: furs and hides, ornamental fish, and live wild animals. Furs and hides had been exported since the early 1930s. This trade first peaked in 1946, with a record exportation of almost a half-million units (Appendix 21). The lack of demand for other products led to an increase of this kind of export beginning in 1963. As a result, a second minor peak occurred in 1966. Between 1966 and 1969, more than 1 million animals—mainly black caimans (*Fam. Alligatoridae*), white-lipped peccaries (*Tayassu pecari*), collared peccaries (*Tayassu tajacu*), red deers (*Mazama americana*), jaguars (*Felis onca*), and otters (*Lutra longicauda*)—were killed for pelts. When in 1975 the government forbade the export of furs and hides through Decree-Law 21147, some of the species exploited were on the verge of extinction, and the remainder had been severely depleted.

Three merchants dominated the trade in furs and hides: Benjamín Samolski, Jorge Toledano, and Luis Valdez Villacorta (Rumrrill and Zutter 1976: 58). The first two had been active in the region as minor merchants since the late 1940s (Sotomayor et al. 1949), but it was not until the 1960s that they achieved prominence as exporters. By then, Samolski, a merchant of Polish-Jewish origin, had become the largest trader in pelts (Haring 1986a: 70), being displaced in the early 1970s by Toledano (Rumrrill and Zutter 1976: 58). In contrast, Valdez Villacorta belonged to a younger generation of traders that emerged in the 1950s and made fortunes in the 1960s (see Box 11.2). Traditional merchant houses, such as Menezes and Suramérica, were also marginally involved in this kind of commerce.

All of these traders continued to resort to the *habilitación* system to provide themselves with furs and hides. However, with the decline of the *fundo* system, the rural trading network was no longer in the hands of *fundo* owners, but in those of river traders, or small retailers and landholders who had settled in independent peasant settlements. These new rural middlemen outfitted many hunters, mostly *ribereño* peasants who had specialized in that kind of activity. At the height of the trade most of the small settlements along the Amazon and Napo Rivers had between four and five of these professional hunters among their inhabitants (San Román 1974).

The export of aquarium fish began around 1954 but took off around 1960. By 1969 some 30,000 *ribereño* peasants were engaged in this kind of extractive activity (Proceso 1969, No. 10). This export cycle peaked in 1976, when more than 20 million units were exported (Appendix 23). Trade in ornamental aquarium fish was very much linked to that of live animals (mostly birds, primates, and reptiles), which began sometime later and had a lesser weight in the structure of the region's exports. In the late 1960s commerce in ornamental fish was controlled by five exporters: Alberto Coriat, Milton Marquillo, Walter and Leo Baumer, Vidal, and the Bustamante brothers, whose aquarium, Moronacocha S.A., was the largest (Proceso 1969, No. 10). Some of these merchants were also involved in the commerce of furs, hides, and live animals.

The trade in ornamental fish was as profitable as that in furs and hides, in some years even surpassing it. For this reason, in the early 1960s a group of Peruvian and U.S. entrepreneurs founded Compañía Peruana Internacional S.A. (COPISA), an air-freight company entirely devoted to the export of ornamental fish and live animals (Rodríguez Ramírez 1968: 62). The company operated in Iquitos, Maracaibo (Venezuela), and Miami, making daily flights to Lima and Miami. Fifty percent of the company's capital was Peruvian, the Coriat brothers being among the most important Peruvian shareholders. The export of live animals was temporarily halted in 1973 with the passing of Supreme Decree 934 and put to an end when in 1975 the government banned the export of pelts and live animals. That law did not affect the export of ornamental fish, which at present continues, though on a smaller scale.

These minor export cycles never amounted to more than 25 percent of the value of the region's exports, which after 1963 became increasingly dominated by raw and processed timber. However, in the context of the general contraction of the export commerce they provided an opportunity for capital accumulation to some of the region's new traders. The high profitability of this trade, which rested on the large difference between the price paid to *ribereño* hunters and that obtained in the international market, allowed some of them to amass fortunes.

The import trade also provided opportunities for enrichment to the new generation of traders. In the past, to become involved in the import trade it was necessary to have a large amount of capital or to have access to national or foreign credit. Thus, only medium to large-sized firms had the financial means to participate. The exemptions established by Supreme Decree 04 and Law 15600 made the import commerce accessible to small traders for the first time. It is thus not surprising that whereas in 1949 there were only 45 importers registered in Iquitos (Sotomayor et al. 1949), in 1973 there were about 300 (Rumrrill and Zutter 1976: 170). By 1974 73 percent of the import licenses conceded by the Ministry of Commerce were given to this group; the rest was distributed among state agencies, industrialists, and private oil companies (Ordeloreto 1978a: 133).

Although the new legislation allowed many small traders to venture into the import trade, very quickly this became concentrated in the hands of a few large firms and individuals. In 1973 29 percent of the value of imports was handled by five firms (Mora 1974: 79). Two of these, Luis Valdez Villacorta and Arquímedes Lázaro (see Box 11.3), belonged to the new generation of traders. The former began his career as a small buyer; later he became an exporter of furs and hides. In contrast, the latter, who had settled in the region in the mid-1960s, capitalized as a small importer and retailer of textile remnants. The other two dominant companies, Iquitos Honda and Ferreyros and Company, were owned by Lima-based capitalists and had only recently opened shop in the region. The fifth firm, Suramérica, was one of the few foreign merchant houses that had managed to survive.

The most profitable import trade was that of durable and nondurable consumer goods. Since the rubber-boom years, Loreto had suffered from periodic scarcities of foodstuffs. Whenever there was an opportunity for the commercial extraction or cultivation of a regional product, rural producers tended to reduce their production of foodstuffs, thus making the region increasingly dependent on imported food for sustenance. This was aggravated during times of extraordinary river floods, when high tidewaters covered the farms of the *varzea* (floodplain) areas.

The 1963–1990 period was no exception. The frenzy of oil exploration between 1970 and 1976 diverted a large number of *ribereño* peasants from agriculture and fishing, resulting in a sharp decrease of food output. Exceptional floods between 1971 and 1974 deepened the trend. As a result, rice production, for instance, fell from 36,000 tons in 1970 to 19,000 tons in 1975 (Appendix 25). The transport demands of the oil industry, and the higher cost of transporting equipment and machinery vis-à-vis foodstuffs, diverted much of the fluvial fleet from the trading in foodstuffs between Pucallpa and Iquitos, contributing further to food scarcity (Proceso 1973, No. 20). Additionally, increasing migration to the region's towns and cities during this period augmented the proportion of consumers over producers.

In the early 1960s the profitability of importing foodstuffs rested on tax exemptions and the large gap between purchasing and selling prices. This allowed a small group of regional and extraregional traders to capitalize and gain gradual control over trade in foodstuffs. In later years this control was enhanced as some traders came to monopolize manufactured foodstuffs produced on the coast (cooking oil, sugar, flour, canned milk, and canned meat and fish), as well as Iquitos's wholesale-retail commerce. Thus, A. Lázaro, who in 1973 was the second largest importer, mainly of consumer goods, controlled a substantial share of the trade in evaporated milk, butter, cheese, and canned sardines produced on the coast (Rumrrill and Zutter 1976: 75). These and other monopolistic practices allowed for the arbitrary control of stocks and prices and, thus, for greater profitability (ibidem: 54).

Although the import of nondurable consumer goods was very profitable, it was the import of durable goods, such as textiles and electrical appliances, that generated the largest profits. Before 1965 imports of nondurable consumer goods exceeded that of durable goods. Thanks to the tax exemptions established by Law 15600 the trend was reversed, and for five years imports of durable goods represented about 75 percent of consumer goods (Ordeoriente n.d.: 237). It was only after the tax exemptions were reduced by 50 percent, in 1968, and foodstuffs became scarce, beginning in 1970, that this ratio was reversed once more.

Part of the trade in luxury goods was consumed within the region, but most of it was consumed by the increasing number of "tourists" who poured into Iquitos from all over the country to buy cheaper goods or was smuggled by Iquitos's traders directly to Lima. The distortion of the aims of Law 15600 became so outrageous that between 1965 and 1968 Iquitos, which has an average annual temperature of 79 degrees Fahrenheit, registered the largest wool consumption per capita within the country (Kuczynski 1977: 81). Although it is difficult to establish whether all of the importers were involved in this kind of smuggling, it is undeniable that some were and made their fortunes from it.

The conspicuousness of such imported luxury goods as jewelry, perfumes, and liquors, as well as rampant smuggling, contributed to the notion that most of the import trade carried out under the incentives of Law 15600 was superfluous. Critics also claimed that this kind of trade only benefited large importers and that it did not serve the law's manifest purpose of promoting the industrialization of the region

(Haring 1986b: 80; Kuczynski 1977: 80). This is only partly true. In the years during which Law 15600 was fully in force (1965–1968), consumer goods represented on average 55 percent of the value of the region's imports, whereas the import of capital goods and raw materials for the agricultural, industrial, and construction sectors amounted to 44 percent (Table 11.2; Appendix 29). In later years the trend toward a decrease in the import of consumer goods went on. Thus, during the 1970s consumer goods represented on average 28 percent of the import trade, whereas capital goods and raw materials, mainly destined for the oil industry, amounted to 63 percent. This structure persisted in the 1980s, when consumer goods represented on average 32 percent of the region's imports.

Economic Diversification

Between 1964 and 1968 tax exemptions allowed the region's new generation of entrepreneurs to capitalize. Although in subsequent years many confined themselves to these activities, a segment of the new elite invested profits from the import-export trade into other activities, particularly industry and shipping. Investment in the industrial sector increased steadily throughout this period. In contrast, investment in the fluvial transport experienced fluctuations.

Some analysts have contended that the takeoff of the industrial sector in Loreto was not the result of the tax incentives established by Law 15600, insofar as most of the new industries were created precisely after these incentives were curtailed by Law 16900 of 1968 (Ordeloreto 1978b: 30). They claim that the reluctance of Loreto's entrepreneurs to invest in this sector was due to their "mercantilist mentality," which led them to search for maximum profits in the shortest time and with the least risks (ibidem: 31). They further argue that given this mentality Loreto's entrepreneurs have preferred to invest in the import trade, which is more profitable, less risky, and requires neither lengthy preparation nor specialized human resources (García 1981: 632). According to this view, it is only during periods when the prof-

Table 11.2   Percentage Distribution of Loreto's Import Trade According to Economic Use of Imports by Period, 1960–1986

Year	Consumer goods[a]	Capital goods[b]	Raw materials[c]	Other	Total
1960–1964	44.2	30.1	18.0	7.7	100
1965–1969	55.0	28.9	14.9	1.2	100
1970–1979	28.4	52.5	10.1	9.0	100
1980–1986	31.9	59.7	7.9	0.5	100

SOURCE: Ordeoriente n.d.: 237–9; Cordelor 1982: 313; Banco Amazónico 1982; INE 1988a: 191.
NOTES: [a] Consumer goods: includes durable and nondurable.
   [b] Capital goods: includes agricultural and industrial capital goods, construction materials, and transport equipment.
   [c] Raw materials and intermediate goods: includes materials and goods for both agriculture and industry, as well as fuels and lubricants.

itability of the import trade declines that these merchants opt to invest in the industrial sector. This would have been the case after 1968.

This might well be true in theory, but this interpretation does not take into consideration the fact that when the government established tax incentives to promote industrialization there was little capital available in the region. Many of the members of the previous generation of entrepreneurs, owners of important traditional merchant houses such as Israel and Company, had closed shop and left the region, taking their capital with them. Those who stayed saw their capital shrink due to the decline of the export economy, which until then had been their main source of wealth. For this reason, most of the industries that opened during the brief period in which tax incentives were fully in force (1964–1968) were mainly financed with extraregional or foreign capital. It was only after a segment of the new generation of entrepreneurs capitalized, taking advantage of the tax exemptions applied to the import-export trade, that they were in a position to invest in industry. And that is exactly what they did, as shown by the commercial biographies of some of the prominent members of the region's elite.

Data on the evolution of the industrial sector in Loreto demonstrates that between 1949 and 1963 the number of industries established in the region remained stagnant at about 120; but in the eight years following the establishment of tax incentives (1964–1972) that number almost tripled (see Table 11.3). This trend continued throughout the following decades.

The evolution of fixed capital in the industrial sector also shows a rapid growth, increasing four times between 1963 and 1974, from US$3 million to US$13 million (Pasquel Ruiz 1989: 417). Likewise, the gross value of production (GVP) of the

Table 11.3   Evolution of the Number of Industries Established in Loreto by Branch of
Activity, 1949–1991

Branch of activity	1949	1963	1972	1981[a]	1987	1991
Food, beverages & tobacco	32	49	162	106	114	154
Textiles, clothes & leather	6	8	47	47	22	39
Lumber production & processing	40	35	62	25	93	138
Chemical industry	4	12	6	10	11	21
Non-metallic minerals	10	9	17	13	36	37
Basic metal industries	2	1	12	11	—	38
Metal prods., machinery & equipment	4	1	24	2	18	22
Construction of transport materials	1	1	2	3	—	14
Paper industry & prints	5	2	5	13	11	37
Other manufacturing industries	15	—	7	3	7	13
Total	119	118	344	233	312	513

SOURCES: Sotomayor et al. 1949; DNEC 1964b; Ordeloreto 1978a; Industria 1981; INEI 1990a; Industria 1991a.

NOTE: [a] Data from 1980 onward exclude industries established in Ucayali; this explains the immediate drop in the number of industries.

industrial activity rocketed from US$4.1 million in 1963 to US$15.6 million in 1968 and to US$98.6 million in 1979 (see Table 11.4).

By 1969 the region's industry had not only expanded but also begun to experience certain diversification. However, like in previous decades, most of the industrial activity was concentrated in three branches: food, beverages, and tobacco, lumber production and processing and, to a lesser extent, chemical industry (see Table 11.5). Throughout the 1970s and 1980s the structure of the region's industrial sector remained quite unchanged, with the three traditional branches of activity producing more than 85 percent of the GVP of the industrial sector (see Table 11.5).

The first investments that the new generation of entrepreneurs made in the industrial sector were mainly in the timber industry. In the first phase, beginning in the late 1960s, investments concentrated on the production of sawn wood for the national and international markets, leaving the installation of more capital-intensive factories for the laminating of timber to foreign firms. By then, up to 80 percent of sawmill owners depended on the *habilitación* system to obtain raw material (Ordeoriente n.d.: 215). In a second phase, beginning in the mid-1970s, the most successful and dynamic of the new entrepreneurs began to invest in the production of plywood, veneers, parquetry, and furniture.

As a result, the number of timber-processing plants increased significantly both in Iquitos and Pucallpa, jumping from thirty-three in 1964 to 168 in 1979 (see Table

Table 11.4   Evolution of Loreto's and Ucayali's Industrial GVP, 1963–1989[b]

| Year | Industrial GVP (US$ million) | |
	Loreto	Ucayali
1963	4.1	—
1968	15.6	—
1970	42.8	—
1975	80.0	—
1976	95.0	—
1977	79.0	—
1979[a]	98.6	—
1982	111.8	52.1
1983	145.7	47.3
1984	138.9	51.1
1985	140.1	87.2
1986	117.7	96.6
1987	114.9	97.2
1988[a]	109.0	112.2
1989[a]	117.1	102.3

SOURCES: Ordeoriente n.d.: 206, 208; Cordelor 1982: 284; INEI 1990a; 1990b.
NOTES: [a] Estimated figures.
[b] Between 1963 and 1980 Loreto's industrial GVP includes that of Ucayali.

Table 11.5   Percentage Distribution of Loreto's Industrial GVP by Branch of Activity, 1969 and 1987

Branch of activity	1969	1987
Lumber production & processing	54.6	20.9
Food, beverages & tobacco	21.7	26.3
Chemical industry	14.4	38.5
Metal prods., machinery & equipment	4.1	8.8
Paper industry & prints	3.1	0.7
Non-metallic minerals	1.0	1.2
Construction of transport materials	0.8	—
Textiles, clothes, & leather	0.2	3.0
Other manufacturing industries	0.1	0.6
Total %	100.0	100.0
Total (US$ million)	9.7	114.9

SOURCES: Ordeoriente n.d.; INEI 1990a: 89.
NOTES: [a] Data for 1969 refer only to the gross value of production of industrial establishments that employ ten or more workers.
  [b] Data for 1987 excludes Ucayali.
  [c] Original figures in soles were converted into U. S., dollars according to the average exchange rates presented by Haring (1986a: 192) and Cuanto (1993).

11.6). More importantly, the number of plants for the manufacture of veneers, plywood, and parquetry increased from two to twenty-seven. This resulted in the growing importance of laminated woods (plywood and veneers) with respect to Loreto's total timber output, which between 1964 and 1979 increased from 8 percent to 27 percent (Appendix 27). Given that this sort of processing plant requires the largest investment and contributes the most added value in regional timber production, such a change reflects a transformation in the economic strategies of the region's elite. Additionally, at this stage most sawmill owners ceased operating on the basis of the traditional *habilitación* system, preferring instead to buy timber directly from a series of middlemen, independent extractors, and shipowners (Mora 1974: 67–9).

Loreto's largest entrepreneurs invested in two other industrial activities: shipbuilding and assembly lines. The decision to go into shipbuilding was prompted by increased demand for fluvial transport as a result of the expansion of the timber industry and the development of the oil industry. In the late 1960s, shortly before the oil boom, the Scavino Levy brothers had established a shipyard in Pucallpa to produce boats for their timber companies. After the oil boom they started providing services for oil companies. By 1973 thanks to a large loan from Banco Amazónico, they were able to expand their shipyard (Proceso 1974, No. 25). This and other regional and foreign shipbuilding companies were very active during the 1970s (Ballón 1991: III, 137, 303). However, with the end of large-scale oil exploration in 1975, the construction of the pipeline to the coast in 1976, and the crisis in the tim-

Table 11.6   Timber-Processing Plants in the Zones of Influence of Iquitos and Pucallpa, by Type of Product, 1964–1996

	Year				
	1964	*1969*	*1979*	*1989*	*1996*
Iquitos					
sawnwood	16	28	46	33	nd
veneer	2	2	1	1	nd
plywood	—	—	5	6	nd
parquetry	—	1	3	—	nd
Subtotal	18	31	55	40	60
Pucallpa					
sawnwood	15	29	94	87	nd
veneer	—	4	1	—	nd
plywood	—	—	4	5	nd
parquetry	—	3	14	22	nd
Subtotal	15	36	113	114	nd
Total	33	67	168	154	nd

SOURCES: DNEC 1964b; Agricultura 1969, 1989; Ordeloreto 1981; Industria 1990; INEI 1998a.

ber industry, beginning in 1981 the demand for fluvial transport shrank once more. By 1987 all private shipbuilding companies had closed.

As to the assembly plants, the first investments were made in the 1970s, mainly by foreign firms, although some local entrepreneurs also invested. Thus, Valdez Villacorta established an assembly line for Suzuki motorcycles in Pucallpa, and Lázaro one for radios in Iquitos. Assembly plants were extremely dependent on tax exemptions; their number oscillated according to changes in the tax legislation. In the 1980s, for instance, there was a boom in Pucallpa of plants mostly devoted to the assembly of electrical appliances for regional and domestic markets. By 1987 this activity contributed 31 percent of Ucayali's industrial GVP (INEI 1990b: 68). However, when in 1991 the government issued Supreme Decree 033, which established that products assembled in Pucallpa but sold outside the region would not benefit from tax exemptions, many of the plants closed (Industria 1991b).

Although there is no doubt that Loreto's industrial sector experienced a quantitative and qualitative growth after 1964, it must be placed in perspective. First, a large number of the new industries were little more than small workshops, employing only five to ten workers. Second, though the volume of fixed capital in the industrial sector grew very rapidly, it amounted to barely US$ 21 million in 1974 and to US$ 36 million in 1987 (INEI 1991a: 85). Third, whereas the gross domestic product of Loreto's industrial activity increased rapidly as a result of the tax incentives, its contribution to the region's GDP never represented more than 10 percent (see Table 11.1). Lastly, a large proportion of the industrial activity continued to be linked to the processing of extractive natural resources (timber and oil) and was thus subject to the recurrent problem of their depletion. Above all, the main problem of Loreto's industrial sector was that a large proportion of its establishments was highly dependent on state subsidies.

All of these elements seem to back those critics who assert that the process of industrialization of Loreto was artificial and that investment was mainly opportunistic. Though there may be some truth in these judgments, it is no less true that Loreto's entrepreneurs had to face extreme odds when venturing into industry. A constrained regional market, long distances from larger domestic markets, poor communications, high transportation costs, insufficient sources of energy, shortage of qualified labor, and ever-changing state policies were the most important of these drawbacks. Given such limitations, it is not surprising that Loreto's entrepreneurs invested only where they had comparative advantages or where state subsidies made it worthwhile to invest. As we shall see, the awareness of these limitations led the region's economic elite to question the industrializing bias of the state's development model for the region.

Whereas investment in the industrial sector was stimulated by state subsidies, participation in the fluvial transport sector was the result of the takeoffs of the timber and oil industries. As we have seen, since the days of the rubber boom Loreto's economic elite endeavored to have a strong hold over fluvial transport, which was crucial to the success of trading activities. At the beginning of the 1960s, however, the shipping sector was immersed in an acute crisis due to shortage of freight and passengers. By then, most of Loreto's large shippers had ceased operating; only three merchant houses, Adolfo Morey and Sons, Comercial Menezes, and Pinto and Company, continued to provide shipping services (INP 1972).

To confront this crisis, the region's largest shippers, convened in 1963 by Joaquín Abensur (see Box 11.1), then head of the trading firm Comercial Menezes, joined forces and founded the Association of Shippers of Loreto. One of the first measures of the association was to distribute freight quotas among members (Rumrrill and Zutter 1976: 250). By 1970 the sector was still in crisis. The shippers' association requested from the authorities of the port of Iquitos the establishment and enforcement of a system of shifts for the loading and unloading of ships and the distribution of freight quotas proportionate to the tonnage of the operating vessels (ibidem). This situation started changing with the beginning of the construction of the airport in Iquitos in 1968, which required the transport of large volumes of gravel and cement from Pucallpa to Iquitos, and with the onset of oil exploration in 1970. In only one year, from 1970 to 1971, the volume of freight increased 33 percent (INP 1972). As a result of the discovery of oil in 1971 and the subsequent oil rush, the demand for fluvial transport soared; very soon the carrying capacity of the region's extant fleet became insufficient.

This made shipping attractive to new entrepreneurs with sufficient capital from external commerce. Almost simultaneously, the most successful invested in ships. Some of them did so shortly before the oil boom to provide services to their timber plants and commercial enterprises. But it was with the oil boom that they became involved in large-scale fluvial and maritime shipping. As a result, between 1972 and 1977 Iquitos's fluvial fleet increased from 192 vessels to 486, excluding seagoing ships (see Table 11.7).

Except for the boats owned by large wholesale-retail traders, such as Hilter Paredes and the Hurtado brothers, who transported food and beverages from Pucallpa to Iquitos, the region's new fleet was primarily devoted to serve the oil industry and the export sector, transporting raw materials, machinery, oil, and timber. The shipping sector was extremely dependent on the oil and timber industries. Thus, after the oil boom busted in 1976 the number of vessels started to diminish, dropping 9 percent between 1977 and 1981. The largest decrease was in the number of barges for the transport of heavy cargo. The crisis in the timber industry beginning in 1981 further affected the shipping sector. As a result, in only four years (1981–1984) the number of vessels shrank 33 percent. It has been said that the involvement of Loreto's entrepreneurs in shipping, like all of their businesses, reflected a speculative attitude (Rumrrill and Zutter 1976: 57). Had this been true, by the end of the oil boom the largest shippers would have withdrawn from the business; owning smaller fleets and working on a smaller scale, all of them remained active and by 1990 continued to control the shippers' association (Armadores 1990).

Around 1980 members of the new generation of entrepreneurs reached the point of maximum expansion and were in the process of consolidating their economic power. As in the past, the economic elite favored a strategy of diversification rather than specialization. By the 1980s Loreto's businessmen carried out a larger range of activities than the merchant houses in previous times. Thus, to the five functions traditionally performed by merchant houses (import, export, wholesale-retail commerce, shipping, and industry), the new entrepreneurs added financing and agriculture. In the past, this wide range of economic activities was carried out by a single

Table 11.7   Iquitos's Fluvial Fleet by Type of Vessel, 1972–1988

Type of vessel	1972	1977	1981	1984	1988
Barges	68	250	206	103	173
Motorboats	39	76	66	75	110
Tugboats	63	130	140	84	202
Scows	22	30	35	74	101
Total vessels	192	486	447	336	586
Net tonnage	19,021	nd	72,992	nd	nd

SOURCES: INP 1972: Cuadros 1–2; Ordeloreto 1979; Cordelor 1982: 334; INEI 1990a: 96.

enterprise—the merchant house—and the activities were highly integrated. In contrast, contemporary entrepreneurs carry out this range of activities through independent firms, of which they are either owners or shareholders.

In general, these firms tend to constitute "conglomerates," the management of which is either in the hands of an individual, a family, or a group of associates (Malpica 1989: 14). This type of organization is favored by the more powerful entrepreneurs who control a large number of firms in different branches of activity. Conglomerates allow resources to be transferred from firms that are highly profitable to those that are not doing as well, thereby spreading the risk and compensating for losses. In Iquitos, most conglomerates are not formally constituted, but in Pucallpa they became known in the 1970s as *organizaciones* and were advertised as such in local magazines and newspapers. The transition from merchant houses to conglomerates, and from integrated activities around a common goal to largely autonomous activities, strongly reflects the diversification and more complex character of Loreto's contemporary economy.

Economic diversification, shifts from commercial to production activities, investments in the industrial sector, and capitalist modes of operation are all signs of the gradual transformation of Loreto's trading elite into a regional bourgeoisie. However, we argue that the most important of these signs was the incorporation of Banco Amazónico in 1962 by several prominent entrepreneurs. In the following section, we analyze the role this bank had in consolidating Loreto's economic elite, as well as its shortcomings in promoting the kind of industrialization considered necessary for regional development.

An Experience in Regional Banking

A recurrent problem of Loreto's economy was the shortage of capital. During the rubber era the main sources of capital were the European merchant banks, matrix companies, or foreign trading partners. Except for two foreign banks founded during the years of decline of the rubber economy, for most of this early period the region lacked a banking system. However, as long as there was a demand for rubber capital continued to flow into the region. In the following period, shortage of capital became more acute, especially between 1928 and 1942, when the demand for regional products shrank. World War II reactivated the region's trade, and for a while new sources of foreign and national capital became available. It was around this time that the Amazon Rubber Corporation was incorporated to supply credit to rubber extractors, and the first Lima-based commercial banks opened branches in Iquitos—Banco Popular in 1938 and Banco de Crédito in 1943.

These commercial banks were not interested, however, in investing in the region. As Fernando Belaúnde put it in 1957: "The [recent] proliferation of bank branches, far from strengthening the provinces' finances, has contributed to weaken them, for rather than bringing new resources to those forsaken places, they attract the provinces' exiguous resources to the capital" (1994: 66). This was certainly the case in Loreto, where between 1943 and 1961 loans by commercial banks represented on average only 43 percent of the savings they attracted (Anuario 1950: 479, 850, 859; Anuario 1954: 155; Anuario 1969: 1016, 1018; INEI 1990a: 122). Although the state-owned Banco Agrícola also opened a branch in Iquitos in 1943, its role as credit supplier was very minor until the 1960s, and it was of little benefit to those in the trading sector.

With the decline of exports in the late 1950s, Loreto's economy entered a period of contraction. One of its manifestations was again a shortage of capital. It was in this context that in 1962 a group of entrepreneurs from Iquitos decided to incorporate Banco Amazónico with an initial capital of only US$373,000 (Proceso 1979, No. 37). The bank was founded to take advantage of legislation passed in previous years by Pres. Manuel Prado, which favored the establishment of regional banks in an attempt to break Lima's financial centralization (Malpica 1989: 760). Six other regional banks were incorporated in other departments almost at the same time, all of them by producers and traders of key export raw materials—sugar, cotton, wool, and minerals.

Banco Amazónico was no exception. Its first president was Arturo Calixto, a prestigious import-export trader of the post–rubber boom era who was already active in 1926 (Treceño 1989; Rodríguez 1928; Guía 1940; Sotomayor et al. 1949). Roberto and Eduardo Power García, sons of one of the founders of Casa Power and Company, a merchant house established in Iquitos in 1911, were the main shareholders and served as the bank's vice president and chief executive, respectively. Its first board of directors included an impressive array of local entrepreneurs: Joaquín Abensur, who in 1957 took over Comercial Menezes, by then one of the few surviving import-export merchant houses; Benjamín Samolski, one of the largest exporters of furs and hides; Antonio W. Acuy, importer and shipper and one of the most prominent members of Iquitos's Chinese colony; Rodrigo López, owner of one of the earliest sawmills in Iquitos; and Alberto Zamora Ganoza, by then one of the region's most important shippers. In subsequent years, and until the bank was audited by the government in 1986, the presidency of the bank underwent few changes, being occupied by A. Calixto (1962–1963), J. Abensur (1964–1969), and E. Power García (1970–1986).

The founders of the bank were interested in attracting and retaining the region's savings so as to create a new source of financing. This objective was expressed in the bank's motto: "Amazonia's money for the Amazonian region." Banco Amazónico had an immediate success, confirming that the founders had been right about the need for a regional bank. Only one year after its opening, the bank came to control 23 percent of the region's savings and 44 percent of its loans; by 1969 these figures had increased to 40 percent and 50 percent, respectively (Banco Amazónico 1963–1969). This was no mean feat considering that three large commercial banks were operating in Iquitos by then: Crédito, Popular, and Banco Internacional (established in 1960). By 1972 Banco Amazónico had more than tripled its capital to US$1.4 million (Proceso 1972, No. 16).

The bank was successful not only in attracting savings and becoming one of the most important suppliers of credit but also in expanding its sphere of influence. Instead of confining its activities to Iquitos, from the beginning the bank's directors opted for a strategy of expansion that would ensure the bank's presence throughout northern Amazonia, opening branches not only in Loreto but in the neighboring departments of San Martín, Amazonas, and Huánuco (see Table 11.8). The order in which these branches were opened reflects the relative economic importance of the cities and towns in which they were established, as well as the strategic criteria of the bank's directors. It is therefore no coincidence that the bank's first branch was opened in Pucallpa, which with Iquitos constituted the poles around which Loreto's economy revolved. In so doing, Banco Amazónico became the first commercial bank to operate in this fast-growing city. In the following years the bank's directors aimed at gaining control of the department of San Martín, which in those years was about to be connected by road to Lima and promised to become an important agricultural center.

In accordance with the interests of the region's economic elite, Banco Amazónico oriented its loans mainly to the commercial and industrial sectors, leaving the agricultural sector, which local entrepreneurs were little interested in, to be served by the state-owned Banco Agrario. During the 1960s, particularly during the years in which Law 15600 was fully in force (1965–1968), the value of loans for commercial activities was twice that for industrial activities (see Table 11.9). During the early years Banco Amazónico became a key component in the financing of the region's import-export trade, thus contributing to the capitalization of a segment of Loreto's new generation of entrepreneurs.

Table 11.8   Branches and Agencies of Banco Amazónico per Year of Opening

Branch or Agency	Year of opening
Pucallpa	1964
Moyobamba	1965
Rioja	1965
Chachapoyas	1966
Tarapoto	1967
Juanjui	1967
Yurimaguas	1972
Tocache	1973
Iquitos	1973
Iquitos	1976
Lima	1977
Iquitos	1977
Tingo María	1980
Contamana	1981
Bellavista	1982

SOURCES: Banco Amazónico 1964–1982.

Table 11.9   Percentage Distribution of Credit Granted by Banco Amazónico According to
Economic Sector, 1962–1984

Year	Commerce	Industry	Other[a]
1962	53.3	33.3	13.4
1964	49.0	41.0	10.0
1966	61.4	34.3	4.3
1968	64.2	32.6	3.2
1970	35.0	47.4	17.6
1972	38.6	48.6	12.8
1974	42.7	47.9	9.4
1976	44.4	47.7	7.9
1978	33.2	33.8	33.0
1980	37.1	52.7	10.2
1982	48.3	46.0	5.7
1984	38.4	52.9	8.7

SOURCES: Banco Amazónico 1962–1984.
NOTE: [a] Includes agriculture and construction.

The bias toward financing commercial activities was reversed beginning in 1970. This shift was reflected in the bank's motto, which in 1969 changed to "Amazonia's money for *the development of* the Amazonian region" (Banco Amazónico 1969, emphasis added). From then on, with the exception of a few years, Banco Amazónico consistently granted a larger proportion of its credit to industrial rather than to commercial activities. Between 1970 and 1984 the bank assigned to commerce an average of 39 percent of the value of its loans, whereas an average of 48 percent was given to industry.

This change was related to three factors: (1) the decline of the external trade as a consequence of the 1968 cuts in tax exemptions, which encouraged those who had capitalized in this sector to diversify their activities; (2) the influence of the modernizing and nationalistic discourse of the military, which in 1970 established new incentives for those investing in the industrial sector; and (3) the increasing demand for timber products in both domestic and international markets beginning in the mid-1960s. Soon thereafter, the increasing needs of the oil industry, which opened new opportunities for industrial investment, mainly in shipbuilding, reinforced the trend.

Through its loans the bank made it possible for a group of Loretan investors to venture into producing laminated woods, an activity that till then had been almost completely in the hands of foreign firms (Caller 1974). It also contributed to the emergence of a regional shipbuilding industry and to a significant expansion of the region's fluvial-maritime fleet. In addition, the bank financed other large industrial ventures, particularly in the food and beverage industry. This shift toward industry did not mean, however, a complete withdrawal from the commercial sector. In fact, between 1974 and 1979, when the volume of the external trade increased as a result of the oil boom, Banco Amazónico financed on average 64 percent and 71 percent of the import and export trades, respectively (Banco Amazónico 1974–1979).

In addition to its own lines of credit through agreements with state banks, Banco Amazónico was entrusted with the administration of important public funds destined to promote the production sector in Loreto. In the past such funds had been entrusted to Lima-based commercial banks. In Iquitos, Banco Amazónico was very successful in displacing its rivals and obtaining the administration of these lines of low-interest credit. One of the first agreements of this kind was that established in 1964 with the state-owned Banco Industrial. In 1972 Banco Amazónico signed an agreement with the Banco Central de Reserva, the country's central bank, to administer its Selective Regional Credit Fund (Banco Amazónico 1974). A more important and more long-term agreement was signed with Ordeloreto, the regional development body created ad hoc by the government in 1977 to plan Loreto's development and administer funds derived from the 10 percent ad valorem oil canon established in 1976. In 1979, after much lobbying, the bank was invited to become part of the corporation's council and was entrusted with the administration of a special fund for the promotion of agriculture, agribusiness, industry, timber extraction, small industry, and tourism (Proceso 1979, No. 37).

Unfortunately, in all of these cases the bank, instead of distributing the resources of promotional credit lines equally among the activities prioritized by the government, placed most of them in activities in which the region's elite had vested interests. In fact, the analysis of how the resources of Cordelor were allocated during the first six years in which the agreement was in force (1979–1984) shows that Banco Amazónico favored not only the region's elite over other less powerful economic sectors but also the interests of the elite of Iquitos over those of the entrepreneurs from other towns (Cordelor 1985). Hence, most of the credit went to the timber, shipbuilding, and food industries, which were considered to be key sectors by Iquitos's elite, whereas agriculture and small industry received little attention. In addition, most of the credit granted went to the entrepreneurs of Iquitos (65 percent in 1979), whereas those from Pucallpa and Yurimaguas received a much lesser share (29 percent and 6 percent respectively).

Banco Amazónico not only tended to channel the Cordelor fund into activities favored by the region's economic elite; it granted a significant proportion of these resources to members of its board of directors or to main shareholders. Thus, for instance, in 1982 the bank granted a loan of US$113,000 to Industrial Maderera Yavarí, a sawmill owned by former bank president J. Abensur. This loan represented 7 percent of the total credit granted that year under the Cordelor agreement. In 1983 the bank granted five loans to Serafín Otero Mutín, who that same year had been elected to the bank's board of directors, for personally and family-owned mills: Molino Marañón S.A. and Industrial García Otero S.A. These loans, amounting to US$97,000, represented 21 percent of that year's Cordelor credit fund. A year later, the bank granted a loan of US$96,000 to Industrial Iquitos S.A., a soda-water plant in which bank president Eduardo Power García was a major shareholder (Cordelor 1985). This loan represented 15 percent of the credit granted under the Cordelor agreement.

There are many more examples, but these suffice to demonstrate that Banco Amazónico funneled both the region's savings and the state promotional credit it administered toward the region's elites. This prompted the bank's critics to claim sarcastically that the bank's motto should have been "Amazonia's money for the Amazonian elite."

In the long run the strategy of granting hefty credits to its shareholders had a boomerang effect. By the early 1980s the bank was holding a large portfolio of debts, most of which were owed by major shareholders, who felt no urge to repay their loans. This situation was aggravated by stagnation in timber industry, in which the bank had invested heavily. The government attempted to save the bank from bankruptcy by pumping public funds into it through the regional development corporations of the departments of Loreto and Ucayali (Malpica 1989: 833). The financial injections, aimed at funding the bank's defaulted debts, were not enough to prevent collapse. By the end of 1985 the bank's uncollectable debts amounted to US$47.7 million. Seventeen businessmen, all of them main shareholders of the bank, owed more than 70 percent of the debt (Malpica 1989: 829–32). In January 1986 the Superintendency of Banking decided to take control of Banco Amazónico.

Banco Amazónico was not the only regional bank to face such difficulties; by the mid-1980s four of the seven regional banks created in the early 1960s had closed their doors or had been absorbed by other commercial or state banks. It has been said that regional banks had too small a capital to be viable, that they attracted only a small proportion of the savings of their respective regions, and that they made no significant contribution to regional development, as they could only grant short-term loans (Kuczynski 1977: 23).

This does not entirely hold true in the case of Banco Amazónico. Although the social capital of Banco Amazónico never amounted to more than US$4 million, the bank did manage to control more than half the savings of Loreto and San Martín, which in 1977 amounted to almost US$10 million. Additionally, the bank was instrumental in financing such capital-intensive activities as timber processing, fluvial-maritime transport, and shipbuilding, thus enabling a segment of the new generation of entrepreneurs to shift from purely commercial endeavors to a combination of activities that involved the extractive, transformation, and service sectors. Above all, that the bank was created at all and that the most prominent new entrepreneurs of Iquitos and Pucallpa were among its shareholders attest to a commitment to invest in the region. This commitment was reaffirmed even after the bank's demise, when despite the violence and deep crisis that affected the country in the late 1980s most of these entrepreneurs continued doing business in the region. That commitment, we maintain, marks their passage from being a transient trading elite to being a rooted regional bourgeoisie.

12

"Without *Patrones* We Lead a Better Life": The Emancipation of *Fundo* Peons

The same factors that led to the disappearance of the traditional merchant houses caused the decline of the landed elite and the disintegration of the *fundo* economy. This led to the massive emancipation of peons from their *patrones*. In this chapter we analyze the elements that furthered this process. We also analyze the consequences of the release of peons from debt-peonage, which included the multiplication of independent settlements, or *caseríos*, the transformation of peons into peasants, and the consolidation of a new social sector, the mixed-blood *ribereño* peasants.

In the 1940s and 1950s a series of government policies favoring small producers weakened the *fundo* economy. The decrease in the international demand for tropical products further contributed to its decline. As *fundos* became less and less important in supplying raw materials for the trading elite, their traditional sources of credit contracted. However, what broke the grip *fundo* owners held over peons was literacy, which began increasing in the 1940s due to the expansion of educational services, and democratization of fluvial transport in the 1950s due to the availability of cheap outboard motors. The first factor enabled *fundo* peons to defend their civil rights. The second broke down the monopoly that *patrones* had over local commerce. Together, these factors undermined the monopoly that *fundo* owners had over land, fluvial commerce, and local authorities, allowing many peons to free themselves by the 1950s and 1960s. Nevertheless, we contend that it was only in the 1970s that *fundo* peons were finally able to liberate themselves from debt-peonage. This was possible because of three factors: (1) the passing of new legislation regulating access to land and resources; (2) the support of some Catholic and Protestant missionaries in confronting *fundo patrones*; and (3) the efforts of the reformist military government to promote the political organization and mobilization of *fundo* peons.

One of the immediate results of the liberation of *fundo* peons was an increase in independent settlements, or *caseríos*, and of native communities. During the

1915–1962 period most *caseríos* were small settlements established within *fundos*, whose inhabitants were attached to *fundo* owners through links of debt-peonage. With the decline and breakdown of *fundos* these settlements became independent. In addition, emancipated *fundo* peons founded numerous new settlements. As a result, the number of independent *caseríos* rapidly increased, thus replacing *fundos* as the dominant feature of the region's rural landscape. The same is true of indigenous settlements previously attached to *fundos*, which, under legislation passed by the military government in the early 1970s, were legally recognized as *comunidades nativas* (native communities).

The emancipation of *fundo* peons from their *patrones* and their organization in independent settlements went hand in hand with their transformation into independent peasants. Although the breaking down of the *fundo* economy led to the elimination of debt-peonage, it did not mean the immediate abolition of the *habilitación* system. In well-connected areas, where access to the market, credit, and information on prices and market conditions was more accessible, the abolition of the *habilitación* system was accomplished early on. In contrast, in peripheral areas, where access to the market continued to be difficult, *fundo patrones* were replaced by a host of smaller *patrones* (generally fluvial traders or medium-sized farmer-traders), and relationships of debt-peonage were replaced by ties of debt-merchandise. By controlling local commerce, these new *patrones* continued to make use of the *habilitación* system to obtain agricultural and extractive products that they then marketed. Although this situation still persists in Loreto's remotest areas, in most cases it was a transitional phase in the conversion of peons to peasants.

This process was accelerated as a result of government policies that increased promotional agricultural credit, ensured guaranteed prices for key commercial crops, and established subsidized marketing networks. These policies also shifted the region's rural economy from extraction to commercial agriculture and from international to domestic markets. The economy of the new peasant sector combined the production of foodstuffs for the regional and national markets with occasional extractive activities and sporadic wage labor. These changes were highly dependent on government subsidies. However, even after Pres. Alberto Fujimori eliminated these supports, in 1990, the structure and orientation of the new rural economy did not change significantly. We conclude that although rural dwellers have greatly benefited from the changes experienced during this period they still have very low levels of income, are subject to constant market fluctuations, and seldom accumulate capital.

The emancipation of *fundo* peons and their conversion into independent peasants marked the consolidation of a new social stratum: that of the mixed-blood *ribereño*, or "riverine," population. *Ribereños* appeared as a distinct social group at the end of the rubber era. The new group resulted from the immigration and interbreeding of peoples from European, Andean, and Amazonian ancestry. Known originally as *loretanos* (Loretans), this group expanded after the rubber bust as a consequence of the further acculturation, geographical displacement, and interbreeding of indigenous, white, and mestizo peoples in the context of the *fundo* economy. However, it was not until the 1970s that *ribereños* became dominant in Loreto's rural areas. It was then that its members came to be known as *ribereño* peasants and that their culture was adopted as representative of the region as a whole, contributing to the development of a strong regional identity.

Proliferation of Independent Settlements

The foundation of nonindigenous settlements in western Loreto can be traced to the rubber era, when white-mestizo immigrants from the Huallaga Basin founded several *caseríos*. Members' activities were ancillary to the rubber economy, such as providing foodstuffs for rubber extractors and firewood for passing steamboats. The former activity included the cultivation of staples, the raising of cattle, and the production of manioc flour, jerked meat, sugar, molasses, and aguardiente. Examples of this kind of settlement are given by Jesús San Román (1974: 87) and Aldo Atarama (1992: 24, 56, 59, 123).

San Román (1975: 180) has argued that the number of *caseríos* expanded after the rubber bust, especially in the 1930s. However, most of the new villages were formed around *patrones* who owned *fundos*, *haciendas*, or extractive posts. Only a few of the villages established after the rubber bust were founded by groups of independent producers (see, e.g., San Román 1974: 29; Atarama 1992: 42, 47, 68). A few additional independent settlements were formed by indigenous peoples who had managed to regain freedom from their *patrones* and had returned to their lands of origin. However, these settlements were rarely able to maintain their autonomy for a long time. Exceptions to this rule were those settlements in which Adventist or evangelical missionaries had settled beginning in the 1930s (Ortiz 1974: II, 643–649). Thus, during the 1915–1962 period most of the rural population resided in *fundo*-bound villages. It was only after the decline of the *fundo* economy that this situation started to change.

The Expansion of Education and Fluvial Transportation

The gradual dissolution of *fundos* and the releasing of *fundo* peons from debt-peonage ties resulted mainly from the decline of Loreto's agroextractive export economy. However, two other factors—higher levels of literacy and cheaper fluvial transportation—played important roles in eroding the monopoly that *fundo* owners possessed over trade, land, and political authority as well as the economic and political holds they had over peons. We have already analyzed the causes of the decline of the regional export economy. We now turn to the expansion of educational and fluvial transportation services.

In 1906 there were only thirty-nine public schools in the three provinces that composed Loreto: Alto Amazonas, Bajo Amazonas, and Ucayali (Fuentes 1906: 478–481). Most were located in Iquitos and smaller urban centers, such as the former colonial mission towns and newly founded district capitals. In addition, 90 percent provided only elementary education and rarely had more than one teacher. In the early 1930s the government passed the Education Law, which stipulated that landholders who had a population of more than thirty children within their properties had the obligation to establish a school and provide free education (DNE 1949: I, 547). However, very few *fundo* owners were willing to comply with this law, fearing that literacy would weaken their hold over peons. In well-connected areas it was easier for local authorities to enforce the Education Law. Thus, schooling was accomplished early in the lower Huallaga Basin (Stocks 1981: 94). In remoter areas enforcement was more difficult.

As a result, by 1940 the level of school attendance in Loreto was still very low: 37 percent for the 6–14 age group, 14 percent for the 15–19 age group (see Table 12.1). Acknowledging that the Education Law was not being implemented, national authorities took new measures to enforce it. In 1941 Pres. Manuel Prado issued a supreme decree ordering the creation of a registry of estates with more than thirty children and the imposition of fines on those landholders not complying with the establishment of schools (DNE 1949: I, 547). The decree also ordered the opening of offices to receive complaints from *fundo* peons. To make it easier for peons to report noncompliance, the decree specified that complaints could be presented orally or handwritten on nonofficial paper. Finally, the decree assigned to the Caja de Depósitos y Consignaciones the task of collecting the fines imposed on negligent *fundo* owners. These measures seem to have been quite effective. By 1962 the number of schools had increased to 167, and the rate of school enrollment had almost doubled (see Table 12.1).

However, from data provided by naval officer Guillermo Faura for 1960, it is apparent that local authorities still found it difficult to enforce the law in remoter

Table 12.1   Rate of School Enrollment per Age Group, 1940–1993

| Area & age group | Percentage of students | | | | |
	1940	1961	1972	1981	1993
Loreto[a]					
6–14	37	63	76	89	81[b]
15–19	14	30	40	46	46
Ucayali					
6–14	—	—	—	93	82[b]
15–19	—	—	—	46	48

SOURCES: Fernández 1985: 80; INEI 1994a, 1994b.
NOTES: [a] Data for Loreto before 1981 include Ucayali.
   [b] Data refer to age group 5–14 years old. Educational facilities for five-year-olds going to kindergarten are usually absent in rural areas; this explains why percentage of school enrollment is lower than in 1981.

areas. Thus, whereas in the Amazon, Ucayali, Marañon, and Huallaga River basins the proportion of settlements with schools was 30–43 percent, in such tributaries as the Morona, Pastaza, and Corrientes it was 10 percent or less (Barclay 1993: 129). Moreover, despite state efforts, until the early 1960s 92 percent of the region's schools had been created by private initiative and were privately supported (Barclay 1991: 70). In most of the *fundos* that had schools, *patrones* charged school-related expenses to peons' accounts; in other cases, as in Negro Urco, expenses were shared by the *patrón* and his laborers (Atarama 1992: 92).

In time, privately run schools were recognized by the Ministry of Education and integrated into the public education system. After the ascension to power of Pres. Fernando Belaúnde in 1963, this process was accelerated. During his first administration Belaúnde devoted up to 33 percent of the national budget to education (Cotler 1978: 367). Rather than building new schools, the government concentrated on improving teachers' salaries, creating new teaching posts, and augmenting school enrollment (Kuczynski 1977: 57). As a result, the number of teachers in the country increased by 67 percent, the number of students by 50 percent (Cotler 1978: 367). In the following years the military government also placed emphasis on improving the country's rate of literacy, especially in the rural areas.

As a consequence of this boost to education, the number of schools in Loreto increased eightfold between 1962 and 1978, whereas the proportion of public schools reached 96 percent (Barclay 1991: 70). Many were bilingual, with teachers trained by the Summer Institute of Linguistics (SIL), a U.S.-based evangelical organization associated with the Wycliffe Bible Translators. The number of those schools in native communities increased from twenty in 1953 to 320 in 1977 (Bravo 1955: 74; Stoll 1985: 157). With more schools and teachers, the rate of elementary school enrollment in Loreto had increased to 76 percent by 1972, whereas the rate of illiteracy had dropped from 51 percent in 1940 to 48 percent in 1957, 34 percent in 1961, 23 percent in 1972, and 15 percent in 1981 (Fernández 1985: 78; CIDA 1963: 489). By 1993 it had decreased to 11 percent (INEI 1996a: 47).

The democratization of education had an immediate impact in levels of schooling and literacy, providing *fundo* peons with a formidable instrument to question the authority of *patrones*. The impact of the democratization of fluvial transport, which rapidly eroded the monopoly that *fundo* patrones had over local commerce, was no less dramatic. Until the 1950s *fundo* owners had almost complete control of local commerce. Being the only ones with enough capital to purchase merchandise and to possess boats and hire shipping services, *patrones* were indispensable as suppliers of manufactured goods. Aided by peons' low levels of literacy, *patrones* were also able to manipulate their terms of exchange.

The appearance of cheaper motorboats in the 1950s broke the monopolies that merchant houses and *fundo* owners possessed over fluvial transportation and trade (Dean 1996: 82–83). A new generation of *regatones* (small fluvial traders) began to operate, not only along the main rivers but also along the remotest tributaries. This trend accelerated during the 1960s, when the Banco de Fomento Agropecuario opened a line of low-interest credit for the purchase of outboard motors (BFA 1962).

The Weakening of Fundo Patrones

Economic deterioration eroded the power of *fundo patrones* on three fronts: monopoly of commerce, monopoly of land, and monopoly of the authority system. Weakened by a decrease in the export trade, pressured by increasingly literate peons who demanded better terms of exchange, and facing greater competition from a host of fluvial traders, *fundo* owners were forced to give up control over local trade and allow *regatones* to call at *fundos* and trade with peons. This was the case of Alfonso Cárdenas, owner of Negro Urco, who in the early 1970s was described as a declining *fundo patrón* whose peons still respected him although they mostly traded with visiting fluvial traders (San Román 1974: I, 89).

These elements also eroded *fundo* owners' control over land. From 1953 on, the Ministry of Agriculture established that alluvial lands in islands and along riverbanks constituted public property, with use being granted on a temporary basis. To gain access, prospective users were required to obtain annual use certificates from the local offices of the Ministry of Agriculture. This also required the possession of personal documents and, hence, literacy. It also meant long trips to the ministry's local offices. Increased literacy and cheaper means of transportation allowed many rural dwellers, whether peons or independent producers, to request access to lands previously used exclusively by *fundo* owners. Most such lands were especially suitable for cultivating rice and vegetables. The impact of this law was enhanced by the expansion of the region's urban populations and the ensuing increase in the demand for local foodstuffs, which guaranteed a market for agricultural production. It was also magnified by the expansion of fluvial trade, which provided new marketing alternatives.

Higher levels of literacy had an even greater impact in breaking the monopoly that *fundo* owners held over public appointments. As we already learned, *patrones* often managed to be appointed as deputy governors; otherwise, they exerted enough influence to see that one of their protegés was designated. To be appointed deputy governor, a candidate had to be twenty-one years old or more and had to possess personal documents. The latter condition required the candidate to be literate so that he could obtain a voting card, or at least to have performed military service and thereby obtained a military card. Before the 1950s very few rural residents could fulfill such conditions. This fact made it easier for *fundo* owners to elect their own candidates.

With higher levels of schooling, however, many *fundo* peons and independent producers were able to obtain personal documents and present themselves as candidates for office. They could also denounce acting deputy governors for offenses and demand removal and replacement. Moreover, with the increase in the number of independent settlements and, concomitantly, in the number of deputy governors, rural dwellers had greater opportunities to manipulate to their own advantage rivalries between authorities.

The Formation of Caseríos and Native Communities

Increased literacy provided *fundo* peons with better means to resist the most exploitative practices of *patrones*. But there is little evidence before the 1970s that they confronted *patrones* openly. However, several external factors challenged the power of *fundo patrones*, bringing forth the disintegration of *fundos* and encouraging the emergence of independent settlements, whether *ribereño* villages or native communities. These factors were: (1) the Agrarian Reform Law passed by President Belaúnde in 1964; (2) the Agrarian Reform Law and Native Communities Law issued by the military government in 1969 and 1974, respectively; (3) the activities of Catholic and Protestant missionaries; and (4) the political proselytization carried out by the National System of Social Mobilization (SINAMOS).

In Loreto, Belaúnde's agrarian reforms were enforced mainly in areas close to Iquitos or along new roads that had been selected as sites for state-sponsored colonization programs. The law was used to update the land registry rather than expropriate operating *fundos*, which affected *fundos* that were abandoned or not undergoing exploitation. Most were less than ten hectares; very rarely were they larger than fifty hectares (Ballón 1992: II, 678–743). However, there were a few exceptions, mostly some old *fundos* and rubber concessions (Ballón 1992: II, 680–681). This law facilitated questioning the legal rights of many *patrones* to claim property rights over areas much larger than they really owned. In addition, the 1964 bylaw ordered the Ministry of Agriculture to enforce Supreme Decree 03 of 1957, establishing procedures for creating indigenous reserves (Ballón 1992: II, 645). As a result, many reserves were created in the Amazon region, specifically Loreto, during the following years.

The Agrarian Reform Law of 1969 had a more direct effect on Loreto's *fundos*. Peons and tenants occupying plots of less than fifteen hectares within Amazonian *fundos* and *haciendas* could now request land titles from the Agrarian Reform Bureau (Ballón 1992: III, 36). As shown by the large number of *fundos* that were reverted to the public domain beginning in 1969 (Ballón 1992: III, 48ff.), the law had an immediate impact. Later, many of these *fundo* lands were granted to former peons. The Agrarian Reform Law also aimed at updating the region's land registry, not only in designated colonization areas but also in all regions. This led to the revocation of large rubber and timber concessions granted to merchant houses and other private companies during the rubber era and up to the 1940s (e.g. Ballón 1992: III, 83, 87, 96–98).

In turn, the Native Communities Law of 1974 had profound repercussions on *fundos* where the peons were mostly indigenous. Particularly in the Napo, Ucayali, and Huallaga River basins it allowed them to request recognition of their settlements as native communities. Additionally, the law provided the means for independent indigenous settlements to obtain legal titles over their lands (see Boxes 8.1–8.4).

Inspired by different objectives, Protestant and Catholic missionaries and institutions played a key role in promoting the organization of indigenous peoples and supporting their claims against *fundo* owners and *habilitadores*. The evangelical missionaries of the Summer Institute of Linguistics, which began operating in Peru in 1945, played an important role in promoting nucleated indigenous settlements around bilingual schools and in obtaining land titles for new communities. Although the SIL linguist-missionaries seldom worked directly with indigenous *fundo* peons (Stoll 1985: 156), their presence ignited conflicts with local *patrones*. The activities of Esther and Paul Powlison among the Yagua in the 1950s, which included the marketing of Yagua products and the supplying of cheaper manufactured goods, "aroused the reaction and protests, sometimes violent, of the *patrones*" (Chaumeil 1981: 84). In 1953 a similar situation arose with Doris and Lambert Anderson, who were working among the Ticuna of Cushillococha. These missionaries persuaded the Ticuna to gather in a large settlement; they helped them obtain titles to their lands and to establish a school, a sawmill, and large plantations. These activities helped the Ticuna "break their dependency with respect to the *patrones*" (Stoll 1985: 215). They also generated significant opposition.

The SIL missionaries were aware that their success depended on extricating indigenous peoples from the influence of *patrones* and guaranteeing them a territory where they could lead independent lives. The evidence indicates that the SIL played an important role in drafting the law establishing indigenous reserves, which was finally passed in 1957 as Supreme Decree 03 (Barclay 1989: 218–219). In fact, most of the first reserves created under that decree were sponsored by SIL missionaries; this was so of Chicais (Aguaruna, 1964), Huau (Piro, 1964), and Utucuro (Shipibo-Conibo, 1964)(Ballón 1992: II, 636–637). Nonetheless, SIL missionaries avoided direct confrontations with local *patrones*. In addition, they favored a discourse of individual effort rather than one of collective struggle and social reform. As has been asserted, members of the SIL, in contrast to some of the Catholic missionaries of the 1960s and 1970s, were never known as "dangerous" missionaries (Cano et al. 1981: 192).

Inspired by Vatican Council II, which added the search for social justice to the traditional notion of salvation, and by the 1968 meeting of Latin American bishops in Medellín, Colombia, which advocated a "liberation theology," the Catholic Church in Peru entered into a period of reflection and reform. In 1973 the assembly of Amazonian bishops issued a pastoral letter calling missionaries to encourage "the organization of the native communities" and to "promote native leaders" (Mercier and Villeneuve 1974: 87, 99). In 1974 the assembly sponsored the creation of the Centro Amazónico de Antropología y Acción Pastoral, later changed to the more secular Centro Amazónico de Antropología y Aplicación Práctica. The center was meant to provide missionaries with guidelines on how to conduct more socially and culturally oriented pastoral activities.

The most active missionary groups in Loreto were the French Franciscans in charge of the Vicariato Apostólico de Pucallpa, and the Canadian Franciscans, in charge of the Vicariato Apostólico de Indiana. The former had jurisdiction over the Ucayali Basin; they worked mostly with the Shipibo-Conibo, supporting their rights and promoting their organization. As a result of their efforts, between 1971 and 1972 Shipibo-Conibo leaders gathered four times to discuss their problems and demand respect for their rights (Chirif 1974: 48). The success of these meetings can be measured by the number of communities represented, which increased from nineteen in the first gathering to seventy-five in the fourth, representing 90 percent of all Shipibo-Conibo settlements. The gatherings caused a stir in the Ucayali Basin, and local *patrones* and authorities accused the missionaries of inciting the Indians to rebel (Villeneuve 1974: 134). With the support of the Franciscans, the Shipibo-Conibo were very successful in securing land titles for their settlements. Between 1971 and 1974 fifteen settlements obtained titles as indigenous reserves (Chirif et al. 1977: 30).

The Canadian Franciscans had jurisdiction over most of the Amazon River and over the Napo, Putumayo, and Yavari Rivers (Villarejo 1965: 424). From their headquarters in Santa Clotilde on the Napo, they redoubled their efforts to promote the organization of the Quichua-speaking Naporuna. The Canadian Franciscans were extremely effective in inciting the numerous Naporuna peons living in local *fundos* to confront *patrones* and to struggle for the recognition of their land rights. With the backing of the missionaries, the Naporuna began to organize. In 1972 representatives of nineteen settlements, many located within *fundos,* gathered for the first time to discuss their problems (Mercier 1974: 118). The spirit of that first meeting is conveyed by one of its main proclamations: "We will not live as slaves forever. We will not serve the *patrones* forever" (Mercier 1979: 309). However, the universal rejection of *fundo patrones* is better summarized by the words of a Naporuna leader: "Without *patrones* we lead a better life" (Mercier 1979: 320). Inspired by these meetings, the Naporuna from 1974 on began cutting links with *patrones* and registering their *fundo*-bound settlements as native communities. The old *fundos* of Pucabarranca, Negro Urco, Huiririma, Camposerio, Monterrico, and Tempestad underwent such change between 1975 and 1976 (AIDESEP 1992)(see Map 3; Boxes 8.1–8.4).

SINAMOS, the agency created by the military government in 1971 to further the rights of the popular sectors, increase popular participation in decisionmaking processes, and promote their organization, also supported the emancipation of *fundo* peons from debt-peonage ties. Immediately after the creation of SINAMOS, its officials began visiting remote rural areas of Loreto, inciting the people to fight for their rights and end their exploitation. SINAMOS sponsored the creation of production and marketing cooperatives and the organization of peasant unions and indigenous associations. It also conveyed grassroots complaints, denunciations, and petitions to the appropriate government agencies.

A group of young anthropologists working for the agency was instrumental in the drafting of the Law of Native Communities. For the first time the law recognized the legal rights of Amazonia's indigenous peoples, establishing clear procedures for the titling of their lands. Unfortunately, as one of the law's authors admitted (Chirif 1985: 220), the lack of more detailed knowledge of the situation in the *selva baja* prevented the group from extending the benefits of the law to the *ribereños.* SINAMOS was nevertheless quite effective in mobilizing both indigenous peoples and *ribereño* peasants to fight for land rights. Relations between SINAMOS officials and missionaries working in Loreto were not always harmonious. Although the agency coordinated some actions with the more radical Catholic missionaries (Villeneuve 1974: 134), the SIL missionaries, who regarded SINAMOS officials as communists, opposed them (Stoll 1985: 218). Furthermore, before closing in 1977 SINAMOS became the object of severe criticism from many popular organizations that resented the agency's constant meddling and attempts to co-opt them. Ironically, many such organizations had been created with the agency's support.

The combination of these factors eroded the economic and political power of *fundo patrones*. This led to the disappearance of *fundos* from Loreto's rural landscape and their replacement by a myriad of independent settlements. In 1940 *fundos* were still the predominant socioeconomic unit in Loreto's rural areas, outnumbering independent settlements by 44 percent (see Table 12.2). In the following ten years, many *fundos* were abandoned and taken over by their peons, becoming independent settlements.

The emancipation of peon families from *fundo* owners and the process of constant fission of old settlements also contributed to the formation of new independent settlements. Between 1940 and 1961 the number of *caseríos* increased from 430 to 1,343. By 1961 there were almost four times as many independent settlements as

Table 12.2 Evolution of Fundos and Independent Settlements, 1940–1993

		Independent settlements	
Year	*Fundos[a]*	*Ribereño[b]*	*Indigenous[c]*
1940	637	430	10
1961	351	1,343	19
1972	42	1,378	51
1981	15	1,674	191
1993	99	1,328	487

SOURCES: DNE 1949; DNEC 1966; INE n.d., 1985a, 1985b; Chirif 1974; AIDESEP 1992; INEI 1994c.

NOTES: [a] *Fundos* include *haciendas, estancias, fincas, granjas,* and *unidades agropecuarias.*
  [b] *Ribereño* settlements include *caseríos, villas, aldeas, poblados, pagos, anexos,* and *comunidades campesinas.*
  [c] Indigenous settlements include *parcialidades, comunidades, colonias, reservas,* and *comunidades nativas* or *comunidades indígenas.*

fundos. By 1972 *fundos* had almost disappeared from Loreto's countryside, and the recognition of indigenous settlements as native communities during the 1970s further increased the number of independent settlements.

From Peons to Peasants

The release of indigenous and *ribereño* peons from *fundo patrones* did not mean automatic disengagement from traditional *habilitado* relationships. The transformation of *fundo* peons into independent peasants that took place between 1963 and 1990 was gradual and did not have the same impact within the department of Loreto. In some cases, *patrones* abandoned *fundos* to migrate to urban centers, leaving their assets behind. In other cases, it was related to the gradual erosion of the economic power and authority of *fundo patrones.* In that case, the transition from peon to peasant was more prolonged and frequently implied the replacement of *fundos patrones* by a new generation of small *patrones* (fluvial traders and medium-sized farmer-traders) and the replacement of debt-peonage bonds by debt-merchandise ties.

The Appearance of Small Patrones

In areas close to urban centers, where levels of literacy were greater and means of transportation more available, the departure of *fundo* owners permitted peons to extricate themselves from debt-peonage and venture into independent production. In remoter areas, such as the Napo River basin, where a local market for agricultural products did not exist and transportation was scarce and irregular, the departure of *fundo* owners did not lead to the immediate liberation of illiterate indigenous peons from the *habilitación* system. In fact, quite often the departure of *fundos* owners generated a crisis among peons, who were left without a source for basic goods. In a few instances, peon families merely searched for a new *patrón*, as in Rumi Tumi on the Napo River.

Rumi Tumi was founded with Naporuna peons by Alejandro Pacaya during the rubber era (San Román 1974: I, 71). In later years three other *patrones* settled the same area with their own peons. Declining profit margins in the 1960s prompted these *patrones* to abandon the area. San Román (ibidem) reports that "this situation of abandonment generated among the Quichua [Naporuna] families a feeling of orphanage." As a result, some of these families migrated to the neighboring *fundo* of Tempestad "in search of a *patrón.*" This was not an isolated case. In areas where there were no possibilities of making a living through independent agricultural or extractive activities, peons whose *patrones* no longer had the economic power to outfit them or who had been abandoned frequently opted to attach themselves to a new *patrón* (Atarama 1992: 74; San Román 1974: I, 69, 89). In other cases, *regatones* filled the void left by departing *fundo patrones* (San Román 1974: I, 75).

Fluvial traders were familiar figures in Loreto's rivers since the nineteenth century. However, before the breakdown of the monopoly that *fundo patrones* held over local trade, *regatones* were constrained to doing business with isolated extractors or the inhabitants of independent settlements, which before the 1960s were not very numerous. Moreover, they generally were confined to petty commerce and did not participate directly in the marketing of profitable boom products (which remained mostly in the hands of *fundo* owners and merchant houses).

The decline of Loreto's *fundos* and trading houses opened the doors for *regatones* to engage former *fundo* peons in *habilitado* relationships. They also became directly involved in the minor export booms of the 1960s and 1970s—*ojé* resin, furs, hides, and ornamental fish. In some cases, as in San Carlos, Jerusalén, and Negro Urco on the Napo, emancipated peons started trading with *regatones* who regularly visited the area (San Román 1974: I, 73, 79, 89). In other cases, as in Rumi Tumi, San Fernando, and Soledad in the Napo Basin, *regatones* settled abandoned *fundos* (San Román 1974: I, 71, 75, 77).

These fluvial traders became known as *patrones de caserío,* or "settlement" *patrones*. Quite often, they built a house, established a small shop, opened pastures, brought in cattle, and even married into the local community. Unlike *fundo patrones*, however, they rarely claimed ownership of the land that belonged to the former *fundos*; their power rested in their control over local commerce. However, they did not have the exclusive trading rights that *fundo patrones* had enjoyed; they had to compete with other traders. In fact, very often several *regatones* settled within the limits of a former *fundo*, competing among themselves for local clients (San Román 1974: I, 71, 75). Some former overseers who remained after owners abandoned their *fundos* also became settlement *patrones*. Like the *regatones*, former overseers did not claim exclusive ownership of the land. They did have, however, enough capital to undertake cattle-raising, establish a retail store, and engage former *fundo* peons in the extraction and production of commercial products.

Whether *regatones* or former overseers, these new *patrones* also operated through the *habilitación* system. During this phase, however, "domination shifted from the field of production to that of commercialization" (San Román 1975: 203). The new *patrones* controlled laborers indirectly through trading relations, rather than directly through the monopoly of land, commerce, and political power. In other words, the coercive debt-peonage system gave way to the less constraining, but no less effective, debt-merchandise system. That system entailed advances in goods in exchange for future delivery of agricultural or forest products. Although the principle underlying debt-peonage and debt-merchandise is similar, from the viewpoint of the *habilitado* laborers the transition to debt-merchandise ties constituted a significant change, as it granted greater personal autonomy and cleared a path to becoming independent peasant producers.

The Influence of Agricultural Promotional Policies

By the early 1970s the labor situation of rural dwellers differed significantly according to their access to the marketplace. Thus, in the Amazon River basin, better connected to the Iquitos market, only 32 percent of *caserío* dwellers were engaged in *habilitado* relationships, whereas in the more isolated Napo River basin the figure was 67 percent (San Román 1974: II, 74). Moreover, whereas in the Napo region 75 percent of *caserío* dwellers sold their products in situ to a wide range of fluvial and local traders, in the Amazon region 63 percent sold their products in other villages or in Iquitos (ibidem: II, 119). Today, the *habilitación* system has been eliminated in most of the region, persisting only in the remotest areas.

The transformation of *habilitado* laborers to independent producers was accelerated after 1980 by an increase in the number of loans and the amount of agriculture credit made available by the government. In 1961 the Banco de Fomento de Agropecuario granted 2,006 agricultural loans, reaching about 10 percent of the region's rural households (see Table 12.3); during the 1970s that did not change substantially. By 1982, however, the number of loans had expanded to 7,532, reaching 23 percent of rural households. By the end of the decade, prior to the closure of its successor—Banco Agrario—in 1992, the number of loans granted had more than quadrupled, to 32,267, reaching at least 41 percent of the region's rural households.

The second factor contributing to the transformation of Loreto's rural laborers into petty commodity producers was the government's establishment of guaranteed prices for the region's main cash crops (rice and yellow corn). To this was added the creation of a network of buying centers along the main rivers, which improved marketing conditions. A third factor was the growth of the region's urban population. It increased almost fivefold from 1961 to 1993, representing 60 percent of the popu-

Table 12.3   Percentage of Rural Households Holding Promotional Agricultural Credit from State Banks and Agencies, 1961–1994

Year	No. loans	No. RHs[a]	% RHs w/loans
1961	2,006	21,194	9.5
1972	2,958	27,073	10.9
1982[b]	7,532	32,319	23.3
1989[c]	32,267	79,516	40.6
1994[d]	2,671[e]	79,516	3.4

SOURCES: Tables 9.3, 10.1; Maletta and Bardales n.d.; INEI 1996a, 1996b.
NOTES: [a] RHs = rural households
　　[b] Data for 1982 and after include the department of Ucayali.
　　[c] For lack of population data for 1982 and 1989, we have used that corresponding to 1981 and 1994, respectively.
　　[d] The notable increase in the number of rural households between 1981 and 1994 mainly derives from differences in the definition of the category "rural household" rather than on an actual increase in population. The 1994 census included in this category households in urban centers that had at least one person dedicated to agriculture.
　　[e] Data on loans for 1994, after the closing of Banco Agrario, include those granted by such government agencies or government-supported institutions as the Fondo Rotatorio of the Ministry of Agriculture, Fondo de Desarrollo Agrícola, Fondo Nacional de Fomento Ganadero and Caja Rural de Ahorro y Crédito.

lation of Loreto and 67 percent of that of Ucayali (see Appendix 30). Logically, this augmented the internal market for regional agricultural products.

The transformation of Loreto's rural laborers is also illustrated by the areas being cultivated for cash crops, family income levels, and the sources of income. Since the 1960s state agricultural credit was specifically directed to the production of rice for the regional and domestic markets and, later, of corn for the Iquitos-based poultry industry. Before the Banco Agrario closed in 1992, and before the cessation of subsidized agricultural credit programs, rice and corn were cultivated mainly for sale and were heavily dependent on access to state or private credit (Cannock and Cuadra 1990: 54). The cultivation of rice and corn expanded along almost all major rivers.

Thanks to the establishment throughout the region of buying centers by Empresa Comercializadora de Arroz S.A. (ECASA, the state rice-marketing enterprise) and Empresa Nacional de Comercialización de Insumos (ENCI, the government agency devoted to the buying and selling of agricultural inputs), the cultivation of rice and corn expanded along almost all the major rivers.

Manioc and plantains, the region's staples, were cultivated mainly for subsistence. However, in settlements close to fast-growing urban centers they gradually became dual-purpose crops, that is, for subsistence as well as commercial sale. In contrast to rice and corn, the cultivation of manioc and plantains was not dependent on credit; their production varied according to fluctuations in prices (Cannock and Cuadra 1990: 54). As a result, during the 1963–1990 period, commercial agriculture expanded steadily. Between 1961 and 1981 the area devoted to cash crops increased by almost 70 percent. With the expansion of the government credit programs during the 1980s, it increased again by almost 40 percent in the short period between 1981 and 1987 (see Table 12.4).

The conversion of Loreto's rural laborers into independent producers is also shown by the increase in average family income. Based on a survey of 742 rural households along the Amazon River, San Román (1974: II, 129) estimated that the

Table 12.4 Cultivated Area of Commercial Crops, 1961–1995 (in hectares)

Year	Rice	Corn	Manioc	Plantain	Total[a]
1961	6,061	3,135	9,928	17,035	36,159
1971	20,200	6,500	7,000	21,000	54,700
1981[b]	26,200	9,600	7,300	17,300	60,400
1987[c]	26,400	30,700	10,600	15,800	83,500
1995	24,161	26,400	23,789	29,090	103,440

SOURCES: ONEC 1972; González 1988; INEI 1996a, 1996b.
NOTES: [a] Data refers to area actually harvested. Hence, figures might be underestimated.
[b] Data for 1981 and after include the department of Ucayali.
[c] For lack of data on the area cultivated in plantains for 1987, we have used data corresponding to 1986.

average annual family income in 1971 amounted to the equivalent of US$333. A study of 501 rural households along the Tahuayo River, a tributary of the Amazon, showed that by 1988 the average annual family income had increased to US$958 (Coomes 1996: 55). Both studies took into consideration the same three sources of income (agriculture, extraction, and wage labor) to estimate annual income. Data provided by Oliver Coomes (1996: 55) show that in Loreto 58 percent of the average annual rural income was derived from the sale of agricultural products, 25 percent from the sale of extractive products, 9 percent from salaried activities, and the rest from the sale of handicrafts, as well as cash remittances.

By the end of the 1963–1990 period independent commercial agriculture had become the main economic activity of Loreto's rural population. In 1994 66 percent of the agricultural units in the departments of Loreto and Ucayali sent most of their produce to market (INEI 1996a, 1996b). However, the significance that commercial agriculture has for the generation of income varies widely according to where producers are located with respect to market centers and networks. Thus, in provinces that include important urban centers and have a low proportion of their population in peripheral areas, this percentage can be as high as 78 percent. In provinces where a large proportion of the population lives in peripheral areas, the percentage of rural households that sells most of their production is about 55 percent. Finally, in isolated provinces this percentage can be as low as 2 percent (INEI 1996a; 1996b).

Consolidation of the *Ribereño* Social Stratum

The emancipation of *fundo* peons from debt-peonage and their gradual transformation into peasants devoted to a combination of subsistence and commercial agriculture marked their consolidation as a new social stratum, the mixed-blood *ribereño* population. Following San Román (1975), Michael Chibnik has argued that "the key period for the formation of *ribereño* identity was from the end of the rubber boom through the first half of the 20th century" (1991: 172, 174). Christine Padoch and Wil de Jong (1990) also espouse this view. In contrast, we maintain that the configuration of the *ribereño* stratum is directly linked to the social and economic events triggered by the rubber boom; it began with the rubber boom, deepened during the post–rubber boom era, and consolidated throughout the 1960s and 1970s.

Origins of the Process

By the mid-nineteenth century, before the rubber boom, Loreto's population was concentrated along the Huallaga River basin, in the department's western fringes. It consisted of a small number of whites living in larger cities, a larger mestizo group residing in towns and their environs, a large population of catechized Indians living in former mission posts, and an undetermined number of uncontacted tribal Indians mostly dispersed in the interfluves. Although mestizos and, to a lesser extent, catechized Indians were of mixed heritage, neither group had the characteristics of what was to become the *ribereño* mixed-blood population. The mestizo population was the product of the intermarriage of people of Spanish stock, who had settled in the region since the foundation of the town of Moyobamba in 1540, with local Amazonian indigenous people and with indigenous and mestizo people from the Andean highlands. However, this mostly urban, Spanish-speaking mestizo population adhered to the European lifestyles and values of the dominant white group. In turn, although catechized Indians had abandoned part of their cultural heritage, had adopted many traits from the Spanish Catholic tradition, and showed some signs of interbreeding, they continued to regard themselves, and to be regarded, as indigenous peoples.

This situation changed with the rubber boom. We propose that four factors contributed to altering the ethnic profile of the region, creating conditions for the formation of the present-day *ribereño* stratum. First was the massive influx of peoples, mostly males, who arrived from the Huallaga Basin, from other parts of Peru, and from other countries. Second was the extended interbreeding between white and mestizo rubber extractors and catechized and tribal indigenous women as a result of the scarcity of nonindigenous women. Third was the assimilation of tribal indigenous children through the widespread practice of *correrías*. The fourth was the disruption of ethnic identities through constant geographical displacement of catechized and tribal indigenous peons.

Around 1870, the beginning of the rubber boom, there was an important inflow of white, mestizo, and indigenous migrants from the Huallaga River basin into eastern Loreto. Most whites and mestizos came as rubber *patrones* or settled as independent farmers. Some mestizos and all catechized Indian migrants came as rubber tappers or collectors. A smaller group of immigrants came from the Andean highlands and from the Pacific Coast, some as *patrones*, others as peons. Finally, there was an important migration of traders and tappers from Brazil and Ecuador and a smaller flow of Europeans, Africans, and Asians.

Most of these immigrants were male; numerous reports remark on the scarcity of men in the Huallaga Basin towns and hamlets, from where most of them emigrated (Derteano 1903: 607). By contrast, there was an acute shortage of white and mestizo women in the rubber fronts (Pesce 1904: 232). This resulted in extensive mating with indigenous women, both catechized and tribal. The relationship between them varied. According to some authors, "Concubinage between whites and savage women is something very natural. . . . Many have even been to Europe and a large number live with their foreign husbands for their entire lives" (Stiglich 1904b: 399). Others, however, claimed that even though "liaisons between Europeans and *cholas* who take care of their households are very frequent," when the European *patrones* return to their countries of origin they usually sell their estates and, with them, their indigenous concubines (Meyendorff in Monnier 1994: 148).

The term *chola* was applied to catechized indigenous women and to tribal Indian women who had been captured in *correrías* and raised in a white-mestizo environment. Often, white and mestizo rubber *patrones* had several *chola* concubines simultaneously. The children of these mixed unions did not want to be considered "as belonging to the same world as their jungle ancestors" (Stiglich 1904b: 399). Brought up by their indigenous mothers but reared in the nonindigenous tradition of their mestizo and white fathers, the offspring of these unions were a major factor in forging a mestizo *ribereño* stratum and identity.

Slave-raids constituted another important means through which the new mixed-blood group was constructed. The main objective of *correrías* was the abduction of boys, girls, and young women, who were brought up by their captors or sold to white or mestizo families living in the countryside or in urban centers. The number of young indigenous people abducted from their tribes through these means must have been extremely high, as it was reported that "from the highest authority, to the lowest farmer or trader, everybody wants to have a savage boy or girl in their service" (Sala 1897: 55). These infant captives were taught "civilized" mores and raised to become loyal domestic servants or peons. Many assumed the surname of their *patrones,* and some were even assimilated into captors' families as low-status members.

The removal of catechized and tribal Indians from their homelands prevented them from maintaining cultural identities and ethnic links. Numerous reports mention the forced enlistment of indigenous peoples from the Huallaga River basin to work as tappers in the lower Amazon. Further displacement within the rubber areas, particularly of indigenous peons engaged in the extraction of castilloa rubber, contributed to the process of uprooting and detribalization. In addition, the practice of transfer of debts promoted the dispersal of members of an indigenous group among a wide range of *patrones,* generating interethnic marriages and causing the loss of ethnic identity. By the early 1900s it was reported that "forced by circumstances, the Indian tribes intermix and mix with rubber tappers forming a new race" (von Hassel 1905: 637)

By the end of the rubber boom Loreto's indigenous population had been severely decimated and displaced. Many of the catechized indigenous peoples of the Huallaga River basin had disappeared, either through assimilation or extermination. Among them were the Hibito, Cholones, Tabaloso, Chamicuro, and Aguano. Others, including the Lamista, Cocamilla, Chayahuita, and Jebero, continued to be dominated by white and mestizo *patrones* but were able to regroup in their lands of origin. A particular case was that of the Shipibo, Setebo, and Conibo of the Ucayali River, Panoan-speaking groups that fused to form a new identity under the domination of white-mestizo *patrones.* In contrast to the catechized Indians of the Huallaga and Ucayali River basins, those from the Marañón and Amazon Rivers were widely scattered and, except for the Urarina, were assimilated into the new mixed-blood group. This was the case with most of the Cocama, Omagua, and Iquitos. On the Napo River, the Quichua-speaking Naporuna were able to maintain a certain degree of ethnic cohesion, although they were still subordinated to *patrones.* Nevertheless, all catechized indigenous peoples lost many members who, isolated from their cultural roots, were assimilated into the mixed-blood group.

Tribal indigenous peoples were also deeply affected by the rubber boom; its impact, however, was not uniform. Some peoples disappeared, as was the case of the Andoa, Remo, and Capanahua; others were decimated to the point that they ceased being viable social units, as with the Capanahua, Zaparo, Arabela, Resigaro, and Aushiri. Other groups managed to extricate themselves from the domination of *patrones* and reconstruct tribal lifestyles, although their social organization, religious traditions, ritual practices, and material culture were highly modified due to the contact with white-mestizos. Among them were the Yaminahua, Cashinahua, Sharanahua, Culina, Mayoruna, Uni, Amahuaca, Murato, and segments of the Ashaninka, Ticuna, and Yagua. Lastly, some remained subject to *patrones* in the new *fundos* that sprang up after the rubber bust. Among them were the Huitoto, Bora, Ocaina, and Mai Huna, as well as other segments of the Ashaninka, Ticuna, and Yagua.

By 1914, the end of the rubber boom, the formation of Loreto's mixed-blood stratum had been under way for almost a half-century. Early-twentieth-century authors called members of this group *loretanos* (Loretans), asserting that they were the result of "a mixture of savages with Quechuas [Andean Indians] and Europeans" and that they were to become "the population of the future" (Stiglich 1904: 408). At the time of the rubber bust at least two generations of *ribereños* existed. Their numbers had grown spectacularly. It has been estimated that at the height of the rubber boom there were 28,000 rubber extractors operating in Loreto, of which 79 percent were catechized and tribal Indians, 21 percent white or mestizo peoples (Varese 1973: 342). After the rubber bust, this ratio was reversed. By 1940 Loreto had 168,611 inhabitants, of which 61 percent were white and mestizo, 38 percent indigenous (DNE 1948: 15).

Expansion of the Ribereño *Social Stratum*

After the rubber bust the expansion of the mixed-blood population was accelerated as a result of further geographical displacement, nucleation of the population in riverine *fundos*, and continued assimilation of indigenous children. Many *patrones* moved from the peripheral rubber fronts to areas closer to the region's urban centers and from the interfluves into the riverine areas. Most of these *patrones* brought along their indigenous and mixed-blood peons. In some instances, they returned to their peons' homelands; in others, they removed them from their native villages. In contrast to the centripetal movement of the *patrones* and their peons, tribal indigenous peons who had been able to free themselves from *habilitado* ties moved in a centrifugal fashion, toward peripheral and interfluvial areas, where they took refuge.

These two processes had the unintended effect of completing the uprooting of many indigenous peons, reinforcing the old colonial boundaries between "civilized" and "savage" Indians. This, in turn, had the effect of bringing civilized Indians nearer to the expanding, mixed-blood population. In subsequent decades the constant displacement of indigenous and mixed-blood peons by *fundo* owners in order to collect different forest products further contributed to their uprooting and inter-breeding with other groups. In their analysis of the history of the settlement of Santa Rosa on the Ucayali River, Padoch and de Jong (1990) present an insightful account of the workings of this type of process.

Nucleation of indigenous and mixed-blood peons in riverine *fundos* had a double effect. In cases where the majority of peons belonged to the same ethnic group, nu-cleation contributed to the maintenance of traditional cultural traits and a certain degree of ethnic cohesion. This took place among the Cocamilla living in *fundos* along the lower Huallaga River (Stocks 1981: 95), the Chayahuita of the Parana-pura and Cahuapanas Rivers (Fuentes 1988: 34), the Piro of the Urubamba River (Gow 1991: 45–46), and among the Naporuna of the Napo River (San Román 1974: I). Where peons belonged to different ethnic groups, with no group having a clear predominance, the tendency was to intermarry and adopt a *loretano* lifestyle.

Slave-raids disappeared after the rubber bust, but the practice of incorporating in-digenous children into the *patrones'* households continued for several decades. This was achieved through the raising of godchildren and the adoption of indigenous or-phans. We have learned that after the rubber bust the institutions of *compadrazgo* and *padrinazgo* became means to disguise the exploitative nature of the relationship between *patrones* and peons, cloaking it with a veneer of spiritual attachment and reciprocal aid. In many cases, godchildren were incorporated into the families of their godparents and raised with their blood children, but they always had a lower status.

Tribal indigenous children, mainly orphans who were given away by adoptive in-digenous families in exchange for valued manufactured goods, also continued to be incorporated into the households of *fundo patrones*. These transactions may have shared some characteristics of a sale, but these children were not considered slaves, and they were not sold or bought in the market. In most cases, they were raised by their *patrones* and incorporated into their households as maids, ayahs, cooks, laun-dresses, and footboys. Even after marriage many remained attached to the house-holds of their *patrones* as peons, perhaps staying on due to bonds of loyalty or for economic convenience.

These elements contributed to the rapid growth of the mixed-blood stratum both in the rural areas as well as in the urban centers. It is worth noting that during the rubber boom and in the following decades this group was not yet referred to as *ribereños*. In the 1930s the Agustinian missionary Father Lucas Espinosa (1935: 14–15, 102) classified Loreto's rural population into four categories: *patrones*, or white entrepreneurs; mestizo landholders with white surnames; Indians reduced to civil life; and savage Indians. In the following decade, Máximo Kuczynski-Godard (1944: 13) reported that most of Loreto's rural dwellers were "poor colonists" with an "Indian-mestizo lifestyle." In the 1950s Pedro Weiss (1959: 16) referred to the "mestizo-Creole culture of the Amazon," describing it as "composed by tribal ele-ments, Andean, native mestizo and Spanish influence, plus some Ecuadorian and many more Brazilian traits." These descriptions do not differ substantially from

Stiglich's 1904 description of the *loretanos*. The defining element of the new stratum was always the fusion of physical and cultural traits from Amazonian, Andean, and European peoples.

The term "*ribereño*," used currently to designate Loreto's mixed-blood rural population, appeared much later. Loretan writer Arturo D. Hernández was apparently the first to use it, in his 1954 novel, *Selva Trágica* (The Tragic Forest). In ornate language, Hernández presents an urban-biased view of the mixed-blood people settled along the region's main rivers: "Pushed permanently by the overwhelming forest, which brandishes the savage vigor of madness and the perseverance of the eternal, *ribereños* turn their backs to the obscure and mysterious interior and direct their sight to the ochery waters of the wide river in an attitude of expectation for all that which flows down with the current and speaks to their imagination of immense distances and vague yearnings" (1970: 222; emphasis added).

Hernández used the term "*ribereño*" not only to indicate geographic location (riverbanks versus interfluves) but also to denote a particular sociobiological group, which he contrasts with both "savage" and "tamed Indians" and to which he attributed a particular "mentality" (1970: 2).

The term retained its literary imagery until the 1970s, when it was incorporated into the discourse of the social sciences. Anthropologist Stefano Varese (1973: 358) was the first to use the term "*ribereño* population" to refer to "small and mid-size farmers with limited access to credit." Interestingly, Varese makes no reference to the ethnic background of this population, except to assert that its members stand in contrast to the "indigenous population" and to "colonists" from outside the region. By restricting the term "*ribereño*" to Loreto's nonindigenous rural population, Varese and subsequent authors narrowed the scope of previous social labels, such as *loretanos*, which referred both to rural and urban mixed-blood populations. This was the first change in the way Loreto's mixed-blood population was conceptualized.

During the following years the use of the term "*ribereño*" became widespread, mostly as an adjective indicating geographical location, though with some ethnic overtones. Thus, Genaro García (in Mora 1974: 65) referred to "*ribereño* populations," and San Román (1974: 10) talked about "*ribereño* farmers." According to San Román, *ribereño* farmers and colonists constitute a mixture of "mestizos from San Martín, Europeans and Asians of diverse origins, some *zambos* [the offspring of Africans and Amerindians], and Amazonian Indians" (San Román 1975: 180). These colonists and farmers could be classified into three subgroups: large colonist-entrepreneurs, or *patrones*; midsized colonists, or small *patrones*; and small, or common, colonists. In other words, in its original meaning, the term "*ribereño*" cut across classes, encompassing both *patrones* and peons.

San Román (1975: 179) asserted that in the process of adapting to the *selva baja* the immigrants from San Martín adopted indigenous ways of life. Such "cultural symbiosis" was expedited by the fact that many of the immigrants took local indigenous women as wives. However, San Román pointed out that although the *ribereño* colonists "adopted many of the cultural traits of the indigenous peoples, they oriented their social attitudes towards the world of the whites and their Western culture." This author was the first to use the term "*ribereño*," not only to indicate geographical location ("riverine areas") but also to refer to occupation ("farmer"), ethnic background ("racial mixture"), and cultural heritage ("semi-Indian lifestyle").

Anthony Stocks (1981: 9) defines *ribereños* as "white-mestizo rural pioneers" who constitute the bulk of the Amazonian rural population and "whose culture is closer to European rather than to native models." Yepes del Castillo (1982: 67) was the first to coin the expression "*ribereño* mestizo population." His characterization of the origins of this sector changed gradually over time (Yepes del Castillo 1982, 1983, 1988). However, in his latest paper on the subject (1988: 60) he suggests that the *ribereño* population emerged as a result of a double process. On the one hand was the acculturation of Amazonian indigenous peoples, who realized that in order "to survive they had to resemble the foreign colonists." On the other hand was the "Amazonization" or "nativization" of the mestizo immigrants, who were "forced to learn . . . the way of the natives" in order to survive in their new environment.

Until then, *ribereños*—whether alluded to as "colonists," "pioneers," or "rural dwellers"—had always been described as "farmers," including large, mid-sized, and small landholders. Jaime Regan (1983: 112) was apparently the first to characterize *ribereños* as "peasants" and to use the expressions "*ribereño* mestizos" and "mestizo peasants" interchangeably. We contend that this change reflected both the disappearance of large and mid-sized *fundo* owners from Loreto's rural scene in the 1960s and 1970s, as well as the transformation of former peons into small producers. This new identification gave rise to the expression "*ribereño* mestizo peasants," used commonly today. It is worth noting, however, that by restricting its use to designate the region's small rural producers, the term "*ribereño*" lost its original cross-class meaning. We contend that this was the second important change in the conceptualization of Loreto's mixed-blood population.

Thus, whereas early writers conceived of the process of interbreeding as one leading in both rural and urban areas to the emergence of a mixed-blood population comprising various occupations and different class segments, contemporary authors have narrowed the focus. They conceive of the process as one leading to the formation of a specific type of rural dweller, namely, the riverine mestizo peasant.

*   *   *

The *ribereño* peasant economy has been the subject of several recent studies. Some have focused on land use patterns and resource management (Denevan 1984; Hiraoka 1985b, 1986; Pinedo-Vásquez 1986; Padoch and de Jong 1987; Padoch et al. 1990). Others have analyzed labor practices and market economic strategies (Hiraoka 1985a, 1987; de Jong 1987; Padoch 1988; Chibnik 1989; Chibnik and de Jong 1992; Coomes 1996a, 1996b). For a more detailed analysis of the economy of present-day *ribereño* peasant producers, we refer the reader to these studies, and particularly to Coomes (1992) and Chibnik (1994). In concluding this chapter, we would like to stress two aspects of the process of emancipation of Loreto's rural laborers and their shift from peons to peasants. First, these changes transformed the economic and political relationships between the rural areas and the urban centers. Second, the state played a central role in this transformation.

The government's efforts to modernize the region's economy by eliminating the *habilitación* system, promoting agriculture over extraction, and redirecting the economy from the international to the domestic market were quite successful. By attacking the *habilitación* system, regulating access to land and natural resources, and promoting the liberation of *fundo* peons from debt-peonage ties, the government further eroded the power of *fundo* owners, ultimately eliminating them from Loreto's rural scene. In turn, by granting promotional agricultural credit, establishing guaranteed prices for key cash crops, and creating a subsidized marketing network, the state reoriented the region's economy from extraction to agriculture.

The state also helped to eliminate the monopoly exercised by traditional merchant houses and reduced the influence that the fluvial traders and settlement *patrones* who succeeded them held over the rural population. These changes were permanent; they did not depend on continued government intervention. Even after the profound economic crisis of the late 1980s, and the termination of subsidized credit programs shortly after President Fujimori's ascension to power in 1990, the area devoted to cash crops continued to grow (see Table 12.4). It is worth noting, however, that even though the transformation of Loreto's rural population from peons to peasants improved their lot, they are by no means well-off. *Ribereño* peasants still have very low levels of income. Their market activities are subject to abrupt ups and downs, and they very rarely accumulate capital. Having replaced the merchant and landed elites as the primary economic agent in the rural areas and as the main link between rural and urban economies, the state has become the target of the demands of the *ribereño* peasants. It has also become the main opponent of other organized social sectors in the region.

13

"People Expect the State to Solve Everything": Popular Organization and Regionalist Demands

By adopting a modernizing, developmentalist doctrine aimed, among other things, at integrating the popular sectors economically and politically, the state became during the 1963–1990 period an important instrument of political organization. Under Gen. Juan Velasco Alvarado during the so-called first phase of the revolutionary military government (1968–1975), the democratization of Peru proceeded at a reasonable pace via greater popular participation in economic and political events. Reforms aimed at preventing Marxist parties from co-opting these population sectors and, thus, blocking the possibility of a communist revolution. In this chapter we analyze the political transformations in Loreto during this period. We begin the analysis by examining the process of organization of Loreto's popular sectors. We define "popular sectors" as the classes, class segments, and other strata occupying a subordinate economic and political position. The circumstances under which the region's different social segments joined forces to form a multiclass movement revolving around a regionalist ideology and political platform will be discussed in detail.

Loreto did not escape the political dynamics triggered by the military government during its first phase. However, some important differences in the early 1960s distinguished Loreto from the rest of Peru and help explain its particular sociopolitical development in later years. First, Loreto's popular sectors had remained largely unorganized. This was due to the fact that the two political parties most interested in promoting popular organization—the populist Alianza Popular Revolucionaria Americana (APRA) and the Moscow-oriented Communist Party—considered Amazonia to be a marginal region in demographic and economic terms. Instead, they concentrated political efforts in the coastal and highland regions. Second, popular sectors in Loreto were rarely involved in this kind of struggle, unlike the rest of the country, where peasants and workers had confronted propertied classes through land invasions and labor strikes. Lastly, whereas most of the country's popular sectors mobilized around sectorial demands, in Loreto most important protests revolved around regional demands.

In Loreto the National System of Social Mobilization (SINAMOS), the government agency created in 1971 to mobilize and organize the country's poor, promoted the organization of such popular sectors as *ribereño* peasants, integrated tribal indigenous peoples, and slum-dwellers. The government also indirectly strengthened existing organizations, such as those grouping industry workers and impoverished, middle-class professionals. In fact, the stimulus to organize also touched the region's new elite, which modernized the venerable chamber of commerce and created new sectorial organizations, such as the shipper's association. We analyze the organizational processes underpinning each of these sectors, emphasizing their demands, platforms, and main forms of mobilization. Although most of the political activity was concentrated in Iquitos, Pucallpa, and their areas of influence, the urge to organize, as we point out, reached the region's remotest areas. Among Loreto's poorest and most disenfranchised sectors, political participation generated a greater awareness of basic rights.

Whereas in the rest of the country popular organizations gathered political experience by opposing economically dominant groups, in Loreto most political action was targeted at confronting the government. In Loreto economic power was based on trade rather than on the property of productive resources. Unlike other regions, in Loreto there was no property for the popular sectors to fight over. Moreover, by passing reformist legislation the state had eliminated potential sources of conflict between the propertied and propertyless classes, especially in rural and marginal urban areas. In effect, an early SINAMOS (n.d.: 1–2) report pointed out that in Loreto's economy there was "no transferable economic base, the objective pre-requisite to foster social mobilization." To put it in Marxist discourse, this meant that in Loreto no strong "concentration of the property of the means of production" existed, either in the agrarian, industrial, fishing, or mining sectors. Any impetus for the political mobilization of the popular sectors was therefore absent.

Members of SINAMOS did not assume conflicts between the regional bourgeoisie and the working classes were nonexistent. They believed, however, that such problems stemmed from the monopoly of commerce, not from the concentration of property. SINAMOS concluded that "it would not be appropriate to initiate a large-scale psychosocial program in the region, including propaganda, raising of political consciousness, training, and organization, until the problem of the economic base of social mobilization has been worked out" (SINAMOS n.d.: 7). In the absence of large property, whereby redistribution could channel political mobilization, SINAMOS opted to organize the popular sectors around the demand for services and rights traditionally provided by the state: schooling, health care, electricity, running water, housing, roads, promotional credit, marketing facilities, land titles, and personal documents.

In addition, the military government, by designing a series of policies favoring the popular sectors, defused points of conflict with the elites. Thus, for instance, by passing more equitable legislation to ensure access to rural and urban lands and to natural resources, the state helped eliminate the circumstances that might have led to an open, violent confrontation between peasants, indigenous peoples, and poor urban dwellers, on the one hand, and large entrepreneurs and landholders on the other hand.

As a result, we contend, instead of confronting the region's elite the popular sectors aimed their guns at the state. A few local government officials were well aware of the problems that could arise from the kind of policies favored by SINAMOS. In 1974 Genaro García, a Loretan economist working for Ordeoriente, the regional development agency, contended that SINAMOS was raising excessive expectations among the popular sectors and that it was running the risk of becoming a gigantic public-works agency. He suggested that stimulating the creative potential of the population using a minimum of state technical assistance would work better (Mora 1974: 74). García warned that "the state does not have enough resources to satisfy so many demands and paternalism engenders a dependency complex, so that, people expect the state to solve everything" (ibidem).

By becoming the region's main economic agent and regulator, the state became the target of most demands by the region's organized social sectors. Conflicts between these organizations and the state manifested themselves not only in sectorial demands but, above all, in regional demands. The most prominent example of the latter is the long struggle of Loretans to obtain a portion of the wealth generated by oil extraction. To defend the special status the region had been granted, whereby it was exonerated of a large number of taxes and duties, Loretans constantly pressed the authorities.

Despite different social, economic, and political standings, Loreto's various social sectors were able in 1978 to coordinate efforts and organize themselves into the Frente de Defensa del Pueblo de Loreto (FDPL). United, they pressed the state into paying an oil canon. We argue that the formation of the FDPL evinces the strength of Loreto's longstanding regionalist ideology, which provided common ground for the region's elite and popular sectors to combine their efforts and reconcile sectorial and regional demands. Our analysis of the agenda and activities of the FDPL reveals, however, the existence of frictions among the right, or center-right, representatives of the entrepreneurs, and the leftist leadership of popular organizations.

Loreto's New Social Sectors

Of the four social sectors that emerged or consolidated during the 1963–1990 period, regional bourgeoisie, *ribereño* peasants, indigenous peoples, and slum-dwellers, only the first had a tradition of corporate organization. Founded in 1890, Loreto's chamber of commerce underwent several transformations as a result of the changing economic interests and activities of the region's elite. Originally a guild of merchants, the chamber changed its name to the Chamber of Commerce and Agriculture around 1917 to reflect the potential of export agriculture and the emergence of a new landed elite. In the early 1960s it changed its name to Chamber of Commerce, Agriculture, and Industry. This transformation responded to the process of economic diversification stimulated by the passing of new legislation in the late 1950s promoting the industrial sector.

In the first half of the 1970s the group changed its name yet again to its current designation: Chamber of Commerce, Industry, and Tourism. The dropping of the agricultural component reflected the demise of the region's export agriculture and the disappearance of large *fundo* owners from the rural scene. The incorporation of tourism followed the creation of the Ministry of Industry, Commerce, Tourism, and Integration by the military government and responded to the fact that some of its members had investments in that industry. The modern chamber came to represent the broad range of interests of the generation of entrepreneurs that emerged in the 1960s. In addition, segments of the region's elite formed more specific organizations. Shippers, for instance, founded the Asociación de Armadores de Loreto in 1963 to confront the crisis in fluvial transportation.

During this period confrontations between Loreto's elite and the central government mostly revolved around tax incentives and, more specifically, the application of Law 15600 and the Peruvian-Colombian Customs Agreement, which had provided Loreto with a special tax status. These incentives had facilitated the accumulation of capital by the new generation of entrepreneurs. Any threat to those legal instruments was seen as a direct attack on the elite's interests, and each time the government attempted to curtail or eliminate them the chamber reacted swiftly and energetically.

It was not difficult for the chamber to persuade the popular sectors that cuts to tax incentives would mean grave consequences for the economy. In fact, this issue provided the first common ground for the diverse social sectors within the region, especially the urban sectors, to join efforts against the government. It also contributed to the creation of Loreto's first regionalist front. However, with the passage of time and the realization that the greatest beneficiaries of these incentives were the traders and industrialists, the popular sectors became increasingly reluctant to side with them.

Peasant Organizations

Because of their ethnic heterogeneity, dispersion, and subordination to *patrones*, Loreto's rural population had no experience in corporate organization before the 1960s. Except for the mutual-aid associations formed in a few independent *caseríos* close to Iquitos in the late 1930s (de Jong 1987: 13), as well as the committees of small producers sponsored by the Servicio Cooperativo Interamericano de Producción de Alimentos in the late 1940s (Sotomayor et al. 1949: 95), the vast majority of *ribereño* peoples were not organized. They thus had no means of fighting for their rights. It was only after the decline of the *fundo* economy, and the political sponsorship of the military government, that emancipated *ribereño* peons began to organize.

SINAMOS had a crucial role in this process. With its support, several agrarian leagues were founded in Loreto in 1975, the most active of which were located in the Amazon and Ucayali River basins (Rumrrill and Zutter 1976: 265; Ruiz Saavedra 1985: 256). That year, those leagues joined to form the Federación Agraria Selva Socialista de Loreto (FASSOL) and affiliated with the Confederación Nacional Agraria (CNA), the national agrarian union created in 1972 by the military government to further the objectives of the 1969 agrarian reforms.

In 1975, however, Gen. Francisco Morales Bermúdez deposed Pres. Velasco Alvarado, initiating the second phase of the military government (1975–1980). In a shift to the right, the new government attempted to stop the process of popular mobilization, which by then had grown out of its control. In 1977 it closed SINAMOS and in 1978 dissolved the CNA. The assets of the CNA were transferred to the Organización Nacional Agraria (ONA), an organization of mid-sized farmers. The government also expropriated FASSOL's assets. Although the CNA and FASSOL continued operating, lack of official support led to the disappearance or weakening of most of the agrarian leagues created in Loreto. Despite its brevity, the experience demonstrated the benefits that could accrue from these movements and prompted the emergence of new organizations.

Since 1973 several independent *ribereño* settlements close to Iquitos had formed the so-called Comités de Defensa de las Cochas to protect their lakes from overexploitation by industrial fishing boats (Ruiz Saavedra 1985: 256). In 1977, after the dissolution of SINAMOS, five such settlements in the district of Las Amazonas, Maynas Province, joined forces to protect their forests and lakes from the intrusion of logging companies, commercial hunters, and industrial fishermen (Atarama 1992: 156). A year later they formed the Federación Distrital de Campesinos de Las Amazonas (FEDICALAM).

In 1980 FEDICALAM, together with similar federations in Maynas Province, founded the Federación Campesina de Maynas (FECADEMA). Union activists linked to the Marxist-oriented national peasants' confederation, the Confederación Campesina del Perú (CCP), were instrumental in the creation of FECADEMA. The new organization also received important support from European development agencies and from the Catholic Church (Chibnik 1994: 194). In contrast to the agrarian leagues and the CNA, FECADEMA defined itself as a "classist" organization, calling for an alliance between peasants and workers (FECADEMA 1981).

FECADEMA supported some popular demands, such as additional promotional credits and the titling of native communities and peasant settlements (FECADEMA 1981: 245–49). They also supported highly political demands with little appeal to the region's *ribereño* peasants, who for the first time were venturing into the production of cash crops for the regional market and were facing very practical economic problems. Furthermore, the new organization was not able to obtain legal recognition from the government, which limited its effectiveness. In 1981, to surmount these problems, FECADEMA decided to sponsor the creation of committees of producers of specific crops. These organizations were recognized under existing legislation (Ruiz Saavedra 1985: 257). The result was the creation in 1982 of the Comité de Productores de Arroz de la Provincia de Maynas (COPAPMA), a provincial committee of rice producers that became affiliated with the CCP and ONA. COPAPMA not only fought for higher prices, a guaranteed market for rice, and better credit conditions; it also endorsed FECADEMA's political agenda. Using its own funds, COPAPMA in 1985 established the Casa Campesina (Peasant House), sharing premises with FECADEMA. Casa Campesina offered legal counseling, technical training, and leadership courses to the affiliates of both organizations. In contrast to FECADEMA, COPAPMA was extremely successful both in recruiting members and in exporting its model to the rest of the department. In 1983 it had a thousand members; four years later, membership had quadrupled. By 1992 COPAPMA had promoted the creation of similar committees in the provinces of Loreto, Requena, Ramón Castilla, Alto Amazonas, and Ucayali; 10,000 members were distributed across 400 settlements (Chibnik 1994: 196; Atarama 1992: 157). In view of COPAPMA's success, FECADEMA also sponsored the creation of committees of producers of jute and corn.

Ribereño peasant unions had two main objectives. First was to obtain better marketing and credit conditions. To ensure this they did not hesitate to resort to measures of force. The occupation of the premises of the state rice-marketing agency in 1985 and the taking of the Banco Agrario in 1988 constitutes expressions of their resolve. They also claimed rights to land and defended collective natural resources such as lakes and forests. This was particularly true after 1980, when Pres. Fernando Belaúnde passed Decree Law 02, encouraging the occupation of the Amazon by large enterprises (Ruiz Saavedra 1985: 258–9).

In 1987 a group of peasant leaders promoted the creation of a union at the departmental level (Atarama 1992: 159). The new organization, the Federación de Campesinos y Nativos de Loreto (FEDECANAL), grouped all provincial committees of producers as well as a few indigenous communities, mainly Yagua. One of FEDECANAL's first actions was to call for a general peasant strike to demand legal recognition from the government. This was obtained in October 1987 following an eight-day strike (ibidem: 160).

Among the demands of the new peasant union were the acceleration of the process of titling Loreto's native communities and the recognition of *ribereño* settlements as "peasant communities." In later years, the titling of native communities became one of the main tasks of the Asociación Interétnica de Desarrollo de la Selva Peruana (AIDESEP), the national association of Amazonian indigenous peoples, which opened a regional office in Iquitos in 1988. In turn, the recognition of *ribereño* settlements as peasant communities was achieved in 1991, after the passing of a bylaw to the General Law of Peasant Communities, which had been issued in 1987.

The organization of the peasant sector in Loreto took place rapidly in the provinces of Maynas and Coronel Portillo but affected Loreto's other provinces only slightly. This suggests that peasant-union activists were most successful where peasants had become more deeply involved in the production of cash crops for local urban markets, that is, Iquitos and Pucallpa. It also explains to some extent the weakness of the peasant movement. As we shall see, although some of the demands of the peasant unions were included in the agenda of Loreto's FDPL, peasant organizations largely remained a second-rank force within regional political movements.

Indigenous Organizations

Loreto's indigenous peoples began organizing earlier than *ribereño* peasants. As we learned, in the early 1970s Catholic missionaries and SINAMOS officials were actively involved in the organization of indigenous peoples. Even before the passage of the Native Communities Law in 1974, several indigenous groups had organized gatherings of settlement leaders. In Loreto, the Shipibo-Conibo and the Naporuna were pioneers. In this early stage, intercommunity gatherings were a means of coordinating demands for land titles from the government, preserving natural resources, obtaining personal identity documents, protesting abuses by traders and *fundos* owners, getting credit support, and improving marketing conditions (Chirif 1974: 50). Later, such meetings were instrumental to forming ethnic federations. Again, the Naporuna and Shipibo-Conibo were the first indigenous peoples in Loreto to form such an organization.

After several *tandarinas* (intercommunity meetings) supported by Canadian Franciscans, the Naporuna created the Wangurina federation in 1978, later renaming it the Organización Kichuaruna Wangurina. The organization of the Naporuna was mainly linked to the efforts of the Catholic Church and was little influenced by SINAMOS. In contrast, SINAMOS managed to push aside the Franciscan missionaries that had originally supported the Shipibo-Conibo movement, promoting instead affiliations with the three government-sponsored agrarian leagues created in the Ucayali Basin (Morin 1999). With the dissolution of the Confederación Nacional Agraria in 1978 and the weakening of the agrarian leagues, the Shipibo-Conibo were left without any organization.

The Summer Institute of Linguistics and the Vicariato de Pucallpa filled the vacuum, competing for the allegiance of the Shipibo-Conibo leadership (Morin 1999). Thus, in 1978 evangelical missionaries sponsored the formation of the Organización de Desarrollo Shipibo, whereas Catholic missionaries promoted the creation of the Frente de Defensa de las Comunidades Nativas del Ucayali. Although both organizations were short-lived, they aggravated existing divisions among Shipibo-Conibo communities. It was only in 1980 that leaders linked to the dissolved agrarian league known as Juan Santos Atahualpa started encouraging settlement leaders to form an ethnic federation. The Federación de Comunidades Nativas del Ucayali was founded in 1981.

In the following years several other indigenous peoples followed the Naporuna and the Shipibo-Conibo, especially after the formation of the Asociación Interétnica de Desarrollo de la Selva Peruana (AIDESEP), the national association of Amazonian indigenous organizations. AIDESEP originated from meetings held between Yanesha, Ashaninka, Aguaruna, and Shipibo-Conibo leaders and Peruvian and foreign professionals who were working in the Amazon region; such meetings had been promoted since 1977 by the Centro de Investigación y Promoción Amazónica (CIPA). In 1978, the indigenous leaders shook off the tutelage of CIPA and formed the Coordinadora de Comunidades Nativas de la Selva Peruana, which in 1980 became AIDESEP.

The main demands advanced by Lima-based AIDESEP were: (1) state recognition for their organizations and respect for their autonomy; (2) the right to determine their own model of development; (3) participation in the design of regional policies that concerned them; (4) recognition of their right to land and immediate titling of all native communities; and (5) recognition of their right of exclusive use of the natural resources extant within their lands (AIDESEP 1981: 641–2). The motto that summarized AIDESEP's political agenda in that early stage was "Land, Language, and Culture."

Often under the auspices of AIDESEP, seventeen additional indigenous organizations were formed in the departments of Loreto and Ucayali during the 1980s and early 1990s (Dandler 1998). Most represented a single indigenous group, whereas others grouped different indigenous peoples sharing the same basin or area. Given the difficulties of maintaining regular communications among organizations and between them and AIDESEP's Lima headquarters, the association opened a regional office in Iquitos in 1988. This office lobbies for better conditions for the indigenous peoples in areas such as education, health, personal documentation, military service, natural resources, and marketing of produce. Above all, it has been extremely successful in securing community land titles. By 1992 257 out of 334 legally recognized native communities in the department of Loreto had secured legal title to their lands (AIDESEP 1992). Of these, 45 percent were titled during the first five years of operation of AIDESEP's Iquitos office, revealing the political clout achieved by the national indigenous confederation within the region. In later years AIDESEP opened new offices in San Lorenzo (Alto Amazonas Province) and Pucallpa; by 1998 it had managed to secure land titles for 372 native communities with a total of 2,115,118 hectares (Región Agraria 1998).

The activities of AIDESEP's Iquitos office and of its member organizations have made indigenous peoples extremely visible, positioning them for the first time as major actors in the region's political arena (see García Hierro et al. 1998). Furthermore, pride in being of indigenous heritage, which was fostered by the new organizations, has led many *ribereños*, who had previously suppressed their ethnic origins, to proclaim their Amerindian ancestry and demand land titles under the Native Communities Law. Good examples are the Cocamilla of the lower Huallaga River, the Naporuna of the central Napo, and, more recently, the Cocama of the lower Ucayali and Marañon Rivers.

As we shall see, AIDESEP has been reluctant to participate in such regional organizations as the FDPL. However, despite its tendency to pursue an autonomous political path, it has established links with organizations formed by other social sectors. Thus, of the nineteen indigenous federations in Loreto, which in the early 1990s were affiliated to AIDESEP, three were also bases of FEDECANAL, the regional union that groups *ribereño* and indigenous organizations. However, even those that were not so affiliated frequently resorted to FEDECANAL or COPAPMA for advice on legal and economic matters (Chirif et al. 1991: 146). Some of the federations affiliated with AIDESEP are also members of the Confederación de Nacionalidades de la Amazonía Peruana, founded in 1987.

Slum-Dwellers' Organizations

New social sectors were also emerging in urban areas. Since the 1940s there has been a sustained process of urbanization in Loreto and Ucayali (see Appendix 30). This is especially true of Iquitos and Pucallpa; their populations increased spectacularly beginning in the 1960s. Between 1961 and 1993 the population of Iquitos more than quadrupled, from 57,777 to 274,759, whereas Pucallpa's increased more than six times, from 26,391 to 172,286 (see Appendix 31). In Iquitos, it was the result of massive migrations from Loreto's rural areas. The standard explanation is that with the beginning of oil exploration in 1971 thousands of peasants were hired by the oil companies and moved their families to Iquitos, where wives or parents could cash their fortnightly checks (Rumrrill and Zutter 1976: 225–30; San Román 1994: 237–8). According to this view, following the end of oil exploration in 1975, these former oil company workers, estimated at 15,000, would have settled permanently in Iquitos, contributing to the creation of new slums and the emergence of a new and influential social force.

Although the oil boom undoubtedly accelerated the process of rural-urban migration, there is ample evidence that heavy migration to Iquitos started much earlier and that the appearance of new slums in Iquitos is a phenomenon that predated the oil boom. Thus, in 1964, eight years before the oil boom, it was reported that there were already fifteen slums in Iquitos containing 41 percent of the city's population (Mora 1974: 79). Most of the marginal urban population (12,000-plus people) lived in one slum, the port of Belén (Dobkin de Ríos 1984: 9). In 1964 it was estimated that 43 percent of the inhabitants of Belén came from rural settlements close to Iquitos, within the province of Maynas, or from other provinces of the department of Loreto (ibidem: 56). A 1969 survey estimated that the immigrant population of Iquitos represented 36 percent (CEPD 1972: 312).

With the support of the Communist Party, slum-dwellers began organizing quite early, founding the Comité Central de Barriadas in 1959. This organization came of age in 1965, when it mobilized its affiliates to oppose the major of Iquitos, who had threatened to dissolve several of the city's *barriadas*, or "shanty towns." By 1968 the number of slums had increased to twenty, and slum-dwellers represented 50 percent of the population of Iquitos (Mora 1974: 79). The arrival of new waves of rural migrants forced many to invade peripheral public and private lands to build homes.

During this time many of the small suburban *fundos* of Iquitos were invaded. This process continued throughout the 1970s and 1980s and became a constant source of conflict among slum-dwellers, owners of peripheral urban lands, and the government.

With the advent of the military government in 1968, the marginal urban sectors acquired new political relevance. Aware of their importance in all of Peru's large cities, the government in 1969 established the Oficina Nacional de Desarrollo de los Pueblos Jóvenes, a national agency to carry out a program providing slums with land titles and basic services, such as electricity, running water, schools, and pavement, the main concerns of slum-dwellers (Driant 1991: 119). The replacement in official discourse of the term *barriada* for that of *pueblos jóvenes*, or "young towns," reflected a shift in the government's perception of slums. From problematic marginal urban areas they came to be seen as promising "areas in the process of becoming cities" (ibidem); from "tumors to be extirpated" they came to be considered as a "positive factor in the process of urbanization" (Delgado 1974: 126). SINAMOS was given the task of promoting the organization of this new sector. In Iquitos, that resulted in the creation of numerous neighborhood committees. The committees of a given shanty town were organized, in turn, into "committees of promotion and development" led by a board of directors, charged with coordinating development actions with SINAMOS.

After the ousting of President Velasco Alvarado in 1975, the new government attempted to deactivate the organizations of slum-dwellers by halting assistance to the *pueblos jóvenes*. As a result, SINAMOS, already suspect in the eyes of these organizations because of its attempts to co-opt them, fell into disgrace. By the time SINAMOS was dissolved in 1977 the slum-dwellers' organizations in Iquitos had created an alternative association, the Comité Central de Pueblos Jóvenes de Iquitos. Leftist parties influenced the new organization which, as we shall see, had an important role in founding the FDPL.

In 1979 the government passed Decree-Law 22162, which established that titled *pueblos jóvenes* would be treated like any other integrated neighborhood. This meant that their organizations would not now be legally recognized and would no longer be eligible for special assistance from government agencies (Driant 1991: 122–3). This caused uproar among the country's marginal-urban organizations. In Iquitos, it led to the founding in 1980 of the Federación de Pueblos Jóvenes de Iquitos (FAPUJI), which became affiliated with the Confederación General de Pobladores del Perú, the national confederation of slum-dwellers, founded that same year under the influence of leftist parties. By 1983 FAPUJI represented thirty *pueblos jóvenes* with an estimated population of 50,000 (Proceso, No. 48).

Slum-dwellers were among the most important urban social sectors because they could mobilize hundreds of people to protest the lack of attention to their demands; they could also rally support for the regional causes championed by the FDPL. There were, however, other organized social sectors in Iquitos and other urban centers that also had a share of political power, insofar as they could suspend the provision of important services or interrupt important economic activities. Among the former were schoolteachers and university educators; among the latter were bank employees and factory workers. Although all of these sectors were present in the region before 1962, after that year they emerged as important social and political forces.

Through the Maynas branch of the Sindicato Unico de Trabajadores de la Educación del Perú, founded in 1972, teachers had the capacity to organize massive strikes and exerted an important influence in regional politics and in the regional fronts of Iquitos and Pucallpa. University students, through the local university students' union founded in 1965 under the auspices of the APRA and taken over in 1968 by a coalition of leftist parties, were prominent in the street marches and strikes called by the regional front (Rodríguez Achung 1981: 12). Bank employees were mostly affiliated to the Federación de Empleados Bancarios (FEB), founded in the 1960s and strongly influenced by the Communist Party. Although FEB had an ambivalent attitude toward the regional front, its support was highly sought after because it could paralyze the region's economic transactions, as in 1965 when it went on strike (García 1979: 382). Finally, factory workers were organized in the Federación Departamental de Trabajadores de Loreto (FEDETL), which in the 1960s affiliated with the Central Nacional de Trabajadores, the national union linked to the Christian Democrat Party. Although the workers' movement in Loreto expanded as a result of industrial expansion during the 1960s and 1970s, compared with other popular organizations it constituted a second-rank force. Furthermore, the political ambivalence of FEDETL's leaders toward the struggles of the regionalist fronts left them isolated and politically weak.

Popular organization during the 1963–1990 period was a phenomenon that involved even the region's remotest areas, as proved by the proliferation of indigenous organizations. However, the process was strongest in Iquitos, Pucallpa, and their respective areas of influence. Thus, most of the region's popular organizations were formed in the provinces of Maynas (Iquitos) and Coronel Portillo (Pucallpa). We contend that this was due to three factors: (1) the rapid expansion of Iquitos and Pucallpa, which became the region's largest markets; (2) the disappearance of the rural elite and the concentration of the activities of the new bourgeoisie in those two cities; and (3) the low population densities in and difficult communications with areas distant from the main urban centers. As we shall see, the urban emphasis of Loreto's organizations was also evident in the nature of the demands made by the regionalist political fronts that emerged in Pucallpa and Iquitos during the late 1970s.

The Struggle for the Oil Canon

The antecedents of the formation of the FDPL, the regionalist front founded in 1978, are found in the local reaction to the government's curtailing of tax exemptions in 1968. Confronting a grave economic crisis and having already decreed a 44 percent devaluation of the national currency, President Belaúnde in early 1968 issued Law 16900, which cut by 50 percent the tax exemptions granted to Loreto three years earlier. This measure, meant to strengthen the country's balance of payments and reduce high inflation rates, mostly affected the commercial sector, specifically the import trade. However, it also affected the lower working sectors, which had to pay higher prices for basic consumer goods. Through the daily *El Oriente*, Loreto's trading elite voiced its discontent, declaring in dramatic terms that "Loreto is experiencing the darkest hours in its history" (Barletti 1985: 9). In order to gain popular support for their cause, the leaders of the chamber of commerce argued that the government's measure would restrict trade and lead to significant layoffs in the commercial and construction sectors.

However, popular discontent did not explode until the government approved a rise in the price of kerosene and gasoline by mid-1968. The national drivers' union called a strike for June 28, which paralyzed Iquitos. Slum-dwellers took advantage of the situation to demonstrate against the government. At dusk the populace started looting stores as they advanced from the large port-slum of Belén toward downtown. Along the way they set a movie theater on fire. As the crowds overwhelmed both the police and the firemen, the government called in the army, declared Iquitos to be in a state of siege, and suspended constitutional rights in Maynas Province (Barletti 1985: 8).

In the wake of the popular uprising the chamber of commerce issued a public communiqué deploring the course of events and requesting punishment for those responsible. By disavowing any direct participation in the rebellion, the group attempted to counter those who had accused it of inciting the popular protest. This was not the last time that the region's elite fomented popular protest, but later it disavowed organized or spontaneous street demonstrations when they affected elites' interests.

In an attempt to regain popular support in the region, the government soon lowered prices for kerosene, gasoline, diesel fuel, and rice, granted titles to slum-dwellers, and promised the chamber of commerce that it would revise a decree prohibiting the import of certain goods until 1969 (Barletti 1985: 12–3). These measures benefited the popular sectors as well as the region's commercial bourgeoisie. After the ousting of President Belaúnde in October 1968 the region's elite profited even more. In November the military government restored tax exemptions for the import of basic foodstuffs.

Members of the regional elite, who adhered to rightist or centrist political positions, learned three important lessons from this massive popular uprising, the first in modern times: (1) they could recast some of its particular demands into widely appealing regional issues; (2) they could profit from the support of the popular sectors; and (3) in any event, because of their divergent interests popular sectors could easily turn against them. As we shall see, during the struggle for the oil canon, the actions of the chamber of commerce revealed such ambivalence. In turn, the urban popular sectors, mostly unorganized except for the slum-dwellers, realized that: (1)

forcible actions paid off; (2) it was necessary to be organized to be effective; and (3) the regional elite was not an ally to be trusted, although common interests could emerge.

As we already learned, under the auspices of the military government and the increasing influence of leftist parties, Loreto's popular sectors entered an accelerated process of organization over the following years. Most of their initial demands were sectorial in nature. It was not until the discovery of oil in 1971 that the request for a share of oil profits gradually acquired the character of a regionalist demand.

In September 1971, two months before Petro-Perú, the state oil company, discovered oil in northern Loreto, Joaquín Abensur, one of the most renowned entrepreneurs in Iquitos, addressed an assembly of authorities, technocrats, military officials, and entrepreneurs convened by Banco de Crédito to discuss the issue of development in the Amazon region. He suggested that a portion of any future oil revenues be allocated to its owner, the department of Loreto (Banco de Crédito 1972: 203). After the discovery of oil, which increased expectations for huge profits, the idea that Loreto should benefit from its oil reserves spread among the region's other social sectors. Their representatives argued that Loreto should learn a lesson from the rubber boom and should not allow the government to be the only beneficiary of the region's riches. This argument was only partly true, insofar as the state had invested heavily in Loreto before the rubber boom and had continued to invest rubber revenues in the infrastructure of Iquitos. However, it caught on, becoming, from then on, a leitmotiv in regionalist discourse.

In 1972, following new oil discoveries by Occidental Petroleum Company, Loreto's local authorities requested the central government to pass necessary legislation to ensure that a portion of the region's oil revenues went "to the construction of vital infrastructure for the cities of the Amazonian region" (Proceso 1972, No. 15). They demanded a tax on each barrel of oil produced by national and foreign companies in Loreto. In this early demand, we already discern the urban emphasis of regionalist struggles.

In the following years, the idea of an oil canon (*canon petrolero*) gained favor and gradually replaced support for an oil tax. The notion of an oil *canon* differed from that of an oil *tax* requested earlier. In the context of mining, a canon, or "quit-rent," is the amount paid by a miner to the owner of the land in exchange for the right of exploitation. This amount is generally calculated as a percentage of the value of the ore extracted. This shift reveals the growing conviction among Loreto's different social sectors that the oil reserves belonged to Loreto and that the state and private companies should compensate the region for the right to exploit it. This contravened all extant laws, which considered subsoil resources as state property. These different perspectives on natural resources intensified the confrontation between Loreto and the state.

Between 1972 and 1975 the oil boom generated new jobs and reignited Loreto's economy. During this brief period of prosperity, which benefited the emerging bourgeoisie, *ribereño* peasants, and the urban poor, the demand for an oil canon subsided. A few local government officials, in yet another warning against repeating the errors of the rubber boom, continued to insist on the need to invest some of the oil revenues into development of the region. However, no organization appears to have made this demand a central issue of its agenda during the oil-boom years.

This situation changed in 1975, when most of the foreign oil companies left the region. By 1976 the demand for an oil canon had taken root among all the social sectors. On October 9, the day the government commemorated the 1968 expropriation of the International Petroleum Company, there was a general demonstration by the population of Iquitos, demanding the granting of an oil canon. The most active groups involved in the demonstrations were slum-dwellers, factory workers, schoolteachers, and university students, mostly led by Trotskyist and Maoist union activists. The police suppressed the demonstration, and several of the leaders were arrested and imprisoned. Surprisingly, a month later, during a visit to Iquitos, President Morales Bermúdez signed Decree-Law 21678, the Oil Canon Law, which granted Loreto 10 percent of the value of the region's crude production for a period of ten years. These funds were to be invested in regional development programs designed by the National Planning Institute and Ordeoriente.

Several regional analysts attributed this victory to popular mobilization in Iquitos (San Román 1994: 242; Dávila 1994: 7). However, rumor has it that President Morales Bermúdez was persuaded to sign the decree during a sumptuous party thrown by prominent members of the regional elite and that his close advisers were shocked, disapproved of his decision, and recommended delaying the implementation of the law. Whether this is true or not, it took almost one year for the bylaw of Decree Law 21678 to be issued and more than two years for the first payments to be made. It is also clear that once the law passed it generated strong opposition in government ranks, as it established a dangerous precedent. In effect, in approving payment of an oil canon to Loreto the government implicitly accepted the view that underground resources did not belong exclusively to the state. In a centralized, nonfederal country such as Peru, this was unacceptable.

It was in this context of confrontation with the state that the regional organization FDPL was founded. Its creation, as well as its actions during the first year of existence, have been well documented (Rodríguez Achung 1981). Here we present only the main events leading to its formation and then examine its later development, focusing particularly on the shifting alliances between the different sectors involved.

After the government's delay in paying the oil canon, massive new street demonstrations took place, showing how crucial the issue had become to the population of Iquitos. Although most of the unions participated, the protests were mostly spontaneous. There was little coordination between different organizations and thus no strong regionalist movement. This explains why the government, two years after passage of the Oil Canon Law, still felt no need to implement it. It also explains why the organizations that had been pressing for payment of the canon designated a committee to organize the FDPL.

The idea of regional "defense fronts" was not new in Loreto. In 1975 popular organizations in Pucallpa founded the Frente de Defensa de los Intereses del Pueblo (FEDIP). FEDIP's most important demand on the government was the provision of basic services and infrastructure for the rapidly growing city. In August 1978 FEDIP became the Frente de Defensa de la Provincia de Coronel Portillo (FREDECOP); its main demand was that Coronel Portillo, Loreto's southernmost province, should become the new department of Ucayali. Two months later, FREDECOP called a general strike, which was extremely effective and became known as the first *pucallpazo*. Its success encouraged the creation of a similar organization in Iquitos.

Representatives of the slum-dwellers' and schoolteachers' unions composed the core of the organizing committee of the Iquitos front. The drivers' union, the federation of university students, and professional associations were also represented. Although the chamber of commerce supported the effort, it always had reservations about the committee's political orientation. Most members of the chamber's board of directors did not attend the act by which the organizing committee was officially installed, claiming that it would be no more than a "communist façade organization" (Rodríguez Achung 1981: 17). Nevertheless, representatives of the chamber continued to attend the committee's gatherings. On the occasion of the second anniversary of the signing of the Oil Canon Law, the committee called for a demonstration by the people of Iquitos to demand immediate payment of the oil canon. Despite little organization, the protest was impressive.

In view of the demonstration's success, in November 1978 the committee convened the First Popular Assembly of the People of Loreto. Delegates represented various unions, as well as the chamber of commerce. During this event the FDPL was formally created and its first board of directors elected. The list of candidates presented by leftist organizations won by a clear 120–23 majority. José Sicchar, a Trotskyist activist of the slum-dwellers' organization, was elected secretary general; other posts were filled by representatives of the schoolteachers' union, the federation of university students, and professional associations, precisely the organizations most strongly influenced by radical leftist parties. Left out were organizations that represented the region's large and small entrepreneurs, such as the chamber of commerce, the shippers' association, and the drivers' union, as well as white and blue-collar organizations like the bank employees' federation and FEDETL, none of which were under the direct influence of the radical left.

The political platform approved by the First Popular Assembly also demonstrates the powerful influence of leftist militants. The slogan that was adopted—*No a la Penetración Imperialista* (No to Imperialistic Intervention)—reveals that even though the FDPL's most popular demand was the payment of the oil canon, that was seen as only a first step in the antiimperialist and revolutionary long-term struggle. That, by necessity, would begin by radically confronting the military dictatorship. In an attempt to gain wider support, FDPL's platform was organized into fourteen sections that addressed the demands of most of the region's popular sectors

(Rodríguez Achung 1981: 35–8), including *ribereño* peasants and indigenous peoples, who had not participated directly in the formation of the FDPL. The platform contained a total of sixty-five demands, most aimed at improving the economy for the region's poor, bettering their living conditions, and empowering them. It also included several political demands for an active say in the administration of the oil canon funds. Some of these demands were designed to give the FDPL some of the attributes of a regional government. For example, the FDPL wanted to (1) oversee the use of oil canon funds by Ordeloreto; (2) supervise all building projects carried out with canon funds; (3) control the hiring of personnel for projects financed with canon funds; (4) control the prices of basic consumer goods; and (5) monitor the region's social-security system (Rodríguez Achung 1981: 35–8). In summary, the leftist leadership turned what started as a broad, multiclass movement revolving around an appealing regional issue into a classist, antiimperialist organization promoting a disparate array of populist demands.

The newly formed FDPL called for a twenty-four-hour general strike in December 1978. Although it was a success, with production, commercial, and service activities being paralyzed, there were still some sectors that were discontent with the FDPL's leadership, namely, the chamber of commerce and the drivers' union (Rodríguez Achung 1981: 16). The antagonism between the leftist leadership and the entrepreneurial sector reached a head in mid-December 1978, when an alliance of the bank employees' federation, a drivers' union faction, and the chamber of commerce proposed to repudiate the FDPL's acting board and elect an alternate. The disruption of the FDPL was barely averted through the incorporation into the board of seven new members belonging to the contesting organizations (Rodríguez Achung 1981: 17).

This, however, only delayed confrontation among these sectors. The FDPL's new board convened a Second Popular Assembly in late December. To attract wider support, they invited delegates from the peasant and indigenous movements. By then the government had offered to pay a share of the oil canon funds that the FDPL claimed was owed Loreto. The main item on the assembly agenda was to determine whether to accept this offer or demand full and immediate payment. The chamber of commerce favored the first option, but the majority of delegates voted for an indefinite general strike beginning in early January 1979 to force the government to transfer all payments due. The chamber of commerce and the drivers' union did not endorse the strike, and it failed on its first day: stores opened, public transportation operated, and even most affiliates of FEDETL, the workers' federation, went in for work (Rodríguez Achung 1981: 19).

Instead of revising their political strategy, FDPL's leftist leadership determined that it had to create a new workers' union that would not be manipulated by traditional union leaders and would confront the exploiting classes (i.e., merchants and industrialists). This, however, was the wrong move, insofar as it alienated large segments of the population that otherwise would have supported the regionalist struggle. In fact, the strike's failure was so devastating that throughout 1979 FDPL was essentially paralyzed. In the meantime, the government began to make the first payments of the oil canon.

When in 1979 the military government decided to call free elections in 1980, the oil canon became an important political issue in Loreto. Sensing the importance of this issue, presidential candidate Fernando Belaúnde, while visiting Iquitos, declared: "I am here to ensure that what was promised be complied with: that the oil canon be paid not as a gift that is given away but as a debt to be honored to a people that deserves it" (Barletti 1985: 13). Belaúnde's declaration was well received by Loreto's voters, 66 percent of whom favored him in the election (Kanatari 1994, No. 500). In contrast, the meager 6 percent obtained by the divided leftist parties shows that despite their political activities through the FDPL they were not able to elicit popular support. No leftist candidates were elected as house representatives. In contrast, five of the seven representatives elected in Loreto belonged to Acción Popular, Belaúnde's party. Among them were members of the region's economic elite who had actively participated in the FDPL.

In July 1980 Antonio D'Onadio was elected FDPL president. D'Onadio was an acceptable candidate for both the chamber of commerce and the popular organizations. An entrepreneur who had been president of the chamber, he was trusted by the region's elite; because of his strong regionalist ideals, the leftist leadership respected him. The election of D'Onadio marked a rapprochement between the entrepreneurial and popular sectors and the beginning of a new phase in the evolution of the regional front. Later that month, only three days after Belaúnde's accession to power, a delegation of representatives of the chamber of commerce and the FDPL visited him to discuss the most important demands of Loreto's population (Ocampo 1983: 496). By the end of 1980 President Belaúnde agreed to increase oil canon payments and appointed a high-level commission to analyze Loreto's problems and issue recommendations within thirty days (Shupihui 1981, No. 17).

To pressure the government, the FDPL organized a successful one-day general strike in early January 1981. Two days later the government commission sent a memorandum to the president that (1) acknowledged that the oil canon payments made until then had been insufficient; (2) established the amount to be paid under the oil canon for fiscal year 1981; and (3) created a broad-based commission composed of government officials and representatives of the civil society, in charge of determining the formula to calculate the oil canon due (Shupihui 1981, No. 17).

The FDPL accepted the recommendations of the government commission with some revisions. Because of its greater lobbying capacity, the chamber now assumed the leading role within the FDPL in the oil canon negotiations. The government and the FDPL agreed that the commission would be composed of high-level technocrats as well as representatives of Loreto's institutions, as determined by the FDPL. The FDPL's choice of representatives reveals changes yet again among the forces within the movement. Of the four delegates chosen, one was linked to the chamber of commerce, whereas the other three belonged to the professional associations of lawyers, economists, and engineers. Union activists like José Sicchar who once had great influence within the FDPL were now confined to the role of occasional observers.

The government technocrats and FDPL representatives were not able to agree on how to calculate the 10 percent oil canon: whether it should be calculated on the basis of the gross value or the net value of oil production. As a result, both formulas were presented to the government. Shortly thereafter, President Belaúnde issued Decree 177-EFC–81, establishing the oil canon on the basis of the net value of oil production after deducting refining and transportation costs, export tariffs, and operational expenditures.

The FDPL rejected that resolution, adopting as its slogan *Pagar el Verdadero Canon Petrolero* (Payment of the True Oil Canon). In the following months, the government not only failed to pay the oil canon as expected but also stopped transferring Loreto's share of the national budget. This enraged Loreto's population. In early December 1981 the FDPL organized a massive popular meeting, where it was decided to declare Loreto in a state of emergency until the government paid the full amount of the oil canon. The FDPL also demanded that Loreto's share of the national budget be restored and that the payment of the oil canon be extended until the region's oil reserves were exhausted.

The general strike had little success, mainly because the chamber did not commit full support, as it was simultaneously negotiating another issue with the government that was crucial to its interests: the extension of the Peruvian-Colombian Customs Agreement. There was a risk that Colombia would not ratify it because of legislation passed by the military government in 1980, whereby Iquitos was granted the status of "free port" (Ocampo 1983: 499–501).

In addition, the FDPL was distracted by conflicts with the newly created department of Ucayali over their respective demarcation (e.g., how the boundaries were drawn). Giving in to the pressures exerted by the highly bellicose Frente de Defensa de la Provincia de Coronel Portillo, the military government, as one of its last acts, created in June 1980 the department of Ucayali. It comprised two southern provinces of Loreto (Coronel Portillo and Ucayali). Although Loretans were resigned to the loss of Coronel Portillo, they fiercely opposed removal of Ucayali. In fact, many who lived in the province opposed its inclusion in the newly formed department. The government used this thorny issue, which was resolved in 1984, when the province of Ucayali was restored to Loreto, in its negotiations with the FDPL over the oil canon. As a result, the FDPL entered a period of paralysis (Rumrrill 1982: 22).

It was not until November 1982 that the FDPL was able to reorganize, convening what was to be the last of its large popular assemblies. Another platform was approved reasserting the prior demands, which were raised once more as central mobilizing issues (Barletti 1983: 27–32). Although the new platform included demands from the popular and entrepreneurial sectors, suggesting the desire to reconcile their respective interests, the FDPL was not able to exert enough pressure to secure its three basic demands with respect to the oil canon. The government never ·

agreed to the first demand: payment of the full amount of the oil canon. As for the second (restoration of Loreto's share of the national budget), in 1987, facing decreasing oil production and prices, the APRA government decided to reincorporate Loreto into the national budget (Panduro 1987: 7).

However, as a result of its pressures, by the end of 1982 the FDPL obtained one important victory: It forced the government to pass Law 23538, which granted Loreto the benefit of the oil canon until the depletion of its reserves. Later, in 1984, President Belaúnde also passed Law 24300, establishing the distribution of oil canon funds. These were to be distributed as follows: 40 percent for Cordelor, the regional development corporation; 40 percent for municipalities; 12 percent for agricultural subsidized credit; 5 percent for the local state university; and 3 percent for the Instituto de Investigaciones de la Amazonía Peruana, a state-sponsored research center. With those two measures, the government undermined the FDPL. From then on, the oil canon issue was submerged; Cordelor, the corporation that administrated the funds, and the region's political forces and population segments would have minor disputes over how canon funds would be invested.

Experts agree that the struggles over the oil canon constituted the backbone of Loreto's regionalist movement. Fewer consensus exists, however, as to which sector deserves the credit for forcing the government to pay up. Representatives of the left have claimed that the passing of the Oil Canon Law and its enforcement was a victory for the organized popular sectors. According to this view, they were the only ones that defended the region's interests. In turn, leaders of the chamber of commerce have, in a scarcely veiled criticism to the leftist parties, argued that "the Chamber has supported both sectorial and regional demands, achieving what other politicized organizations have not been able to accomplish" (Cámara 1990: 3). Our analysis of the events reveals that neither deserve full credit. Divergent political interests and constant strife prevented either from exerting enough pressure on the government and actually delayed the enforcement of the Oil Canon Law. Their conflicts also hindered the development of a stronger regionalist movement, one that would have effectively supervised investment of the oil canon funds.

In the ensuing years the FDPL became little more than a phantom organization, resurrected whenever an issue with regional appeal surfaced. This happened in 1988, when leftist parties, in the name of the FDPL, adhered to a national strike called by the Central General de Trabajadores del Perú, the leftist national workers' confederation, to protest the ruinous economic measures of the APRA government (Panduro 1993: 19). Later that year, the chamber of commerce, together with the opposition parties, Acción Popular and Partido Popular Cristiano, and other local forces, created an alternative organization, the Frente de Defensa de la Región del Amazonas. Its purpose was to oppose a law imposing a 10 percent tax on the sale of beer and a 1 percent value-added tax on the sale of goods and services (Panduro 1993: 19, 27). Putting aside their differences, the two fronts joined forces temporarily to protest, unsuccessfully, this law.

This was the last gasp of the FDPL. In later years, several attempts were made to create a regional frontlike organization under different names: Comisión Cívica de Loreto (1989), Frente Cívico (1992), and Frente Cívico Patriótico (1995). Diverse political parties and social sectors hoped to benefit from the almost mythical prestige of the former FDPL to further their sectorial interests. However, until 1990 none succeeded in mobilizing the population like the FDPL had during the early years of the struggle over the oil canon.

Elite organizations and popular sectors may have failed to build a strong regionalist movement, but no doubt remains that during the 1963–1990 period extraordinary social mobilization reshaped the region's political profile. Prior to that, the merchant elite was the only organized sector having the means to confront and negotiate with the government. During this period most urban and rural popular sectors organized at the regional and national levels. Even indigenous peoples, the region's most oppressed social group, were able to exert enough pressure to obtain important political and economic concessions. Above all, political mobilization during this agitated period contributed to enhance political awareness and strengthen the region's civil society. The state—whether acting as promoter or punching bag—contributed greatly during these years to the incorporation of Loreto's population into the national life and, therefore, to the taming of the frontier.

Conclusions

Loreto has undergone radical transformations since the government's first efforts to integrate the region into Peruvian national life some 150 years ago. These transformations have led to the taming of the Loretan frontier. At present most of the traits characteristic of frontier economies have disappeared or are confined to the region's remotest areas. Despite claims that the state has done little for Loreto, we maintain that it has played a crucial role in the taming of the frontier. The extension of civil rights, the emergence of a regionalist ideology, and the consolidation of a regional identity constitute the three most important areas in which this process has found expression.

Civil Rights

Beginning in the 1940s the democratization of education was the state's principal strategy to integrate Loreto's population into civil life. A larger investment in the education sector in the 1960s produced drops in illiteracy rates. This was crucial to enhance political participation, for only literate people could apply for a voting card and qualify for elected or appointed local public positions. In addition, given that in Peru the voting card constitutes the main identity document, lack of it brings a series of other civil limitations. This was especially the case in rural Loreto.

In Peru there are three basic identity documents: birth certificate, military card, and voting card. District municipalities issue birth certificates. To obtain one, rural dwellers had to make long, costly trips to the district's capital (Villeneuve 1974: 139). Additionally, newborns had to be registered within one month of birth, otherwise parents were fined. As most parents were not able to register children in time, and as many did not have the money to pay the fine, a great number of children were never registered. Lack of birth certificates prevented parents from registering children in public schools, contributing to the vicious circle of illiteracy.

Without birth certificates people were also prevented from obtaining voting cards. Hence, from the 1950s military service, which was compulsory for men at age eighteen, was one of the few means for illiterate people (many without birth certificates, of course) to obtain a personal document: the military card. It was also a means for rural poor to learn how to read and write, to get acquainted with their civil rights, and to gain a certain amount of self-respect. Thus, there are many testimonies of men who, after serving in the military, realized how they were being exploited by their *patrones* and decided not to work for them anymore (San Román 1975: 188; Agüero 1994: 229).

Because of the benefits of military service, many men in Loreto's rural areas opted to serve even if not drafted. As late as 1985 in some *ribereño* settlements up to 66 percent of adult men had done military service (Chibnik 1994: 166). Higher levels of literacy and acquisition of personal documents by serving in the military allowed *ribereño* peasants to be appointed as deputy governors, an office long monopolized by local *patrones*. This, in turn, allowed them to oppose deputy governors favorable to *fundo* owners and local traders, further breaking their political power.

In the 1970s the government continued investing in schools and teachers. More importantly, it favored civil integration by encouraging the organization of the more marginal population sectors. Through the activities of these organizations, peasants, indigenous peoples, and slum-dwellers became more aware of their rights, especially those they lacked. With the support of leftist parties, progressive missionaries, and socially oriented nongovernmental organizations, a new generation of leaders emerged at the local level. The creation of alternative mass means of communications, such as the radio station La Voz de la Selva, supported by the Catholic Church, contributed to a greater political awareness among the region's popular sectors. Through meetings, assemblies, and other collective activities, the notion that political organization and struggle was necessary to ensure and enhance civil rights reached the region's most isolated settlements.

During the 1970s the government also addressed the problem of lack of personal documents, especially acute among indigenous peoples. Thus, for instance, in a 1975 survey of Shipibo-Conibo settlements, only 16 percent of all men and 13 percent of all women had birth certificates. In addition, only 8 percent of adult men and less than 1 percent of adult women had voting cards, and only 12 percent of adult men had military cards (Chirif et al. 1977: 112). In more isolated areas, such as the Purus, Yavari, and Putumayo River basins and the upper tracts of the Morona, Tigre, and Corrientes Rivers, the percentage of indigenous people possessing personal documents was even lower. This situation drastically changed after the implementation of the 1974 Law of Native Communities, which allowed the opening of civil registers in every community, permitting indigenous authorities to issue birth certificates. Also, the creation of new districts, which increased from forty-six in 1961 to fifty-seven in 1993 (in both Loreto and Ucayali), as well as cheaper and faster fluvial transport, facilitated the obtaining of birth certificates by *ribereño* peasants (INE 1984: 5; 1989b: 104, 122).

The 1979 constitution also promoted greater civil participation by extending voting rights to illiterates and reducing the voting age from twenty-one to eighteen. Together with higher levels of literacy, easier means to obtain personal documents, greater political experience, and enhanced civil rights awareness, this has resulted in a dramatic increase in the number of people included in Loreto's electoral register (excluding Ucayali). Between 1979 and 1993, it doubled, from 125,780 to

252,996, representing 77 percent of the voting population (those eighteen years old and above) (Tuesta 1994: 150; INEI 1997: 141).

In contemporary Loreto, not only can a larger proportion of rural people exercise their voting rights; many have become actively involved as candidates in local elections; this is particularly true of the region's indigenous peoples (García Hierro et al. 1998: 10). Taking advantage of the 1980 Law of Municipalities, which allows non-partisan independent candidates to participate in municipal elections at the district and provincial levels, indigenous organizations have begun to present candidates (Chirif et al. 1991: 115). In the past, even in areas where the population was mostly indigenous, municipal officials were always white-mestizos closely associated with the local trading or landed elites. This situation has gradually changed. Thus, since 1983 indigenous organizations have been contending in municipal elections, and in 1989 their candidates were elected in the districts of Morona, Cahuapanas, and Torres Causana in the department of Loreto, and in Atalaya and Yurua in Ucayali. Furthermore, in some of these districts indigenous mayors and counselors have been re-elected several times. This has revolutionized politics at the local level.

A recent study on levels of citizenship in Peru shows that Loreto is not so badly positioned compared to the rest of the country (López 1997). The study takes into account three aspects of citizenship—civil, political, and social—and identifies a series of variables that allow quantification of each aspect at the district and provincial levels. After obtaining a global index, it correlates the resulting level of citizenship with the respective levels of poverty. The study finds that 7.5 percent of the people of Loreto has high levels of poverty and citizenship; 39 percent has a high level of poverty and a middle level of citizenship; lastly, 37 percent has middle levels of poverty and citizenship (ibidem: 504). All in all, according to this study, 83 percent of Loreto's population enjoys middle to high levels of citizenship, a situation that contrasts starkly with that of the Andean departments, which are equally poor but in general have lower levels of citizenship. However, 17 percent of Loreto's population still lives with a high level of poverty and a low level of citizenship. This situation must necessarily change.

The gradual empowerment of the region's marginal population sectors has led to local confrontations with powerful interests. Nonetheless, what distinguishes Loreto as a tamed frontier is that its different population segments have been able to temporarily put aside conflicts and coalesce in order to fight for common demands. The forging of a regionalist ideology has made possible such multiclass alliances.

Regionalist Ideology

The emergence of regionalism in Loreto is closely related to the fact that it was a politico-administrative unit with full political rights, including the election of representatives to the legislature, even during its beginning as a new frontier in the middle of the nineteenth century. In contrast, most frontier regions in the Brazilian, Colombian, Venezuelan, and Ecuadorian Amazons had, at least during the first stages of colonization, the status of special "territories" administered directly by the central government. After 1906, when the department of San Martín separated, Loreto had the right to elect two senators and six house representatives, two for each of its three provinces. Although some were outsiders, most were native to the region, thus ensuring representation of the region's interests at the national level.

The first signs of Loretan regionalism can be traced back to the 1880s. By then, it expressed itself only as a vague sentiment, frequently mixed with separatist ideas and manipulated by the region's elite for its own purposes. In 1886 separatist ideas were voiced in public by supporters, mainly members of the trading elite whose interests had been negatively affected by the establishment of the Iquitos customs in 1881 and the imposition of new duties (González 1886: 344). However, rather than expressing serious intent to separate from Peru and form a new entity, these ideas were used to pressure the government to lower or eliminate tax burdens.

In 1896 conflicts between the trading elite and the government found expression in the uprising of Col. Ricardo Seminario. The merchants of Iquitos, who resented more determined efforts in the collection of taxes, were the main supporters of this movement. By then, regionalist feelings were no longer manifested through separatist ideas, which lacked popular support, but rather through a federalist discourse. Although the government denounced this insurrection as a separatist attempt, attributing it to the lack of patriotic feeling among Loretans, there is little evidence to support such a view. Despite being an outsider, Prefect Hildebrando Fuentes (1908: 237) was aware of the unsubstantiated nature of the accusations. However, in the early 1900s he warned that federalist ideals were catching on because Loretans judged that the government, despite the region's large contribution to the national treasury, was not properly attending to Loretan needs. To suppress such ideas, which he considered to be harmful for the country, he recommended granting Loreto greater autonomy in managing its fiscal resources (Fuentes 1906: 523–5). Fuentes's recommendations went unheeded, and regionalist feelings continued to mount.

With the foundation of La Liga in 1913, regionalist ideas were no longer monopolized by the merchant elite, and a broad regionalist movement emerged. La Liga, a political party composed of educated native Loretans, opposed the political and trading elites, most of whom were outsiders (whether Peruvians or foreigners) and organized into a loose association, La Cueva. Members of La Liga resented discrimination toward Loretans. They struggled to undermine the hegemony of the elite and gain greater political and financial autonomy for the region. The crisis brought about by the drop of rubber prices in 1910 and 1914, and the state's tardiness in providing relief to the region fueled resentment and generated conditions for the insurrection of Capt. Guillermo Cervantes in 1921.

Unlike previous uprisings, that of Captain Cervantes did not reflect the interests of the merchant elite, although it was supported by most of the large Peruvian merchants. Furthermore, it garnered widespread popular support, involving people in Iquitos as well as many rural areas. Thus, it was the first genuine regionalist uprising in Loreto. The rebels denounced the corruption involved in the collusion between larger trading firms and local authorities, the greediness of the merchant elite, and the government's delay in paying salaries of public servants. In addition, they condemned the government for its attempted frontier agreement with Colombia and what they considered to be shameful territorial concessions.

The crushing of the insurrection put an end to this first regionalist movement. But discontent with the government's strong centralist stance lingered. In the following decades Loretan regionalism was expressed mostly as opposition to foreign policy and not to economic issues. The most notorious confrontation arose from the cession to Colombia in 1930 of the territory between the Caqueta and Putumayo Rivers (Morey Menacho 1993; Barletti 1994). Control over that region had led to several clashes between Peruvian and Colombian rubber extractors and to one important armed confrontation in 1911. Peru claimed that the territory was added to the colonial province of Maynas when it was transferred from the jurisdiction of the Audiencia of Quito to the Viceroyalty of Peru in 1802. Colombia claimed that the territory had belonged to the Viceroyalty of Nueva Granada and that Colombians were the first to settle there in the 1880s. In 1916 Colombia and Ecuador settled disputes in the Amazonian frontier with the Suarez–Muñoz Vernaza Treaty. To impede an alliance between Colombia and Ecuador and to isolate the latter, whose territorial claims posed an even greater threat to the integrity of Peruvian Amazonia, in 1922 Pres. Augusto Leguía signed a treaty with Colombia. Peru ceded to Colombia not only the territory in dispute but access to the Amazon River by way of Leticia. This was the price to be paid to ensure Colombia's neutrality in case of armed confrontation with Ecuador. Leguía demanded that the treaty be kept secret so as not to alert Ecuador (Donadio 1995: 61). It was considered to be a diplomatic victory for Peru in that it shattered Ecuadorian aspirations over the region north of the Amazon (ibidem: 80). However, when the treaty went public in 1926, Loretans considered it a betrayal on Leguía's part. Despite angry popular protests in Iquitos and the firm opposition of Sen. Julio C. Arana, who had vested interests in the area, both countries ratified the treaty in 1928.

The official handover of Leticia to Colombia in 1930 generated much local unrest. Two years later prominent members of the regional elite founded the Junta Patriótica, its main objective was to recover Leticia by force of arms. A group of volunteers, mostly civilians and a few lower-ranking officers, financed by the Junta, captured Leticia in September 1932. News of the bloodless seizure aroused widespread enthusiasm in Iquitos. Officers of the army and the navy, who had been previously sounded out by the Junta but had not pledged their backing, were forced by popular clamor to support the action.

Pres. Luis Sánchez Cerro, who until then had remained silent on the issue, was also forced to support the unilateral takeover of Leticia. However, his assassination in early 1933, and the pressures exerted over the new Peruvian government by the League of Nations, put an end to the armed confrontation. In 1934 Peru signed a new treaty, finally ceding the Putumayo region to Colombia. Loretans perceived that as adding insult to injury and confirming the government's disregard for the region. Whereas in the past either the merchant elite or the working classes had monopolized regionalist claims, in this case all social sectors combined to challenge the state. The seizure of Leticia constituted the first instance of multiclass regionalist political action in Loreto.

Between the 1940s and 1960s Loreto's regionalist sentiments did not find expression in any concrete political actions. This is explained partly because the elite and working classes were experiencing profound changes; also, regional politics was taken over by national parties, such as the Alianza Popular Revolucionaria Americana (APRA) and Acción Popular. It was only in the 1970s that regionalism emerged once more as a powerful political instrument. The struggle against the curtailment of the special status granted to the region in the early 1960s and the demand for an oil canon provided grounds for forming a regionalist movement and platform. This took shape in the Frente de Defensa del Pueblo de Loreto (FDPL), founded in 1978. However, the existence of a regionalist ideology did not prevent intense competition among the organizations of the elite and those of the popular sectors for hegemony within the FDPL. This antagonism resulted in several major political defeats for the FDPL. It also led to a realization among the elite and popular sectors that only by joining forces could they attain their common objectives. That these forces were sometimes able to leave their differences aside to fight for common goals is clear evidence of the taming of the Loretan frontier.

In summary, although regionalism has a long tradition in Loreto, on only a few occasions have regionalist sentiments materialized into a regionalist political platform capable of mobilizing all sectors of the region's society. Beginning as little more than a vague feeling expressed in separatist ideas and monopolized by the trading elite, regionalism has become a driving force in Loreto's civil society. This major shift is linked to the extension of civil rights, increased organization of the working classes, and greater political participation. It is also associated with the consolidation of a regional identity, which, we argue, constitutes the most important expression of the taming of the frontier.

Regional Identity

The emergence of a regional identity in Loreto is very much tied to the process of *ribereño*ization, the gradual expansion of the mixed-blood social stratum that originated during the rubber era. Members of this group were hailed by early-twentieth-century authors as "genuine Loretans" and as a new breed that would constitute "the population of the future." In this they were right. In time, members of this emerging group, currently known as *ribereños*, became the predominant population of Loreto in both rural and urban areas. The main traits of their hybrid culture have come to define the modern Loretan identity.

According to early descriptions (Stiglich 1904: 406–410; López 1904: 268; Fuentes 1906: 392), *ribereños* spoke Spanish with an accent, syntax, and vocabulary that distinguished them from other Spanish-speaking Peruvians. In addition, they spoke or understood either an Amazonian indigenous language, highland Quechua, or Inga, or *lingua geral*, the lingua franca based on Tupi languages that was imposed by the Jesuits in Brazilian Amazonia. They lived along the main rivers; both men and women were expert canoe pilots. Women excelled in farming, whereas men were remarkable hunters, fishermen, and extractors of forest products. Most *ribereño* social gatherings revolved around the Catholic calendar of festivities. The most important of these celebrations was Saint John's Day, for which a special dish, *juanes* or *fanes* (balls of rice stuffed with chicken), was prepared. *Ribereños* also celebrated Christmas, New Year's, Carnival, and Easter in distinct ways. During such festivities they danced to the accompaniment of flutes, fifes, drums, and concertinas, and drank *aguardiente* (*cachaza*), sugarcane wine (*ventisho*), and manioc beer (*masato*). For Carnival and Saint John's Day they erected and felled ornamented palm tree trunks (*úmisha*) amid dancing and drinking. They also celebrated *veladas*, keeping vigil and dancing solemnly in honor of the image of a saint, and participated in shamanic activities that combined Amazonian, Andean, and Christian elements.

From these early reports it becomes apparent, however, that at the beginning of the twentieth century *ribereño* culture was very much confined to the rural areas and was markedly different from that of the region's mostly white, European-oriented elites in urban areas. In Iquitos *ribereño* culture was still marginal, being restricted to the neighboring rural settlements of San Juan and Punchana, although the population as a whole had adopted a few *ribereño* festivities. Thus, by 1909 people of all social positions gathered in San Juan to celebrate Saint John's Day, and in Punchana to celebrate the Day of the Immaculate Virgin (Kanatari 1988: 9; 1991: 7). However, these festivities were still the objects of two parallel celebrations: the popular gathering and the private dinners and dancing parties organized by members of the elite.

After the 1914 rubber bust, the situation started to change. The growth of the mixed-blood stratum, as well as the consolidation of a landed elite that acted as an intermediary between the rural and urban populations, created the conditions for the gradual expansion of *ribereño* culture into the region's urban centers. This was especially true in the case of Iquitos, where changes in the way Carnival was celebrated during the 1920s and 1930s constitute a good example of this process.

By 1926 the Iquitos elite, representing official culture, still celebrated Carnival following the Spanish tradition. That included a parade of cars and wagons, each decorated with different allegorical motifs, headed by one carrying the grotesque effigy of *Ño Carnavalón*, epitomizing the spirit of Carnival (CETA 1995). This public event was organized by a committee of distinguished members of the elite appointed by the municipality. The celebration also included private costume balls and beauty pageants held in family residences and social clubs, during which the Queen of Carnival was elected from among the elite's belles.

This could not contrast more with the way in which rural and urban *ribereños* celebrated Carnival. It included the closing of streets and the erection by a family of an *úmisha*, a palm trunk decorated with trinkets, presents, and ribbons. Guests, generally neighbors and family, danced around it to the sound of drums, flutes, and accordions, taking turns to strike it with an ax until it fell and everybody wrestled to grab the presents. The couple who felled the *úmisha* had the responsibility of organizing and financing the following year's celebration. Both ways of celebrating Carnival coexisted, but whereas the elite's celebration took place in the city's main streets, that of migrant *ribereños* was confined to its suburbs.

Ribereño culture continued to assert itself in Iquitos throughout the 1930s. The seizure of Leticia in 1932 advanced this process, insofar as it generated a regionalist feeling that crossed class boundaries. In Iquitos this subtle change found expression in the way Carnival was celebrated. In 1935 the municipal committee in charge of organizing the festivities adopted the *úmisha* celebration instead of the European-style Carnival, arguing that it was "an authentic expression of [the region's] popular customs" (Kanatari 1990: 10). An apparently minor ruling, it nevertheless marked an important step forward in the transformation of *ribereño* culture into the pillar of Loretan culture and identity.

War with Ecuador in 1941 also rekindled regionalist sentiments, although most of the fighting took place on the Pacific Coast and not in the Amazon, where neither country had a strong military presence. In 1942, after Peru's victory, both countries signed the Rio de Janeiro Protocol. This granted Peru territories that were considered Ecuadorian according to the 1936 status-quo frontier, namely, the upper tracts of the Pastaza, Corrientes, and Tigre Rivers and a few kilometers along the Napo River. The signing of this protocol was opposed in Ecuador, where it was seen as condoning a shameful loss of territories. It was also opposed in Peru, where it was considered to be too favorable to Ecuador, for it left in Ecuadorian hands large tracts of land originally included in the colonial province of Maynas. In contrast, in Loreto, where people still resented the handover of Leticia to Colombia, the new territorial gains resulted in a renewed sense of regional pride. In fact, the signing was hailed by Loretans as "a turning point for a people like us, that has waited a hundred years" (Protocolo 1942). By this they meant that for the first time the state had taken resolute measures to secure Loreto's territorial integrity. Nineteen forty-two was also a turning point in the emergence of a regional identity.

That year, Loretans celebrated the four-hundred-year anniversary of Spain's discovery of the Amazon River. Pres. Manuel Prado's designation of Lima and Iquitos as the official seats for the celebration caused great satisfaction in the region. As part of the commemorative acts, the government sponsored the publication of two books by Loretan authors—the novel *Sangama*, by Arturo Hernández, and *Sachachorro*, a collection of short stories by César Lequerica—which signaled a radical change in the region's literary production. Since the publication in 1869 of the *Oda al Río Amazonas*, by Fabriciano Hernández, the first example of regional literature, Loreto's literary tradition had tightly adhered to European parameters and sensibilities (Ramírez 1983: 8). The books by Hernández and Lequerica departed from this tradition by adopting as their subject the *ribereño* way of life. *Sangama* concerned rural *ribereños*; *Sachachorro* involved both rural *ribereños* and the migrant *ribereños* living on the periphery of Iquitos. Although still written in a folkloric tradition that kept a distance between the author and his or her subjects, these two works exalted the *ribereño* worldview and turned it into a legitimate topic of official literature.

During the 1940s and 1950s regional literature flourished with the publication of numerous novels and collections of short stories. Among the best known are *Ayahuasca*, by Arturo Burga Freitas (1941); *Tunchi*, by Juan E. Coriat (1944); *Selva Trágica*, by Arturo Hernández (1954); and *El Motelo*, by Víctor Morey Peña (1958). This literary cycle came to an end in 1963 with the publication of *Paiche* by César Calvo de Araujo (Santos-Granero 1991c: 3). *Trocha*, a literary magazine founded in 1941, became the most important means to disseminate the works of this generation of writers.

Changes in regional literature went hand in hand with a renewal of the fine arts. César Calvo de Araujo is the best-known painter among a small group that depicted the lives of the indigenous and *ribereño* peoples with new eyes and a new aesthetic. Most of these writers and painters belonged to prominent families of Loreto's landed and trading elites. Although not always wealthy themselves, their privileged position ensured that their works reached the regional elite, contributing to the *ribereño*ization of the regional culture.

Massive migration of *ribereños* to Iquitos throughout the 1950s, when the *fundo* economy was declining, drew the region's rural and urban spheres closer. By 1971 73 percent of the population of Iquitos lived in peripheral slum areas. Most slum-dwellers were *ribereños* who migrated to the city in search of better economic opportunities. The organization of the popular sectors in both the rural and urban areas that took place in the 1970s made the *ribereño* population even more visible. It did the same for the indigenous peoples, who until then had been perceived by urban dwellers as remote, exotic, and savage.

The increased influence of the left wing in the national and Latin American political scenes also shifted attention to the popular sectors. These changes were reflected in Loreto's literature. In 1965 a new generation of writers founded Bubinzana, a literary group that criticized the "folkloric approach" of previous authors. They called on writers to stop being "simple spectators of crepuscular or auroral landscapes" and to stop "imitating or replacing regional popular culture" (Morey Alejo 1988: 21). They also proclaimed the need to search for the roots of the regional identity, which, according to their view, lay with the indigenous and *ribereño* peoples, and to "assume their magic worlds from within" (ibidem). Members of the literary group Oruga Acción Cultural, which was founded in 1985, took a similar stance. Adopting and recreating literary forms taken from indigenous and *ribereño* oral traditions, members of this group have concentrated efforts on writing children's stories, many of which have become official textbooks in Loreto's schools.

Renewed looks at the worlds of the *ribereño* and indigenous peoples also characterize Loreto's contemporary painters. Samuel Coriat and César Ching have explored the reality of the *ribereños* of Iquitos's periphery, where urban landscapes and mores merge into the countryside. In a constant search for the roots of Loreto's culture, Nancy Dantas has turned her eyes to the magic world of the forest, incorporating local materials and pigments into her art. More importantly, this new generation of artists includes successful *ribereño* painters, such as Pablo Amaringo of Pucallpa, who depicts in rich colors the complex and symbolically hybrid visions he had as a traditional shamanic practitioner (see Luna and Amaringo 1991).

In recent years several nongovernmental institutions have strived to revalue regional culture. Through its weekly *Kanatari* and the several cultural activities it organizes, such as an annual book festival, the Centro de Estudios Teológicos de la Amazonía, an organization associated with the Catholic Church, has played a crucial role in revaluing regional history and strengthening cultural identity. Governmental institutions have followed suit. In the early 1980s the Ministry of Industry, Commerce, and Tourism sponsored the organization of a festival of folk music, which included groups of indigenous and *ribereño* musicians and dancers. At present, these festivals have become central to the celebration of Saint John's Day. Although the music and choreography that is presented as indigenous or *ribereño* is frequently elaborated by nonindigenous, non-*ribereño* people, these annual festivals have been very successful in disseminating regional cultural values among urban dwellers. In turn, the municipality of Maynas has financed the publication of classical and new Loretan literary works.

Through this process, Loretans are reinventing their cultural tradition. In so doing, they are building a more encompassing regional identity that contrasts with the fragmented identities prevalent in the not-so-distant past. The incorporation of *ribereño* and indigenous cultural expressions into the official culture has shaped the regional identity more in accordance with the region's multicultural reality. Moreover, the recognition and dissemination of *ribereño* and indigenous culture has changed the facile stereotyping and overt discrimination that was characteristic of the opening of the frontier.

*   *   *

Frontier expansion in Loreto has been a long and hazardous process: violent displacement and dispossession of indigenous peoples, coercive forms of labor, irrational exploitation of natural resources, enrichment of a few at the expense of the majority, and manipulation of law for the benefit of a powerful minority. It has left indelible marks in both the people and the landscape. The extermination of entire indigenous peoples, the forced acculturation of many others, the imprint of a *habilitado* mentality resulting from long-term subjection, and the impoverishment of lakes, rivers, and forests are some aspects that will not be easy to forget or overcome.

However, in the past decades Loreto has undergone a process of change that can best be understood as the taming of the frontier, that is, the suppression of the negative economic, social, and political traits characteristic of Amazonian frontier economies. This in no way means that the taming of the Loretan frontier has brought about a sustainable economy, a harmonious society, and full political participation. It has not led to the elimination of extreme economic and social inequalities. However, there can be no doubt as to the magnitude of the positive changes undergone by the region. Loreto has come a long way since the rubber era and is no longer governed by the logic of frontier expansion.

Epilogue

When we finished gathering the data for this book in 1992 it was clear that the ascension to power of Pres. Alberto Fujimori in 1990 had marked the end of a period in the economic history of Loreto. By then, however, it was difficult to ascertain how deeply the neoliberal policies implemented by Fujimori would alter the region's economy and society. For that reason we thought it appropriate to end our analysis in 1990. When we finished writing the first draft of this book in 1997, however, some of the changes resulting from the shift in the political paradigm were already visible. Taking advantage of the need to revise the manuscript for publication, we decided to write an epilogue analyzing the 1990–1999 period.

In 1990 Peru was experiencing a deep economic and political crisis. The populist economic policies of Pres. Alan García (1985–1990) had led the country to hyperinflation, fiscal bankruptcy, and a state of ineligibility for international credit. In addition, the government's incapacity to halt the terrorist activities of Sendero Luminoso (Shining Path) and the Movimiento Revolucionario Túpac Amaru (Tupac Amaru Revolutionary Movement), insurgent groups that appeared during the early 1980s, had driven Peru into a spiral of violence. As a result, thousands of persons were killed, the country's economic infrastructure was seriously damaged, and there was a widespread sense of demoralization.

When Fujimori assumed power he had three objectives: defeat terrorism, solve the economic crisis, and settle frontier conflicts. The first two goals occupied a central place in the government's discourse. We maintain that the last one, although less explicit, was crucial to Fujimori's economic strategy. In effect, Fujimori considered that only by settling pending frontier issues with Chile, Bolivia, and Ecuador could the government redirect substantial human and economic resources that were spent in national defense toward economic development and the defeat of terrorism.

The main pillar of the government's strategy to defeat the insurgent groups was a firm political and economic support of the army. Under Pres. Fernando Belaúnde, who was ousted by the military during his first administration (1963–1968), and under President García, whose party (APRA) had a historical enmity with the military, the relationship between the government and the army had been ambivalent at best. The army was given the responsibility but not the resources to combat insurgents. In addition to establishing a solid alliance with the army, Fujimori placed greater emphasis on intelligence rather than armed confrontation. The government also promoted the organization of self-defense groups, established more expedient judicial procedures, imposed harsher penalties for terrorism, and passed legislation favoring repentance of terrorists.

The government's neoliberal economic strategy called for the liberalization of Peru's economy. This was to be achieved through the elimination of price and for-eign-exchange controls, the eradication of subsidies, the reduction of duties and tar-iffs, the attraction of foreign investment, the privatization of state assets, and the re-duction of the state apparatus. These measures were to be complemented by others aimed at eliminating the fiscal deficit and reinserting the country in the interna-tional finance system, namely, through the reinforcement of tax collection, stricter control over public expenditures, and a firm commitment to pay the external debt.

Lastly, the government's strategy to settle all frontier issues with neighbors en-tailed three steps. First was to provide Bolivia access to the Pacific Ocean and a free-trade zone in a Peruvian port. Second was to solve pending issues with Chile derived from the 1879 war and the 1929 treaty. Third, and most important, was to settle the old frontier conflict with Ecuador, derived from the 1941 war and the Rio de Janeiro Protocol.

In contrast to previous administrations, Fujimori's did not give the Amazon re-gion a central role in the development of the country. Fujimori did not have a spe-cific agenda for the Amazon region in general or for Loreto in particular. Thus, the government confined itself to applying macropolicies designed for the country as a whole. Since terrorism was never a major problem in Loreto, the actions oriented to undermine the power of the insurgent groups did not affect the region. In contrast, the implementation of the economic program and diplomatic negotiations with Ecuador had a great impact and generated much local unrest. Loretans opposed both the agreement with Ecuador and the repeated attempts at curtailing the re-gion's special status. This period is, therefore, characterized by confrontations be-tween the government and diverse regional fronts that emerged at the time.

Economic Reforms

The government's program included the opening-up of the country's economy. This implied the reduction of duties on imported goods that had frequently been im-posed to protect national industry. In the case of Loreto this measure negatively af-fected the timber industry, for it allowed the import of cheap Asian and Ecuadorian laminated woods. This and the prohibition on the export of fine timber, mainly cedar and mahogany, led Loreto's timber industry to a crisis that it has yet to over-come.

The government's economic program also entailed the elimination of promo-tional agricultural credit and subsidies. During his first years of government, Fuji-mori closed and sold the assets of Banco Agrario and of the state agencies in charge of marketing agricultural produce and supplying agricultural inputs. As a result the production of rice, Loreto's main commercial crop, contracted. Although peasants protested the measures, they were not able to generate a more generalized reaction. In 1993 rice production recovered, attaining the high volumes characteristic of the 1980s and showing that the elimination of subsidies had not impaired either peasant production or urban demand, as many thought it would (see Appendix 25). In contrast, the elimination of subsidies to basic goods and services such as gasoline, water, electricity, and telephone had a negative impact on the urban population and thus generated greater resistance.

A keystone of the government's program was the privatization of state companies and the reduction of state bureaucracies. In Loreto, the most important public company was Petro-Perú, the national oil company. The government privatized its marketing facilities and part of its refining and prospecting operations. Although Petro-Perú was not completely dismantled, the people of Loreto opposed its privatization for fear it would lead to a sharp reduction in personnel. Such fear was realized: Between 1989 and 1996 the company's personnel was reduced by 65 percent (Nájar y Grandez 1996: 10). In addition, between 1991 and 1996, through incentives and layoffs, the government reduced the number of public servants in Loreto by 14,000 (ibidem).

This loss of jobs was partly compensated beginning in 1994 with the arrival in the region of eight new oil-prospecting companies that received a concession of eleven oil fields (La Torre 1998: Anexo 2; Mora and Zarzar 1997: 18). This was the result of a change in the previous model of oil concessions to attract foreign investment. Loreto's economy, which since 1987 had entered a recession as a result of the economic measures of President García and the decrease in oil production (see Appendix 28), was reactivated by the presence of these oil companies. Nevertheless, the oil concessions, frequently located in protected areas and in indigenous lands, have been contested not only by those directly affected but also by segments of the urban population. Thus, in 1991 the inhabitants of Iquitos successfully protested government attempts to grant the Texas Crude Company an oil field in the Pacaya-Samiria Reserve on the confluence of the Marañón and Ucayali Rivers.

In April 1992 Fujimori dissolved Congress, where he did not have the majority, and assumed full powers with the support of the army. This self–coup d'etât, widely supported by the people, allowed Fujimori to bypass congressional opposition. Pressured by the Organization of American States, however, Fujimori was forced to call elections for a Constitutional Democratic Congress. This Congress was to reform the 1979 constitution and legislate until 1995. To further concentrate power in the executive branch, but also to control fiscal deficits and create surpluses to pay external debt, Fujimori also suspended regional governments and dissolved regional assemblies, which had been elected for the first time in 1989.

The creation of regional governments had been long demanded by the provinces. To promote decentralization, the 1979 constitution mandated the creation of regions to replace the old departments, as well as the election of regional governments. In some cases the new regions were composed by more than one department. This generated much discontent. Loreto's regional government was the first to be elected in the country. Regional governments had economic and administrative autonomy. They lacked, however, political autonomy, a fact that was denounced by Loreto's more radical regionalist politicians (Kanatari 1990: No. 317). Less than two years after the regional government was created, most Loretans considered it far from efficient. In fact, in November 1990 the FDPL, resurrected specifically for this purpose, urged Loretans to protest the regional government's corruption and poor administration. In April 1992 Fujimori dissolved the regional assembly and replaced the elected regional government by a transitory council of regional administration, composed of a president and five counselors appointed by the executive branch. Loretans were discontented but did not take to the streets. They did, however, five months later, when the president of the transitory council, who was a Loretan, was dismissed and replaced by an outsider (Kanatari 1992: No. 418).

Loreto's elected regional government was in charge of administering funds derived from the 10 percent oil canon assigned to Loreto. The transference of canon funds to Loreto had always been problematic. It caused permanent conflicts between the central government, which claimed that these funds were not properly used, and regional authorities, which countered that the region was not receiving the full amount due. In accordance with his plan of fiscal austerity, Fujimori attempted to remove the administration of the canon funds from Loreto's regional government. In the early 1992 Fujimori decreed that the income derived from the oil canon should be incorporated into the budget of the central government. This measure caused widespread opposition. In October 1993 Fujimori called a referendum to approve the new constitution, which included the possibility of his reelection. In an effort to elicit the support of Loretans, Fujimori announced that the constitution reestablished the oil canon (Kanatari 1994: No. 527). Despite that move, Loretans voted against it. The oil canon was restored, but it was never paid in full. Thus, this issue has continued to be a source of friction with the central government.

Prior to that, however, Fujimori had curtailed the power of the regions by reforming the electoral system at the time of the election of the constitutional Congress. The new system was based on single electoral districts. Before then, each department or region had the right to elect a given number of house representatives and senators according to demographic weight. Under the new system, voters can only vote for the list of candidates presented by a given party. In the case of national parties, that list may or may not include candidates from the voter's region or department. The new electoral system, which was sanctioned by the 1993 constitution, has been considered yet another expression of Fujimori's authoritarianism and as a stratagem favoring centralism. As such, Loreto's political class has also questioned it (Kanatari 1994: No. 530).

When Congress was drawing the 1993 constitution, the opposition suspected that Fujimori would seize the opportunity to abolish the system of regional governments. Popular pressure in the provinces forced Congress to maintain the system, albeit with some changes. Thus, taking advantage of the rivalries between the different departments that composed the 1989 regions, the government established that new regional governments would not be implemented until the people decided via referendum the regions to which they wanted former departments to belong. As a result, the transitory councils were retained. The referendum was never called, and in 1998 the government passed legislation whereby the 1989 regions were reconverted into the original twenty-four departments. The regions lost their economic and administrative autonomy, and the central government once more came to concentrate all financial resources in its hands. The transitory councils were dissolved, but their presidents were maintained, this time subordinated to the Ministry of the Presidency. This was the final blow to the incipient process of decentralization initiated in 1989. Although the law was not particularly aimed at Loreto, Loretans perceived it as such. Thus, the call for an "authentic" decentralization became a central demand in the political platforms of the popular organizations of Loreto.

One of the implicit goals in dismantling the regions was to better control public expenditures and overcome the fiscal deficit. A second measure aimed at attaining a balanced budget was to reform tax legislation and the tax-collection system. Tax laws were simplified, and tax exemptions established in different promotional laws, such as the Law of Industry, were eliminated. In addition, the government created a new, extremely successful tax-collecting agency, the Superintendencia Nacional Tributaria. In Loreto the government attempted to eliminate all tax exemptions, including those related to the import and export trades. Taking advantage of the fact that Law 15600, which exonerated the Amazonian departments from paying many taxes, was valid only until December 1990, the government tried to revoke Loreto's special tax regime.

Popular opposition led the government to temporarily extend the validity of Law 15600. This was done several times in the following two years. In December 1992, however, the government annulled Law 15600 and passed new tax legislation. Through Decree-Law 25980 the government imposed an 18 percent municipal promotion tax on sales. This, in fact, was equivalent to the 18 percent general sales tax that was applied throughout the country, from which the Amazon region was exempted. Additionally, through Decree-Law 25990 the government annulled the benefits established by the Peruvian-Colombian Customs Agreement. In Loreto these measures aroused the protests of both the popular organizations and the chamber of commerce and led to the formation of a regional front. Street manifestations were so massive that the government had to back off and temporarily suspend the second measure. The other, however, was applied and created great resentment among the region's entrepreneurs. The obligation to pay taxes was reinforced by the 1993 constitution, which eliminated the legal mechanism of special tax regimes.

By the end of 1993 the government passed new tax legislation. Decree-Laws 775 and 778 restored the tax exemptions included in the Peruvian-Colombian Customs Agreement, thus revoking in practice the much-denounced Decree-Law 25990.

However, the new laws established that the exemptions would be valid only for merchandise entering the port and airport at Iquitos and not the ports of the Pacific Coast. This was meant to stop smuggling of exempted products into areas not exonerated from payment of duties. However, since until then most of the products imported under this agreement entered through the Pacific Coast, Loreto's entrepreneurs had mixed feelings. On the one hand, they hailed these decrees as a triumph of the people of Loreto; on the other hand, they resented the curtailment of the benefits of the customs agreement. However, when President Fujimori extended the validity of these laws until the year 2000, Loreto's entrepreneurs expressed their satisfaction.

Despite much give and take the government was quite successful in applying its economic program in Loreto. There were, however, two areas in which Fujimori had to give in to the pressures of the region's popular and entrepreneurial organizations: the oil canon and the exoneration of duties. We argue that if the government was not adamant in applying in full its economic program in Loreto it was because it subordinated the goal of liberalizing the economy to the need of settling border disputes with Ecuador. Fujimori compromised on some economic issues to soften opposition among Loretans to the negotiations with Ecuador. The ultimate concession, as we shall see, was the restoration in 1998 of a special tax regime for Loreto and other Amazon areas.

The Ecuadorian Issue

The 1941 war between Peru and Ecuador over the territories north of the Marañón-Amazon axis ended with a Peruvian victory and the signing of the Rio de Janeiro Protocol, which established the border between both countries. In the following years a binational commission began demarcating the frontier. However, in 1949 the commission reached a deadlock, unable to agree on two areas: a ten-kilometer tract on the headwaters of the Lagartococha and Güepi Rivers and a 130-kilometer tract along the Cordillera del Cóndor (Yepes del Castillo 1996: 171). This led Ecuadorian Pres. José María Velasco Ibarra to declare in 1960 that the Rio Protocol was "inapplicable" and "invalid." Since then, the activities of the armies of both countries in the areas not demarcated were the cause of numerous clashes and of a more serious confrontation in 1981.

Until 1990 the position of Peru's chancellery was that there was no frontier problem with Ecuador, that the Rio Protocol was clear as to the demarcation of the frontier, and that it was only a matter of demarcating the remaining areas. This position, meant to deter any possibility of revising the Rio Protocol, became an unmovable tenet of Peruvian diplomacy.

In July 1991, a year after Fujimori assumed power, there was a clash between Peru and Ecuador at the headwaters of the Santiago River. The confrontation ended with a "gentlemen's pact" whereby both countries established precise diplomatic procedures to address future border disputes. This introduced a first fissure in Peru's monolithic diplomatic position on Ecuador. In September 1991 in a speech before the United Nations, Ecuadorian Pres. Rodrigo Borja proposed that both countries submit the frontier dispute to arbitration by the Pope. This was an inspired move. By moving away from its traditional position, Ecuador aimed at forcing Peru to move away from its own position and recognize that there was a pending territorial dispute with Ecuador.

To avoid arbitration, Fujimori, in a letter to President Borja, countered by offering to apply the Rio Protocol to its full extent. This included signing a treaty of navigation and commerce granting Ecuador free navigation rights along the Amazon and its tributaries, which had never been implemented. To make the offer more attractive he expanded the original scope of the proposed treaty by offering to grant Ecuador port facilities in the Amazon (Benalcázar 1992: 232). The offer was well received in Ecuador. In Peru, however, it generated angry comments by former diplomats, as well as resistance from many high-ranking officers of the chancellery. Similar reactions were registered in Loreto, where it was claimed that Fujimori was acting "awkwardly . . . weakening our negotiating position" (Kanatari 1991: No. 373, 8). To eliminate opposition from the more traditional diplomats, Fujimori in 1991 restructured the chancellery, dismissing more than a hundred officers.

In January 1992 Fujimori visited Ecuador, becoming the first Peruvian president to visit that country on an official trip. The visit was a success, and Fujimori was given a warm welcome. In Loreto, his trip was viewed with suspicion, and Fujimori's declarations, which included the offer to Ecuador of a free-trade zone on the Amazon, were criticized as "compromising our sovereignty and our national and territorial integrity" (Vásquez Valcárcel 1992: 6). In December, Fujimori made an unofficial visit to Ecuador to talk with the new president, Sixto Durán Ballén, who took the opportunity to demand a sovereign port on the Amazon. This aroused much opposition in Loreto, where it was suspected that Fujimori would grant Ecuador portions of Loreto, as Pres. Augusto Leguía had done in the past with Colombia. Critics declared that "Loreto will always resist arbitrary decisions over its historical territories that are not based on the will of its people" (Kanatari 1992: No. 435, 3).

Until then Fujimori's economic and political measures with respect to Loreto, namely, elimination of tax exemptions, dissolution of the regional government, and withdrawal of the oil canon, had created much discontent but not active opposition. Fujimori's negotiations with Ecuador triggered the creation of a new regional front. As the Civic Front of Loreto, the chamber of commerce, the professional guilds, and worker and peasant organizations took action. In early January 1993 the Civic Front called a general strike against Fujimori's economic measures and the risk of "territorial mutilation." Fujimori's second official visit to Ecuador, also in January, generated greater opposition. The secrecy in which the negotiations were carried out and the fact that Loretans were not represented persuaded many Loretans that Fujimori was acting "treacherously." In February the Civic Front called a two-day strike against centralism and the granting of a free-trade zone to Ecuador on the Amazon.

The street march organized by the Civic Front was extremely successful, gathering, according to some sources, 100,000 persons (Kanatari 1993: No. 439).

From then on economic reforms and the Ecuadorian issue became the two main pillars of political mobilization in Loreto. There was deep resentment against centralism and Fujimori's authoritarian ways. In this context the demand for a federal state and greater economic and political autonomy reappeared on the region's political scene. Some regionalist leaders and members of the chamber of commerce even proposed holding a referendum on the federal system (Kanatari 1993: No. 449, No. 456).

Whether it planned to or not, the Civic Front, by linking the economic demands to the protests against negotiations with Ecuador, was successful in forcing Fujimori to postpone or temper his economic measures. It was clear that reaching agreement with Ecuador was one of Fujimori's priorities. By opposing talks with Ecuador, the Civic Front forced the government to grant Loreto certain economic concessions. In effect, to placate Loretans after the January 1993 strike the government announced the building of the Iquitos-Nauta Road, which was an old aspiration of the people of Iquitos. Immediately after the February strike it announced the postponement of the decree-law that eliminated the benefits of the Peruvian-Colombian Customs Agreement.

These measures neutralized Loretan opposition. The Civic Front remained inactive until October 1993, when the leftist teachers' union urged other trade unions and professional guilds to campaign against the approval of the 1993 constitution: 58 percent of Loretans voted against the new constitution (Tuesta 1994: 129). Such success led some leaders to propose the creation of a more stable, frontlike organization to act as a "civic force to struggle permanently against authoritarianism". In May 1994 the teachers' union attempted to organize a federation of popular organizations. The professional guilds declined, and the chamber of commerce was never invited, so the idea never took off (Kanatari 1994: No. 506). Things changed after new border clashes between Peru and Ecuador.

In the late 1994 there were several encounters between troops stationed at the headwaters of the Cenepa River. Beginning in January 9 the clashes became low-intensity confrontations, and by January 26, 1995, they had become full-scale combats. As always, both countries blamed the other. It is clear, however, that the presidents of both countries benefited from not putting a quick end to the hostilities. The popularity of the Ecuadorian president, which amid a generalized economic crisis had been at its lowest, increased immediately. The war also benefited Fujimori, whose new constitution had been approved by a very narrow margin and who needed a boost in popularity to be reelected.

The outcome favored Ecuador, which occupied Tiwintza, a small tributary of the Cenepa River. The timely intervention of the guarantor countries of the 1942 Rio Protocol (Brazil, Argentine, Chile, and the United States) put an end to the confrontation and encouraged both countries to initiate diplomatic negotiations to settle differences. This was achieved through the signing of the Itamaraty Agreement, whereby Ecuador agreed to negotiate under the conditions established by the Rio Protocol, whereas Peru admitted that there were pending frontier issues.

Negotiations continued throughout 1995 and 1996 without causing much disquiet in Loreto. In early 1996 the trade union of Petro-Perú, the state oil company, urged Loreto's popular organizations to resurrect the old regional front. Members of the new organization, the Patriotic Front of Loreto, named after the Patriotic Junta that recaptured Leticia in 1932, elected Antonio D'Onadio as its president. D'Onadio had been FDPL president during the 1970s and enjoyed wide acceptance among all classes and local political sectors. The creation of this new front was clearly linked to the efforts of Loreto's public servants to forestall layoffs announced by the government. In April 1996 the Patriotic Front organized its first street march with moderate success (Kanatari 1996: No. 606). The organizers attempted to capitalize on the people's discontent with Fujimori's approach to Ecuador to further their own interests, namely, to stop privatization of state companies and to defend the oil canon.

With the signing of the Santiago Agreement in September 1996, negotiations with Ecuador entered into a new phase. That agreement established that diplomatic negotiations would be held without interruption until a definitive solution was reached. In addition, it committed the parties to "reciprocal concessions." This generated much discontent, for it was feared that any agreement with Ecuador would entail concessions in Loreto's territory. As the Patriotic Front did not react to this news, in July 1997 the teachers' union urged representatives of trade unions, political parties, and other popular organizations to reconstitute the Patriotic Front. In the following two years and until the ratification by Congress of a frontier agreement and a treaty of commerce and navigation with Ecuador in November 1998, the Patriotic Front organized numerous successful strikes and street protests.

The Patriotic Front's demands varied over time depending on politics. Full payment of the oil canon, no more privatizations, and restitution of the regional government were chief among them. However, opposition to any concession to Ecuador other than those explicitly mentioned in the Rio Protocol rallied the different organizations in the Patriotic Front. In 1997 and 1998 it urged more than ten public actions; on some occasions the Association of Municipalities of Loreto joined the cause. During those years popular and entrepreneurial organizations managed to set aside their differences to work toward two common goals: the defense of national sovereignty and the achievement of "authentic" decentralization.

Loreto's regionalist leaders, intellectuals, and mass media fueled nationalist and regionalist sentiments to increase opposition to negotiations with Ecuador. Until 1998 *Kanatari*, the local weekly associated with the Catholic Church, was one of the main promoters of discontent. Comparing the Ecuadorian issue to the handover of Leticia to Colombia, contributors in *Kanatari* and other local media exacerbated fears that the government would make significant territorial concessions. Early Ecuadorian demands of a sovereign port on the Amazon and a sovereign road connecting Ecuador to that port increased the apprehension.

The formation of the Patriotic Front was hailed by the media as a modern expression of the federalist spirit that had animated Loreto since the late nineteenth century. The organized protests were compared to past riots, uprisings, and patriotic mobilizations, characterized, irrespective of ideologies and political platforms, as "federalist" actions (Kanatari 1993: 450; Vásquez 1998). Thus, the Patriotic Front was compared to Seminario's 1896 uprising, which took place amid rubber prosperity, was supported by the merchant elite, and assailed the government for increasing tariffs and duties (Morey Menacho 1996a). But it was also compared to Cervantes's 1921 movement, which was supported by the urban and rural popular sectors, denounced lack of state support to overcome the rubber crisis, and opposed the merchant elite for aggravating the crisis with their economic practices (Morey Menacho1996b). The regionalist spirit was particularly heightened by making reference to the epic events of the 1932 recapture of Leticia. Beginning in 1995 regionalist leaders began celebrating the anniversary of this victory with displays of the Colombian flag captured in Leticia and the sword surrendered by the Colombian commander in charge of the town as symbols of Loretan bravery (Kanatari 1995: No. 574; 1996: No. 624).

As a result of the intensification of nationalist and regionalist feelings and Ecuador's military and diplomatic victory in the 1995 confrontation, public manifestations became increasingly hostile in terms of discourse and imagery. Signs calling Ecuadorans "liars" and "treacherous" became common in street marches. Caged monkeys were also prominently displayed in a direct reference to the derogatory term by which Ecuadorians are known in Peru. Although some local newspapers, such as *Kanatari* (1995: No. 542: 3), warned against excesses, anti-Ecuadorian feeling mounted. This led to the popular explosion that took place during October 24–25, 1998, shortly after the content of the agreements to be signed by Peru and Ecuador were made public.

It has been argued that the violence resulted from a combination of factors (Chirif 1999). First was the creation by the government of the Committee in Support of Peace and Development to counter the Patriotic Front, convening a public meeting in support of the agreements with Ecuador. This was perceived by regionalists as a provocation. Second was the intervention of Iquitos's mayor, who brought to the meeting a group of young roughnecks to harass speakers. Third was the confusion created by the Patriotic Front, which through a very lax interpretation of the agreements with Ecuador misinformed the population, generating greater dissatisfaction. Fourth was the economic recession, which in Loreto had led to unemployment and deeper resentment for the government. The last factor was the government's decision to allow the violence to continue to bring disrepute to Loreto's regionalist movement.

Whether or not the rally to support the agreements was an intentional provocation on the government's part, the police and army did nothing to stop the looting that lasted two full days and left five dead, more than ten buildings burned, and numerous banks and businesses pillaged. The government's strategy paid off. The excesses were repudiated not only in Loreto (Kanatari 1998: No. 737) but also throughout Peru.

On October 26, 1998, Peru and Ecuador agreed on a definitive frontier and signed two agreements: a treaty of commerce and navigation, and an agreement on frontier integration. The issues that generated greater opposition in Loreto were: the concession to Ecuador of two centers of commerce and navigation for a period of fifty years; the granting of navigation rights on the Marañón-Amazon axis and its northern tributaries; the construction of a road connecting Ecuador's and Peru's Amazon territories; and the granting in private property of a square kilometer in the location of Tiwintza. All of these measures were perceived as favoring Ecuador's "colonization" of Loreto. Shortly after the signing, the Patriotic Front and the Association of Municipalities held a referendum on approval of the agreements and whether to install an autonomous regional government, an idea already proposed in 1993. Some 98 percent of voters rejected the agreements and supported the idea of an autonomous government.

Although Fujimori dismissed the results of the referendum, the government accelerated plans to provide Loretans compensation for what they perceived as an affront. In April 1998 the chamber of commerce had presented a project to the government for a Law of Sustainable Development for Amazonia. The government agreed to consider the matter in three months, but it never did. After Loreto's referendum the chamber wrote a letter to the vice president requesting full payment of the oil canon, the granting of promotional credit to small enterprises and, above all, the restoration of the special tax regime (Kanatari 1998: No. 742). Fujimori soon met with members of the chamber of commerce in Lima. In late December Congress finally passed the Law of Promotion of the Integral Development of Peruvian Amazonia (Law 27037). It incorporates some of the points included in the project proposed by the chamber. It promotes investment in the region by exonerating enterprises that sell at least 70 percent of production in the regional market from all taxes except for a 5 percent income tax. It also exonerates gasoline sold in the region from taxes. Finally, it grants various other benefits for a period of fifty years.

The chamber of commerce was not fully satisfied, for the law focused on promoting new rather than established enterprises. However, Loreto's entrepreneurs saw as extremely positive the elimination of some of the worst aspects, namely, Decree-Law 25980, and the restoration of a special, albeit less beneficial, tax regime for the region. In contrast, the leaders of the Patriotic Front radically opposed the law, contending it was neoliberal, only offered tax exemptions, and did not include measures to guarantee human and social development. The Patriotic Front continues to oppose the agreements with Ecuador, and in a public communiqué it warned that it will do everything to impede the handover of centers of commerce and navigation to Ecuador (La Región 2/22/99).

* * *

Events in Loreto in the 1990s constituted an extreme expression of the three factors we associate with the taming of the frontier: the assertion of civil rights, the
shaping of a regional identity, and the development of a regionalist ideology. We say
"extreme," for the struggle against negotiations with Ecuador has been characterized
by a hardline anticentralist—though at the same time nationalist—stand. The massive support that the Patriotic Front has rallied against the central government is a
sign of healthy dissent, as it encompasses all social segments. The discourse through
which dissent has been transformed into political action is based on the federalist aspirations of previous movements and appeals to regionalist sentiments presented as
basic to Loretan identity. This discourse, however, acquired chauvinistic overtones
due to several factors that have little to do with the actual relationship between
Loretans and Ecuadorians, which was basically a "nonrelationship" in which each
party ignored the other. In effect, since the 1941 war and the closure of the frontier
Loreto ceased to have economic and cultural exchanges with Ecuador, and Loretans
ignored Ecuadorians with the indifference of the victorious. Ecuadorians, in turn,
ignored Loretans, because they constituted an uncomfortable reminder that Peruvians inhabited territories claimed as Ecuadorian.

We argue that Loreto's firm opposition to reach an agreement with Ecuador resulted from four factors: (1) rejection of Fujimori's economic program; (2) resentment generated by the elimination of regional governments; (3) indignation caused
by not being consulted on the negotiations; and (4) fear of loss of power derived
from Loreto's traditional geopolitical importance.

Loretans disliked Fujimori ever since he ran for the presidency. In fact, Loreto
was the only department where Fujimori lost in the second round of the 1990 election. Fujimori's economic program, with its emphasis on restricting the economic
role of the state and liberalizing the economy, eliminated the prerogatives that had
sustained Loreto for almost thirty years. Moreover, it ended the special relationship
Loreto maintained with the state since the mid-nineteenth century. Although Loretans have always complained of state indifference toward the region, Loreto has always enjoyed special treatment. Moreover, the state has always been an important
source of employment within the region. All of this was threatened by Fujimori's
economic policies. Fujimori's dissolution of the regional government, which constituted one of the historical demands of Loreto's people, was perceived as adding insult to injury.

The fact that Loreto's leaders and intellectuals were not regularly informed about
the development of negotiations with Ecuador until quite late increased resentment.
Although Fujimori made no secret of his intent to reach a definitive agreement with
Ecuador, negotiations were largely carried out in secrecy. This was so because the
government was bound by Peru's traditional position: that the Rio Protocol was
clear on the demarcation of the frontier and that there was nothing to negotiate
with Ecuador. To make things worse, Fujimori had alienated the sympathies of
Loreto's elite and leadership with his policies and would not have been able to obtain their support even if he wanted. The lack of information led to speculation and

increased fear as to the government's intentions. Fujimori's authoritarian ways did not help.

Although the Patriotic Front and its various member organizations never actually expressed the fear of losing negotiating power as a result of the settlement of frontier disputes with Ecuador, we believe that notion has very much been in the back of their minds. There can be no doubt that throughout its history Loreto has received special treatment and greater attention than did equally poor and remote departments. This was due to geopolitical reasons, namely, Ecuadorian claims over Loretan territories. Now that the frontier dispute has been settled, it is not clear whether the state will continue to grant similar priority to the region. In fact, although the government has once more granted Loreto a special tax regime, this is not as generous as previous systems.

Most authors studying Amazonia attribute its critical situation to the failure of the modern state. According to this view, state intervention has not led to the economic and political incorporation of Amazonia into the nation-states that share it. Although in Loreto state intervention has had a mixed outcome, there is no question that it has played a crucial part in integrating the region into national life. As a result, Loreto is no longer a frontier. However, the process of modernization is not yet completed, mostly because some rural areas have not fully benefited from it, but also because the region's leadership has concentrated efforts in Iquitos. Further democratization, institution-building, and extension of civil rights in Loreto will very much depend on the capacity of its people and leadership to imagine and design new strategies of political participation and economic development that encompass the region as a whole.

Appendixes

Appendix 1   Loreto's Rubber Exports by Species and Qualities, 1886–1913 (in metric tons)

Species & qualities	1886	1889	1892	1895	1898	1900	1901	1903	1904	1908	1909	1910	1911	1912	1913
Hevea brasiliensis															
Fine	143.0	316.0	187.8	155.5	886.0	461.8	791.4	962.8	1066.5	952.9	1120.7	1024.4	1035.5	1303.8	875.6
Entrefine	—	—	—	—	—	296.8	478.1	651.0	746.6	669.6	813.4	742.7	671.8	871.9	613.1
Scrappy	—	—	—	—	—	22.0	44.3	45.3	19.2	—	—	—	93.4	69.8	28.0
Other Heveas	—	—	—	—	—	143.0	269.0	266.5	300.7	283.3	307.3	281.7	270.3	362.1	234.5
Weak fine	—	—	—	—	—	—	4.0	18.1	—	548.3	520.3	442.4	339.6	647.3	614.0
Castilloa	1000.4	675.0	1336.6	857.3	925.0	397.6	577.4	1009.2	1093.9	883.9	881.0	827.5	706.9	863.0	859.9
Slabs	—	—	—	—	—	82.0	60.1	58.0	53.0	32.7	30.4	42.5	38.8	54.7	31.2
Balls	—	—	—	—	—	315.6	517.3	951.2	1040.9	851.2	850.6	785.0	668.1	808.3	828.7
Total volume	1143.4	991.0	1524.4	1012.8	1811.0	859.4	1372.8	1990.1	2160.4	2385.1	2522.0	2294.3	2082.0	2814.1	2349.5

SOURCES: Maúrtua 1911: 147; Mavila 1902: 548; Pennano 1988: 183–4; Bonilla 1974.

Appendix 2   Value of Loreto's Import-Export Trade and Commercial Balance, 1900–1914

		Value in U.S. dollars[a]		
Year	*Imports*	*Exports*	*Imports and Exports*	*Balance*
1900	732,713	1,714,735	2,447,448	982,022
1901	1,060,765	2,561,067	3,621,832	1,500,302
1902	1,254,643	1,898,208	3,152,851	643,565
1903	1,491,420	2,982,845	4,474,265	1,491,425
1904	2,863,751	3,706,700	6,570,451	842,949
1905	2,831,425	4,558,615	7,390,040	1,727,190
1906	3,232,764	5,123,100	8,355,864	1,890,336
1907	4,000,000	3,983,375	7,983,375	− 16,625
1908	1,847,000	2,803,000	4,650,000	956,000
1909	2,387,000	5,148,500	7,535,500	2,761,500
1910	4,518,500	5,588,000	10,106,500	1,069,500
1911	2,275,500	2,553,000	4,828,500	277,500
1912	2,189,000	6,049,500	8,238,500	3,860,500
1913	1,943,500	3,815,000	5,758,500	1,871,500
1914	697,000	1,789,000	2,486,000	1,092,000

SOURCES: Maúrtua 1911: 147, for 1900–1907; Ordeoriente n.d.: 228–34, for 1908–1914.

NOTE: [a] Original figures in *soles* were converted into U.S. dollars according to the average exchange rates presented by Pennano (1988: 110) and Haring (1986a: 192).

Appendix 3   Value of Loreto's Import-Export Trade and Commercial Balance, 1915–1962

Value in U.S. dollars[a]

Year	Imports	Exports	Imports and Exports	Balance
1915	671,845	2,318,447	2,990,292	1,646,602
1916	1,570,388	2,173,783	3,744,171	603,395
1917	2,266,505	2,292,233	4,558,738	25,728
1918	1,179,612	2,121,359	3,300,971	941,747
1919	1,100,000	3,203,883	4,303,883	2,103,883
1920	1,396,117	1,856,311	3,252,428	460,194
1921	458,738	264,078	722,816	– 194,660
1922	419,417	1,120,388	1,539,805	700,971
1923	1,357,281	1,445,631	2,802,912	88,350
1924	1,687,864	1,456,311	3,144,175	– 231,553
1925	2,011,165	2,582,524	4,593,689	571,359
1926	2,296,117	2,104,854	4,400,971	– 191,263
1927	1,364,078	1,627,670	2,991,748	263,592
1928	880,000	732,500	1,618,500	– 147,500
1929	811,500	757,000	1,568,500	– 53,700
1930	1,200,000	920,000	2,120,000	– 280,000
1931	724,234	779,944	1,504,178	55,710
1932	492,611	394,089	886,700	– 98,522
1933	635,514	336,449	971,963	– 299,065
1934	957,684	489,978	1,947,662	– 467,706
1935	1,045,131	593,824	1,638,955	– 451,307
1936	1,047,382	872,818	1,920,200	– 174,564
1937	1,259,843	944,882	2,204,725	– 314,961
1938	1,384,977	633,803	2,018,780	– 751,174
1939	942,699	609,982	1,552,681	– 327,717
1940	762,712	627,119	1,389,831	– 135,593
1941	907,692	646,154	1,553,846	– 261,538
1942	815,385	938,462	1,753,847	123,077
1943	1,015,385	1,107,692	2,123,077	92,307
1944	969,231	2,046,154	3,015,385	1,076,923
1945	1,092,308	2,938,462	4,030,770	1,846,154
1946	1,630,769	3,107,692	4,738,461	1,476,923
1947	1,507,692	3,169,231	4,676,923	1,661,539
1948	1,123,077	1,015,385	2,138,462	– 107,692
1949	423,310	846,619	1,269,929	423,309
1950	849,802	1,640,316	2,490,118	90,514
1951	1,179,183	2,555,995	3,735,178	1,376,812
1952	1,543,408	2,308,682	3,852,082	765,274
1953	1,552,538	2,296,340	3,848,878	743,802
1954	3,306,247	3,605,891	6,912,138	299,644
1955	4,105,263	3,889,474	7,994,737	– 215,789
1956	4,526,316	3,947,368	8,473,684	– 578,948
1957	3,947,368	4,942,105	8,889,473	994,737
1958	3,751,645	4,462,484	8,214,129	710,839

(continues)

Appendix 3   *(continued)*

	Value in U.S. dollars[a]			
Year	Imports	Exports	Imports and Exports	Balance
1959	2,883,703	4,386,867	7,270,570	1,503,164
1960	3,624,161	4,746,458	8,370,619	1,122,297
1961	4,742,729	3,985,831	8,728,560	- 756,898
1962	6,580,910	7,073,080	13,653,990	492,170

SOURCE: Ordeoriente n.d.: 228–34.

NOTE: [a] Original figures in *soles* were converted into U.S. dollars according to the average exchange rates presented by Pennano (1988: 110) and Haring (1986a: 192).

Appendix 4   Value of Loreto's Import-Export Trade and Commercial Balance, 1963–1988

	Value in U.S. dollars[a]			
Year	Imports	Exports	Imports and Exports	Balance
1963	5,425,056	4,172,260	9,597,316	- 1,252,796
1964	8,381,805	4,407,159	12,788,964	- 3,974,646
1965	14,492,915	4,299,031	18,791,946	-10,193,884
1966	29,694,258	4,395,973	34,090,231	-25,298,285
1967	21,580,240	2,677,402	24,257,642	-18,902,838
1968	13,980,649	3,213,545	17,194,194	-10,767,104
1969	10,258,005	3,185,902	13,443,907	- 7,072,103
1970	7,740,152	3,112,186	10,852,338	- 4,627,966
1971	8,900,000	2,500,000	11,400,000	- 6,400,000
1972	19,300,000	3,700,000	23,000,000	-15,600,000
1973	27,300,000	3,800,000	31,100,000	-23,500,000
1974	41,100,000	3,035,614	44,135,614	-38,064,386
1975	42,400,000	nd		
1976	33,500,000	nd		
1977	13,600,000	nd		
1978	nd	nd		
1979	28,700,000	8,900,000	37,600,000	-19,800,000
1980	37,100,000	12,900,000	50,000,000	-24,200,000
1981	48,700,000	13,175,160	61,875,160	-35,524,840
1982	58,200,000	8,440,000	66,640,000	-49,760,000
1983	16,260,790	4,691,464	20,952,254	-11,569,326
1984	17,926,041	3,783,024	21,709,065	-14,143,017
1985	13,285,271	2,547,240	15,382,511	-10,738,031
1986	59,818,707	1,746,625	61,565,332	-58,072,082
1987	48,189,000	1,370,668	49,559,668	-46,818,332
1988	14,102,500	1,357,786	15,460,286	-12,744,714

SOURCES: Ordeoriente n.d.: 228–34, for 1963–1970; Pasquel Ruiz 1989: 412, for 1971–73; Orde-loreto 1978b: 27, for imports 1974–1977; Ordeloreto 1978a: 95, for exports 1974; Perú 1981: 8, for 1979–1980; Banco Amazónico 1982; INE 1988a, for exports 1981–82; INE 1989a: 128–9, for 1984–1988; elaborated by the authors.

NOTE: [a] Original figures in *soles* were converted into U.S. dollars according to the average exchange rates presented by Haring (1986a: 192).

Appendix 5   Main Products Exported Through Iquitos, 1928

Products exported	G.W. (tons)	Value (US$)[a]	Value (%)
Balata	883	152,627	28.5
Cotton	835	151,023	28.2
Coffee	180	40,855	7.6
Ivory nuts	2,617	40,698	7.6
Fine Hevea	207	38,158	7.1
Fine timber[b]	3,649	29,695	5.6
Weak Hevea	121	19,415	3.7
Fine scrappy	99	11,835	2.2
Dessicated animals	1	11,475	2.1
Cotton seeds	1,449	9,535	1.8
Others	264	30,032	5.6
Total	10,305	535,348	100.0

SOURCE: Guzmán Rivera 1929; elaborated by the authors.
G.W. = gross weight
NOTES: [a] Conversion of Peruvian *soles* is based on an average exchange rate of 4.00 soles per U.S. dollar (Haring 1986a: 192).
[b] Mahogany and cedar.

Appendix 6   Main Products Exported Through Iquitos, First Semester 1939

Products exported	G.W. (tons)	Value (US$)[a]	Value (%)
Barbasco	651	113,248	34.9
Cotton	285	58,563	18.1
Furs and hides	149	52,751	16.3
Fine timber	1,828	27,609	8.5
Coffee	389	27,602	8.5
Ivory nuts	747	15,047	4.6
Balata	83	14,421	4.5
Caspi milk	179	8,817	2.7
Hevea	35	3,054	0.9
Cotton seed paste	270	2,728	0.8
Others	1	18	0.0
Total	4,617	323,858	100.0

SOURCE: Guía 1940; elaborated by the authors.
NOTE: [a] Conversion of Peruvian *soles* is based on an average exchange rate of 5.41 soles per U.S. dollar (Haring 1986a: 192).

Appendix 7   Main Products Exported Through Iquitos, 1948

Products exported	G.W. (tons)	Value (US$)[a]	Value (%)
Barbasco roots	1,429	—	—
Barbasco powder	166	398,891[b]	41.0
Washed caspi milk	535	297,210	30.5
Furs and hides	89	—	—
Caiman hides	65	129,108[c]	13.3
Fine timber[d]	2,479	123,951	12.7
Cotton	26	15,740	1.6
Ojé powder	4	5,471	0.6
Laminated balata	7	4,037	0.4
Ivory nuts	141	nd	nd
Others[e]	5	nd	nd
Total	4,946	974,408	100.0

SOURCE: Sotomayor et al. 1949; elaborated by the authors.
NOTES: [a] Conversion of Peruvian *soles* is based on an average exchange rate of 6.50 soles per U.S. dollar (Haring 1986a: 192); value of Loreto's exports has been calculated on the basis of average export prices (in US$) per kilogram provided by SCIPA (1959) for the 1946–50 period.
[b] Joint value of barbasco roots and powder.
[c] Joint value of furs, hides and caiman hides.
[d] Mahogany and cedar.
[e] Additionally Loreto exported 1,145,207 gallons of kerosene and diesel, as well as 106,150 gallons of ethylic gasoline.

Appendix 8   Main Products Exported Through Iquitos, 1955

Products exported	Value (US$)	Value (%)
Rosewood oil	1,022,932	26.3
Caspi milk	536,747	13.8
Coffee	521,190	13.4
Barbasco	420,063	10.8
Furs	361,721	9.3
Cotton	326,716	8.4
Fine timber	241,147	6.2
Oil	210,032	5.4
Others	248,926	6.4
Total	3,889,474	100.0

SOURCE: Ordeoriente n.d.: 238.

Appendix 9   Main Products Exported Through Iquitos, 1962

Products exported	Value (US$)	Value (%)
Caspi milk	2,941,834	41.6
Oil	1,733,781	24.5
Coffee	462,342	6.5
Cotton	439,970	6.2
Rosewood oil	313,199	4.4
Furs	302,013	4.3
Fine timber	257,271	3.6
Barbasco	96,943	1.4
Others	525,727	7.5
Total	7,073,080	100.0

SOURCE: Ordeoriente n.d.: 238.

Appendix 10   Main Products Exported Through Iquitos, 1969

Products exported	Value (US$)	Value (%)
Timber	668,049	20.9
Coffee	550,564	17.3
Oil	522,921	16.4
Ornamental fish	317,899	10.0
Cotton	228,058	7.2
Caspi milk	202,718	6.4
Furs	191,200	6.0
Rosewood oil	119,788	3.8
Barbasco	46,072	1.4
Others	338,632	10.6
Total	3,185,901	100.0

SOURCE: Ordeoriente n.d.: 238.

Appendix 11   Main Products Exported Through Iquitos, 1974

Products exported	Value (US$)[a]	Value (%)
Timber	1,766,327	58.3
Furs	398,052	13.1
Ornamental fish	353,574	11.6
Rosewood oil	248,908	8.2
Palmito	108,732	3.6
Barbasco powder	85,900	2.8
Cotton	56,249	1.9
Ornamental plants	6,600	0.2
Ojé powder	6,400	0.2
Live animals	3,965	0.1
Others	907	0.0
Total	3,035,614	100.0

SOURCE: Ordeloreto 1978a: 95.
NOTE: [a] Figures refer to expected exports according to export permits granted and not necessarily to actual exports.

Appendix 12   Main Products Exported Through Iquitos, 1981

Products exported	Value (US$ FOB)	Value (%)
Timber and paper	10,895,270	82.7
Textiles[a]	1,019,844	7.8
Ornamental fish	667,369	5.1
Handicrafts	502,002	3.8
Rosewood oil	44,620	0.3
Ojé powder	18,842	0.1
Barbasco powder	14,710	0.1
Aquatic plants	12,512	0.1
Total	13,175,169	100.0

SOURCE: INE 1988a: 188–89.
NOTE: [a] It probably refers to textiles being re-exported.

Appendix 13   Main Products Exported Through Iquitos, 1986

Products exported	Value (US$ FOB)	Value (%)
Timber and paper	1,164,283	66.7
Ornamental fish	317,858	18.2
Metal work	23,298	1.3
Barbasco powder	21,703	1.2
Ojé powder	10,587	0.6
Aquatic plants	500	0.0
Other agroforestry products	207,005	11.9
Others	1,291	0.1
Total	1,746,625	100.0

SOURCE: INE 1988a: 188–9.

Appendix 14   Loreto's Ivory Nut Exports, 1903–1948

Year	Exports (tons)	Value (US$)[a]
1903	54	nd
1904	128	nd
1906	27	nd
1907	0.3	nd
1908	4	nd
1910	9	nd
1911	450	nd
1912	1,186	nd
1913	3,588	139,340
1914	2,816	nd
1923	1,770	nd
1925	5,889	nd
1928	2,617	40,698
1930	1,167	23,340
1939[b]	1,494	30,094
1940	1,303	66,254
1945	500	nd
1948	141	nd

SOURCES: Bonilla 1976: III; Villarejo 1988: 136; Extracto 1924; Appendixes 5–7.
NOTES: [a] Conversion of Peruvian currency into U.S. dollars is based on average exchange rates provided by Haring (1986a: 192).
[b] The original 1939 figure referred to volume exported during the first semester; we have doubled it to obtain an approximate figure of that year's exports.

Appendix 15   Loreto's Cotton Exports, 1910–1974

Year	Exports (tons)	Value (US$)[a]
1910	0.1	nd
1911	0.1	nd
1919	2,345	nd
1925	1,626	nd
1928	835	150,102
1935	751	nd
1939[b]	570	117,126
1945	160	nd
1948	26	15,740
1949[c]	13	nd
1950	nd	19,763
1955	nd	326,316
1960	1,112	111,857
1961	nd	145,414
1962	nd	439,970
1963	nd	156,600
1964	nd	104,400
1965	nd	55,928
1966	nd	171,514
1967	nd	13,646
1968	nd	66,805
1969	nd	228,058
1970	nd	292,559
1974	nd	56,249

SOURCES: Bonilla 1976: III; Villarejo 1988: 136; Ordeoriente n.d.: 238; Appendixes 5–7, 9–11.

NOTES: [a] Conversion of Peruvian currency into U.S. dollars is based on average exchange rates provided by Haring (1986a: 192).

[b] The original 1939 figure referred to volume exported during the first semester; we have doubled it to obtain an approximate figure of that year's exports.

[c] Loreto's cotton boom ended in 1949 when exports of this product decreased to an insignificant thirteen tons. In subsequent years most of the cotton exported through Iquitos was produced in San Martín.

Appendix 16   Loreto's Fine Timber Exports, 1912–1962

Year	Exports (tons)[a]	Value (US$)[b]
1912	4	nd
1913	103	nd
1914	290	nd
1923	3,644	nd
1925	8,650	nd
1928	3,649	29,695
1930	6,572	nd
1935	18,508	nd
1939[c]	3,655	54,138
1940	16,993	nd
1946	9,110	45,958
1948	2,479	129,108
1949	21,937	nd
1955	nd	241,147
1960	3,862	278,747
1962	nd	257,271

SOURCES: Bonilla 1976: III; Villarejo 1988: 134; Appendixes 5–7.
NOTES: [a] Original figures in square feet have been converted into tons on the basis of the equivalence of 1.7 kg per square foot of hardwoods suggested by Watson (1964: 79).
   [b] Conversion of Peruvian currency into U.S. dollars is based on average exchange rates provided by Haring (1986a: 192).
   [c] The original 1939 figure refered to volume exported during the first semester; we have doubled it to obtain an approximate figure of that year's exports.

Appendix 17   Loreto's Balata Exports, 1925–1948

Year	Exports (tons)	Value (US$)[a]
1925	1,545	513,713
1926	2,138	764,335
1927	743	92,875
1928	883	152,627
1930	614	nd
1939[b]	166	28,842
1940	133	nd
1948	7	4,037

SOURCES: Guzmán Rivera 1929: 130; Villarejo 1988: 136; Appendixes 5–7.
NOTES: [a] Conversion of Peruvian currency into U.S. dollars is based on average exchange rates provided by Haring (1986a: 192).
   [b] The original 1939 figure referred to volume exported during the first semester; we have doubled it to obtain an approximate figure of that year's exports.

Appendix 18   Loreto's Coffee Exports, 1925–1974

Year	Exports (tons)	Value (US$)[a]
1925	30	nd
1928	180	40,855
1930	189	nd
1935	700	nd
1939	778	55,204
1946	136	nd
1948[b]	ne	ne
1950	nd	592,885
1955	nd	521,190
1960	803	604,027
1961	nd	480,984
1962	nd	462,342
1963	773	423,409
1964	nd	861,298
1965	nd	648,770
1966	nd	641,312
1967	nd	390,284
1968	nd	854,642
1969	nd	550,564
1970	nd	393,918
1974	ne	ne

SOURCES: Haring 1986a: 36; Watson 1964: 67; Ordeoriente n.d.: 238; Appendixes 5–7.

NOTES: [a] Conversion of Peruvian currency into U.S. dollars is based on average exchange rates provided by Haring (1986a: 192).

[b] Loreto's coffee boom ended in 1948 when no exports of this product were registered. In subsequent years most of the coffee exported through Iquitos was produced in San Martín and commercialized through agents of Lima-based coffee export houses.

Appendix 19   Loreto's Caspi Milk Exports, 1928–1970

Year	Exports (tons)	Value (US$)[a]
1928	13	1,293
1935	365	17,179
1939[b]	358	17,634
1948	535	297,210
1950	nd	138,340
1955	nd	536,842
1956[c]	697	611,000
1957	951	918,400
1958	1,181	940,100
1959	1,047	808,497
1960	914	706,252
1961	1,148	1,121,871
1962	nd	2,941,834
1963	814	358,300
1964	nd	242,356
1965	nd	316,928
1966	nd	320,356
1967	nd	305,677
1968	nd	264,916
1969	nd	202,718
1970	nd	41,465

SOURCES: Guzmán Rivera 1929; Ríos Zañartu 1995: 128; SCIPA 1959: 32; CONETSCAR 1964: 165; Ordeoriente n.d.: 238; Appendixes 6, 7, 9, 10.

NOTES: [a] Conversion of Peruvian currency into U.S. dollars is based on average exchange rates provided by Haring (1986a: 192).

[b] The original 1939 figure referred to volume exported during the first semester; we have doubled it to obtain an approximate figure of that year's exports.

[c] Figures provided by SCIPA for 1956–58 and by CONETSCAR for 1959–61 and for 1963 refer to Peru's exports; however, as most caspi milk was produced by Loreto, we assume them to be almost equivalent to Loreto's exports.

Appendix 20 Loreto's Barbasco Exports, 1931–1986

Year	Exports (tons)	Value (US$)[a]
1931	1	71
1932	9	488
1933	14	1,133
1934	245	22,154
1935	438	61,070
1936	359	222,920
1937	394	197,000
1939	1,105	198,891
1940	1,208	nd
1946	5,459	nd
1948	1,596	398,891
1949	3,132	nd
1950	nd	289,855
1955	nd	420,063
1960	1,221	237,808
1961	nd	141,685
1962	nd	96,943
1963	nd	156,600
1964	nd	70,843
1965	nd	193,885
1966	nd	167,785
1967	nd	95,524
1968	nd	59,894
1969	nd	46,072
1970	nd	39,161
1974	nd	85,900
1981	31	14,710
1982	nd	35,058
1983	nd	18,532
1984	nd	11,029
1985	nd	21,786
1986	nd	21,703

SOURCES: Villarejo 1988: 137; Wille et al. 1939: 111; Delboy 1952: 17; Agricultura n.d.; Ordeoriente n.d.: 238; INE 1988a: 188; Appendixes 7, 9–13.

NOTES: [a] Conversion of Peruvian currency into U.S. dollars is based on average exchange rates provided by Haring (1986a: 192).

Appendix 21 Loreto's Fur and Hide Exports, 1935–1974

Year	Exports (units)	Value (US$)[a]
1935	73,045	nd
1939[b]	—	105,502
1940	171,723	nd
1946[c]	497,741	1,127,231
1947	—	473,076
1948	—	129,108
1949	—	223,452
1950	152,992	273,979
1951	120,688	294,796
1952	88,449	145,520
1953	118,382	217,119
1954	178,008	271,789
1955	nd	361,721
1956	221,000	395,211
1960	238,749	432,513
1961	nd	354,213
1962	nd	302,013
1963	235,514	610,179
1964	nd	290,828
1965	nd	186,428
1966	324,556	648,253
1967	266,565	420,643
1968	251,223	422,608
1969	272,447	453,078
1970	nd	555,172
1973	nd	542,072
1974	nd	398,052

SOURCES: Haring 1986a: 36; Piazza 1952: 32; Córdova 1958: 46; Watson 1964: 12; Ordeoriente n.d.: 238; BCR 1974; Appendixes 6, 7, 9–11.

NOTES: [a] Conversion of Peruvian currency into U.S. dollars is based on average exchange rates provided by Haring (1986a: 192).

[b] The original 1939 figure referred to volume exported during the first semester; we have doubled it to obtain an approximate figure of that year's exports.

[c] Figures for 1946–1956 refer to Peru's exports; as most furs and hides were produced by Loreto, we assume Peru's figures to be almost equivalent to Loreto's exports.

Appendix 22   Loreto's Rosewood Oil Exports, 1952–1983

Year	Exports (tons)	Value (US$)[a]
1952	13	127,439
1955[b]	158	1,120,541
1956	228	1,169,800
1957	159	777,200
1958	262	878,000
1959	205	638,006
1960	112	376,792
1961	172	492,867
1962	nd	313,199
1963	nd	402,685
1964	nd	372,856
1965	nd	290,828
1966	nd	178,971
1967	55	198,051
1968	nd	149,735
1969	nd	119,788
1970	nd	29,947
1974	nd	248,908
1981	3	44,620
1982	nd	35,096
1983	nd	41,904

SOURCES: SCIPA 1959: 31; Watson 1964: 16; Villarejo 1988: 137; Ordeoriente n.d.: 238; Cordelor 1982: 200; INE 1988a: 188; Appendixes 9–12.

NOTES: [a] Conversion of Peruvian currency into U.S. dollars is based on average exchange rates provided by Haring (1986a: 192).

[b] Figures for 1955–1958 refer to Peru's exports; however, as most rosewood oil was produced by Loreto, we assume them to be almost equivalent to Loreto's exports.

Appendix 23   Loreto's Ornamental Fish Exports, 1954–1986

Year	Exports (units)	Value (US$)[a]
1954	450,000	nd
1955	1,230,000	nd
1956	2,428,000	nd
1957	2,083,000	nd
1958	2,779,000	nd
1959	2,880,000	nd
1960	5,189,000	nd
1961	4,978,000	199,100
1962	5,054,000	nd
1963	4,807,000	nd
1964	6,303,000	nd
1965	4,356,000	217,800
1966	8,164,000	408,200
1967	11,947,000	597,300
1968	12,229,000	489,100
1969	11,934,000	358,000
1970	14,587,000	437,600
1973	15,093,489	352,049
1974	nd	353,574
1975	15,405,400	511,920
1976	20,151,900	920,815
1977	19,908,400	940,017
1980	8,234,771	624,911
1981	8,698,193	682,171
1982	nd	649,694
1983	7,233,946	641,709
1984	nd	583,265
1985	nd	364,810
1986	nd	317,858

SOURCES: Agricultura n.d.; San Román 1974: II, 114; BCR 1974; Cordelor 1982: 249, 265; INP 1984: 20; INE 1988a: 188; Ríos Zañartu 1995: 167; Appendixes 10–13.
NOTES: [a] Conversion of Peruvian currency into U.S. dollars is based on average exchange rates provided by Haring (1986a: 192).

Appendix 24   Loreto's Live Animal Exports, 1963–1973

Year	Exports (units)	Value (US$)[a]
1963	40,223	103,400
1964	39,522	115,896
1965	32,799	78,769
1966	30,896	73,134
1967	53,452	68,760
1968	120,821	112,808
1973	nd	105,373

SOURCES: Rumrrill 1973: 110; Agricultura n.d.; BCR 1974.
NOTES: [a] Conversion of Peruvian currency into U.S. dollars is based on average exchange rates provided by Haring (1986a: 192).

Appendix 25   Loreto's Rice Production, 1936–1997

Year	Production (tons)[a]
1936	2,283
1937	1,740
1939	867
1941	151
1942	572
1948	1,261
1951	994
1952	1,739
1954	2,130
1963	14,480
1964	13,300
1965	10,230
1966	20,116
1967	23,217
1968	29,545
1970	36,000
1971	36,764
1972	25,400
1973	23,496
1974	19,320
1975	19,440
1976	21,501
1977	38,369
1978	36,164
1979	51,842
1980[b]	51,475
1981	54,447
1982	61,776
1983	51,347
1984	48,550
1985	44,000
1986	39,396
1987	44,600
1988	40,184
1989	50,807
1990	34,909
1991	38,097
1992	36,528
1993	47,012
1994	56,128
1995	45,487
1996	47,100
1997	56,100

SOURCES: Extracto 1936–1954; CONETSCAR 1964–1969; INEI 1990a; INEI 1996a; INEI 1998a.
NOTES: [a] Refers to rice in hull.
   [b] From 1980 onward figures do not include the production of the newly created department of Ucayali.

Appendix 26   Loreto's Sawn Wood Production by Area, 1941–1997

	Production in cubic meters[a]		
Year	Iquitos	Pucallpa	Total
1941	11,562	—	11,562
1942	8,291	—	8,291
1943	12,687	—	12,687
1944	9,211	906	10,117
1945	2,480	3,335	5,815
1946	10,382	6,131	16,513
1947	12,388	9,053	21,441
1948	22,337	11,965	34,302
1949	18,623	11,566	30,189
1950	15,649	14,925	30,574
1951	27,485	17,053	44,538
1952	25,764	26,519	52,283
1953	19,597	25,816	45,413
1954	20,282	27,621	47,903
1955	16,935	33,595	50,530
1956	17,832	34,277	52,109
1957	16,090	37,996	54,086
1958	12,584	30,715	43,299
1959	7,594	37,611	45,205
1960	14,597	41,000	55,597
1961	14,597	40,120	54,717
1962	19,156	46,131	65,287
1963	18,486	41,248	59,734
1964	31,582	44,989	76,571
1965	31,747	58,070	89,817
1966	48,512	61,513	110,025
1967	37,876	50,653	88,529
1968	40,606	46,228	86,834
1969	38,411	48,965	87,376
1970	27,501	50,339	77,840
1971	34,449	56,718	91,167
1972	36,512	52,812	89,324
1973	33,949	64,331	98,280
1974	106,196	59,249	165,445
1975	nd	72,000	nd
1976	77,415	155,569	232,984
1977	33,448	76,856	110,304
1978	27,990	78,116	106,106
1979	40,294	141,759	182,503
1980	31,336	145,405	176,741
1981	39,986	147,994	187,980

(continues)

Appendix 26   *(continued)*

	Production in cubic meters[a]		
Year	Iquitos	Pucallpa	Total
1982	33,281	144,926	178,207
1983	21,320	121,445	142,765
1984	30,398	147,315	177,713
1985	19,041	229,982	249,023
1986	40,522	201,948	242,470
1987	39,895	198,578	238,473
1988	40,172	232,843	273,015
1989	40,583	167,307	207,890
1990	24,761	nd	nd
1996	71,500	280,708	352,208
1997	111,070	441,821	552,891

SOURCES: Anuario 1954: 155; Banco de Crédito 1972: Cuadro 23; Ordeloreto 1979; INEI 1990a: 66; INEI 1990b: 52; INEI 1998a; INEI 1998b.
NOTES: [a] Original figures in square feet were converted: 1,000 sq. ft = 2.36 m³.

Appendix 27   Percentage Distribution of Loreto's Timber Industrial Production by Type of Product, 1964–1997

| | Percentage distribution | | |
Year	Laminated[a]	Sawn wood[b]	Total (m³)
1964	7.7	92.3	82,900
1965	12.1	87.9	102,200
1966	13.9	86.1	127,700
1967	15.8	84.2	105,100
1968	20.4	79.6	109,100
1969	21.8	78.2	111,800
1970	31.1	68.9	112,900
1976	11.7	88.3	263,800
1977	35.4	64.6	170,700
1979	26.9	73.1	249,800
1980[c]	68.1	31.9	88,600
1981	62.0	38.0	90,600
1982	58.5	41.5	64,600
1983	63.8	36.2	45,300
1984	54.8	45.2	49,800
1985	60.2	39.8	36,900
1986	45.8	54.2	57,400
1987	45.0	55.0	59,400
1988	48.4	51.6	59,900
1996	26.4	73.6	97,162
1997	33.1	66.9	166,109

Sources: Banco Amazónico 1976; Agricultura 1975: 97–98; Ordeloreto 1981: 79–80; INE 1988a: 124–5; INE 1989a: 92.
Notes: [a] Laminated wood includes plywood and veneers.
  [b] Figures of total sawn wood production vary in some cases from those presented in Appendix 26 because they are based in different sources.
  [c] Figures for 1980 onward exclude the production of Ucayali.

Appendix 28   Loreto's Oil Production, 1939–1997 (in thousands of barrels)

Year	Production
1939	10
1943	8
1945	65
1946	89
1947	117
1948	121

(continues)

Appendix 28   *(continued)*

Year	Production
1949	140
1950	149
1951	169
1952	200
1956	403
1957	780
1958	712
1959	859
1960	1,014
1961	993
1962	1,352
1963	1,260
1964	1,254
1965	1,252
1966	1,123
1967	1,178
1968	1,013
1969	1,026
1973	606
1974	899
1975	2,994
1976	4,315
1977	10,894
1978	33,407
1979	47,066
1980	46,634
1981	45,292
1982	45,342
1983	43,011
1984	44,905
1985	45,071
1986	41,809
1987	38,309
1988	32,533
1989	29,990
1990	29,483
1991	26,452
1992	27,818
1993	29,786
1994	30,659
1995	29,300
1996	28,971
1997	27,968

SOURCES: Extracto 1939; Anuario 1943–1969; Valcárcel 1991: 191; INEI 1998a.

Appendix 29   Percentage Distribution of Loreto's Import Trade According to Economic
Use of Imports, 1960–1986

| | *Percentage distribution* | | | | | |
Year	*Consumer goods*[a]	*Capital goods*[b]	*Raw materials*[c]	*Other*	*Total*	*Value*[d] *(US$M)*[e]
1960	50.3	31.9	9.3	8.5	100	3.4
1961	38.7	35.7	20.7	4.9	100	4.6
1962	38.3	22.3	32.1	7.3	100	5.5
1963	43.6	31.7	16.2	8.5	100	4.9
1964	50.0	28.7	11.8	9.5	100	5.9
1965	65.4	19.3	14.9	0.4	100	12.9
1966	45.3	42.7	11.8	0.2	100	25.5
1967	52.4	28.7	16.3	2.6	100	18.6
1968	56.0	23.9	18.9	1.2	100	11.1
1969	55.8	29.7	12.8	1.7	100	8.9
1970	43.7	21.2	17.5	17.6	100	7.5
1979	13.1	83.7	2.7	0.5	100	28.8
1980	46.0	46.0	7.1	0.9	100	37.7
1981	35.4	54.8	8.2	1.6	100	8.7
1982	31.0	45.0	21.6	2.4	100	58.2
1983	31.7	64.5	3.7	0.1	100	16.3
1984	49.3	48.7	2.0	0.0	100	17.9
1985	34.5	61.7	3.8	0.0	100	13.3
1986	15.4	73.7	10.9	0.0	100	59.8

SOURCES: Ordeoriente n.d.: 237–9; Cordelor 1982: 313; Banco Amazónico 1982; INE 1988a: 191.
NOTES: [a] Consumer goods = durable and non-durable.
   [b] Capital goods = agricultural, industrial, construction materials, transport equipment.
   [c] Raw materials and intermediate goods = agricultural, industrial, fuels, lubricants.
   [d] Absolute figures differ in some cases from those in Appendixes 3–4 because they are based on different sources.
   [e] Original figures in *soles* were converted into U.S. dollars according to the average exchange rates presented by Haring (1986a: 192) and Cuánto (1993).

Appendix 30   Urban and Rural Populations, 1940–1993

	Loreto			Ucayali		
Year	% Urban	% Rural	Total	% Urban	% Rural	Total
1940	31.9	68.1	158,597	41.0	59.0	10,014
1961	36.8	63.2	272,933	46.3	53.7	64,161
1972	47.8	52.2	375,007	56.2	43.8	120,501
1981	51.9	48.1	483,685	64.7	35.3	162,726
1993	59.3	40.7	798,646	66.8	33.2	366,912

SOURCES: Rodríguez Achung 1991; INEI 1996a, 1996b.

Appendix 31   Populations of Major Urban Centers, 1913–1993

Year	Iquitos	Pucallpa	Yurimaguas	Requena	Contamana
1913	12,498	nd	nd	nd	nd
1928	22,575	nd	nd	nd	nd
1940	31,828	2,368	5,503	1,774	2,860
1961	57,777	26,391	11,655	3,931	4,708
1972	110,242	57,095	17,268	7,285	5,056
1981	173,629	97,925	21,966	7,861	5,378
1993	274,759	172,286	30,658	14,954	10,177

SOURCES: Rodríguez Achung 1991; INEI 1996d.

Reference List

Agricultura. (Ministerio de Agricultura). n.d. Diagnóstico de la Región Oriente. Iquitos.
_____. 1969. Memoria Anual, 1969. Zona Agraria VIII. Iquitos.
_____. 1975. Memorial Bienal, 1973–1974. Zona Agraria VIII. Iquitos.
_____. 1989. Memoria Anual, 1989. Zona Agraria VIII. Iquitos.
_____. 1990. Libro de Registro de Certificados de Posesión. Ministerio de Agricultura/Reforma Agraria. Pucallpa.
AIDESEP. 1981. "Manifiesto de los Indígenas Amazónicos del Perú ante la Primera Reunión Amazónica de Asuntos Indígenas." *Shupihui*, 20: 639–642.
_____. 1992. *Directorio de Comunidades Nativas: Región Loreto*. Oficina Regional. Iquitos: Asociación Interétnica de Desarrollo de la Selva Peruana.
Albornoz, Mariano M. 1885. "Breves Apuntes sobre las Regiones Amazónicas por el Presidente de la Sociedad 'Obreros del Porvenir de Amazonas', Doctor don . . . ." In C. Larrabure i Correa, *op. cit.*, Vol. VII: 386–427.
Alemani, Agustín. 1904. "Viaje al Alto Ucayali por el P. . . . , de la Prefectura Apostólica de San Francisco del Ucayali." In C. Larrabure i Correa, *op. cit.*, Vol. IV: 259–263.
Almirón, Víctor M. 1905. "Resumen de las Exploraciones que del Año 1896 a 1902 Practicó en los Ríos Ituxi, Curuquetá i Alto Purús el Señor Don . . . ." In C. Larrabure i Correa, *op. cit.*, Vol. IV: 369–380.
Alvarez Rodrich, Augusto. 1995. "Del Estado Empresario al Estado Regulador." In Julio Cotler (ed.) *Perú, 1964–1994. Economía, Sociedad y Política*, pp. 69–91. Lima: Instituto de Estudios Peruanos.
Amazonas. 1990. Memoria Anual, 1990. Dirección de Recursos Naturales y Medio Ambiente. Iquitos: Región Amazonas.
Anonymous. 1938. *Hombres del Amazonas*. Iquitos: Empresa de Publicidad Oriente.
_____. 1941. "Noticias." *La Vida Agrícola*, 18(215): 809.
_____. 1944a. "La Rehabilitación de la Industria Extractiva de Gomales." *Colonias y Foresta*, 1(1): 37–41.
_____. 1944b. "Notas." *La Vida Agrícola*, 21(249): 632.
_____. 1944c. "El Barbasco en Nuestro Oriente." *La Vida Agrícola*, 21(250): 733–738.
_____. 1945. "Explotación de Productos Naturales de la Selva." *La Vida Agrícola*, 22(256): 287.
_____. 1955. "La Industria del Palo de Rosa." *Colonias y Foresta*, 6(12): 6–7.
_____. 1974. "Velasco Entrevistado." *Participación*, 3(5): 82.
_____. 1988. "Algunos Levantamientos de la Historia de Loreto." *Kanatari*, 200: 25; 6/17/1988.
_____. 1990. "Comunidad Campesina Protege sus Cochas." *Kanatari*, 304: 3–10; 7/15/1990.
_____. 1992. "Los que Hicieron Posible Loreto." *Kanatari*, 400: 4–11; 5/17/1992.

———. 1993a. "La Liga y La Cueva. Los Escándalos del Putumayo. (Versiones de Jorge Basadre)." *Kanatari*, 450: 16–25; 5/2/1993.

———. 1993b. "La Historia de Saqueos Continúa." *Kanatari*, 453: 6–8; 5/23/1993.

Anuario. 1944–1978. *Anuario Estadístico del Perú*. Lima: Dirección Nacional de Estadística-Oficina Nacional de Estadística y Censos.

Arana, Julio C. 1913. *Las Cuestiones del Putumayo: Declaraciones Prestadas ante el Comité de la Cámara de los Comunes y Debidamente Anotada*. Barcelona: Imprenta Viuda de Luis Tasso.

Armadores. (Asociación de Armadores de Loreto). 1990. Directorio de Empresas Asociadas. Iquitos.

Atarama, Aldo. 1992. *De Nativos a Ribereños: Un Recorrido a lo Largo de su Historia Comunal*. Lima: Servicio Holandés de Cooperación Técnica.

Ballón. Francisco. 1991. *La Amazonía en la Norma Oficial Peruana, 1821–1990*. Lima: Centro de Investigación y Promoción Amazónica (4 vols.)

BA (Banco Agrícola). 1942–1952. *Memorias Anuales*. Lima.

Banco Amazónico. 1962–1989. *Memorias Anuales*. Iquitos.

Banco de Crédito. 1972. *Realidad, Perspectivas y Problemas de la Selva Peruana: Mesa Redonda*. Lima: Banco de Crédito del Perú.

BAP (Banco Agrario del Perú). 1970–1987. *Memorias Anuales*. Lima.

Barandiarán, Carlos. 1890. "Informe Presentado á la Comisión Especial al Departamento de Loreto, por el Capitán del Puerto de Iquitos, Don . . . ." In C. Larrabure i Correa, *op. cit.*, VII: 428–441.

Barba López, Aura Teresa. 1990. "Colonización Dirigida y Espontánea en la Región Integrada del Departamento de Santa Cruz-Bolivia." In Claudio M. Flores and Thomas A. Mitschein (org.), *Realidades Amazónicas no Fim do Século XX*, pp. 213–264. Serie Cooperação Amazónica: . Belém: Associacão do Universidades Amazónicas/Universidad Federal do Pará.

Barclay, F. 1989. *La Colonia del Perené: Capital Inglés y Economía Cafetalera en la Configuración de la Región de Chanchamayo*. Iquitos: Centro de Estudios Teológicos de la Amazonía.

———. 1991. "Protagonismo del Estado en el Proceso de Incorporación de la Amazonía." In Barclay et al., *op. cit.*: 43–100.

———. 1993. "La Evolución del Espacio Rural en la Amazonía Nororiental del Perú." In Lucy Ruiz (coord.), *Amazonía: Escenarios y Conflictos*, pp. 95–146. Quito: Centro de Investigación de los Movimientos Sociales del Ecuador/Abya Yala/Facultad Latinoamericana de Ciencias Sociales-Sede Ecuador.

———. 1995. "Transformaciones en el Espacio Rural Loretano tras el Período Cauchero." In Pilar García Jordán (coord.), *La Construcción de la Amazonía Andina (Siglos XIX–XX)*, pp. 231–280. Quito: Abya-Yala.

———. 1998. "Sociedad y Economía en el Espacio Cauchero Ecuatoriano de la Cuenca del Río Napo, 1870–1930." In Pilar García Jordán (ed.), *Fronteras, Colonización y Mano de Obra Indígena en la Amazonía Andina*, pp. 125–238. Lima: Fondo Editorial Pontificia Universidad Católica del Perú.

Barclay, Frederica, and Fernando Santos-Granero. 1991. "La Situación General de la Niñez en la Amazonía." In *Medio Ambiente Amazónico y Niñez*. Lima: UNICEF/Gobierno Regional de Loreto.

Barclay, Frederica, Martha Rodríguez Achung, Fernando Santos-Granero, and Marcel Valcárcel. 1991. *Amazonía, 1940–1990: El Extravío de una Ilusión*. Lima: Centro de Investigaciones Sociológicas, Económicas, Políticas y Antropológicas/Terra Nuova.

Bardella, Gianfranco. 1989. *Un Siglo en la Vida Económica del Perú, 1889–1989*. Lima: Banco de Crédito.

Barham, Bradford L., and Oliver T. Coomes. 1994a. "Reinterpreting the Amazon Rubber Boom: Investment, the State, and Dutch Disease." *Latin American Research Review*, 29(2): 73–109.

_____. 1994b. "Wild Rubber: Industrial Organization and the Microeconimics of Extraction during the Amazon Rubber Boom (1860–1920)." *Journal of Latin American Studies*, 26: 37–72.

_____. 1996. *Prosperity's Promise: The Amazon Rubber Boom and Distorted Economic Development*. Dellplain Latin American Studies, No. 34. Boulder: Westview Press.

Barletti, José. 1985. *Loreto y las Elecciones*. Iquitos: Centro Cultural Francisco Izquierdo Ríos.

_____. 1993. "El Movimiento Federalista de Loreto de 1896." *Kanatari*, 450: 4–22; 5/2/1993.

_____. 1994. "Luchas Autonómicas Anticentralistas." *Kanatari*, 500: 9–11; 4/17/1994.

BCR (Banco Central de Reserva). 1974. *Boletín Estadístico*, 1. Iquitos.

_____. 1992–1993. Informes Trimestrales. Iquitos.

Belaúnde, L. Elvira. 1992. Gender, Commensality, and Community among the Airo-Pai of Western Amazonia. Ph.D. Dissertation. London School of Economics and Political Science.

Belaúnde, Fernando. 1994 [1959]. *La Conquista del Perú por los Peruanos*. Lima: Studium.

Bellier, Irène. 1991. *El Temblor y la Luna: Ensayo sobre las Relaciones entre las Mujeres y los Hombres Mai Huna*, T. 1. Quito: Abya-Yala.

_____. 1994. "Los Mai Huna." In F. Santos-Granero and F. Barclay (eds.), *op. cit.*, pp. 1–179.

Benalcázar, César A. 1992. *Ecuador y sus Fronteras*. Quito.

Bendayán, Teddy R. 1993. "Guillermo Cervantes Vásquez y la Amazonía." *Kanatari*, 450: 6–26; 5/2/1993.

BFA. (Banco de Fomento Agropecuario). 1944–1970. *Memorias Anuales*. Lima.

Bodley, John H. 1973. "Deferred Exchange Among the Campa Indians." *Anthropos*, 68: 589–596.

Bonilla, Heraclio. 1974. "El Caucho y la Economía del Oriente Peruano." *Historia y Cultura*, 8: 69–80.

_____. 1993. "Estructura y Eslabonamientos de la Explotación Cauchera en Colombia, Perú, Bolivia y Brasil." *Data-Revista de Estudios Andinos y Amazónicos*, 4: 9–22.

_____. 1994. *Guano y Burguesía en el Perú: El Contraste de la Experiencia Peruana con las Economías de Exportación del Ecuador y Bolivia*. Quito: Facultad Latinoamericana de Ciencias Sociales–Sede Ecuador.

Bonilla, Heraclio (comp.) 1976. *Gran Bretaña y el Perú, 1826–1919: Informes de los Cónsules Británicos*. Lima: Instituto de Estudios Peruanos/Fondo del Libro del Banco Industrial del Perú. (3 vols.)

Bravo, César. 1955. "Informe sobre las Escuelas Bilingües y la Obra del Instituto Lingüístico." In *Dos Lustros entre los Selvícolas (1945–1955)*, pp. 72–76. Lima: Instituto Lingüístico de Verano.

Brown, David. 1912. "Informe sobre el Comercio de Iquitos Correspondiente al año 1912." In H. Bonilla (comp.), *op. cit.*, Vol. III: 247–56.

Bunker, Stephen. 1984. "Modes of Extraction, Unequal Exchange, and the Progressive Underdevelopment of an Extreme Periphery: The Brazilian Amazon, 1600–1980." *American Journal of Sociology*, 89(5): 1017–1064.

———. 1985. *Underdeveloping the Amazon: Extraction, Unequal Exchange, and the Failure of Modern State.* Chicago: University of Illinois Press.

Burga Freitas, Arturo. 1941. *Ayahuasca: Mitos y Leyendas del Amazonas.* Lima.

Bustamante, Teodoro. 1991. "Sobre Conflictos, Victorias y Derrotas." In M. Restrepo et al., *op. cit.*, pp. 89–98.

Butt, Gualterio R. 1873. "Exploración de los Ríos Nanai, Itaya, Morona, Pastaza i Tigre por el Segundo Ayudante de la Comisión Hidrográfica del Amazonas. Parte del Ayudante . . . ." In C. Larrabure i Correa, *op. cit.*, Vol. III: 103–9.

Caenazzo, Mara. 1986. "La Población de Pucallpa." *Shupihui*, 37: 29–71.

Caller, Vladimir. 1974. Informe sobre Inversiones Extranjeras en la Región. Iquitos: Instituto Nacional de Planificación.

Calvo, César. 1963. *Paiche: Novela Amazónica.* Arequipa.

Cámara. (Cámara de Comercio, Industrias y Turismo de Loreto). 1990. Boletín Informativo. Iquitos.

———. 1991. Directorio Industrial. Iquitos.

Cannock, Geoffrey, and Víctor Cuadra. 1990. "Políticas de Ajuste Económico y Producción Agrícola en la Selva." *Debate Agrario*, 9: 43–67.

Cano, Ginette et al. 1981. *Los Nuevos Conquistadores: El Instituto Lingüístico de Verano en América Latina.* Quito: CEDIS/FENOC.

Capelo, Joaquín. 1900. *Razón General de Precios y Datos Comerciales de la Plaza de Iquitos (Febrero de 1900).* Lima: Imprenta de la Escuela de Ingenieros-J. Mesinas.

Caravedo, Baltazar. 1981. "El Debate Nacional sobre el Descentralismo, 1930–1980." In Carlos Amat y León and Luis Belaúnde (eds.), *Lecturas sobre Regionalización.* Lima: Universidad del Pacífico.

Casagrande, Joseph B., Stephen I. Thompson, and Philip D. Young. 1964. "Colonization as a Research Frontier: The Ecuadorian Case." In R.A. Manners (ed.), *Process and Pattern in Culture: Essays in Honor of Julian H. Steward*, pp. 281–325. Chicago: Aldine Publishing Co.

Casement, Roger. 1988. *Putumayo Caucho y Sangre: Relación al Parlamento Inglés (1911).* Quito: Abya-Yala.

Castre, Emilio. 1906. "El Departamento de San Martín y Nuestras Regiones Orientales." *Boletín de la Sociedad Geográfica de Lima*, 19(2): 125–82.

Cazes, David. 1910. "Informe sobre el Intercambio Comercial de Iquitos para el Año de 1910." In H. Bonilla (comp.), *op. cit.*, Vol. III: 221–26.

CEPD. (Centro de Estudios de Población y Desarrollo). 1972. *Informe Demográfico del Perú.* Lima.

CETA. (Centro de Estudios Teológicos de la Amazonía Peruana). 1995. *Almanaque.* Iquitos: CETA/Biblioteca Amazónica.

Cha, Chungsuk. 1969. *El Rol de la Selva en el Desarrollo Agrícola del Perú.* Lima: Banco Central de Reserva.

Chaumeil, Jean-Pierre. 1981. *Historia y Migraciones de los Yagua de Finales del Siglo XVII hasta Nuestros Días.* Lima: Centro Amazónico de Antropología y Aplicación Práctica.

_____. 1983. *Voir, Savoir, Pouvoir: Le Chamanisme chez les Yagua du Nord-Est Péruvien.* Paris: Editions de L'Ecole des Hautes Etudes en Sciences Sociales.

_____. 1994. "Los Yagua." In F. Santos-Granero and F. Barclay (eds.), *op. cit.*, pp. 181–307.

Chibnik, Michael. 1989. "Riesgo, Crédito y Producción de Arroz en Loreto." *Amazonía Indígena,* 9(15): 26–39.

_____. 1991. "Quasi-Ethnic Groups in Amazonia." *Ethnology,* 30(2): 167–182.

_____. 1994. *Risky Rivers: The Economics and Politics of Floodplain Farming in Amazonia.* Tucson: The University of Arizona Press.

Chibnik, Michael, and Wil de Jong. 1992. "Organización de la Mano de Obra Agrícola en las Comunidades Ribereñas de la Amazonía Peruana." *Amazonía Peruana,* 11(21): 181–215.

Chirif, Alberto. 1974. "Los Congresos de las Comunidades Nativas: El Inicio de la Participación." *Participación,* 3(5): 45–53.

_____. 1985. "25 Años de Política de Desarrollo Rural en la Amazonía Peruana y sus Repercusiones en las Sociedades Indígenas de la Región." In Jürg Gasché and José María Arroyo (eds.), *Balances Amazónicos: Enfoques Antropológicos,* pp. 171–223. Iquitos: Centro de Investigación Antropológica de la Amazonía Peruana.

_____. 1999. "Desmanes y Algo Más: Recordando la Ira en Iquitos." *Ideéle,* 116, (Marzo).

Chirif, Alberto, Carlos Mora, and Roque Moscoso. 1977. *Los Shipibo-Conibo del Ucayali: Diagnóstico Socio-Económico.* Lima: Sistema Nacional de Movilización Social.

Chirif, Alberto, Pedro García, and Richard Ch. Smith. 1991. *El Indígena y su Territorio.* Lima: Coordinadora de las Organizaciones Indígenas de la Cuenca Amazónica/Oxfam America.

CIDA (Comité Interamericano de Desarrollo Agrícola). 1963. *Relaciones entre la Tenencia de la Tierra y el Desarrollo Socio-Económico de la Agricultura Peruana: Informe Preliminar.* Lima: Instituto de Reforma Agraria y Colonización.

Collier, Richard. 1981. *Jaque al Barón: La Historia del Caucho en la Amazonía.* Lima: Centro Amazónico de Antropología y Aplicación Práctica.

CONETSCAR. 1964–1969. *Estadística Agraria.* Lima: Universidad Agraria/Ministerio de Agricultura.

Coomes, Oliver T. 1992. Making a Living in the Amazon Rain Forest: Peasants, Land, and Economy in the Tahuayo River Basin of Northeastern Peru. Ph.D. Dissertation. University of Wisconsin–Madison.

_____. 1996a. "State Credit Programs and the Peasantry under Populist Regimes: Lessons from the APRA Experience in the Peruvian Amazon." *World Development,* 24(8): 1333–1346.

_____. 1996b. "Income Formation among Amazonian Peasant Households in Northeastern Peru: Empirical Observations and Implications for Market-oriented Conservation." *Yearbook,* Conference of Latin Americanist Geographers, 22: 51–64.

Coomes; Oliver T., and Bradford L. Barham. 1994. "The Amazon Rubber Boom: Labor Control, Resistance, and Failed Plantation Development Revisited." *Hispanic American Historical Review,* 74(2): 231–257.

COPAPMA (Comité de Productores de Arroz de la Provincia de Maynas). 1986. Propuesta Para la Plataforma de Lucha. Iquitos.

Cordelor (Corporación Departamental de Desarrollo de Loreto). 1982. *Anuario Estadístico Regional, No. 1.* Iquitos.

_____. 1985. Convenio Cordelor-Banco Amazónico. Préstamos Otorgados Desde 1979 a Junio de 1985. Iquitos.

Córdova, Daniel. 1958. "La Explotación de Cueros y Pieles de Animales Silvestres." *Pesca y Caza*, 8: 44–48.

Coriat, Juan E. 1943. *El Hombre del Amazonas: Ensayo Monográfico de Loreto*. Iquitos: Librería Coriat.

_____. 1944. *Tunchi*. Lima.

Corporación. n.d. *Ampliación y Modificación del Estatuto de la Corporación Peruana del Amazonas y Reglamento Interno*. Lima: Corporación Peruana del Amazonas.

Cotler, Julio. 1978. *Clases, Estado y Nación en el Perú*. Lima: Instituto de Estudios Peruanos.

Crabtree, John. 1992. *Peru Under García: An Opportunity Lost*. Pittsburgh: University of Pittsburgh Press.

Cuánto. 1993. *Cómo Estamos: Revista Trimestral de Análisis Social*, Marzo. Lima: Instituto Cuánto.

Dandler, Jorge. 1998. *Pueblos Indígenas de la Amazonía Peruana y Desarrollo Sostenible*. Lima: Oficina Internacional del Trabajo.

d'Ans, André-Marcel. 1982. *L'Amazonie Péruvienne Indigène*. Paris: Payot.

Dávalos y Lissón, Pedro. 1930. *Diez Años de Historia Contemporánea del Perú, 1899–1908*. Lima: Librería e Imprenta Gil.

Dávila, Carlos. 1994. "Descentralización, la Lucha Continúa." *Kanatari*, 500: 5–8; 4/17/1994.

Dean, Bartholomew C. 1996. Chanting Rivers, Fiery Tongues: Exchange, Value, and Desire Among the Urarina of Peruvian Amazonia. Ph.D. Dissertation. Harvard University. Ann Arbor: University Microfilms International.

Dean, Warren. 1987. *Brazil and the Struggle for Rubber*. Cambridge: Cambridge University Press.

de Jong, Wil. 1987. "Organización del Trabajo en la Amazonía Peruana: El Caso de las Sociedades Agrícolas de Tamshiyacu." *Amazonía Indígena*, 7(13): 11–17.

Delboy, Emilio. 1938. "Historia y Romance de la Caoba." *Boletín de la Dirección de Agricultura, Ganadería y Colonización*, 9(28–31): 211–33.

_____. 1952. "Memorandum sobre la Selva del Perú." *Boletín de la Sociedad Geográfica de Lima*, 69(1–2): 3–52.

Delgado, Carlos. 1974. *Problemas Sociales en el Perú Contemporáneo*. Lima: Instituto de Estudios Peruanos.

Denevan, William M. 1984. "Ecological Heterogeneity and Horizontal Zonation of Agriculture in the Amazon Floodplain." In Marianne Schmink and Charles H. Wood (eds.), *Frontier Expansion in Amazonia*, pp. 311–336. Gainesville: University of Florida Press.

Derteano, César. 1903. "Visita del Subprefecto del Alto Amazonas, Don … á los Distritos de Santa Cruz, Lagunas, Jeberos i Cahuapanas." In C. Larrabure i Correa, *op. cit.*, VII: 601–10.

Descola, Philippe. 1982. "Territorial Adjustments Among the Achuar of Ecuador." *Social Science Information*, 21(2): 301–20.

Diaz, Paulino. 1903. "Memoria Presentada por el Prefecto Apostólico de San León del Amazonas al Ministro de Justicia i Culto." In C. Larrabure i Correa, *op. cit.*, IX: 215–28.

DNE (Dirección Nacional de Estadística). 1949. *Censo Nacional de Población de 1940*, Vol. 9. Lima: DNE.

DNEC (Dirección Nacional de Estadística y Censos). 1964a. *Directorio de Comercio al por Menor: Directorio de Comercio al por Mayor.* Primer Censo Nacional Económico, 1963. Lima.

_____. 1964b. *Directorio de la Industria Manufacturera con Cinco o Más Personas Ocupadas.* Primer Censo Nacional Económico, 1963. Lima.

_____. 1966. *VI Censo Nacional de Población*, Vol. 3. Lima.

Dobkin de Ríos, Marlene. 1984. *Visionary Vine: Hallucinogenic Healing in the Peruvian Amazon.* Prospect Heights: Waveland Press.

Dole, Gertrude. 1999. "Los Amahuaca." In F. Santos-Granero and F. Barclay (eds.), *Guía Etnográfica de la Alta Amazonía*, Vol. 3. Quito: Abya-Yala/Smithsonian Tropical Research Institute.

Domínguez, Camilo. 1988. "De Quito al Amazonas. Naturaleza y Hombre." In Polidoro Pinto, Ana Cecilia Montoya, and Roberto Franco (eds.), *De Misahuallí a Chaguaramás: En Canoa del Amazonas al Caribe*, pp. 71–92. Bogotá: Instituto Nacional de los Recursos Renovables y del Medio Ambiente/Universidad Nacional de Colombia/Comisión Colombiana del V Centenario del Descubrimiento de América.

_____. 1989. "Poblaciones Humanas y Desarrollo Amazónico en Colombia." In *Populações Humanas e Desenvolvimento Amazónico*, pp. 93–124. Serie Cooperação Amazónica. Belém: Organização dos Estados Americanos/Universidade Federal do Pará.

Domínguez, Camilo, and Augusto Gómez. 1990. *La Economía Extractiva en la Amazonia Colombiana, 1850–1930.* Bogotá: Tropenbos Colombia/Corporación Araracuara.

_____. 1994. *Nación y Etnias: Los Conflictos Territoriales en la Amazonia, 1750–1933.* Bogotá: Disloque Editores.

Donadio, Alberto. 1995. *La Guerra con el Perú.* Bogotá: Planeta.

Dourojeanni, Marc. 1990. *Amazonía ¿Qué Hacer?* Iquitos: Centro de Estudios Teológicos de la Amazonía.

Dradi, Maria Pia. 1987. *La Mujer Chayahuita: ¿Un Destino de Marginación? Análisis de la Condición Femenina en una Sociedad Indígena de la Amazonía.* Lima: Fundación Friedrich Ebert.

Driant, Jean-Claude. 1991. *Las Barriadas de Lima: Historia e Interpretación.* Lima: Instituto Francés de Estudios Andinos/DESCO.

Durand, Juan. 1980. "Promoción de Exportación de Productos Forestales." In *Seminario sobre Extracción y Transformación Forestal.* Pucallpa: Ministerio de Agricultura/Food and Agriculture Organization.

El Comercio. 1917. *Cuestiones Económicas de Loreto.* Iquitos: Imprenta y Librería H. Reátegui.

Espinar, Enrique. 1901. "Exploración del Río Yavarí por el Capitán de Navío . . . ." In C. Larrabure i Correa, *op. cit.*, Vol. IV: 53–60.

_____. 1902. "Viaje al Igara-Paraná, Afluente Izquierdo del Río Putumayo, por el Capitán de Navío . . . ." In C. Larrabure i Correa, *op. cit.*, Vol. IV: 218–23.

Espinosa, Lucas. 1935. *Los Tupí del Oriente Peruano: Estudio Lingüístico y Etnográfico.* Madrid: Librería y Casa Editorial Hernando.

_____. 1955. *Contribuciones Lingüísticas y Etnográficas sobre Algunos Pueblos Indígenas del Amazonas Peruano*, T. I. Madrid: Instituto Bernardino de Sahagun.

Expedientes. 1976. Expedientes de Nombramiento y Creación de Tenencias de Gobernación. Archivo de la Sub-prefectura de Maynas. Iquitos.

Extracto. 1918–1942. *Extracto Estadístico*. Lima: Ministerio de Fomento/Ministerio de Hacienda y Comercio.

Faura, Guillermo. 1965. *Los Ríos de la Amazonía Peruana: Estudio Geográfico, Político, Militar de la Amazonía Peruana y de su Porvenir en el Desarrollo Socio-Económico del Perú*. Lima: Colegio Leoncio Prado.

FECADEMA. 1981. "Convocatoria a la II Asamblea Provincial de la Federación Campesina de Maynas." *Shupihui*, 17: 99–100.

_____. 1981. "Pronunciamiento de la Federación Campesina de Maynas." *Shupihui*, 18: 245–49.

Fernández, Hernán. 1985. "El Problema Educativo." In Carlos Peñaherrera et al., *La Selva Peruana: Realidad Poblacional*. Lima: Asociación Multidisciplinaria de Investigación y Docencia en Población.

Fernández Maldonado, Jorge. 1974. "Petróleo y Selva: Entrevista." *Participación*, 3(5): 15–17.

FitzGerald, E.V.K. 1991. *ECLA and the Formation of Latin American Economic Doctrine in the Nineteenforties*. Working Paper Series No. 106. The Hague: Institute of Social Studies.

Flores Marín, J. Antonio. 1987. *La Explotación del Caucho en el Perú*. Lima: Consejo Nacional de Ciencia y Tecnología.

Fomento (Ministerio de Fomento). 1902. *Leyes, Decretos y Resoluciones Relativas a la Región Oriental*. Lima: Imprenta del Estado.

Foweraker, Joe. 1981. *The Struggle for Land: A Political Economy of the Pioneer Frontier in Brazil from 1930 to the Present Day*. Cambridge: Cambridge University Press.

Fuentes, Aldo. 1988. *Porque las Piedras no Mueren: Historia, Sociedad y Ritos de los Chayahuita del Alto Amazonas*. Lima: Centro Amazónico de Antropología y Aplicación Práctica.

Fuentes, Hildebrando. 1905a. "Memoria del Prefecto de Loreto . . . ." In C. Larrabure i Correa, *op. cit.*, Vol. XVI: 41–62.

_____. 1905b. "Relaciones de los Empresarios Caucheros con sus Peones." In C. Larrabure i Correa, *op. cit.*, Vol. XIV: 29–33.

_____. 1906. "Apuntes Geográficos, Históricos, Estadísticos, Políticos i Sociales de Loreto, por el Ex-prefecto de ese Departamento . . . ." In C. Larrabure i Correa, *op. cit.*, Vol. XVI: 139–536.

_____. 1908. *Loreto: Apuntes Geográficos, Históricos, Estadísticos, Políticos y Sociales*. Lima: Imprenta de La Revista. (2 vols.)

García, Genaro. 1981. "Zona Franca y Desarrollo Regional." *Shupihui*, 20: 629–34.

García, Joaquín. 1979. "Ensayo de Cronología de los Movimientos Populares en la Amazonía Peruana. Desde la Conquista hasta el Año 1970." *Shupihui*, 9: 374–384.

_____. 1995. "Tanto Bregar para Volver a lo Mismo." *Kanatari*, 585; 12/3/1995.

García Córdova, Gustavo. 1905. "Memoria del Subprefecto de la Provincia del Alto Amazonas, Don . . . Anexo al Anterior Oficio." In C. Larrabure i Correa, *op. cit.*, Vol. XVI: 38–41.

García Hierro, Pedro, Soren Hvalkof, and Andrew Gray. 1998. *Liberación y Derechos Territoriales en Ucayali—Perú*. Documento IWGIA No. 24. Copenhagen: International Work Group for Indigenous Affairs.

García Jordán, Pilar. 1991. *Iglesia y Poder en el Perú Contemporáneo, 1821–1919*. Cusco: Centro de Estudios Rurales Andinos "Bartolomé de las Casas."

_____. 1993. "El Infierno Verde. Caucho e Indios, Terror y Muerte. Reflexiones en torno al Escándalo del Putumayo." *Anuario del Instituto de Estudios Histórico Sociales*, 8: 73–85.

_____. 1994. "La Misión del Putumayo (1912–1921). Religión, Política y Diplomacia ante la Explotación Indígena". In Pilar García Jordán, M. Izard, and J. Laviña (coords.), *Memoria, Creación e Historia: Luchar contra el Olvido*, pp. 255–272. Barcelona: Publicacions Universitat de Barcelona.

_____. 1998. "Misiones, Fronteras y Nacionalización de la Amazonía Andina: Perú, Ecuador y Bolivia." In Pilar García Jordán and Nuria Sala i Vila (coords.), *La Nacionalización de la Amazonía*, pp.11–37. Barcelona: Publicacions Universitat de Barcelona.

García Rossell, Ricardo. 1905. "Indice de los Descubrimientos, Expediciones, Estudios i Trabajos llevados á cabo en el Perú para el Aprovechamiento i Cultura de sus Montañas, en Especial las de Loreto por . . . ." In C. Larrabure i Correa, *op. cit.*, Vol. XV: 582–645.

Gasché, Jürg. 1982. "Las Comunidades Nativas Entre la Apariencia y la Realidad. El Ejemplo de las Comunidades Huitoto y Ocaina del Río Ampiyacu." *Amazonía Indígena*, 3(5): 11–31.

_____. 1983. "La Ocupación Territorial de los Nativos Huitoto en el Perú y Colombia en los Siglos 19 y 20. Apuntes para un Debate sobre la Nacionalidad de los Huitoto." *Amazonía Indígena*, 4(7): 2–19.

Girard, Raphael. 1963. *Les Indiens de l'Amazonie Péruvienne*. Paris: Payot.

Gonzales, Alberto. 1988. Crédito y Producción Agraria en los Departamentos de Selva. Datos Estadísticos.

Goulard, Jean-Pierre. 1994. "Los Ticuna." In F. Santos-Granero and F. Barclay (eds.), *op. cit.*, pp. 309–442.

Gow, Peter. 1991. *Of Mixed Blood: Kinship and History in Peruvian Amazonia*. Oxford: Clarendon Press.

Gregorio y Alonso, B. 1953. "Acción Misionera de los PP. Agustinos en Loreto bajo su Triple Aspecto Religioso, Cultural y Científico." In Misiones Agustinianas, *op. cit.*, pp. 13–74.

Guerra, Margarita. 1984. *Historia General del Perú*, Tomo 12. Lima: Milla Batres.

Guía. 1940. *Guía de Loreto*. Iquitos: El Oriente.

Guzmán Rivera, Toribio. 1929. *Guía de Loreto Industrial, Comercial y de Propaganda*. Iquitos: La Razón.

Haring, Maria Margaretha (Rita). 1986a. *Boomtown an de Amazone: Een Historisch-sociologische Studie over de Peruanse Amazonasregio en de Stad Iquitos, emt Nadruk op de Periode, 1880–1980*. Utrecht: Institut voor Culturele Antropologie.

_____. 1986b. "Burguesía Regional de la Amazonía Peruana, 1880–1980." *Amazonía Peruana*, 13(7): 67–84.

Harner, Michael J. 1973. *The Jivaro: People of the Sacred Waterfalls*. New York: Anchor Press/Doubleday.

Henkel, Ray. 1982. "The Move to the Oriente: Colonization and Environmental Impact." In J.R. Ladman (ed.), *Modern-Day Bolivia: Legacy of the Revolution and Prospects for the Future*. Tampa: Arizona State University.

Hernández, Arturo D. 1942. *Sangama*. Lima: Torres Aguirre.

_____. 1970. *Selva Trágica*. Lima: Atlántida.

Herrera, José Fermín. 1905. "Estado Comercial de la Región Peruana del Amazonas el Año 1872, por . . . ." In C. Larrabure i Correa, *op. cit.*, Vol. XVI: 104–138.

Higbee, Edward C. 1949. *Lonchocarpo, Derris y Piretro*. Publicación Agrícola, Nos. 159–160. Washington D.C.: Unión Panamericana.

_____. 1951. "Of Man and the Amazon." *Geographical Review*, 41(3): 401–420.

Hiraoka, Mario, 1985a. "Cash Cropping, Wage Labor, and Urbanward Migration: Changing Floodplain Subsistence in the Peruvian Amazon." In Eugene Parker (ed.), *The Amazon Caboclo: Historical and Contemporary Perspectives*, pp. 199–242. Studies in Third World Societies, No. 32. Williamsburg: College of William and Mary.

_____. 1985b. "Floodplain Farming in the Peruvian Amazon." *Geographical Review of Japan*, 58(1): 1–23.

_____. 1986. "Zonation of Mestizo Riverine Farming Systems in Northeast Peru." *National Geographic Research*, 2(3): 354–371.

_____. 1989. "Patrones de Subsistencia Mestiza en las Zonas Ribereñas de la Amazonía Peruana." *Amazonía Indígena*, 9(15): 17–25.

House Documents. 1913. "Slavery in Peru. Message from the President of the United States Transmitting Report of the Secretary of State, With Accompanying Papers, Concerning the Alleged Existence of Slavery in Peru." House of Representatives, 62nd Congress, 3rd Session, US. Washington D.C.: Government Printing Office.

Huckin, V. 1913. "Informe sobre el Movimiento Mercantil de Iquitos para el Año de 1913." In H. Bonilla (comp.), *op. cit.*, Vol. III: 257–82.

_____. 1914. "Informe sobre el Intercambio Comercial de Iquitos para el Año 1914." In H. Bonilla (comp.), *op. cit.*, Vol. III: 283–99.

Hugh-Jones, Stephen. 1992. "Yesterday's Luxuries, Tomorrow's Necessities: Business and Barter in Northwest Amazonia." In Caroline Humphrey and Stephen Hugh-Jones (eds.), *Barter, Exchange, and Value: An Anthropological Approach*, pp. 42–74. Cambridge: Cambridge University Press.

Industria. (Dirección Regional de Industria, Turismo e Integración). 1973. Perfil Industrial del Complejo Maderero Napo. Iquitos

_____. 1981. Directorio Industrial. Iquitos.

_____. 1982. Anexo al Directorio Industrial. Iquitos.

_____. 1990. Relación de Empresas Industriales Establecidas en la Región Ucayali. Pucallpa: Secretaría Regional de Asuntos Productivos y de Transformación/Dirección de Industrias.

_____. 1991a. Directorio Industrial. Iquitos.

_____. 1991b. Directorio Industrial. Pucallpa.

INE (Instituto Nacional de Estadística). n.d. *Censos Nacionales VII de Población y II de Vivienda, Departamento de Loreto*. Lima. (2 vols.)

_____. 1984. *Estadísticas Demográficas, Loreto—Ucayali, 1940–1981*. Iquitos.

_____. 1985a. *Censos Nacionales VIII de Población y III de Vivienda, Departamento de Loreto*. Lima. (2 vols.)

_____. 1985b. *Censos Nacionales VIII de Población y III de Vivienda, Departamento de Ucayali*. Lima. (2 vols.)

_____. 1988a. *Compendio Estadístico—Loreto, 1986*. Iquitos.

_____. 1988b. *Producto Bruto Interno por Departamentos, 1970–1987*. Lima.

_____. 1989a. *Región del Amazonas—Compendio Estadístico, 1988*. Lima.

_____. 1989b. *Perú: Población y Superficie a Nivel Distrital*. Lima

INEI (Instituto Nacional de Estadística e Informática). 1990a. *Región Amazonas—Compendio Estadístico, 1989–1990*. Lima.

_____. 1990b. *Región Ucayali—Compendio Estadístico, 1989–1990*. Lima.

_____. 1994a. *Resultados Definitivos a Nivel Provincial y Distrital: Departamento de Loreto*. Censos Nacionales 1993, IX de Población, IV de Vivienda. Lima. (2 vols.)

_____. 1994b. *Resultados Definitivos, No. 14. Departamento de Ucayali.* Censos Nacionales 1993, IX de Población, IV de Vivienda. Lima.

_____. 1994c. *Directorio Departamental de Centros Poblados, Loreto.* Lima.

_____. 1995a. *Departamento de Loreto—III Censo Nacional Agropecuario—Resultados Definitivos.* Lima. (3 vols.)

_____. 1995b. *Departamento de Ucayali—III Censo Nacional Agropecuario—Resultados Definitivos.* Lima. (2 vols.)

_____. 1996a. *Loreto—Compendio Estadístico Departamental, 1995–1996.* Lima.

_____. 1996b. *Ucayali—Compendio Estadístico Departamental, 1995–1996.* Lima.

_____. 1996c. *Cuentas Regionales: Producto Bruto Interno, 1970–1995.* Lima.

_____. 1996d. *Dimensión y Características Urbanas del Perú, 1961–1993.* Lima.

_____. 1997. *Directorio Nacional de Municipalidades Provinciales y Distritales, 1997.* Lima.

_____. 1998a. *Compendio Estadístico Departamental, 1997–1998.* Lima.

_____. 1998b. *Ucayali: Estadísticas de Medio Ambiente, 1997.* Pucallpa.

INP (Instituto Nacional de Planificación). 1971. Oficio No. 012-71/AJ-INP del Jefe del INP (G. Marco del Pont) al Ministro de Industria (A. Jiménez de Lucio). Lima 11/2/1971.

_____. 1972. Comisión para el Estudio de los Diferentes Aspectos del Problema Tarifario del Transporte Fluvial en la Región del Oriente. Estudio e Informe. Iquitos.

_____. 1984. Evaluación Socio-Económica del Plan Departamental de Desarrollo de Loreto, 1983–1984. Iquitos.

Izaguirre, Bernardino. 1922–1929. *Historia de las Misiones Franciscanas: Narración de los Progresos de la Geografía en el Oriente del Perú, 1619–1921.* Lima: Talleres Tipográficos de la Penitenciaría (14 vols.)

Izquierdo Ríos, Hildebrando. 1976. *Comandancia General de Mainas: Aspectos de Mainas Libre.* Lima: Ultra.

Junta. (Junta de Vías Fluviales). 1907. *Ultimas Exploraciones Ordenadas por la Junta de Vías Fluviales a los Ríos Ucayali, Madre de Dios, Paucartambo y Urubamba: Informes de los Señores Stiglich, von Hassel, Olivera y Ontaneda.* Lima: La Opinión Nacional.

Kanatari. 1988. "¿Cómo era San Juan Antiguamente?." *Kanatari,* 197: 9; 6/26/1988.

_____. 1991. "La Parroquia de la Inmaculada de Punchana. Recuerdos de Viejos Tiempos." *Kanatari,* 350: 7–8; 6/2/1991.

Katzman, Martin T. 1977. *Cities and Frontiers in Brazil: Regional Dimensions of Economic Development.* Cambridge and London: Harvard University Press.

Kelly, Brian, and Mark London. 1983. *Amazon.* New York: Holt, Rinehart, and Winston.

Killip, E.P., and A.C. Smyth. 1930. "The Identity of the South American Fish Poison." *Journal of the Washington Academy of Sciences,* 20(5): 74–81.

Kuczynski, Pedro-Pablo. 1977. *Peruvian Democracy under Economic Stress: An Account of the Belaúnde Administration, 1963–1968.* New Jersey: Princeton University Press.

Kuczynski-Godard, Máximo. 1944. *La Vida en la Amazonía Peruana: Observaciones de un Médico.* Lima: Librería Internacional del Perú.

La Combe, Ernesto. 1902. "Expedición de Puerto Bermúdez á Iquitos i de este último Puerto al Istmo de Fiscarrald, Dirigida por el Coronel. . . . " In C. Larrabure i Correa, *op. cit.,* Vol. XII: 200–276.

Lamb, Bruce F. 1966. *Mahogany of Tropical America.* Ann Arbor: The University of Michigan Press.

———. 1974. *Wizard of the Upper Amazon: The Story of Manuel Córdova-Ríos.* Berkeley: North Atlantic Books.

Laos, Ricardo. 1902. "La Industria Gomera en el Perú." In *Leyes, Decretos y Resoluciones Relativas a la Región Oriental,* Ministerio de Fomento. Lima: Imprenta del Estado.

Larrabure i Correa, Carlos. 1905–1909. *Colección de Leyes, Decretos, Resoluciones i Otros Documentos Oficiales Referentes al Departamento de Loreto.* Lima: La Opinión Nacional. (18 vols.)

La Región. 1999. "Comunicado de Reunificación. Frente Patriótico de Loreto." *La Región,* 2/22/1999.

La Torre, Lily. 1998. *Sólo Queremos Vivir en Paz: Experiencias Petroleras en Territorios Indígenas de la Amazonía Peruana.* Documento IWGIA, 25. Copenhagen: International Workgroup of Indigenous Affairs.

Lausent-Herrera, Isabella. 1986. "Los Inmigrantes Chinos en la Amazonía Peruana." In *Primer Seminario sobre Poblaciones Inmigrantes: Actas,* Vol. 2. Lima: Consejo Nacional de Ciencia y Tecnología

———. 1996. "Los caucheros y comerciantes chinos en Iquitos a fines del siglo XIX (1890–1900)." In Pilar García Jordán et al. (coords.), *Las Raíces de la Memoria. América Latina,* pp. 467–481. Barcelona: Publicacions Universitat de Barcelona.

Legislatura. 1943. *Diario de los Debates del Senado: Legislaturas Extraordinarias de 1941,* Vol. I. Primera Legislatura Extraordinaria. Lima: Torres Aguirre.

Lehm, Zulema. 1993. Milenarismo y Movimientos Sociales en la Amazonía Boliviana: La Búsqueda de la Loma Santa y la Marcha Indígena por el Territorio y la Dignidad. Tesis de Maestría en Ciencias Sociales. Facultad Latinoamericana de Ciencias Sociales–Sede Ecuador.

León, Numa P. 1905. *Informe de la Comisión Mixta Peruano-Brasileña de Reconocimiento del Alto Yuruá.* Lima: n.d.

Lequerica, César. 1942. *Sachachorro.* Iquitos.

López, Agustín. 1904. "Viaje al Río Blanco por el Padre . . . , de la Prefectura Apostólica de San Francisco de Ucayali." In C. Larrabure i Correa, *op. cit.,* Vol. IV: 263–71.

López, Sinesio. 1997. *Ciudadanos Reales e Imaginarios: Concepciones, Desarrollo y Mapas de la Ciudadanía en el Perú.* Lima: Instituto de Diálogo y Propuestas.

Luna, Luis Eduardo, and Pablo Amaringo. 1991. *Ayahuasca Visions: The Religious Iconography of a Peruvian Shaman.* Berkeley: North Atlantic Books.

Maletta, Héctor, and Alejandro Bardales. n.d. *Perú: Las Provincias en Cifras, 1876–1981,* Vol. 1. Lima: Ediciones AMIDEP/Universidad del Pacífico.

Malpica, Carlos. 1989. *El Poder Económico en el Perú.* Lima: Mosca Azul.

Martínez Riaza, Ascensión. 1998a. "Estrategias de Ocupación de la Amazonía. La Posición Española en el Conflicto Perú-Ecuador (1887–1910)." In Pilar García Jordán (ed.), *Fronteras, Colonización y Mano de Obra Indígena en la Amazonía Andina (Siglos XIX–XX),* pp. 241–335. Lima: Pontificia Universidad Católica del Perú/Universitat de Barcelona.

———. 1998b. "La Incorporación de Loreto al Estado-Nación Peruano. El Discurso Modernizador de la Sociedad Geográfica de Lima (1891–1919)." In Pilar García Jordán and Núria Sala I Vila (coords.), *La Nacionalización de la Amazonía,* pp. 99–126. Barcelona: Publicacions Universitat de Barcelona.

Maskrey, Andrew, Josefa Rojas, and Teocrito Pinedo (eds). 1991. *Raíces y Bosques: San Martín Modelo para Armar.* Lima: Tecnología Intermedia.

Matrícula. 1910. *Matrícula de Contribuyentes: Provincia de Bajo Amazonas, Departamento de Loreto.* Lima: Talleres Tipográficos de La Revista.

Mattos, João Wilkens de. 1984. *Diccionario Topographico do Departamento de Loreto na Republica do Perú por* . . . Iquitos: Centro de Estudios Teológicos de la Amazonía.

———. 1854. "Roteiro da Primeira Viagem do Vapor Monarcha, desde a Cidade da Barra do Rio Negro, da Provincia do Amazonas até a Povoação de Nauta, na Republica do Perú; feito . . . ." In J. W. de Mattos (1984), *op. cit.*

———. 1874. "Diccionario Topographico do Departamento de Loreto na Republica do Perú por . . . ." In J. W. de Mattos (1984), *op. cit.*

Maúrtua, Aníbal. 1911. "Geografía Económica del Departamento de Loreto." *Boletín de la Sociedad Geográfica de Lima,* 21(2): 121–180.

Mavila, Oscar. 1902. "Estudio sobre el Departamento de Loreto, Presentado á la Sociedad Geográfica de Lima por el Alférez de Fragata Don . . . ." In C. Larrabure i Correa, *op. cit.,* Vol. VII: 534–63.

———. 1904. "Exploración de los Ríos Tigre, Pastaza, Morona, Curarai, Apaga, Potro i Cahuapanas, practicada por el Alférez de Fragata . . . de Orden del Prefecto de Loreto, Coronel Pedro Portillo. Informe del Alférez . . . ." In C. Larrabure i Correa, *op. cit.,* Vol. IV: 244–59.

McKinley, Michelle. 1997. "Contested Exchanges: Debt-Peonage and the Politics of Urarina Social Mobility." Unpublished paper.

Memoria. 1862. *Memoria que el Ministro de Gobierno, Policía y Obras Públicas Presenta al Congreso Nacional de 1862.* Lima: La Epoca.

———. 1896. *Memoria que el Ministro de Gobierno y Policía Presenta á la Legislatura Ordinaria de 1896.* Lima: El País.

———. 1899. *Memoria que el Director General de Correos y Telégrafos Presenta al Sr. Ministro de Gobierno Dando Cuenta de la Marcha Administrativa de Ambos Ramos Durante el Año de 1895.* Lima: El País.

Memorial. 1904. "Memorial de los Caucheros de Loreto pidiendo la Dación de un Reglamento de Locación de Servicios para la Industria del Caucho." In C. Larrabure i Correa, *op. cit.,* Vol. XV: 495–502.

Mensaje. 1939. *Mensaje presentado al Congreso por el Gral. de División Don Oscar R. Benavides, Presidente Constitucional de la República.* Lima.

Mercier, Juan Marcos. 1974. "Tandarina de Yumbos Quichuas del Río Napo." In J.M. Mercier and G. Villeneuve (eds.), *op. cit.,* pp. 187–191.

———. 1979. *Nosotros los Napu-Runas. Napu Runapa Rimay. Mitos e Historia.* Iquitos: Centro de Estudios Teológicos de la Amazonía/Ministerio de Educación.

Mercier, Juan Marcos, and Gaston Villeneuve (eds.). 1974. *Amazonía ¿Liberación o Esclavitud?* Colección Iglesia Liberadora, 8. Lima: Ediciones Paulinas.

Misiones Agustinianas. 1953. *Misiones Agustinianas: Album Recordatorio del Cincuentenario de la Llegada de los Padres Agustinos a Loreto, 1901–1951.* Lima: Antonio Lulli.

Mitchell, G.B. 1911. "Informe sobre el Comercio de Iquitos correspondiente al Año 1911." In H. Bonilla (comp.), *op. cit.,* Vol. III: 227–45.

Monnier, Alain (ed). 1994. *L'Amazonie d'une Baronne Russe.* Sources et Témoignages: I. Nadine de Meyendorff. Geneva: Musée d'Ethnographie de Genève/Société des Amis du Musée d'Ethnographie/Société Suisse des Américanistes.

Montero, Hugo, and Carlos E. Crespo. 1989. "Poblaciones Humanas y Desarrollo de la Amazonía Ecuatoriana." In *Populações Humanas e Desenvolvimento Amazónico,* pp. 125–191. Serie Cooperação Amazónica. Belém: Organização dos Estados Americanos/Universidade Federal do Pará.

Mora, Tulio. 1974. "Amazonía Entrevistada." *Participación,* 3(5): 63–79.

Mora, Carlos, and Alonso Zarzar. 1997. "Aspectos Generales de las Comunidades Indígenas en la Amazonía Peruana." In Antonio Brack and Carlos Yáñez (eds.), *Amazonía Peruana: Comunidades Indígenas, Conocimientos y Tierras Tituladas*, pp. 11–28. Lima: Tratado de Cooperación Amazónica.

Morey Alejo, Humberto. 1988. "Narrativa Amazónica fuera de Contexto." *Revista de Cultura Amazónica*, 2: 19–22.

Morey Menacho, Raúl. n.d. Origen de la Familia Morey en el Perú y Genealogía. Iquitos.

———. 1993. "La Insurgencia Loretana por la Entrega de Leticia." *Kanatari*, 450: 12–27; 5/2/1993.

———. 1996a. "La Historia no escrita de Loreto. A 75 Años de la Revolución del Capitán Cervantes." *Kanatari*, 620: 7–10; 8/4/1995.

———. 1996b. "El Estado Federal de Loreto de 1896." *Kanatari*, 607: 9–18; 5/5/96.

Morey Peña, Víctor. 1958. *El Motelo: Cuentos*. Lima: Juan Mejía Baca.

Morin, Françoise. 1999. "Los Shipibo-Conibo." In F. Santos-Granero and F. Barclay (eds.), *Guía Etnográfica de la Alta Amazonía*, Vol. 3. Quito: Abya-Yala/Smithsonian Tropical Research Institute.

Muratorio, Blanca. 1987. *Rucuyaya Alonso y la Historia Social y Económica del Alto Napo, 1850–1950*. Quito: Abya-Yala.

Nájar, Fernando, and Roger Grandez. 1996. "Pobreza y Desempleo en Iquitos." *Kanatari*, 608: 9–11; 5/12/1996.

Navarro Cáuper, Alfonso. 1988a. "El Movimiento Federalista de Loreto." *Kanatari*, 200: 4–10; 7/17/1988.

———.1988b. "Forjadores de la Identidad Nacional." *Kanatari*, 200: 18–9; 7/17/1988.

Ocampo, Esteban. 1983. "Política Fiscal y Descapitalización de la Amazonía Peruana." *Shupihui*, 28: 493–510.

Olivera, José María. 1907. "Informe del Jefe de la Comisión Exploradora del Alto Madre de Dios por la Vía de Puerto Maldonado, Teniente Primero de la Armada Nacional, Don . . . ." In Junta, *op. cit.*, pp. 295–439.

ONEC (Oficina Nacional de Estadísticas y Censos). 1972. *Censos Nacionales de Población, Vivienda y Agropecuario—Departamento de Loreto*, Vol. 14. Lima.

Ordeloreto (Organismo Regional de Desarrollo de Loreto). 1978a. *Boletín de Estadística Regional*, No. 1. Iquitos.

———. 1978b. *Régimen Tributario de la Región de Selva—Propuesta para Promover el Desarrollo Regional*. Documento de Trabajo. Iquitos.

———. 1979. *Boletín de Estadística Regional*, No. 2. Iquitos.

———. 1980. *Ordeloreto: Memoria del Desarrollo*. Iquitos: Proceso Editores.

———. 1981. *Boletín de Estadística Regional*, No. 4. Iquitos.

Ordeoriente n.d. Borradores para Diagnóstico de la Región Oriente. Iquitos.

Ordinaire, Olivier. 1988. *Del Pacífico al Atlántico y Otros Escritos*. Monumenta Amazónica D1. Iquitos: Centro de Estudios Teológicos de la Amazonía/Instituto Francés de Estudios Andinos.

Ortiz, Dionisio. 1974. *El Alto Ucayali y el Pachitea: Visión Histórica de dos Importantes Regiones de la Selva Peruana*. Lima: San Antonio. (2 vols.)

———. 1984. *Pucallpa y el Ucayali: Ayer y Hoy*, Tomo 1. Lima: Apostolado de la Prensa.

———. 1986. *Pucallpa y el Ucayali: Ayer y Hoy*, Tomo 2. Lima: Científica.

Overing Kaplan, Joanna. 1975. *The Piaroa, a People of the Orinoco Basin: A Study in Kinship and Marriage*. Oxford: Clarendon Press.

Padoch, Christine. 1986. "The Campesinos of Santa Rosa: History and Ethnicity in an Amazonian Community." Paper presented at the Annual Meeting of the American Anthropological Association, Philadelphia.

———. 1988. "The Economic Importance and Marketing of Forest and Fallow Products in the Iquitos Region." *Economic Botany*, 5: 74–89.

Padoch, Christine, Jomber Chota Inuma, Wil de Jong, and John Unruh. 1990. "La Agroforestería Orientada Hacia el Mercado en Tamshiyacu." In William M. Denevan and Christine Padoch (eds.), *Agroforestería Tradicional en la Amazonía Peruana*, pp. 195–208. Documento 11. Lima: Centro de Investigación y Promoción Amazónica.

Padoch, Christine, and Wil de Jong. 1987. "Traditional Agroforestry Practices of Native and Ribereño Farmers in the Lowland Peruvian Amazon." In H.L. Gholz (ed.), *Agroforestry: Realities, Possibilities, and Potentials*, pp. 179–194. Dordrecht: Martinus Nijhoff.

———. 1990. "Santa Rosa: El Impacto del Comercio de Productos Forestales Sobre un Poblado Amazónico y sus Habitantes." Unpublished paper.

Padrón. 1939. *Estado del Padrón General de Terrenos de Montaña al Año 1937*. Lima: Ministerio de Fomento.

Palacios, Samuel. 1890a. "Primer Informe del Presidente de la Comisión Especial, Coronel . . . ." In C. Larrabure i Correa, *op. cit.*, Vol. IV: 383–431.

———. 1890b. "Segundo Informe del Presidente de la Comisión Especial, Coronel . . . ." In C. Larrabure i Correa, *op. cit.*, Vol. IV: 431–561.

Palacios Rodríguez, Raúl. 1990. *Historia Marítima del Perú*, Tomo 12(1). Lima: Instituto de Estudios Histórico-Marítimos del Perú.

———. 1991. *Historia Marítima del Perú*, Tomo 12(2). Lima: Instituto de Estudios Histórico-Marítimos del Perú.

Panduro Coral, Moisés. 1993. "1985–1990: Las Trincheras que Ocupamos." *Kanatari*, 450: 18–27; 5/2/1993.

Paredes, Rómulo. 1912. "Report to the Minister of Foreign Affairs of Peru in reference to the Putumayo region and the crimes therein committed by certain individuals connected with the Peruvian Amazon Co." In House Documents, *op. cit.*

Pasquel Ruiz, Antonio. 1989. "Liberalismo Tributario en la Amazonía Peruana." In Edna M. Ramos de Castro and Rosa E. Acevedo Marin (org.), *Amazónias em Tempo de Transição*, pp. 391–429. Serie Cooperação Amazónica. Belém: Organização dos Estados Americanos/Universidade Federal do Pará.

Pennano, Guido. 1988. *La Economía del Caucho*. Iquitos: Centro de Estudios Teológicos de la Amazonía.

Perú. 1981. *Plan Departamental de Desarrollo de Loreto—Plan Nacional de Desarrollo, 1982–1983*. Iquitos: Oficina Departamental de Planificación de Loreto.

Pesce, Luis. 1904. "Informe sobre las Industrias Agrícolas Florestales de la Hoya Amazónica Peruana i la Medicina e Higiene en la Misma por . . . Primera Parte." In C. Larrabure i Correa, *op. cit.*, Vol. XV: 5–99.

Petey, Beatriz Célia C. de Mello. 1972. "Aspecto da Economia Amazónica na Epoca da Depressão (1920–1940)." *Boletim Geografico de Rio de Janeiro*, 31(229): 1–178.

Piazza, Alvaro. 1952. "Los Pécaris en la Selva del Perú." *Pesca y Caza*, 4: 21–32.

Pineda Camacho, Roberto. 1993. "La Vida Cotidiana en los Barracones de la Casa Arana." In Roberto Pineda Camacho and Beatriz Alzate Angel (eds.), *Pasado y Presente del Amazonas: Su Historia Económica y Social*, pp. 55–66. Bogotá: Universidad de los Andes.

Pinedo-Vásquez, Miguel. 1986. "Annually Flooded Lands of the Peruvian Amazon: Use and Tenure." Paper presented at the Annual Meeting of the American Anthropological Association, Philadelphia.

Plane, Auguste. 1903. *Le Pérou*. Paris: Plon.

Pontoni, Alberto. 1981a. *Transnacionales y Petróleo en el Perú: Análisis de las Políticas Petroleras, 1968–1980*. Lima: Centro de Estudios para el Desarrollo y la Participación.

_____. 1981b. "Recursos Petroleros, Excedentes y Desarrollo Regional en la Selva Norte." Paper presented to *Coloquio Sobre la Nueva Conquista de la Selva*, Iquitos, Noviembre 1981.

Portillo, Pedro. 1900. "Exploración de los Ríos Apurímac, Ene, Tambo, Ucayali, Pachitea i Pichis por el Prefecto de Ayacucho, Coronel Don . . . ." In C. Larrabure i Correa, *op. cit.*, Vol. III: 463–550.

_____. 1909. *Acontecimientos Realizados con los Ecuatorianos, Colombianos y Brasileros en los Ríos Napo, Putumayo, Yurúa y Purús Durante los Años 1901 á 1904 Siendo Prefecto del Departamento de Loreto el Coronel D. . . .* Lima: Tipografía del Panóptico.

_____. 1914. "Departamento del Madre de Dios. Memoria que presenta el Coronel D. . . . , Ministro de Fomento, en Comisión." *Boletín de la Sociedad Geográfica de Lima* 30(1–2): 139–87.

Proceso. 1966–1989. *Proceso* (magazine), 1–67. Iquitos.

Protocolo. 1942. *El Protocolo de Río de Janeiro ante la Historia*. Lima: San Martín.

Raigada, Eduardo. 1875. "Exploración del Río Napo por el Comandante Don . . . ." In C. Larrabure i Correa, *op. cit.*, Vol. III: 170–3.

Raimondi, Antonio. 1859. "Primer Viaje del Naturalista Don . . . al Departamento de Loreto. Relación." In C. Larrabure i Correa, *op. cit.*, Vol. VII: 35–114.

_____. 1862. "Estudio de la Provincia Litoral de Loreto, por . . . Informe." In C. Larrabure i Correa, *op. cit.*, Vol. VII: 118–278.

_____. 1869. "Segundo Viaje del Naturalista Don . . . de Chachapoyas á Tabatinga en la Frontera con el Brasil." In C. Larrabure i Correa, *op. cit.*, Vol. VII: 280–359.

_____. 1879. *El Perú: Historia de la Geografía del Perú*, Vol. 3. Lima: Imprenta del Estado.

Ramírez, Luis Hernán. 1983. "Panorama de las Letras Amazónicas." Preface to Roger Rumrill, *Vidas Mágicas de Tunchis y Hechiceros*. Lima: Ital Perú.

Ramírez, Roberto. 1989. "Caquetá: Colonización, Haciendas y Conflictos Sociales en el Siglo XX." In Edna M. Ramos de Castro, Rosa E. Acevedo Marin (orgs.), *Amazónias em Tempo de Transição*, pp. 25–68. Serie Cooperação Amazónica, 4. Belém: Organização dos Estados Americanos/Universidade Federal do Pará.

Regan, Jaime. 1983. *Hacia la Tierra Sin Mal: Estudio de la Religión del Pueblo en la Amazonía*. Iquitos: Centro de Estudios Teológicos de la Amazonía. (2 vols.)

Región Agraria. 1998. Directorio de Comunidades Nativas. Región Agraria de Loreto/PETT. Iquitos.

Registro. 1902. *Registro Oficial de Fomento, Minas, Industrias y Beneficencia: Sección Industrias y Colonización*. Primer Semestre. Lima: Imprenta Calle de Palacio.

Relaciones. 1972. Memorandum Reservado de la Dirección de Soberanía Territorial y Fronteras a la Sub-Secretaría de Asuntos Económicos e Integración del Ministerio de Relaciones Exteriores. Lima, 27 de junio.

Restrepo, Marco, María Eugenia Tamariz, and Teodoro Bustamante. 1992. *Frontera Amazónica: Historia de un Problema*. Quito: Casa de la Cultura Ecuatoriana.

Reyes, Rafael. 1985. *Memorias, 1850–1885*. Bogotá: Fondo Cultural Cafetero.

Ribeiro, Darcy. 1971. *Fronteras Indígenas de la Civilización*. Mexico: Siglo XXI.

Ríos Zañartu, Mario César. 1995. *Historia de la Amazonía Peruana: Texto Para Educación Básica y Superior Para Ser Desarrollado de Acuerdo a la Programación Curricular Microrregional y Local*. Iquitos: El Matutino.

Robledo, Luis M. 1903. "El Bajo Urubamba." *Boletín del Ministerio de Fomento*, 1(10): 33–80.

Rodríguez, E. 1928. *Guía de Iquitos Comercial, Industrial y de Propaganda*. Iquitos: H. Reátegui.

Rodríguez Achung, Martha. 1981. *El Frente de Defensa del Pueblo de Loreto: Ensayo de Interpretación de un Movimiento Social*. Serie: Estudios e Investigación. Lima: Pontificia Universidad Católica del Perú.

———. 1986. "Poblamiento de la Amazonía desde el Siglo XIX hasta 1940." *Shupihui*, 37: 7–28.

———. 1991. "Proceso de Ocupación y Construcción Social del Espacio." In F. Barclay et al., *op. cit.*: 103–159.

Rodríguez Ramírez, Ricardo. 1967. *Guía de Pucallpa*. Pucallpa.

———. 1968. *Guía Centenaria de Loreto*. Iquitos: La Razón.

Romero, Fernando. 1983. *Iquitos y la Fuerza Naval de la Amazonía (1830–1933)*. Lima: Ministerio de Marina.

Rosas, Belisario. 1898. "Exploración del Yuruá-Mirim por Don Ignacio Espinar i Don . . . Diario de viaje elevado por . . . ." In C. Larrabure i Correa, *op. cit.*, Vol. III: 423–30.

Rosenzweig, Alfredo. 1967. "Judíos en la Amazonía Peruana, 1870–1949." *Maj'shavot*, 6(1–2): 19–30. (Buenos Aires).

Roux, Jean-Claude. 1994. *L'Amazonie Peruvienne: Un Dorado Dévoré par la Forêt, 1821–1910*. Paris: L'Harmattan.

Ruiz Saavedra, José. 1985. "La Organización Campesina en la Región de Iquitos." In Jürg Gasché and José María Arroyo (eds.), *Balances Amazónicos: Enfoques Antropológicos*, pp. 255–260. Iquitos: Centro de Investigación Antropológica de la Amazonía Peruana.

Rumrrill, Roger. 1973. *Reportaje a la Amazonía*. Lima: Ediciones Populares Selva.

———. 1974. "Amazonía. Más de Cien Años de Soledad." *Participación*, 3(5): 5–14.

———. 1982. *Amazonía Hoy: Crónicas de Emergencia*. Iquitos: Centro de Estudios Teológicos de la Amazonía/Centro Amazónico de Antropología y Aplicación Práctica

———. 1984. *Guía General: Amazonía Peruana*. Lima: Rumrrill Editores.

Rumrrill, Roger, Carlos Dávila, and Fernando Barcia. 1986. *Yurimaguas: Capital Histórica de la Amazonía Peruana*. Yurimaguas: Concejo Provincial de Alto Amazonas.

Rumrrill, Roger, and Pierre de Zutter. 1976. *Los Condenados de la Selva*. Lima: Horizonte.

Sala, Gabriel. 1897. "Exploración de los Ríos Pichis, Pachitea, Alto Ucayali i de la Región del Gran Pajonal, por el Padre . . . ." In C. Larrabure i Correa, *op. cit.*, Vol. XII: 7–154.

Salazar, Ernesto. 1989. *Pioneros de la Selva: Los Colonos del Proyecto Upano-Palora*. Quito: Banco Central del Ecuador.

Samanez y Ocampo, José B. 1980. *Exploración de los Ríos Peruanos Apurímac, Eni, Tambo, Ucayali y Urubamba*. Lima: SESATOR.

Sánchez del Aguila, Manuel. 1963. *Contribución al Desarrollo Agroeconómico de Loreto y San Martín*. Lima: Dirección de Colonización del Ministerio de Agricultura.

San Román, Jesús. 1974. *Estudio Socio-Económico de los Ríos Amazonas y Napo*. Iquitos: Investigación y Promoción de la Amazonía/Centro de Estudios Teológicos de la Amazonía. (2 vols.)

_____. 1975. *Perfiles Históricos de la Amazonía Peruana.* Lima: Ediciones Paulinas/Centro de Estudios Teológicos de la Amazonía.

_____. 1994. *Perfiles Históricos de la Amazonía Peruana.* Iquitos: Centro de Estudios Teológicos de la Amazonía/Centro Amazónico de Antropología y Aplicación Práctica/Instituto de Investigaciones de la Amazonía Peruana. (second edition, augmented and corrected by Martha Rodrígez Achung and Joaquín García).

Santos-Granero, Fernando. 1980. "Belaúnde y la Colonización de la Amazonía: De la Fantasía a la Realidad." *Amazonía Indígena,* 1(2): 7–18.

_____. 1991a. *The Power of Love: The Moral Use of Knowledge Amongst the Amuesha of Central Peru.* Monographs on Social Anthropology, 62. London School of Economics. London: The Athlone Press.

_____. 1991b. "Frentes Económicos, Espacios Regionales, y Fronteras Capitalistas en la Amazonía." In F. Barclay et al., *op. cit.,* pp. 227–287.

_____. 1991c. "Derroteros de la Literatura Amazónica Contemporánea." *Poesía y Narrativa Amazónica Contemporánea.* Lima: Copal/Grupo Cultural Oruga.

_____. 1992. *Etnohistoria de la Alta Amazonía, Siglos XV-XVIII.* Colección 500 Años, 46. Quito: Abya-Yala.

_____. 1993. "Burguesías Locales y Espacios Regionales en la Amazonía Norperuana: Los Casos de Loreto y Ucayali." In Lucy Ruiz (coord.), *Amazonía: Escenarios y Conflictos,* pp. 95–146. Quito: Centro de Investigación de los Movimientos Sociales del Ecuador/Abya Yala/Facultad Latinoamericana de Ciencias Sociales-Sede Ecuador.

Santos-Granero, Fernando, and Frederica Barclay. 1994. *Guía Etnográfica de la Alta Amazonía,* Vol. 1. Quito: FLACSO-Ecuador/Instituto Francés de Estudios Andinos.

_____. 1998. *Selva Central: History, Economy, and Land Use in Peruvian Amazonia.* Washington D.C./London: Smithsonian Institute Press.

Santos, Roberto. 1980. *História Económica da Amazónia (1800–1920).* São Paulo: TAO.

Schaper, Günther. 1949. "¿Es la Amazonía una Zona Agrícola de Porvenir?" In Sotomayor et al., *op. cit.,* pp. 80–84.

Schmink, Marianne, and Charles H. Wood. 1992. *Contested Frontiers in Amazonia.* New York: Columbia University Press.

SCIPA. 1959. *Comercio Exterior de Productos Agropecuarios, 1946–1958. Manual Estadístico.* Lima: Servicio Cooperativo Interamericano de Producción de Alimentos.

Seymour-Smith, Charlotte. 1988. *Shiwiar: Identidad Etnica y Cambio en el Río Corrientes.* Quito: Abya Yala/Centro Amazónico de Antropología y Aplicación Práctica.

Sicchar, Víctor Rubén. 1979. "Las Luchas Populares en Iquitos." *Shupihui,* 12: 385–387.

SINAMOS. n.d. Problemática de la Movilización Social: Región Oriente. Sistema Nacional de Movilización Social.

Sotomayor, Humberto, Günther Schaper, and Antonio Arévalo. 1949. *Guía de Loreto.* Iquitos: Jorge Reátegui Burga.

Spence, D. (ed.). 1908. *Lectures on India Rubber.* London: International Rubber and Allied Trades Exhibition.

Stearman, Allyn M. 1978. "The Highland Migrant in Lowland Bolivia: Multiple Resource Migration and the Horizontal Archipelago." *Human Organization,* 32(2): 180–185.

Stiglich, Germán. 1904a. "Viaje que por Encargo de la Junta de Vías Fluviales Practicó en los Ríos Pachitea, Bajo Ucayali, Amazonas, Alto Ucayali i Urubamba el Alférez de Fragata Don . . . ." In C. Larrabure i Correa, *op. cit.,* Vol. IV: 272–367.

———. 1904b. "La Región Peruana de los Bosques, por el Teniente Segundo de la Armada Nacional, Don . . . ." In C. Larrabure i Correa, *op. cit.*, Vol. XV: 308–495.

———. 1907. "Informe del Jefe de la Comisión Exploradora de las Regiones del Ucayali, Fiscarrald i Madre de Dios, Teniente Segundo de la Armada Don . . . ." In Junta, *op. cit.*, pp. 3–258.

Stocks, Anthony W. 1981. *Los Nativos Invisibles: Notas sobre la Historia y Realidad Actual de los Cocamilla del Río Huallaga, Perú.* Lima: Centro Amazónico de Antropología y Aplicación Práctica.

Stoll, David. 1985. *Pescadores de Hombres o Fundadores de Imperio? El Instituto Lingüístico de Verano en América Latina.* Lima: DESCO.

Tamariz, María Eugenia. 1991. "El Diferendo Limítrofe Ecuador-Perú: Haciendo de Tinterillo del Diablo." In M. Restrepo et al., *op. cit.*, pp. 57–86.

Taussig, Michael. 1987. *Shamanism, Colonialism, and the Wild Man: A Study of Terror and Healing.* Chicago and London: The University of Chicago Press.

Tizón i Bueno, Ricardo. 1905. "El Progreso del Oriente Peruano, por . . . ." In C. Larrabure i Correa, *op. cit.*, Vol. XV: 541–557.

Thorp, Rosemary, and Geoffrey Bertram. 1985. *Peru, 1890–1977: Crecimiento y Políticas en una Economía Abierta.* Lima: Mosca Azul/Fundación Ebert/Universidad del Pacífico.

Torres Videla, Samuel. 1923. *La Revolución de Iquitos, Loreto, Perú.* Pará: Tipografía España.

Tovar, Enrique D. 1966. *Vocabulario del Oriente Peruano.* Lima: Universidad Nacional Mayor de San Marcos.

Tovar, Carlos, and M. Vizcarra. 1981. "El Rol Propulsor de la Corporación Financiera de Desarrollo COFIDE en el Sector Forestal." In *Seminario Sobre Extracción y Transformación Forestal.* Pucallpa: Ministerio de Agricultura/Food and Agriculture Organization.

Trahtenberg, León. n.d. *Los Judíos de Lima y las Provincias del Perú.* (photocopy)

Transportes. (Dirección Regional de Transporte, Vialidad y Comunicaciones). 1990a. Motonaves con Registro en el Puerto de Iquitos. Iquitos.

———. 1990b. Motochatas con Registro en el Puerto de Iquitos. Iquitos.

Treceño, Silvino. 1989. "Hace Muchos Años." *Kanatari*, 265: 10; 10/15/1989

———. 1990. "Hace Muchos Años." *Kanatari*, 311: 10; 9/2/1990.

———. 1990. "Hace Muchos Años." *Kanatari*, 301: 10; 6/24/1990.

———. 1991. "Hace Muchos Años." *Kanatari*, 346: 10; 5/5/1991.

Tuesta, Fernando. 1994. *Perú Político en Cifras: Elite Política y Elecciones.* Lima: Fundación Ebert.

Ucayali. (Región Ucayali). 1990. Libro de Registro de Barreales por Campaña. Sub-Dirección de Aguas y Riegos. Pucallpa.

Ugarteche, Pedro. 1933. *Documentos que Acusan (El Tratado Salomón-Lozano).* Lima: Estanco del Tabaco.

Urmeneta, Darío. 1905. "Monografía de la Provincia de Ucayali por el Subprefecto. . . ." In C. Larrabure i Correa, *op. cit.*, Vol. XVI: 67–74.

Varese, Stefano. 1973. *La Sal de los Cerros: Una Aproximación al Mundo Campa.* Lima: Retablo de Papel.

Vásquez, Iván. 1998. *Más de un siglo de luchas contra el centralismo.* Iquitos.

Vásquez Valcárcel, Jaime. 1992. "Ante la Agresión cómo Responder." *Kanatari*, 383: 2; 1/19/1992.

———. 1993. "Historia que Motiva." *Kanatari*, 450: 25; 5/2/1993.

Villanueva, Manuel P. 1902. "Los Ríos Fronterizos del Departamento de Loreto, por el Comisionado Especial, Don . . . ." In C. Larrabure i Correa, *op. cit.*, Vol. VII: 563–601.

Villarejo, Avencio. 1965. *Los Agustinos en el Perú (1548–1965)*. Lima: Ausonia.

_____. 1988. *Así es la Selva.* Iquitos: Centro de Estudios Teológicos de la Amazonía.

Villeneuve, Gaston. 1974. "Los Shipibo del Ucayali." In J.M. Mercier and G. Villeneuve (eds.), *op. cit.*, pp. 133–153.

von Hassel, Jorge M. 1902a. "Estudio de los Varaderos del Putumayo por el Ingeniero . . . Informe." In C. Larrabure i Correa, *op. cit.*, Vol. IV: 106–13.

_____. 1902b. "Expedición de Puerto Bermúdez a Iquitos i de este último Puerto al Istmo de Fiscarrald, dirigida por el Coronel Ernesto La Combe. Informe del Ingeniero . . . ." In C. Larrabure i Correa, *op. cit.*, Vol. XII: 376–411.

_____. 1902c. "Estudio de los Varaderos del Purús, Yuruá i Manu por el Ingeniero . . . ." In C. Larrabure i Correa, *op. cit.*, Vol. IV: 209–213.

_____. 1903. "Viaje del Ingeniero . . . á los Ríos Napo i Curarai. Informe del Ingeniero . . . ." In C. Larrabure i Correa, *op. cit.*, Vol. IV: 228–39.

_____. 1905. "Las Tribus Salvajes de la Región Amazónica del Perú, por Don. . . . " In C. Larrabure i Correa, *op. cit.*, Vol. VII: 637–677.

_____. 1907. "Informe del Jefe de la Comisión Exploradora del Alto Madre de Dios, Paucartambo i Urubamba por la Vía del Cuzco." In Junta, *op. cit.*, pp. 259–394.

Wagley, Charles. 1953. *Amazon Town.* New York: Macmillan.

Walker, Charles. 1987. "El Uso Oficial de la Selva en el Perú Republicano." *Amazonía Peruana*, 14(8): 61–89.

Watson, Eduardo. 1964. *Comercio y Tendencias del Mercado en los Productos de la Región de la Selva Peruana.* Lima: Universidad Agraria.

Wechsberg, Joseph. 1966. *The Merchant Bankers.* Nueva York: Simon and Schuster.

Weinstein, Barbara. 1983. *The Amazon Rubber Boom, 1850–1920.* Stanford: Stanford University Press.

_____. 1985. "Persistence of Caboclo Culture in the Amazon: The Impact of the Rubber Trade, 1850–1920." In Eugene Parker (ed.), *The Amazon Caboclo: Historical and Contemporary Perspectives*, pp. 89–113. Studies in Third World Societies, 32. Williamsburg: College of William and Mary.

Weiss, Pedro. 1959. "Los Lamas son un Pueblo Misterioso y Legendario que Vive en el Huallaga: Historia y Costumbres." *Perú Indígena*, 8(18–19): 13–26.

Wille, J.E., J.A. Ocampo, A. Weberbauer, and D. Schofield. 1939. *El Cube (Lonchocarpus utilis) y otros Barbascos en el Perú.* Boletín No. 16. Lima: Ministerio de Fomento/Instituto de Estudios Agrícolas del Perú.

Witt, N.H. 1908. "Notes on the Growth and Production of Para Rubber in Brazil." In D. Spence (ed.), *op. cit.,* pp. 40–46.

Wolf, Howard, and Ralph Wolf. 1936. *Rubber: A Story of Glory and Greed.* New York: Covici-Friede Publishers.

Woodroffe, Joseph F. 1914. *The Upper Reaches of the Amazon.* London: Methuen and Company.

Yepes del Castillo, Ernesto. 1982. "El Poblador Ribereño de la Amazonía Peruana. Un Contingente Social por Estudiar." *Análisis*, 11: 67–70.

_____. 1983. "El Poblador Ribereño de la Amazonía Peruana." *Shupihui*, 28: 437–449.

_____. 1988. "Ribereños No-Indígenas del Bajo Ucayali." *Perú Indígena*, 12(27): 59–71.

Yepes del Castillo, Ernesto (ed.). 1996. *Mito y Realidad de una Frontera: Perú-Ecuador, 1942–1949. El Informe McBride: Un Testimonio Inédito del Departamento de Estado.* Lima: Ediciones Análisis.

Zarzar, Alonso. 1985. "Nacer es un Ritual: Compadrazgo, Cuvada y Padrinazgo Indígena." *Amazonía Peruana,* 6(11): 65–86.

Zarzar, Alonso, and Luis Román. 1983. *Relaciones Intertribales en el Bajo Urubamba y Alto Ucayali.* Lima: Centro de Investigación y Promoción Amazónica.

Zegarra García, Enrique. 1945. *Mi Contribución al Resurgimiento de la Industria Cauchera en el Perú.* Lima: Corporación Peruana del Amazonas.

_____. 1949. "El Problema Número Uno del Oriente Peruano Radica en la Regularidad de sus Comunicaciones." In Sotomayor et al., *op. cit.*, pp. 23–27.

Zumaeta, Pablo. 1913. *Las Cuestiones del Putumayo: Memorial de Pablo Zumaeta, Gerente de "The Peruvian Amazon Co. Ltd." en Iquitos.* Folleto No. 1. Barcelona: Imprenta Viuda de Luis Tasso.

Interviews

Abensur, Joaquín. 1991. Fundo Pucabarranca: interview of former owner. Iquitos.

Cárdenas, Aurelio. 1991. Fundo Negro Urco: interview of son of former owner. Iquitos.

Dávila Shapiama, María Elena. 1997. Fundo Panguana: interview of daughter of former owner. Panama.

Gómez Perea, Oscar A. 1991. Fundo Berlín: interview of son of former owner. Iquitos.

Herrera, N.N. 1991. Fundo Monterrico: interview of former manager. Iquitos.

Lequerica, Germán. 1991. Compañía Comercial Suramérica S.A.: interview of former clerk of the company. Iquitos.

Paíno López, Gerardo. 1991. Fundo San Rafael-Versalles: interview of son of former owner. Iquitos.

Riera Vásquez, Luis. 1991. Fundo Paraíso: interview of son of former owner. Iquitos.

Rojas Vela, Nicanor. 1991. Fundo Puritania: interview of former manager. Iquitos.

Index